▨ Colour Plates [between pp. 132 & 133]

For Morag Chisholm

Foreword

I AM DELIGHTED TO BE ABLE TO WRITE THIS INTRODUCTION TO A long-overdue biography of a remarkable composer, performer and musical polymath. I met Erik Chisholm in Cape Town during a four-month stint there with the Cape Town Municipal Orchestra. We got on very well, partly because of a common interest in Janáček at a time when there were not so many experts on this composer as there are now. Ever since then I have held Erik Chisholm in high esteem and am very happy that through this volume his creativity and individuality will become better known.

Erik Chisholm was a musician of rare capabilities. He was a pianist and organist, a conductor, a composer, a lecturer on music, an entrepreneur and administrator, and to all these he brought a unique blend of originality, flair and energy. After an early start as a performing pianist, Chisholm established himself in Glasgow as an important influence on the progress of music in Scotland and Scottish music in general. He founded the Active Society for the Propagation of Contemporary Music and through this and the Glasgow Grand Opera Society he brought many first performances to that city. Berlioz's *Les Troyens*, for example, was first heard in the UK under his baton, as was *Beatrice and Benedict* and Mozart's *Idomeneo*. He formed many other organisations, including the Scottish Ballet Society, and in the meantime composed prolifically. Chisholm's passion for traditional Scottish music should also be noted. His time in South Africa, notably as Principal of the South Africa College of Music and Professor of Music at Cape Town University, was equally productive. Here he focused on the promotion of opera (including some of his own fascinating works) and introduced much new music to South Africa.

John Purser's biography is written with great affection for Chisholm the man and musician. He takes us on an exciting journey from his early Scottish and Pibroch-influenced works to his Hindustani influences, his interests in Russian music and his vital essays in modernism. Chisholm's restless nature and his extraordinary passion and originality, is truly captured in a biography of great quality.

Sir Charles Mackerras CH, AC, CBE

Acknowledgments

My chief acknowledgment is to Erik Chisholm's three daughters, Morag, Sheila and Fiona. It is they who have encouraged and informed me; handled my queries and probings with patience and honesty; shown me hospitality and shared, in their very different ways, their great and entirely justified pride in their father's achievements. In particular, Dr Morag Chisholm has not only been a guide and helper of extraordinary energy – an energy which she surely inherits from her father – she has also chaired the Erik Chisholm Trust since its inception and has, through it, commissioned the first version of this book, the copying of scores and parts, the promoting of concert performances and the production of CDs. She has given me many useful contacts, has read through the drafts and suggested improvements and corrected errors. It is to her that I dedicate this book and I am honoured by her gracious acceptance.

I also owe a deep debt of gratitude to the Birmingham Conservatoire (University of Central England) and, in particular, George Caird and Peter Johnson. UCE were commissioners with the Erik Chisholm Trust of the book's first version, and without both their moral and financial support it would not have been possible.

My very particular thanks go to Chisholm's widow, Lillias Scott Forbes, who has given me many personal insights and permission to reproduce one of Erik's settings of her verses in its entirety; also to Virginia Fortescue, a long-time colleague of Chisholm's, who has been equally open and frank and has also read through my draft chapters and corrected several errors. Ronald and Marjorie Stevenson also gave me many insights into Chisholm's complex character and spoke openly about their time with him in Cape Town.

I never knew Erik Chisholm myself, although our lives, and even our careers as Scottish composers, overlapped. The sad truth is that South Africa became a pariah country, and cultural communications became less open for over two decades. All that has changed dramatically, so my next acknowledgment goes to the staff of the Manuscript and Archives Department of the University of Cape Town. They could not have been more helpful. They are Lesley Hart, Janine Morgan, Santie de Jongh and Albee Odendaal. Lesley Hart, in particular, has been unfailingly kind and good enough to read through and comment on an earlier version of this book. Also, while working in Cape Town, I was given much support and hospitality by Gus and Nicky Ferguson, and much information by Michael Tuffin, David Tidboald and Lily Savitz.

In Glasgow, Sally Clegg of the Mitchell Library dug out fascinating material and also curated an excellent Erik Chisholm exhibition; and, as ever, the Scottish Music Centre dealt with my many requests with their usual patience and forbearance – particularly in the form of Alasdair Pettinger, who has done a good deal of work himself on Erik Chisholm. Elsewhere in Scotland, Alex Beveridge and Maurice Lindsay provided early memories of Chisholm, Ken Walton shared his knowledge and enthusiasm and Dr Stuart Campbell likewise.

Special thanks go to Alistair Hinton and the Sorabji Archive for permission to quote extensively from Sorabji's letters to Chisholm.

My thanks also go to the Trustees of the Erik Chisholm Trust, amongst them Dr Fiona Wright, Alastair Chisholm (no relation), Martin Dalby, Michael Jones and Hugh MacDonald. It is the Trust's money which has supported this publication, never mind the initial commission.

Without the many performers who have given their time, skills and energies to Chisholm, much of his music would have remained in obscurity. Murray McLachlan has done more than any one performer to bring this wonderful music to light, learning a vast quantity of technically challenging material in a unique idiom, frequently from barely legible scores. His achievement has been little short of heroic, backed by Jim Pattison and Dunelm Records, whose dedication to the cause has been exemplary.

Other performers who have done much for Chisholm include Ronald Brautigam, Clark Rundell, Angelo Gobato and the students at UCT Opera School, Michael Jones, Alastair Chisholm, Jack Keaney and Jean Hutchison.

With respect to Chisholm's association with the arts in general, notably with ballet, both Jonathan Burnett and Jim Hastie have been most generous with their time, providing me with images and even a video of a scene from *The Forsaken Mermaid* danced in the original costume to the original choreography. Anne Crosbie, widow of the artist William Crosbie who designed the sets and costumes for *The Earth Shapers*, has also been most helpful, as have Crosbie's main dealers, Ewan and Carol Mundy.

Many others have assisted who are not named here, and I only hope that what follows does justice to Chisholm and to all those who have helped me. One does one's best not to perpetrate error, but even facts refuse to be as fixed as one might wish. I accept responsibility for any mistakes and omissions. Every effort has been made to obtain necessary permissions. If I have failed in this respect, I trust forgiveness will be forthcoming. In any event, I indemnify my publishers, Boydell & Brewer, to whom thanks, and especially to Bruce Phillips, the first of their number to champion this book. Special thanks to David and Jeanne Roberts and Margaret Christie for their vital help and expertise. The typesetting, music examples and the index are their work respectively, and they have gone far beyond the calls of duty.

Finally, my wife, Barbara, has once again put up with all the inconveniences of a husband working late, being away, being tired and short-tempered when he's at home, and generally failing to undertake his proper share of the domestic necessities. She deserves a long holiday from the making of many books, of which, in the words of Ecclesiastes, there does indeed seem to be no end.

CHAPTER 1

Glasgow: Kailyard or Coal Yard?

To HAVE BEEN BORN IN GLASGOW IN THE EARLY TWENTIETH century is not seen as a recommendation for a budding musician. Paris would carry weight, or Dublin, in the midst of a great literary revival. But much of the literature of Scotland at the time is described uncharitably as of 'the kailyard school', the kale yard being where coarse greens were grown at the back of small, self-satisfied homes, where folk were 'douce' and 'couthy', humour was 'pawky'; sentiment ruled over realism, and the parochial over the international. In this school, J. M. Barrie has been unfairly cast as the leading dominie, when, in reality, the bulk of the 'kailyard' publications were produced for the English, not the Scottish market.[1] As for the radical significance of Conan Doyle, R. L. Stevenson, George Douglas, Lewis Grassic Gibbon, young MacDiarmid and others, it has yet to be fully understood outside Scottish literary circles.

As for Glasgow, it was an industrial city, wealthy and poor in equally extravagant measure; filthy with the smog and smuts of millions of coal fires; lurid with the flares of the Bessemer Converters at the mammoth steel works; and with its ears ringing with the sound of riveting in some of the greatest shipyards of the world.

These stereotypical views held sway even in Scotland well into the latter half of the twentieth century, since when appreciation of the artistic life in Glasgow in the early 1900s has largely centred round the visual arts. 'The Glasgow Boys' and the work of Charles Rennie Mackintosh now command international respect. But of music we hear and read practically nothing, and what we do read is not encouraging:

> Mr Scott, the only Scottish composer technically abreast of the highest developments of modern music in Europe and the only composer today who is endeavouring to establish a Scottish national idiom – who, in other words, has got beyond kailyairdism.[2]

Thus Hugh MacDiarmid, writing from a position of ignorance, apparently unaware of the work of J. B. McEwen or young Chisholm, but none the less imparting a home truth. It was not only the composers who were lacking. Scotland had no full-time professional orchestra, and professional opera and ballet came only with touring companies. The leading Scottish composers, Alexander Mackenzie, Hamish MacCunn and John McEwen, were in London and, though two of them had been knighted, their reputations are only now emerging from under the shadows of their English counterparts. As for Glasgow's two great pianist-composers, Eugen d'Albert and Frederic Lamond, they were both in Germany. Traditional music was largely represented by the influential but somewhat distorted arrangements of Marjory Kennedy-Fraser; through the fading skills of the violinist James Scott Skinner; and the folksy caricatures of the music hall, for which Harry Lauder is most unreasonably criticised. Chisholm himself was not shy of expressing his dismay at the musical shortcomings of his home city:

> [I]n a town the size of Glasgow it would be extremely fortunate to find *one hundred* of its inhabitants taking a vital interest in music *as an art* (as distinct from regarding it either as so much ear-tickling or as a means to gaining an easy reputation among one's friends as a 'high-brow' by airing a little knowledge in their society).[3]

On the other hand, the part-time Scottish Orchestra sustained a substantial season of concerts in the outstanding acoustic of the St Andrew's Halls, with visiting conductors and artists of the highest distinction. Chisholm wrote:

> As a youth living in Glasgow, I remember the annual visits of the Beecham Opera Company (and under later titles) at which I and indeed the musical public of Britain heard for the first time, major operatic works like 'Boris Godunov', 'Prince Igor', 'Otello', 'Falstaff', 'Khovanschina' and 'Rosenkavalier'; with the best available English singers and an orchestra of 100 players, not at Covent Garden, but in Glasgow's own Colosseum Variety Theatre.[4]

There were also many amateur choirs, there was no shortage of pianists and organists and (not entirely lost to the lovers of classical music) a very real presence of genuine traditional music. This had been seriously researched by figures such as Lucy Broadwood, Ann Geddes Gilchrist, Frances Tolmie and John Glen, and could also be heard in piping competitions or in Gaelic-singing kirks in the city. There was also the Glasgow Athenaeum, which was the forerunner of the Royal Scottish Academy of Music, and to which Erik Chisholm naturally gravitated.[5]

But there is no denying that, in the absence of any outstanding locally based role-models, whether individual or institutional, success for a Glaswegian in the world of music was likely to depend upon a combination of inborn talent, personal determination and parental support. Chisholm had all three in profusion.

Erik Chisholm was born in Cathcart, Glasgow, on 4 January 1904, the son of John Chisholm (illus. 1) and Elizabeth McGeachy MacLeod. He was the middle of three brothers, John Sinclair ('Jack') being born in December 1899 and Archibald MacLeod ('Archie') in October 1907. Archie was an accountant, became Treasurer of the Active Society for the Propagation of Contemporary Music (Erik's brainchild), and was later to follow Erik to South Africa.

Chisholm's father ran the family firm of painters and decorators, which had its offices at 63 Berkeley Street, Glasgow. It was a well-established business, built up over three generations, John Chisholm being a master painter. In the early years of his marriage, Erik was occasionally to add to his meagre income by working for the company, but in his childhood and youth the Chisholm household was

1 Erik Chisholm's father,
   John Chisholm, *c.* 1916

financially secure, and there were no early pressures on young Erik to pay his way in the world, which is just as well, for he was not a strong child. He had had influenza as a baby[6] and had to stop formal schooling at thirteen.[7] His mother once declared, 'you could blow peas through Erik's ribs'.[8]

He was not happy at school and was, no doubt, relieved to leave it, although he seems to have been able to make other people less than happy, too:

> Playing kick the can, ringing door bells or tying opposite door knobs together, pushing younger and weaker lads into beds of stinging nettles, were some of my favourite games, when I was at Junior School.[9]

He had buck teeth, but had them all taken out while still in his twenties, and wore spectacles all his life to counteract his short-sightedness, sometimes having to remove them and bring whatever he was studying right up to his eyes.[10] When the Second World War broke out, he was classed as Grade 4 and so rejected for military service.[11] He had also broken his arm when he fell off the Crocodile Rock at Millport, where the family regularly holidayed; and since it had not been reset straight, he was unable to hold a rifle properly.[12] Fortunately it did not inhibit his organ or piano playing.

Throughout his life he suffered from severe, sometimes incapacitating migraines. His student, Alex Beveridge, recalled the pallor in his face and his having to ask to be helped to another room, and Chisholm describing 'stars falling – falling all over my eyes'.[13] Frightening visual disturbances of this nature are associated with chronic migraines. It was something he had to learn to cope with, and he coped 'very well' in the view of one of his doctors.[14] In other respects, he seems to have been a thoroughly normal child, and he recalls family life with disarming humour and a story-teller's proper use of exaggeration. It is worth quoting extensively from the following childhood recollections, which give a delightful insight into upper-middle-class society of the period:

> It was my father's dearest wish to keep his three sons 'off the street' ... He added an extra storey on the top of our semi-detached house at 28 Corrour Road, Newlands, Glasgow, which would accommodate a full-size billiard table (incidentally, burning down the whole house and that of our next door neighbour in the process!) He bought us a 35mm projector, complete with arc lamp, slide attachment, a selection of cowboy films and newsreels, but no motor. There were none in those days. So every time we had a cinema show, which was usually Friday or Saturday nights, my eldest brother, Jack, had to 'caw the haun'le' (turn the handle) of the projector to make it go. It was a pretty strenuous task – for a 350m. reel lasted 15 minutes. It was no joke to keep turning without a break for a quarter of an hour or more. ...
>
> My brother Jack came in for more than his fair share of turning the handle of the ice-cream freezer, packed around with ice, which became harder and harder to push as the ice embedded itself closer into the freezer. My Mother's ice cream – made from real cream and fresh strawberries – was marvellous. There's nothing like it, nowadays, with the mass-produced, slick, sleek, tasteless, synthetic, characterless, professional manufactured stuff, mis-called 'ice cream'. ...
>
> To return to the cinematograph, bioscope or movie, our proud family record in this field goes back before even the invention of the movie camera. In 1903, or thereabouts, my Uncle James blew himself through the ceiling when an acetylene contraption he was adjusting went wrong. If I close my eyes right now, I can see the hole in the ceiling where he went through.
>
> Another early memory of the movies was the gorgeous time when Father took us all for a holiday to the Island of Millport. ... Three or four times a week as soon as it was dark, there was an open-air film show. From our sitting-room windows we could watch the whole show free in the comfort of our own home. ... [T]he thrilling climax, when the Mounties stormed in to release the captured garrison and hacked to bits the treacherous Red Indians, always made fine viewing. Especially when accompanied by the strains of the *William Tell* Overture. A doing-his-best-so-don't-shoot-me-five-bob-an-hour movie pianist played this on a museum piece, all-but upright piano.
>
> When I got older, my Dad bought me a Pathe-Baby Cine Camera with stand and my brother Archie and I started up a Glasgow Cine Club for making our own movies. One of the pictures we shot on 9.5 mm stock, was called *The Gas Trap*, a thriller with camera work by the Chisholms which made that of Clair, Einstein, Fritz Lang and D. W. Griffiths look just plain silly.[15]

But what of music in the midst of all this entertainment? According to Chisholm's daughters, the family was not musical, but when asked what was the chief turning-point in his career, the first one Erik mentioned was hearing Beethoven's 'Moonlight' Sonata on a pianola-roll at the age of about seven – 'a magical revelation which still remains with me'.[16] When his daughters attempted the same piece, they could never live up to that seminal moment and felt quite crushed by his criticism.

Apart from the 'Moonlight' Sonata experience, there is only one other clue as to the origins of Chisholm's interest in music, found in a casual remark at the end of a 1950 review of a Chisholm work, referring to his mother as a 'still well-known singer'.[17] None of Chisholm's daughters has any recollection of their grandmother singing. They recall her as a somewhat forbidding lady, well turned out in hat and gloves: a good wife and mother to her boys, but with less interest in her grandchildren.

There is no clear account of when Erik started composing, but in 1950 a newspaper reported that his mother, 'Forty years ago … heard her young son Erik playing the piano – he was idling with variations on a little Scots folk-tune. A year later it became his first opus (unofficial)'.[18] This would make him six or seven years old. Some three years later came another seminal moment, with the gift of Patrick MacDonald's *A Collection of Highland Vocal Airs*, published in 1784.

> I first came across Macdonald when I was a boy of 10. My parents used to take us all to the Island of Millport for our summer holidays. On one occasion we stayed at a boarding house run by a friendly Scots family of the name of Stewart. They presented me with a bundle of old music, and in a very handsome leather volume bound in along with 'Home Sweet Home and Variations', 'The Dying Poet', 'Battle March of Delhi' (Overture to Maritana) was the Macdonald collection of Highland vocal music. I very soon realised that this latter was of some value, and it is many, many years since I tore it from its bourgeoise surroundings, and have trailed it around with me ever since.[19]

Indeed he had. His much-used, much-annotated copy shows that he had turned these pages often.[20] Many of the airs were subsequently used for his *Scottish Airs for Children* and *A Celtic Song Book*, and several of his other Scottish works. Such must have been his interest in the MacDonald collection, and in music in general, that he was allowed to leave school to pursue music. Perhaps his parents also realised that his musical talents were not being adequately nurtured in the class-room:-

> When I was 13, and a pupil of Queens Park Secondary School our music mistress was a Miss Polly White who during a rehearsal by Class 1a of which I was a rebellious pupil of 'A hundred pipers and a' and a" said to me, 'Erik do please stop singing. You are dragging the whole class out of tune.'[21]

Whatever Miss White's opinion of his singing, Erik left school and moved on to study at the Glasgow Athenaeum School of Music (now the Royal Scottish Academy of Music and Drama).[22] There is no record of his education, musical or otherwise, for the next four years. According to Diana Chisholm he gave his first (organ) recital in Hull in 1915, when he would have only been eleven years old.[23] More certain information comes from a programme in which he appears as a pianist playing a Mozart minuet in 1917[24] and Debussy's *Arabesque No. 2* at a Students' Musical Afternoon on 9 March 1918.[25] At some point during this period he was being taught organ by Herbert Walton, and piano by Philip Halstead, both in Glasgow,[26] and he must have been producing music of his own:

> My early masterpieces included a piano suite on Browning's *Pippa Passes* about which I was crazy at the time (I mean about Browning, not my Suite), a lyric movement for string quartet, and my chef d'oeuvre, a Chaconne (35 variations on a ground bass), triple fugue and epilogue for large orchestra.
>
> I can still remember the subjects of the fugues. As it was never my way to do things by half it so happened that I was in love with three girls at the time, and each subject was supposed to sum up the charms of my fair enslavers. The first fugue was for strings only, the second fugue for wind only, and the third for brass only; so the first time you heard the full orchestra was when all three subjects were combined – rather a clever idea don't you think? The three girls were:
>
> My String girl: – Gretchen Walton, daughter of the Glasgow Cathedral organist, Herbert Walton. … My woodwind girl was Effie Ross, daughter of the owner of famous Ross's Dairies of Glasgow. … My brass girl, Phemie Lang, was the daughter of the general manager of Weir's Engineering Works. It was coincidence, I hope, that they were all classy gurls whose fathers had substantial incomes. … Well, when this work was finished, I was mightily pleased with it, and I remember wondering who would be the lucky conductor to be allowed to give its first performance. Sir Landon Ronald? Too old fashioned – unlikely at his age (he was 47) to understand the out-pouring of an ardent (albeit contrapuntal) young heart! Sir Henry Wood? Better, certainly, but too slap-dash, and tied up with old-fashioned fogies like Strauss and Scriabin.
>
> Sir Hamilton Harty? Not bad; a little too Irish – leprecorny [*sic*], perhaps, but we'll keep his name on the list meantime.[27]

The foregoing might suggest that Chisholm was potentially arrogant, but his daughter Fiona described him more truly as 'a Puck among the professors'.[28] In any case, he was one of the first to find merit in and promote the works of those whom he might have considered to be his rivals. He composed because he had to, not because he sought to aggrandise himself. David Tidboald, who had met him during the war years, and knew him in Cape Town, where Tidboald was conducting the Municipal Orchestra, said that if you happened upon him at work and asked him what he was composing, he would reply: 'Oh, some rubbish … just some rubbish … you'd have to cut off my hand before I could stop composing.'[29]

On another occasion he declared 'composition is a disease',[30] and, writing to Hindemith, he confessed:

> I had a wonderful time here with Szymon Goldberg – he's the most delightful fellow in the world – and how he played my violin concerto! I keep writing stuff because I can't stop – did a concerto for orchestra and a one-act opera 'Dark Sonnet' this year – nobody seems to think anything I write is any good, so probably they are right![31]

All composers need a high degree of self-belief, but most are full of doubts, and Chisholm was no exception, and it says a great deal for his father that he took his son seriously as a composer, as Erik himself recounts:

> The first composer I ever met in my life was John Ireland, and that was because my father made an appointment for him to see me and hear some youthful compositions of mine. Ireland was then living at 14a, Gunters Grove, Chelsea. I would be about 15 or 16, so this would be around the years 1919–20.
>
> Ireland led us down the garden to a large, dark-looking studio. I remember his piano was covered with dust and cigarette ash. Ireland scanned through my scores with a rather bored look, but perked up a bit when he came to my marvellous triple fugue. He said he would be prepared to give me composition lessons if I would come down and live in London.
>
> My father said this was not the idea at all. He wanted to know if Mr. Ireland would give his son lessons by post? Ireland said this was impossible, so my Dad rushed me across London to Muswell Hill for a second opinion. This time from Hubert Bath, composer of the popular *Cornish Rhapsody* (said by some, to be more corny than Rhapsy). Nothing doing again. But finally my Dad did settle for correspondence lessons from Dr. A. Eaglefield Hull. But that is another story.[32]

During this period Chisholm seems to have started on a scrapbook of newspaper cuttings of reviews of Beecham performances, Ernest Newman's writings, concert programmes and the like, the selection revealing that catholicity of taste which was to mark his entire career as composer, performer, teacher and musicologist.[33]

At this stage, Chisholm's piano playing and composition developed in tandem. In 1921 he played the Liszt Piano Concerto No. 1 in Hull, to considerable acclaim;[34] and in March 1922 he performed his own Sonatina at a British Music Society members' concert in Glasgow.[35] The piece was perceived to be of the impressionist school and treated with the usual condescension accorded to young composers' early works, the reviewers stating that he had yet to find his own voice, but that he showed promise. The *Glasgow Herald* also reveals that he had performed a Liszt concerto (presumably the First, in a two-piano reduction) with his teacher, Herbert Walton.[36]

Encouragement for Chisholm as a composer came also from David Stephen, to whom he had sent the above-mentioned Chaconne along with a work for violin and piano and other unspecified pieces. Stephen, himself a composer and Director of the School of Music in Dunfermline where he worked for the Carnegie Trust, congratulated Chisholm on his variety of style and his orchestration, and expressed a liking for the violin and piano piece. But he warned against the Chaconne as a form which might perhaps be more useful academically than practically.[37]

Young Erik undoubtedly had a typical tyro's contrapuntal leanings, but in the *Straloch Suite* he had already achieved a fair degree of mastery without having to employ counterpoint for show. The work was completed in 1933 in arrangements for orchestra and string orchestra, as well as piano. However, two other piano versions date from 1923, when Chisholm was only nineteen. The printed suite has three movements, others have five, but all are based upon tunes from the Robert Gordon of Straloch lute book of 1627, which is now lost. G. F. Graham's copy of part of the manuscript, which he made in 1847, is all that Chisholm had to go on, and only a few of the tunes Graham copied have been transcribed from lute tablature into staff notation. The three-movement version is the one considered here.

After an imposing *Grave* introduction, the first movement *Allegro con spirito* makes neo-classical contrapuntal play with the tune 'Ostende', eventually turning it into a brief fugue and concluding with a repeat of the *Grave*. The title of the tune refers to Spinola's extended siege of Ostend, which took three years and three months, killed over 70,000 men and was the occasion of Isabella Eugenia, Governante of the Netherlands, refusing to change her underwear until the town surrendered in 1604, thus obliging the ladies of the court to dye theirs 'in order to keep their vice-regal mistress in countenance', as William Dauney reports. Chisholm knew Dauney's work on the Skene manuscript, which contains the earliest version of this tune, and this story may explain the mixture of the humorous with the heavyweight in the treatment, as well as accounting for the down-beat quiet return to the *Grave*, perhaps representing the city's ultimate defeat.

The *Allegro con energia – Allegro scherzando* of the second movement features three tunes from the manuscript. It starts with a deliberately laboured, thick-textured setting of 'Have over the Water', which is itself an aggressive and insistent tune, probably used for the song

> Farre well adew, that courtlycke lyfe,
> To warre we tend to gowe,

which was sung to the tune of 'Have Ouer ye Water to Floride Or Selengers Round'. A war-like intention would certainly fit this music, but Chisholm contrasts this with a setting of gentle lyricism of 'The Canaries'. His lingering and lovely treatment, with rich harmonies based around pedal notes, recalls the Brahms Op. 117 Intermezzo inspired by the words of 'Lady Anne Bothwell's Lament', though not based on the tune. Donald Tovey's admiration of Brahms, manifest in his own compositions, no doubt rubbed off on Chisholm, who was his admiring student, although Margaret May recalled that Chisholm 'appeared to have a dislike of Brahms'.[38] True or not, he certainly was familiar with the Intermezzi:

> Medtner has often been called the 'Russian Brahms' which means that both composers have a certain gravity of musical demeanour, and take themselves and their art with great seriousness. There is more in it than that, though. In the second movement of this piano concerto *Romanza*, the opening sentences might easily be taken for a typical Brahms intermezzo.[39]

'Have over the Water' returns in a variation derived from one provided in Straloch itself. The centre-piece of the movement is a bright version of 'An Thou Wert My Own Thing', a love song whose cheerful immediacy is captured in the easy-running quavers which are also in the original. 'The Canaries' and 'Have over the Water' are then repeated in varied form.

The last movement (*Mesuré – Andante espressivo e tempo rubato – Mesuré*) starts with the tune 'Galua Tom' with splendid off-beat chords, which might be attributed to the influence of Bartók, were it not that they are there in the original Straloch version from over 300 years ago (ex. 1).

But at the heart of the movement is another haunting rendering of a tune, 'I Long for Thy Virginitie', whose title (although mistranscribed as 'I Long for My Virginitie') no doubt spoke to Chisholm as enticingly as did its beautifully shaped melody. The texture and harmonies with which Chisholm adorns this tune draw out its beauties with native sympathy (ex. 2).

Around this period Chisholm must have joined the Pouishnoffs in London, with whom he lived and studied for two or three years,[40] including the periods when they were on holiday in Cornwall (see below). During this time he

Ex. 1 *Straloch Suite*, III, bars 9–16

Ex. 2 *Straloch Suite*, III, Andante espressivo e tempo rubato, first 10 bars

composed the *Cameos* for piano solo, which he copyrighted in 1926. Considering that he was only twenty-two, their publication by Curwen must have given him cause for pride.[41]

Each of the eight little pieces is given a title, some with quotations from an eclectic gathering of sources, showing that Chisholm's interests were broad ones from the start. Is there an echo in Chisholm's *Cameos* of 1926 of Alfredo Casella's mixture of mischief, sentiment and cynicism in the *Pupazzetti* of 1915, and which the two performed together in 1931, Chisholm having to assert his smaller bulk on the piano stool against the well-built militaristic Casella?[42] Or might one not equally turn to McEwen, whose music was known to Chisholm, who himself called for better recognition for his predecessor?[43]

'A Jewel from the Sidereal Casket' is headed by an unsourced quotation, 'B. [Beta] Cygnus – a drop of blood red with an emerald green companion', which refers to the spectacular double star, also described as orange and blue.

The solemn tread of the melody is punctuated by octaves in the bass marked 'quasi timp.' and later four-note chords are marked 'quasi Cor', implying the possibility of subsequent orchestration involving timpani and horns. This is done not just 'in the manner of' but assuming fixed tuning on the timps and a middle register for the four horns. He did partly orchestrate the 'Procession of Crabs'[44] and may have intended to orchestrate others. 'The Mirror', on the other hand, seems too pianistic for orchestral treatment. It has echoes of Chopin and McEwen, but has its own still mysteries, as though this were a mirror of water rather than of glass.

'The Witch-Hare' is inspired by Walter de la Mare's 'she eye'd the moon so bright / And she nibbled on the green' with 'celeste' and 'celestial' instructions to the pianist – or possibly organist, who might use a Celeste stop. Its jerky chromatic skippings could have been penned by McEwen, whose own character pieces *Vignettes from la Côte d'Argent* were composed in 1913 and published in 1918. From them, 'Crépuscule du Soir Mystique' and 'La Rosière' display similar varieties of texture and post-impressionist harmonic twists; but closest in character and rhythm is the 'Humoreske' from the *Four Sketches* of 1909. Also McEwen-like are the growling bass line and whole-tone fragments in 'The Companion to Sirius', 'around which revolves a dark planetary world, the solitary known instance of a stellar planet' – as the heading to the score quotes (ex. 3). The companion, Sirius B, is what we now know as a white dwarf.

'The Rolling Stone' is a delightfully observed sound picture of a stone rolling downhill with occasional near stops en route. John Drinkwater provided the text, 'I thank the Lord I'm a rolling stone / With never a care to carry'. Contrary motion and polytonality add to the unstable effects of the start-and-stop rhythms.

Ex. 3 *Cameos*, 4 'The Companion to Sirius', first 10 bars

'The Procession of Crabs', equally well observed, perhaps on summer holiday at Millport on the Clyde estuary, marches determinedly, using variety of harmonic density to help punctuate the rhythm, and the theme of motion is continued by 'The Sweating Infantry' as described by Walt Whitman: 'the dust-cover'd men / In columns rise and fall to the undulations of the ground.' The drum tap of the left-hand major sevenths is accompanied at first wearily, then more purposefully with a trumpet call at its climax (marked 'Trp.' in the score), before it dies away into the distance.

The *Cameos* are concluded with an exuberant piece 'after a picture by Miss Ellerton-Hill' called 'Happiness'. It is subtitled 'Laugh and be merry' in a draft version. The off-beat left-hand chords give it a reckless immediacy suggestive of general tomfoolery, in which Chisholm indulged throughout his life.

Taken as a whole, these are remarkably sophisticated and assured pieces, full of character, variety of texture and harmonic and rhythmic adventure. Melodically, they are less effective, but that is not really the nature of the scenes they evoke. A brief snapshot of Chisholm at the time of their composition is given by Watson Lyle, writing in 1932:

> Some nine or ten summers ago I was staying with friends, M. and Mme. Pouishnoff, in a cottage they had taken for the season, delightfully situated at a sequestered part of the rugged coastline of North Cornwall. Through my open bedroom window the voice of the ocean would croon a *berceuse*, or seek with yells to overawe me to sleep, according to its mood; but the character of my *aubade* never varied. Promptly at 8 a.m. began the industrious application of the pianist's pupil, Erik Chisholm, to his morning's work at the keyboard. His afternoons were generally occupied at composition, though occasionally he would trudge off with me along the coast, or go swimming with his teacher while Mme. Pouishnoff and myself, from the comfort of the beach, watched them brave the breakers of the Atlantic. Well into the night, I believe, Chisholm read, or studied the planetary system through an enormous telescope. I suppose there were hours when he slept; but having just completed a commission for a book within scheduled time, his tireless energy seemed a reproach to my righteous laziness of those few weeks.[45]

Leff Pouishnoff had studied at St Petersburg in the early 1900s but had settled in London in the 1920s with his wife Dorothy, a former pupil and also a concert pianist. The opportunity not just to study but to live with such a couple who had experienced the heyday of Russian culture must have been an extraordinary one for a teenager, and no doubt was partly responsible for opening Erik's ears to a wide variety of repertoire. Certainly, in 1926, he gave the first complete performance in Scotland of Mussorgsky's *Pictures at an Exhibition* in a recital for the Russo-Scottish Society, which included his own 'Procession of Crabs' (illus. 2).[46] Pouishnoff, meanwhile, was performing the *Cameos* on his American tour, with great success,[47] and Leigh Henry was looking for Chisholm to orchestrate

'Procession of Crabs' and 'Companion to Sirius' for a season at the Scala Theatre of *Il Teatro delle Piccolo Maschere*.[48] Only a draft orchestration for 'Procession of Crabs' appears to survive.

The following year (1927), Chisholm put on a concert for the Spanish Society of Scotland which included works by de Falla (two Spanish dances with piano duet, female voices and solo dancer), Debussy's Rhapsody for Saxophone and Piano and *Musiques pour le Roi Lear* and pieces by Lord Berners, Albéniz, Granados, López Chavarri and Soro.[49] The music critic Dunton Green had made some suggestions for the programme and had also some advice on Chisholm's own compositions: 'Neither "Viewed from a Starpoint" nor the "Cuckoo and the Nightingale variations" are altogether to my taste … There is a certain lack of grip about these two pieces in larger dimensions and a resultant dryness of which you have to beware'.[50] This was good advice, which Chisholm might have done well to heed on other and later occasions, for his prolific facility in making thorough use of his basic material is occasionally overdone. The concert was well reviewed, and Chisholm was described as having 'a fluent technique, and a sensitive feeling for rhythm and tone colour'.[51]

Rather less good advice was coming from his piano teacher Leff Pouishnoff who, in a long and highly critical letter written in 1927, almost totally demolishes a piano sonata of Erik's and accuses him of having little emotional life or, if he has it, of suppressing it. The sonata in question was the *Cornish Dance Sonata*, and consisted of character pieces treated characterfully. Sketches for the sonata (dated October 1926[52] and originally dedicated to Miss Jessie Moodie[53]) are declared by Chisholm to be predecessors of his First Symphony (See Chapter 5).[54] Pouishnoff objected to the subject-matter, satirising the titles of the movements, writing 'clodded hoofs to the slaughter' for 'With Clogs on', though 'Chin & Tongue Waggle' was indeed an actual title.

> Why not be silly one day? Why not throw aside the desire of being 'modern', fancy for wild, queer tunes, prickly rhythms, weird dischords? And to unbutton your waistcoat & flannel shirt & let the sun penetrate to your suffering heart, suffering with what? And to burst in peels of young, happy laughter? Throw yourself on the warm earth at noon and drink the nature beautiful aromas?

How Chisholm responded to this effusion of exhortations in occasionally quaint English, and frequently quainter thoughts, is not known. If he was wise, he would have let the whole business quietly drop, for behind it all there clearly lies the failure of Pouishnoff to engage with modernism and dissonance, for the tone of the letter, despite its many strictures, is affectionate and even admiring.[55] Chisholm did, in fact, resurrect this sonata in symphonic form. Some years later, however, it seems that Pouishnoff had blotted his copy book more seriously, at least in Sorabji's eyes.

The more I think about Pouishnoff's behaviour the more scandalous and

RUSSO-SCOTTISH SOCIETY.

Pianoforte Recital

OF

Russian Music

BY

ERIK CHISHOLM

IN

M'Lellan Galleries, Glasgow,

TUESDAY, 16th FEBRUARY, 1926,

AT 8 P.M.

TICKETS, reserved **2/4**; unreserved **1/3** (including Tax).

Booking at PATERSON SONS & CO., Ltd.,
182 Buchanan Street, Glasgow.

PROGRAMME.

(1)

"PICTURES AT AN EXHIBITION"
Modeste Petrovitch Moussorgsky.

The motive which led to the composition of this work was the exhibition in 1874 of drawings by the architect, Hartmann. Moussorgsky paid him tribute by "drawing in music" the best of his sketches.

The introduction is entitled "PROMENADE," and at its re-occurence represents the passing of the musician from one picture to another.

1. GNOMUS.
   A drawing representing a little gnome dragging himself along with clumsy steps by his little twisted legs.

2. IL VECCHIA CASTELLO.
   A castle of the Middle Ages, before which a troubadour is singing.

3. TUILERIES.
   Children disputing after their play.

4. BYDLO.
   A Polish wagon with enormous wheels drawn by oxen.

5. BALLET OF CHICKENS IN THEIR SHELLS.

6. SAMUEL GOLDENBERG AND SCHMUYTE.
   Two Polish Jews, the one rich, the other poor.

7. LIMOGES, THE MARKET PLACE.
   Market women dispute furiously.

8. CATACOMBS.
   Hartmann portrays himself examining the interior of the Catacombs in Paris by the light of a candle.

9. THE HUT ON FOWLS' LEGS.
   The drawing showed a clock in the form of the hut of Baba-Yaga, the fantastical witch, on the legs of fowls. Moussorgsky added the witch rushing on her way, seated on her mortar. An episode is suggestive of the Death Witch stirring the cauldron over a roasting fire.

10. THE GATE OF THE BOHATYRS AT KIEV.
    (First Complete Performance in Scotland).

(2)

"FIVE SONGS FOR CHILDREN,"   ...   *Igor Stravinsky*
(The Magpie—Song of the Bears—The Raven
—Tillimbom—The Jack Daw).

Misses Campbell, Thomson, Bain, Shiels, Miller & Elliot
(Sung in Russian).
At the Piano,   -   -   Miss Jessie Moodie.
(First Performance in Britain).

(3)

NOCTURNE in "B." flat   ...   .   *Paderewski*

PROCESSION OF CRABS, ...   *Erik Chisholm*
Published by Curwen.

TANGO, ...   *Erik Chisholm*

(4)

JAVA SUITE, ...   *Leopold Godowsky*

1. GAMELAN.
   This is the title of the native music, played by the Javanese on their indigenous instruments.

2. WAYANG PURWA (Puppet Shadow Plays).

3. CHATTERING MONKEYS
   At the Sacred Lake of Wendit.

4. THE BROMO VOLCANO,
   And the Sand Sea at Daybreak.
   (First Performance in Britain).

(5)

SONG OF THE VOLGA BARGEMEN,   ...   *Glazunov*

PETITE VALSE, ...   *Pouishnoff*

IN A THREE-HORSE SLEIGH,   ...   *Tschaikowsky*

GOPAK, ...   *Moussorgsky*

PRELUDE in "C" sharp minor, ...   *Rachmaninoff*

2   The programme of Chisholm's 1926 Russo-Scottish Society recital

outrageous it becomes. 'Great artists cant be treated like that' indeed!! Treated like what? And who ever said he was a great artist to begin with?[56]

But others will have to reveal to what behaviour Sorabji is referring.

In the interim, Chisholm had crossed the Atlantic to take up appointments as organist and choirmaster at the Westminster Presbyterian Church, New Glasgow, Nova Scotia, and music master at Pictou Academy.[57] It is very probable that an uncle of Chisholm's was living in Nova Scotia at the time, hence the opportunity to work there. The family, however, is unable to confirm the existence of Uncle George, never mind his place of residence, so the only evidence is a letter some four years later, from 'Your affec: Uncle' to Erik.[58]

In Nova Scotia, he gave a number of successful recitals, in February 1928 performing the Tchaikovsky B♭ minor Piano Concerto, accompanied on the organ by George Scott-Hunter.[59] 'Erik Chisholm's work as soloist in the concerto was dazzling. There is no denying that technically the piece was in the palm of his hand, so to speak. It was a performance long to be remembered.' And the critic was equally enthusiastic about his group of piano solos, which included Ravel's *Jeux d'Eau*. Later that month, also in Westminster Church Hall, New Glasgow, he and Bernice Stultz gave the first of five recitals including all the Beethoven violin sonatas, alongside songs and modern works.[60] Chisholm also directed what was claimed to be the first performance in Canada of Bach's *St Luke Passion* with the Westminster Choir.[61]

But Pictou and New Glasgow were no match for Old Glasgow, especially with a bribe from his father of a new piano and a studio,[62] and Chisholm was back home to stay by the end of the year.

CHAPTER 2

The Active Society

Bringing the Heroes of Modernism to Glasgow

THE DOINGS OF THE ACTIVE SOCIETY FOR THE PROPAGATION OF Contemporary Music are of such interest and so well written up by Chisholm and his wife, Diana, that this chapter is not only a long one, but has extended quotations from the 150 pages of Chisholm's unpublished lectures on *Men and Music*, which describe his encounters with some of the most famous composers and performers in twentieth-century music. They constitute a unique document, and their publication is long overdue. In the meantime, what follows here, in Chapter 4 and in Interlude: The Love of Sorabji will have to satisfy the curiosity of scholars of Bartók, Bax, Casella, Van Dieren, Hindemith, Ireland, Medtner, Petri, Schmitt, Cyril Scott, Sorabji, Szymanowski, Tovey, Lamond, Walton and others. But to begin with, it is helpful to establish the relatively modest but youthfully exuberant background from which Chisholm produced this extraordinary series of concerts.[1]

In September 1928, Leff Pouishnoff wrote, glad that Chisholm was 'back in England [*sic*]', but hoping for greater things for him and offering to disseminate an orchestral score (unidentified) of Chisholm's. On his return from Nova Scotia, Chisholm took up piano teaching in Glasgow. Margaret May describes him as 'a very encouraging, if somewhat strict, teacher'. He taught the Leszetycki method 'insisting on straight wrists at all times. He appeared to have a dislike of Brahms, and most of my pieces were by modern composers, especially Bartok.'[2]

The lessons were given at a Chinese piano, in the conservatory at his parents' home in Caerlaverock Road. It was 'covered with (fearful) dragons' (Margaret was four years old when she first encountered them); and there was a pipe organ in the hall, which Erik's father had given him as a birthday present. Alas, the piano did not survive the journey to Cape Town after the war. Chisholm was also appointed organist at St Matthew's Church in Glasgow, and it is probably for the excellent instrument there that he composed the *Symphony from the Hebrides* for organ, which is missing its conclusion.

Chisholm was still seeking composition lessons, though illness seems to have prevented him from visiting Holst, who recommended Gordon Jacob and Herbert Howells.[3] But, composition apart, his musical education was very far from complete, and realising, thanks to the persuasive good sense of his wife-to-be, Diana Brodie,[4] that he needed a degree if he was to further his career, Chisholm applied for university entrance. In this he was supported by a recommendation from Pouishnoff:

I beg to certify that Mr Erik Chisholm has studied with me the art of piano playing for a number of years and that in the course of our work together he proved
to be the possessor of a keen brain and highly developed intelligence. Although
deprived by his poor health of the opportunity of going through the ordinary rou-
tine of a school education, he, by means of reading and exchanging his opinions
with worthy people, filled this gap most successfully ... I may add that my opinion
of him as a musician is of a very high degree and I shall be greatly surprised (and
disappointed) if he fails to make his name and position a subject of pride for his
fellow-countrymen.[5]

Such recommendations were necessary as Chisholm had never completed his
schooling and had none of the requisite qualifications. An equally glowing testimonial came from Hugh Roberton, conductor of the internationally renowned
Glasgow Orpheus Choir.[6]

I have known Mr. Eric [sic] Chisholm for a number of years and regard him as
the most brilliant and promising of our younger Scottish musicians. In his music
he is both daring and original. Apart from music, I regard him as a young man of
much more than ordinary intelligence. ... [H]e has that kind of native intelligence
in literary and kindred matters which may be called a gift.

I have no doubt he would bring nothing but credit to any University which
admitted him.

A couple of years later, commenting on Roberton's knighthood, Chisholm's
own view of the choir took the form of a back-handed, but entirely accurate compliment:

We have a new musical knight, Sir Hugh S. Roberton, whose famous Orpheus
Choir still continues to amaze by its faculty of gaining the maximum of artistic
effect from the minimum of musical quality.[7]

Chisholm was duly accepted by the University of Edinburgh, but his studies
with Donald Francis Tovey appear to have been as unorthodox as his admission. Most Tuesday mornings he would travel to Edinburgh to attend Professor
Tovey's lectures and Reid Orchestra rehearsals, which were themselves illustrated lectures of sorts. He would then walk across Edinburgh with Tovey to
his house for lunch, the latter discoursing the whole way. Lunch was followed
by Tovey looking at Chisholm's compositions, which provided the occasion for
more lecturing on music. Under the influence of the lunchtime wine, Chisholm
confessed to dozing off occasionally, but Tovey never noticed.[8]

Early in 1929, Chisholm gave recitals in St Matthew's United Free Church,
including some of his own transcriptions of Elgar, Strauss, de Falla and the
'Rondes Printanières' from *The Rite of Spring*.[9] Chisholm's own account of these
quite wonderful, even hilarious ventures cannot be bettered:

In the church there was a fine three-manual organ on which I gave a number of organ recitals. Respectable works like Bach Preludes and Fugues and Choral Preludes, Karg-Elert's big Op. 66 [in fact Op. 65], (which occupied three evenings) and transcriptions I had made (for I knew no better!) of Stravinsky's *Sacré du Printemps* [*sic*], Strauss' *Don Quixote*, Elgar's *Falstaff* and other exciting orchestral works. They were mostly pieces that had not yet found a place in the programmes of the Scottish Orchestra.

The three Karg-Elert evenings were favourably reviewed in *Musical Opinion*: 'By his playing, Mr. Chisholm fully justified his courage and enterprise in undertaking these recitals.'[10] Erik continues:

> I asked a bright young student friend of mine, Patrick Shannon, to assist me in these orchestral transcriptions, to the extent of placing himself inside the organ case, and banging cymbals, side drums, triangles, castanets and so on, at appropriate places in the score. Of course, nobody knew he was there, and I didn't fail to make a flowery gesture with hand or foot to show the audience it was all my own work. The music-liking Glaswegians (it would be an exaggeration ever to call them music-lovers) began to sit up and take notice of Chisholm and his unique orchestral organ. The upshot was that Pat Shannon and I became confirmed partners in musical crime, and one extravagance led to another.
>
> Pat was a gifted and versatile young musician, playing piano for a sketchy living (in bioscope, cafe, pub and music hall). He was also a fine organist, played all percussion instruments, and – given a week's notice – was prepared to tackle any string, wood-wind or brass instrument ever invented. ... He lived with his sister and widowed mother in Pollokshields, and his mother adored her brilliant, harum-scarum loveable son. ... We next launched a series of what we called *National Musical Recitals* – again in the kirk – roping in some singer friends, using the church choir and gradually building up a performing unit of keen, talented and adventurous young musicians.
>
> With Pat playing the orchestral parts on the organ, and I the solo piano parts, we performed the Delius concerto, *Nights in a Garden in Spain* [*sic*], Medtner's second concerto, Bartok's first, the Franck *Symphonic Variations* and *Les Djinns*.
>
> To keep up the reputation of the organ itself we had, of course, to find a new recruit to play percussion in the organ case.
>
> All that I remember about this new chap is that his face was covered with pimples, and he had a lisp. More to the point – he couldn't count rests properly. There was a revealing incident when Miller, or whatever his name was, crashed his cymbals fortissimo in a quiet bit in a slow movement. After that disaster, Pat and I decided it was safer to let the organ look after its own reputation.[11]

Somewhat improbably, it might seem, Patrick Shannon turned religious and became Provost of St Andrew's Cathedral, Aberdeen; whether in later life he jollied up the hymns with cymbals, drums and castanets is not recorded, though he did instigate 'Kathedral Kapers' with the Youth Fellowship and the curates of the cathedral and is fondly remembered to this day.[12] In any event, Erik and Patrick and the arithmetically challenged Miller were not the only performers:

> We got the choir to sing a difficult work like Kodaly's *Psalmus Hungaricus* with one of our own boys, Logan Annand, doing the solo tenor part. Annand was an ambitious singer, whose intonation could be distressing, and he had a habit of cupping his right ear in his hand as though trying to sell coal in the Cowcaddens.
>
> But his enthusiasm and eagerness to learn new works amply compensated for these little foibles. One of his most accurate performances was in the difficult *Sonata Vocalise* of Medtner where the voice is used as a solo wind instrument, without words. This requires a voice of beauty and great purity of tone to bring it off successfully, and our Logan's voice was more noted for quantity than quality.[13]

As regards quantity as opposed to quality, the coalmen of Glasgow were without peer. In Chisholm's day the Cowcaddens area of the city contained some of its oldest and most characterful, as well as poverty-stricken, housing. Coalmen (usually small, if not actually stunted and bow-legged from childhood rickets) would project their melancholy cries of 'coooaaal' towards the top floors of five-storey tenements, and then cup their ears to hear the reply from hastily raised sash windows. If coal were needed, these same men would carry hundred-weight sacks up five flights, day after day. It is small wonder they occasionally cheated their customers.

Quantity rather than quality might also apply to the compositional output of the conductor Ian Whyte (1901–60), who was invited to contribute to the concerts. The following assessment is, from many other accounts, entirely fair.[14]

> Whyte's vital (if dour), musical (if uninspired), self-assured (if slightly condescending), personality was a new and exciting experience, and we saw at once the possibilities of having guest artists. If we could get some really Big Shots to play for us, it could be possible to increase the range of our concerts and thus attract a wider public.[15]

All of this spirited adventure was soon to take on a new and even more impressive role in the form of the accurately, if ponderously named 'Active Society for the Propagation of Contemporary Music'. There is no doubt that Chisholm was the leading instigator, and from the start the Society dreamed grand dreams and approached leading individuals at home and abroad. The Society was probably founded around June 1930,[16] but was not formally constituted until 13 October 1930 in the showrooms of Chisholm Decorators at 63 Berkeley Street, Glasgow.[17] The headed notepaper bears an impressive list of names, most of which were on the first prospectus, sometimes holding slightly different offices. The Duchess of Atholl succeeded Tovey as President, and the Honorary Vice-Presidents included Bartók, Bax, Lord Berners, Bliss, Casella, Delius, Van Dieren, Hindemith, Medtner, Sibelius and Walton.[18]

The Foreword outlined the familiar problems of so-called music lovers who 'will not listen to music unless it is written in a well-defined tradition', pointed out the necessity for change and outlined the aims of the Society, so that 'the intolerant attitude of most musical organisations towards all music composed later than about the end of last century' might be led to at least study and endeavour to understand the new music before rejecting it.[19] Among those approached was the famous Scottish writer Neil Gunn, who reluctantly declined:

> Dear Mr Chisholm,
>
> I am now a member of so many Scots Societies whose meetings I can never attend, that it's really little use my joining your Active Society ... But I am extremely interested in what you have sent & shall do my best to bring the astonishing news before whatever music lovers I may meet and, where I can, mention it in writing. I am always interested in Sorabji's notes in the <u>New Age</u> and wish I could hear him at the piano on Dec 1, when C. M.Grieve [Hugh MacDiarmid] tells me he will be in Glasgow ... assuring you that I shall do my best to spread the glad tidings.
>
> Yours sincerely,
> Neil M Gunn[20]

To further these aims, Chisholm proposed that lectures be given and that scores acquired by the Society be loaned to the Mitchell Library for study prior to the concerts.[21] He also published programme notes in the *Scottish Musical Magazine*, reproducing an essay by his fellow Scot, Cecil Gray, on Van Dieren.[22]

The concerts, which ran from 1930 to 1937, were impressive in their scope, showing breadth of taste and an ability to attract some of Europe's most significant composers and performers. A list of the prospectuses and programmes with an outline of their contents is given in Appendix 1.[23] They included Walton conducting his *Façade*; Hindemith playing his own sonatas for viola and viola-d'amore, with Chisholm at the piano; Sorabji giving his one and only performance of his *Opus Clavicembalisticum*; Medtner premièring his *Sonata Romantica*; Casella conducting his *Serenata* and playing piano solos; Bax playing the piano in his viola sonata; Bartók performing a number of his piano works and accompanying his songs; John Ireland playing the piano for some of his songs and his *Phantasie* Trio in A minor: Bartók, for a second visit, performing his own early music transcriptions, pieces by Kodaly, and his Sonata in E: and Chisholm playing the Shostakovich Twenty-four Piano Preludes, among many other works scarcely known at that time. Egon Petri also came and performed Busoni, but attracted an audience of little over a hundred. Chisholm, having cautiously engaged one of the smallest concert halls in Glasgow, was none the less caustic about this turnout:

> Then, of course, the present economy urge which is sweeping the country just now is a heaven-sent excuse for the mean-fisted ... to do without what they don't

3 Erik Chisholm, March 1933

want. A new car or fur coat … Ah! but that is different. We *must* have our bit of fresh air and fun, mustn't we?[24]

In this sense of frustration, he was joined by no less a figure than Hugh Roberton. In greeting the formation of the Active Society he mixed his personal enthusiasm with a proper sense of caution. After listing some of the famous names about to come to the city, he wrote:

> You will now understand why that prospectus nearly took my breath away. I felt very much as an old ferryman must feel when a motor boat first dashes from point to point of his oft-rowed river. … I see in this a young man's revolt … a revolt against the innate conservatism of musical bodies; the cry of the children for liberty to express themselves. … A brilliant start is being made, such a start as could only be made by young men. Glasgow is thereby honoured. Will Glasgow rise to the occasion? I wish I could answer the question in the positive. Alas, the walls of Philistinism are deeply founded. This we know. But we know also that the giant Goliath was slain by a certain stripling called David. Good luck, my lads![25]

These generous sentiments from Sir Hugh deserve attention, for he had not long before received short shrift from the rebarbative pen of Hugh MacDiarmid, who branded him as a reactionary, liable to do long-term damage to Scottish musical culture.[26] That MacDiarmid appears never to have given credit to Chisholm for his work, either as concert promoter or as composer, is equally worthy of attention.

However stout the walls of Philistinism, Chisholm himself must have gained hugely from these experiences, not only meeting with his fellow composers, watching them conduct or hearing them play their own music; but performing with them, absorbing their styles, not by imitation or grim academic study, but through the fingers and the body movements of the men with whom he conversed and performed. But it was at a cost.

> The contemporary music concerts I ran and financed almost single-handed for about 10 years in Glasgow … brought me in no income. On the contrary, they resulted in well nigh wrecking my own private practice as a music teacher, it being whispered around – 'if we send our children to Chisholm for music, they will get nothing but the music of Bartok and Schönberg to play.'[27]

Chisholm was still composing during all these activities. The *Straloch Suite* was finalised in 1933 (see Chapter 1), and a first version of the *Piobaireachd* Concerto was finished in 1932 (see Chapter 3). In 1933 Chisholm premièred his *Dance Suite for Orchestra and Piano* with the Scottish Orchestra under Barbirolli and then at the ISCM Festival in Amsterdam with Constant Lambert conducting,[28] and the overture for small orchestra *The Freiris of Berwick* was also completed in 1933. But there is no doubt that the Active Society must have taken up a huge amount of his time.

Not all the concerts involved the invitation of foreign celebrities. On 2 May 1933, for example, the programme included works by Bloch, Szymanowski and Schmitt, performed by Chisholm, Wight Henderson, a string quartet and singer Sally Thomson; but it was followed by Cyril Scott, who came to perform his own works in the same month; and that autumn Chisholm was trying to set up an exchange with Peruvian composers.[29]

The opening W. G. Whittaker concert did not, unsurprisingly, raise any eyebrows, but was well received. It was celebrated with appropriate dignity, if lacking a subsequently characteristic panache. Sir Daniel Stevenson, as Vice-President, gave a speech; and letters of support from the Duchess of Atholl (who agreed to become Honorary President), Barbirolli, Bartók and Delius were read out by Erik.[30] He kept his mouth shut on other matters, however:

> Whittaker – a noted Bach scholar – was really no great shakes as a composer and he resented our band of young musical hooligans leading the musical life of Glasgow under his nose. On more than one occasion he threw a spanner in our works, and so, though lip service was paid to the incumbent of the Gardiner Chair of Music, there was no love lost between us.[31]

By contrast, Chisholm's relationship with the Reid Professor of Music in Edinburgh was one of intense admiration of pupil to master, and the 1931–2 season of the Active Society opened with a concert given by Tovey (piano) and the flamboyant Gasparini (cello). Tovey's Sonata in F major and *Elegiac Variations*, the Röntgen Sonata Op. 56 and the Debussy Cello Sonata made up the programme, Beethoven having been ousted.[32] Tovey's music is somewhat Brahmsian in character, but immensely accomplished and at times both beautiful and exciting.[33] Chisholm primarily regarded him as an academic mentor, for he avoids any reference to his compositions, but the affection and regard he felt for him shines through every paragraph of his study of him.[34]

If the Whittaker concert provided a somewhat low-key start to the 1930–1 season, a fortnight later, Walton's *Façade*, with Parry Gunn giving out Sitwell's parodic nonsense via a megaphone positioned in a hole in the backdrop, set a more appropriate tone and attracted a large audience to the Stevenson Hall. Walton noted that twenty-four poems had been advertised and wrote:

> The programme should really consist of 18 poems, but I see in your magazine there are 24. The last 6 I should like to be cut out as they aren't particularly good specimens & are only there to lengthen the programme if it is being done alone – the 18 last about 45 mins, which is more than enough for anyone.[35]

Chisholm recalled the occasion with amusement and perhaps a little self-satisfaction:

> For the two Glasgow performances, we hired the special curtain from Oxford University Press. On this were two clowns –one on each side of the centre piece

– a Facade-y looking building: one clown is holding a guitar and reciting, the other holding a pipe and playing on it, representing the two elements in *Façade*, speech and music. Our first performance was on Tuesday October 28, 1930.

Walton 'had little practical experience of conducting' and Parry Gunn, the narrator, had trouble fitting in with the music:

> Walton was tentative, quiet and shy, and even at the final rehearsal made practically no comments to the players. He seemed quite happy at the way they played his music, and although obviously he could hear that Parry Gunn was rather shaky in his entries, was invariably polite, friendly and appreciative.
>
> Before the performance, however, he seemed a little nervous. The synchronisation of the orchestra and narrator was on the whole satisfactory, until we came to the fourth group – three rather elusive pieces – *By the Lake, A Man from a far Countree* and *Country Dance* when Gunn seemed to backfire on himself and got hopelessly out in the rhythms. Walton turned a little pale, looked faint, and made a feeble gesture in my direction which I interpreted as a wish that I should take over the stick from him.
>
> We were, of course, all hidden behind the screen so no one in the audience was aware that conductors had changed mid-stream. Oddly enough, in a letter from Walton which I received in November 1963, he refers to this incident. 'I well recall the *Façade* performance, but how or why it ended with the baton in your hand, I cannot remember.'[36]

Not only was Gunn out of time, he was also largely incomprehensible, if not inaudible, according to the *Daily Express*. But on the whole, *Façade* was received favourably in the spirit in which it was always intended.[37] Walton wrote to Chisholm, thanking him for payment and pleased that a repeat of *Façade* was proposed. 'All the notices seemed encouraging', he wrote.[38]

Hindemith followed a fortnight later. He had just written a game for children, *We Build a Town* for children's voices and any three instruments. Typical of his *Gebrauchsmusik* (Music for Everyday Use), it is unpretentious, tuneful and unambitious. Chisholm got hold of a score and gave it to Agnes Duncan, who rehearsed it with her Junior Orpheus Choir. On the night, they gave a word-and-note-perfect performance, at which Hindemith was both amused and delighted. The concert included Hindemith playing the sonatas for solo viola; for viola and piano, Op. 11 No. 4; and for viola d'amore and piano, Op. 25 No. 2. Chisholm writes:

> I was the pianist, and, although I played a great deal in those days, I certainly had qualms about being a competent partner for such a world-famous composer and virtuoso player.
>
> Hindemith had an international reputation from 1921 onwards, and I see that our local music critics (by no means au fait with the then futuristic music) however much they may have been puzzled by his music, all referred to him as the

'famous' Hindemith. One such critic described the viola sonata as representing a rare buoyancy of spirit, perhaps better described as a kind of powerful restlessness.[39]

With the assistance of a local viola player (Mrs Shannon – our Pat's mother) I had been practising the piano part for several weeks before the concert. Hindemith was kindness itself at the rehearsals. He seemed pleased that I was quick on the uptake, immediately caught on to his tempi, and was not afraid to give him plenty of support. ... I remember that in a certain passage in the viola d'amore sonata, Hindemith said: 'Would it not be better if you played it this way – with such and such a finger? And do use more downward wrist movement for a cantabile touch'. I quickly slipped off the piano stool and he gave me a convincing demonstration.

It was fun, too, to hear and accompany a viola d'amore. This was, indeed, the first time I had ever heard the instrument. It is similar in size to the ordinary viola, but had six or seven gut strings, tuned in 3rd and 4th, and a secondary set of fine steel strings lying close to the belly. In Hindemith's instrument it was decorated with a circular rose and a blindfolded Cupid on the head. I believe this ornamentation was original.

Hindemith played with great gusto, sweeping the bow powerfully across the strings in the many arpeggio-ed six-note chords.[40]

4 Paul Hindemith

Hindemith's request for more downward wrist movement in order that Chisholm could produce a better cantabile suggests that the Leszetycki school, with its insistence on permanently straight wrists, if followed too rigidly, could lead to rigidity in playing. But to be fair to Chisholm, the viola d'amore is scarcely a well-matched partner for a modern concert grand.

The next concert contained songs by F. G. Scott. It would be a pity if the more famous names associated with the Active Society were to push aside a composer of Scott's quality. His songs are intensely beautiful, and his idiom a wonderful blend of native Scottish lyricism and energy, with the modernist techniques of polytonality, unprepared dissonance and the like. If Henri Duparc can hold an international reputation on the basis of a few songs, then F. G. Scott deserves at least as much. Chisholm knew it, and he knew the world should know it. He wrote about 'F.G.' as being 'not only the best thing in Scottish music today, but … a composer whose work bears comparison with the best that is being written anywhere at the present time.' Chisholm went on to recognise in Scott something he himself had been working on since childhood, the development of a Scottish idiom that was 'long since past the stage of direct imitation', and praised him for his fastidiousness and conscientiousness.[41] He might also have praised him, along with all the other Glasgow-based musicians, for his generosity:

> Apart from Sorabji (who had pots of money anyway – Dad was a millionaire) we gave all our distinguished visitors as large a fee as we could afford in addition to paying their travelling expenses and hotel bills, if private hospitality was not available. On the other hand, in the 10 years of the Society's existence, none of our local performers ever got a penny for their services – there just wasn't any money left over.[42]

As one of the singers had fallen ill, Scott sang, apologising for his voice – unnecessarily in the view of the *Daily Express* and the *Evening News*, who enjoyed his characterisation of the songs.[43]

As if Walton, Hindemith and Scott were not a rich enough offering of varied fare, the next in line was Leon Dudley Sorabji. Well, that was the name on his birth certificate, but he changed it, and the world now knows him as Kaikhosru Shapurji Sorabji – to which one is tempted to add 'of that ilk'. But Sorabji and Chisholm together demand treatment on their own (see Interlude: The Love of Sorabji). Suffice it to say here that Sorabji's performance of his own *Opus Clavicembalisticum* deserves to remain numbered among the great iconic events of the modernist movement in music.

Bernard Van Dieren was to have come next, for a concert in December 1930, and he did indeed arrive. Had Cecil Gray told Chisholm in advance that Van Dieren knew nothing at all about the physical side of conducting and that he suffered from constant and incurable kidney pain, the invitation to conduct might have been reconsidered. Chisholm did recognise 'a curiously elusive quality about Van Dieren's music, which makes a good performance unusually difficult …

Much of his music is without bar lines, and a characteristic "prosy" quality makes it yield up its secrets only after prolonged and intensive study.' These, at any rate, were the explanations he gave for what he described as Van Dieren's 'shocking' behaviour.[44]

Van Dieren and his wife, Frida Kindler, a noted pianist, came up a few days before the concert to allow him to take the last few rehearsals of the chamber orchestra. The singer, John Goss, was coming later for the final rehearsal.[45] The concert had attracted a lot of attention and some people were even coming up specially from London. The orchestra had been selected from the best available players; everything was in place and all boded well. Let Chisholm (leaning heavily on Diana's version)[46] take up the tale:

> Lunch with them [the Van Dierens] on the Sunday was an enjoyable affair over which he enthused about such less accepted musical gods as Meyerbeer, Busoni, Alkan and Berlioz. He complimented us highly on the pioneering work of the Active Society and it was in a particularly happy frame of mind that I escorted them along to the rehearsal. But beware of vanity. ... After a polite little speech ... Van Dieren got down to business. He looked at the orchestra, awkwardly lifted his arms and started waving them around. The orchestra looked at him expectantly – what was he doing? Once more he repeated the same gestures and this time one brave member of the orchestra scratched on his fiddle. Van Dieren began to look peeved, and rattled his baton for attention. Again he gesticulated wildly with his arms in mid-air, but not a squeak came out of the players.
>
> Van Dieren glared balefully at the orchestra, who was now beginning to look puzzled and not a little scared. The fact was that Van Dieren had failed to give them the necessary preliminary up-beat. Eventually they did come in and the rehearsal proceeded. Right from the start it was painfully obvious that this composer didn't think much of our band. Over and over again he stopped them, seldom letting them even finish a phrase. ...
>
> The interval came at long last. The players were looking either sulky or downright mutinous. Van Dieren stalked off madly into the artist's room and slammed the door. I followed after him to try and soothe his ruffled feathers, but was told to get out. In about 10 minutes time he flung open the door, stampeding into the room, for all the world like a raging bull. His face was scarlet, his eyes flashing, his lips set in a grim angry line. Heaven help anyone who made a mistake this time!
>
> We learned afterwards that he had taken a dose of cocaine – to ease his mental and physical agony. If the injection alleviated the pain, it certainly did not improve his temper. ... He stamped, raged, almost foaming at the mouth, and finally with a furious gesture flung his baton down and said the rehearsal was over.
>
> He said that he would go back to London that night and wire John Goss to stop him coming north. 'Couldn't we understand plain English THE CONCERT WAS CANCELLED.' For an hour or so we tried to persuade him to change his mind:

he was adamant – there would be no concert! So, the Van Dierens took the night Scot to London (after wheedling out of me cash to buy first-class train tickets – they had neither tickets nor money).[47]

Chisholm persuaded the orchestra to carry on under his own baton, and then spent half the night working up the pieces Mrs Van Dieren was intended to play, and a substitute singer, Robert Watson, who was an excellent sight-reader agreed to take up Goss's role. But it proved in vain. Watson developed laryngitis and the concert was cancelled.[48] It was to be one of those rare occasions on which Chisholm was defeated.

As for Van Dieren, he rushed off to see Philip Heseltine (alias Peter Warlock), apparently to unburden himself of his Glasgow disappointment. Warlock was an Honorary Vice-President of the Active Society and a great friend and supporter of Van Dieren. He was also in negotiation with the Active Society for a concert of his works; but he was a depressive and gassed himself that night, so Van Dieren was the last person to see him alive and also 'the first person to find Heseltine in the gas-filled room'.[49]

Sorabji wrote:

Van Dieren may realise the amount of labour you put into these concerts: but I doubt it ... And I am determined to make it my business to inform Van Dieren thereof and the heroic efforts you put out to make them a success.

I've just heard to my horror that Philip Heseltine has committed suicide.[50]

A subsequent correspondence, raking over the coals of the whole sorry affair, appeared in the *Glasgow Herald* and, as usual, resolved nothing.[51]

Things calmed down briefly with recitals of quintets by David Stephen, Gavin Gordon and Ian Whyte, with a little Satie thrown in, Satie almost qualifying as a Scottish composer on account of his mother, Jeannie Anton.[52] Pouishnoff came north and performed an all-Russian programme (hence no Chisholm?), including some Szymanowski. Next appeared Medtner with a programme of his own music, following on his appearance as soloist with the Scottish Orchestra in his Concerto No. 2. It is a measure of the respect in which the Society was held by such well-established figures that Medtner honoured Glasgow with the first performance of his *Sonata Romantica*. The concert in the Stevenson Hall, which is not large, was poorly, but enthusiastically attended, although one critic voiced similar reservations about the textures of his music to those made about Sorabji's *Opus Clavicembalisticum*, namely that they were too thick and unrelieved.[53] Chisholm himself occasionally allows his fingers to run away with his compositional self-control, but it is a rare occurrence and perhaps only really obvious in the sonata *An Rioban Dearg*, which is discussed separately (see Chapter 3) and which remained unrevised. Medtner would have hated the work. He disliked anything that smacked of modernism and wrote to Chisholm in the autumn of 1931 asking for his and his wife's names to be withdrawn from membership of the

Active Society: 'I consider the activities of the composers active army [*sic*] (the majority of them) not only hostile to our art but even pernicious.'[54]

The Medtner concert was repeated in St Andrews, but only after the removal of all the portraits from the walls, which unnerved Medtner, who also refused to play the new sonata on the grounds that the piano had not had enough time to recover from its journey. In the end, Chisholm was relieved that A. M. Henderson and his wife had monopolised the Medtners, who were, in any case, grateful to them for previous kindnesses – to such an extent that Medtner dedicated the *Sonata Romantica* to Henderson. Years later, Chisholm met the widowed Mrs Medtner in Moscow and they laughed gently together over Henderson's determination to keep the Chisholms at arm's length (see Chapter 9).[55]

Three weeks after Medtner, Casella was in town, conducting and performing his *Serenata*.

> Casella was tall, thin and military looking, wore white trousers and sports canvas shoes and had sunken sleekly, southern sexy eyes. He came to Glasgow in 1931 to give a concert of his works for us on February 23, and intended to repeat the programme three days later in Dundee.[56] When he arrived in Glasgow a telegram awaited him with news that his mother was gravely ill. So he felt compelled after the Glasgow concert, to rush off to Northern Italy, which left me to find substitutes for the missing items.
>
> Casella composed sunny, cheerful, tuneful, attractive quasi-Neapolitan music: diatonic stuff with a modern slant. In 1916, he wrote *Five Puppet Pieces* (March, Berceuse, Serenade, Nocturne and Polka) which exist in two versions – orchestral and for piano duet, and which were popular.
>
> Casella played primo and I secondo at the Glasgow concert. It was all great fun. He was much taller and broader than I (in those days I was very thin, indeed my Mother used to say you could blow peas through Erik's ribs) and I had to hold my head high and generally assert myself on the music stool not to be pushed off by Casella's leonine but militaristic bulk.
>
> I remember that while rehearsing the Serenade movement (where in the middle the left hand of the top player has to play a passage below the right hand of the bottom player) we had to stop and rewind. The accompanying pattern at the beginning of the *nocturne* required my right hand to nip right smartly away and out at the end of each quaver chord, to avoid lacerations from Casella's pinky nail.
>
> After the performance he clapped me chummily on the back and was very matey.
>
> At the rehearsal of his concerto for string quartet, Casella conducted the players, but of course, left them to their own resources at the concert. I asked him what the narrow strip of red ribbon in his buttonhole of his jacket signified. He replied that he was a member of the Italian Fascist party, as I suppose most of the Italian national intellectuals were in 1931. ... Casella held himself very erect and

had a keen military look about him. Before conducting his delightful *Serenata for clarinet, bassoon, trumpet, violin and cello*, he clicked his heels together as though on the parade ground.[57]

It is one of the many ironies of war that the next time Chisholm and Casella were to meet was during the Allied advance northward through Italy, when Chisholm took the opportunity to send the Casella household some much-needed supplies, as the Casellas were too poor to make use of the black market (see Chapter 6).

If poor old Casella was to end up wondering at the consequences of a marriage between Italy and Germany in the cause of fascism, Busoni had revelled in the artistic fusion between the two countries which features so strongly in assessments of his work. Perhaps only an Italian in love with the German intellect could treat Bach as did Busoni. Liszt had, of course, set a precedent: but with Bach himself, virtuosity (whether at the keyboard or as composer) was always the servant, not the master. Busoni's practices were taken to their extremes by Sorabji, and, given Chisholm's own predilections and pianistic skills, it is to his credit that he denied himself the emotional self-indulgence of Sorabji, the intellectual self-indulgence of Busoni and the pianistic self-indulgence of both. In his later years, he was able to view Busoni with a degree of detachment:

> I doubt very much if many Busch works were performed anywhere during the 1950s and the early 1960s. This is not to say he was a bad composer. It's simply that his music, like that of Tovey, Joachim, Rontjen, Busoni, Van Dieren and a 1000 others, is not just good enough to stay in the world repertoire.[58]

It was much to his disgust, however, that he missed the next concert on account of flu, as it was Egon Petri playing Busoni. Petri was a pupil of Busoni's and the leading interpreter of his often fiendishly difficult music. Such was his devotion to his master that he played for £15 instead of his usual 100 guineas. There was, sadly, a poor turnout. Busoni himself had performed in Glasgow two years before his death,[59] and Petri performing the *Fantasia Contrappuntistica* might alone have drawn more to the event, never mind the F minor *Fantasie nach Bach*, and the *Indianisches Tagebuch*, which was based upon Native American musical motifs.[60]

The next concert was postponed and the programme altered, but Ethel Smyth's Trio for Horn, Violin and Piano got a hearing alongside Brahms's work for the same combination.[61] This was a coupling not without its ironies, as the somewhat forbidding Smyth had been thoroughly put out when she met the equally forbidding Brahms. They were much more at their ease with the horn. But the real treasures of the concert were the F. G. Scott songs, which included 'Moonstruck' and the wonderfully-sustained and haunting 'St Brendan's Graveyard'.[62] Scott himself proposed the two groupings: 'The Wee Man', 'Chanson', and 'Country Life'; and 'Moonstruck', 'St Brendan's Graveyard' and 'Hey the Dusty Miller', commenting that 'That would give them a bit o' fat wi' the lean and not too much of either.'[63]

Bax followed in January 1932. His music had featured in two earlier concerts (see Appendix 1), and he and Chisholm became good friends. It was natural that they should. Bax had a penchant for Irish qualities in his music, and had a general leaning towards things Celtic (which included a degree of political radicalism no doubt also appealing to Chisholm). His style was even likened to the elaborate embellishments of Celtic design by one critic,[64] and in this he might be said to parallel some of the techniques of embellishment found in *piobaireachd*, Gaelic psalm singing and Irish sean-nós singing. Bax and Chisholm both played the piano, as did Dr Mary Grierson, a colleague of Tovey's from Edinburgh.[65] Meanwhile, Erik was trying to persuade Prokofiev to come and play for the Society. It was not to be. A convoluted correspondence kept stumbling over dates, fees, exchanges and the like.[66]

Compton Mackenzie (of *Whisky Galore* fame and perhaps not to be too closely associated with *The Monarch of the Glen*, given the eponymous television series) was at this time a keen supporter of the Active Society. He had recently been elected Lord Rector of Glasgow University, so was in Glasgow quite frequently and, as editor of *The Gramophone*, was potentially of considerable use.[67]

If the names of Bax and Compton Mackenzie failed to give the Active Society some status in the world, the next to come was perhaps the greatest coup of all. Schoenberg might have equalled it, but he demanded £1,000 per concert, which, as Chisholm observed, was one way of saying 'no'.[68] Bartók came twice to Glasgow, in February 1932 and November 1933, and these two concerts are treated here together. Despite his renowned shyness, he was altogether a more accessible person than Schoenberg. His fee was £15. He was glad to come for that,[69] and was at the piano throughout the evening of 29 February 1932 in the Stevenson Hall, which was, on this occasion, well attended.

The critics were duly deferential, particularly admiring his piano technique, though some found it excessively percussive, but also responding favourably to his interest in folk music, a characteristic which dominated the concert.[70] The programme is listed in Appendix 1.

There was trouble over the employment of Angela Pallas (one of Tovey's students) to sing a group of Bartók songs, resulting in Tovey's resignation from the Incorporated Society of Musicians. The ISM in London opposed the granting of a petition (to which Tovey was a signatory) sent to the Home Office on behalf of the singer, who was Greek. The letter from the ISM General Secretary exonerated the Edinburgh branch but failed to acknowledge the London branch's interference, so Tovey's resignation stood. Fortunately, the Home Office granted permission at the last minute.[71]

On both of Bartók's visits he stayed in the Chisholm household and it would appear that Diana, though not yet married to Erik on the occasion of the first visit, acted as hostess, no doubt also in her capacity as Secretary of the Active

Society. Many years later, and conflating the two visits, she described his arrival in Glasgow with her usual stylishness and powers of observation:

> When we knew Bartók was coming to Glasgow to stay with us, the first thing, which worried us, was – language difficulty. None of us, of course, could speak one word of Hungarian ... you can imagine my disappointment, when, on meeting Sir William Burrell [Hungarian Consul in Glasgow] a few minutes before the train was due to arrive (8.35 p.m. on February 28 1932), he said he hoped that either my husband or I could speak Hungarian because he could not. ... But we need not have worried. When the Flying Scotsman arrived and the passengers alighted from the train it was quite simple to recognise him. There was only one Béla Bartók! A small white-haired man, wearing a black Homburg hat, thick black coat with a heavy Astrakhan collar and armed with a music case in one hand and an umbrella in the other. Who I wondered had forewarned him about Glasgow's weather?
>
> Sir William went forward at once to greet him, and I swear I saw a look of relief flit across the consul's face when Bartók said in a softly spoken, broken English accent, 'Bartók is my name'. After that all went smoothly.

Diana felt that Bartók had 'built an invisible barrier of defence for himself against the outside world'. She also noticed that, apart from his heavy overcoat, his suits, though well tailored and well pressed, were equally well worn, and his shirts were frayed at the cuffs and collars.

> Altogether he gave one the impression of 'putting a face' on things generally, and being harassed by some secret worry. The face of a pathetic little man – but an intensely proud one who was also a musical genius.[72]

He told them very little about himself, apart from the fact that he had a wife and son; but he made a great fuss of their baby daughter, Morag, and seemed to be very fond of children, and, where music was concerned, he would and could talk at length. The Chisholms thoroughly enjoyed his stay, and appreciated his almost fanatical love of folk music – not just Hungarian or Slav, but of all countries. Normally his face looked rather stern and taut; but when he spoke of these vital aspects of his life: 'his whole face lit up and his eyes became pools of liquid fire'.

And if initially he seemed distant and unapproachable:

> [W]hen he found he could relax, and was in no danger of being 'lionised' (the soul-searing penalty the celebrity pays for being a celebrity) and that he was among friendly, sympathetic people, his whole personality seemed to change, to become electrified.
>
> Then one became aware of the terrifically forceful personality of this seemingly quiet, shy, self-effacing musician. Here was someone with dynamic strength of will to achieve what he had set out to do with his life. Erik asked him if he had

ever come across the folk music of Scotland, and in particular, if he had heard any of our ancient piobaireachd (Pibroch) music. Bartók confessed that this was one branch of folk music he had had no opportunity to study.[73]

How Bartók reacted to *piobaireachd* is dealt with in Chapter 3, but his reactions to his hospitality showed an equally characteristic curiosity:

> We served him a typical Scottish high tea – a plate of meat or fish supported with cake, scones, butter, jam and tea. I asked him if he would like gooseberry or straw-berry jam. He said, 'No thank you,' then as an afterthought – 'Is it manufactured or homemade?' I said it was homemade. 'Then I'll have some' he replied: 'Home-made jam has character and taste, bought jams neither.' …
>
> On another occasion he lunched at the home of my friend, Ernest Boden. He hardly spoke at all during the meal, but once expressed interest in the fish course, which happened to be halibut. Apparently he had neither heard of nor tasted halibut before.[74]

Bartók left behind him some of the scores from which he had performed (they are unmarked) and also a copy of his *Über die Herausgabe ungarischer Volkslieder* of 1931, signed, 'To Mr. Eric Chisholm with kind regards Béla Bartók. Glasgow, the 29th Febr. 1932.'[75] As for his attitude to his own compositions, Diana noted that he spoke of them with detachment 'almost as though someone else had writ-ten them'. His greatest failure, he said, had been *The Miraculous Mandarin.* '"The story,' he said with a sly smile, 'was considered immoral by some theatre manag-ers and consequently had only a few performances." '[76]

It would seem that Bartók shared with Chisholm a sense of mischief. He had asked Erik to turn the pages during both rehearsal and concert:

> Just before the rehearsal Bartók pointed out a particularly difficult passage in the score and asked Erik if he would play the notes in the bass for him. Somewhat surprised but anxious to please Bartók he agreed to do this. When it came to the actual playing of the part at the concert, Bartók gave my husband a flashing imp-ish grin, and, of course, played the whole passage brilliantly.[77]

Bartók's second appearance in Glasgow was for a concert on 2 November 1933. The programme contained some of his transcriptions of works by Purcell, Marcello and others:

> After he had played through these pieces, on the morning of his concert, Bartók turned to me saying: 'You know, Mr. Chisholm, that whenever I play these tran-scriptions, the critics always complain that I have made considerable modifica-tions in the originals. As a matter of fact, I have not altered a single note.'
>
> Although I didn't say so at the time, I could see why this mistake had been made. Bartók played this music in his own dynamic, rhythmically arresting fash-ion, so that, even if all the notes were the same, the music sounded as though Bartók had altered it.[78]

A group of Kodaly pieces followed, and the recital ended with Bartók's Sonata in E, some shorter pieces, and the Sonata in Three Movements of 1926. But, sadly, the review in the *Glasgow Herald* does little more than describe the programme and gives practically no sense of Bartók either as composer or performer[79] – a deficiency made up for in Diana Chisholm's own account:

> I have never heard anything to equal the rhythmic intensity, the sheer percussive vitality, the dash and abandon, the actual physical reality (some critics called it brutality) of the sound content in Bartók's playing of the first and last movements. The only pianist of this time who approached Bartók in this respect is the Hungarian and unofficial pupil of Bartók, Andor Foldes. When he played, the legs of the piano seemed to be twitching in an effort to join in this animalistic, choreographic, Pan-worship rite.[80]

On the second visit, Bartók had in his music case the manuscript of some of his Forty-four Duos for Violins. 'These, he said, had their origin in folksong material which he had adapted for educational purposes: the violinistic counterpart to his earlier collection of easy teaching pieces in the *For the children* volumes and similar works.'[81] Also in the case was the full score of the Second Piano Concerto.

> It was written in the composer's own precise, cleanly pointed and highly characteristic pen work on transparent draughtsman's paper. ...
>
> Bartók knew I had played the solo part of his first piano concerto and asked how I thought the piano writing compared in the two concertos. At the time he was sitting on the edge of his bed turning over the pages and I was on the armchair. I saw that No. 2 did not seem so rhythmically complex as No. 1, and that there were some uncomfortably big stretches – chords consisting of two piled-up perfect fifths in each hand: later a whole string of rapid semiquavers in block chords. Bartók did not have particularly large hands, and yet managed to play these passages without undue difficulty.
>
> I knew from the previous year's concert that he had wrists of steel, and was a virtuoso pianist. The opening of the second movement struck me as a typical Bartók slow movement. ... I passed over some pages until I reached the *presto* section of this two-sided movement, which combines slow movement and scherzo, and raised my eyebrows enquiringly at my first sight of tone clusters. He smiled, then replied in that soft, almost inaudible voice of his: 'Not my invention, I'm afraid. I got the idea from a young American composer, Henry Cowell.'
>
> Bartók was a very quiet, shy, calm and thoroughly collected person and disliked being made a fuss of. It was said that when gushing admirers addressed him as 'Master' or 'Maestro' he would reply, with barely concealed irritation, 'My name is Mr. Bartók.' So I did not press him for any further information about Henry Cowell.[82]

Many years later, visiting Nicolas Slonimsky in Boston, Chisholm met Cowell by chance. He was well acquainted with Cowell's work and found him 'a most likeable and fascinating fellow, and like Bartók himself, fanatical about folk music.'

> He told me, that when he was in London in 1923, Bartók accidentally overheard him playing some of his own music, which employed tone clusters. He was extremely interested in this new technique, and later wrote asking if he might be permitted to use similar tone clusters in his own compositions.
>
> Cowell said that his chance encounter with Bartók was one of the most exciting episodes of his life. Bartók had invited him to come to Paris and demonstrate his revolutionary technical devices to some of Bartók's friends, including Ravel, Roussell and Manuel de Falla.[83]

With Bartók we shall leave this chapter and the Active Society. Not that the latter became inactive, but its doings were, perhaps, less dramatic and arresting and can be recorded as they fit in with Chisholm's emerging passion for opera – the direct result of a new and challenging appointment, for which he was ideally adapted and which is covered in Chapter 4. But this one cannot be closed without pointing out that throughout all of these activities, Chisholm was still composing and, for a study of some of the Scottish fruits of those labours, the reader is directed to the next chapter.

CHAPTER 3

Chisholm's Scottish Inheritance

IF THERE WAS ONE THING THE ACTIVE SOCIETY FOR THE PROMOTION
of Contemporary Music did not do for contemporary music, it was to support
Erik Chisholm. It did occasionally focus on Scottish composers, but there was
no attempt to pursue a Scottish agenda, whether in terms of native composers
or native idioms. Chisholm redressed the balance through his own compositions
and by resurrecting the Dunedin Association (see Chapter 4).

Scotland had, and has, highly distinctive native idioms,[1] and no one was more
aware of this at the time than Chisholm himself. The latter half of this chapter is
given over to discussion of several of the works in which he explored the Scottish
idiom, but it is useful to begin with the background from which his unique and
challenging contribution emerged.

There are those who, thinking to prove themselves cosmopolitan, consider any
focus upon particular national styles a kind of offence against internationalism
– a word rendered meaningless if there is no such thing as nationalism. In most
sophisticated cultures this is not an issue: unfortunately, in Scotland it was and
remains a major issue, and it was one which Chisholm himself had to confront.[2]

> There are two attitudes generally adopted … to native composers: the first is
> summed up as follows: when the great Scottish composer does come along we
> will welcome him – we will play his work and acclaim him and do honour to his
> genius but so far Scottish music has only had talents and frankly we are not inter-
> ested in anything but the very best.
>
> And the second point of view is that unless we are willing to encourage what
> creative talent we do possess we are extremely unlikely ever to produce great
> musical composers. … Such an attitude is not likely to exist unless it is evolved and
> matured over a fairly long period and generally arrives as part of a rising national
> consciousness in the people. Take the case of the Bohemian and Finnish peoples
> towards their composers. The Czechs did everything possible to encourage their
> own musicians … and in a century they produced at least two men of outstanding
> genius in Dvorak and Smetana, besides a host of other important composers. At
> the time of the German occupation of Czechoslovakia I am told that in the pro-
> grammes of many concert organisations the predominance of native music was as
> high as 80%.[3]

The passage goes on to declare that 'Scotland is one of the least national-
minded races in the world', and in this concern he was far from being alone.
Hugh MacDiarmid, with splendid polemic, trumpeted the need for the nurturing and development of native styles,[4] but he consistently ignored Chisholm's
fundamental contributions, having time and space only for the significant but,

by comparison, relatively minor achievements of F. G. Scott. The reason for this was that Scott had been his teacher and virtually all his music consisted of settings of words – frequently MacDiarmid's. MacDiarmid himself had no musical appreciation whatever.[5]

Nothing daunted, Chisholm honoured his native idiom more fully than practically any composer before or since, and he must have taken particular delight in Bartók's presence in his own household, as a leading proponent of the study and use of folk music and one ready to engage with Scottish music also. Erik's wife, Diana, recalled Bartók's interest, and Erik incorporated her recollections into his own talk on Bartók:

> To many continentals Scotland just seems to be the top-part of England with no particular characteristics of its own. How wrong they are! If they travel to the North of Scotland and make contact with the Gaelic-speaking population, see our tartans, Celtic Crosses, and hear our piobaireachd music, they may realise that we have certain Asiatic qualities which are not shared by the Sassenach. ...
>
> Now, Scottish folk music, and especially Piobaireachd happened to be my husband's pet subject and particular study at that time. For years he had been doing considerable research in this line, so of course, he brought out various collections of folk music and gramophone records, and Bartók listened and studied these for hours. The result of this conversation was that the next day Bartók went to a well-known shop in town which supplied all Highland requisites, and came home with a tartan rug, a chanter, all the piobaireachd music he could lay his hands on, and told us that the manager of the firm had arranged with one of our most noted Pipe-Majors to come next day to the Grand Hotel to play the bagpipes to him (this was one thing my husband hadn't been able to do!). Bartók was enchanted.[6]

Such endorsement was, of course, welcome, but in Chisholm's case, unnecessary. His own interest had been sparked all those years ago when he chanced on Patrick MacDonald's *A Collection of Highland Vocal Airs* (illus. 5), as described in Chapter 1.

Quite apart from that one volume, Chisholm's interest in – indeed profound involvement with – Scottish traditional music is readily demonstrated.

> I started off being a Scottish national composer, but came under the influence of Northern Indian music when I lived in that country, and later the current dodecaphonic music. I have a hunch that I would like to end my musical days in Scotland: whereas the national dances of almost any country you could mention, have been stylised and worked into art music by national composers (in Bohemia, Smetana and Dvorak: in Poland, Chopin and Szymanowski, etc.) in Scotland – leaving vocal music out of it – there is not a single example of a March-Strathspey-Reel which exists outside traditional bagpipe music.[7]

Whether that is true or not, Chisholm composed a large body of works based on Scottish musical forms, tunes and styles; he arranged a considerable number of

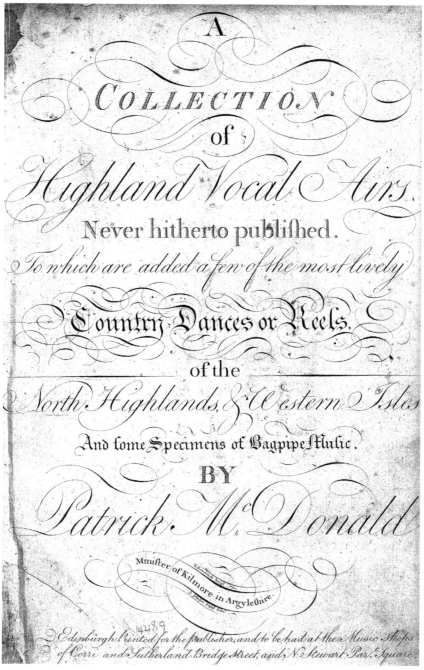

5 The cover of Patrick MacDonald's *A Collection of Highland Vocal Airs*, 1784

Scottish airs; and he published a collection of his own arrangements of Scottish song which culminated in the *Celtic Song Book*, for which he selected suitable texts. He also listed his Scottish works in a notebook;[8] to which may be added the *Highland Sketches* and the *Night Song of the Bards* and the settings of Lillias Scott's poems, which are in Scots and which Chisholm has set in a Scottish style (see Chapter 10).

The fact that Chisholm chose even to list such works indicates his sense of their significance as a genre in his music, and that they include so many major pieces indicates his seriousness of purpose with respect to his native culture and idioms. In this he was following in a long tradition (still very much alive), harking back to eighteenth-century composers such as MacLean, Oswald and Munro, who were already writing sonatas based on Scottish tunes.[9]

Chisholm was also aware of the traditions associated with his own clan, writing in 1945 that '"The Chisholm Salute", for example, is only to be played when the chief is in residence at Beauly Castle, at the birth of an heir, or on some important occasion in the life of that particular clan'.[10] He probably also knew of the Chisholm bagpipe chanter which would spontaneously crack on the death of the chieftain. It therefore bore several silver fillet repairs and, on one occasion, 'the family piper, when from home at a wedding, heard his chanter crack, and at once started up, saying he must return, for The Chisholm was dead. And he was.'[11]

He even seems to have thought of himself as a direct musical descendant of the MacCrimmons, citing his own McLeod ancestry:

> I now find myself speaking, musically, in the characteristic idiom of the Mac-
> Crimmons (a great family of Piobaireachd composers), through a twentieth cen-
> tury technique, and writing for the modern orchestra instead of for the Highland
> bagpipe. Virtually a descent of the MacCrimmon line, and I am occupied with the
> same emotions to which to give expression. My mother is a McLeod, thus giving
> me descent from two Highland clans.[12]

The MacCrimmons were one of the leading dynasties of pipers and composers of *piobaireachd*, and in Chisholm's day their pre-eminence was undisputed. Added to this family connection is a clear interest in the cultural history of the Celts and, specifically, the Gaels, manifest in the Preface to his book *Celtic Folk Songs*,[13] in which the tunes are derived from the Patrick MacDonald collection, and in the Celtic mythological basis of several of his ballets and operas.

Further clues to the breadth of Chisholm's knowledge of traditional Scottish music can be found in works to which he refers or which were listed from his library.[14] He must have had quite a few to show Bartók,[15] and his personal copy of Patrick MacDonald's *A Collection of Highland Vocal Airs* is heavily marked. Chisholm was also familiar with the *Straloch Lute Book* (see Chapter 1), and he copied many of the tunes from William Dauney's publication of the Skene MS

6 Chisholm's copy of Patrick Macdonald's *Collection of Highland Vocal Airs*

in G. F. Graham's transcriptions.[16] He also knew the *Forbes Cantus Book*,[17] and Campbell's *Albyn's Anthology*.[18] Of course, Johnson's *Scots Musical Museum*, with its many Burns settings, was well known to him, along with George Thomson's publications, with further Burns settings. He had access to the *Celtic Monthly*, and he had copies of articles on Gaelic music.[19]

With respect to the Gaelic language, he practically always uses the Gaelic spelling of *piobaireachd* when the Anglicised 'pibroch' was the norm, and he contributed to a concert in Glasgow in 1927 with his name printed in Gaelic as 'Uilleam Siosal'. However, his own knowledge of Gaelic was clearly scanty, consistently misspelling *aotrom* as 'antrum', and the like. His debt for the gift of the Patrick MacDonald book (see Chapter 1) was paid in music, not words.

■ The Patrick MacDonald works for piano

> I have read with much interest your collection of Gaelic melodies, airs & dances, & congratulate you on your excellent arrangements, especially those for more advanced players.[20]

It would seem from Granville Bantock's remark above that Chisholm had started work on the Patrick MacDonald airs as early as 1929. With three exceptions, all of the tunes for these four collections of pieces were drawn from MacDonald's *A Collection of Highland Vocal Airs ...* published in 1784. Many of the airs selected overlap with the *Celtic Song Book*, which contains some 200 vocal settings. But between the *Airs from the Patrick MacDonald Collection*, the *Petite Suite*, the *Scottish Airs* and the *Scottish Airs for Children*, there is only one tune out of sixty settings of MacDonald used twice – MacDonald's No. 5.

This suggests that these four groups were conceived as complementary and could possibly be assembled into a kind of *gradus ad Parnassum*, starting with the *Scottish Airs for Children*. For studies of the individual pieces, the reader is directed to the liner notes for *Erik Chisholm, Music for Piano*, vols. 1–4, Dunelm Records, DRD0222–0225. A list of the airs and their MacDonald equivalents is given in Appendix 2.

■ Scottish Airs for Children

Chisholm wrote 'For the children' on the title page (presumably his own three daughters), with the further intention of publishing them in three graded volumes, for which he had drawn up lists.[21] The manuscript is undated, but the airs were arranged in the 1940s, when he was still in Scotland and the children were still young. Not all have titles in the MacDonald source, and occasionally Chisholm intended a different title deemed more suitable for children. These he mostly crossed out, perhaps because he also planned for the pieces to be accompanied by poems by A. T. W. (as yet to be identified) and drawings by Wm. C. – presumably William Crosbie, who designed the sets and costumes for Chisholm's ballet *The Earth Shapers*.

These are pieces of great beauty, their sensitivities enhanced rather than diminished by the directness and simplicity of treatment required for children. The variety of texture he achieves with what is basically the simplest of two-part writing is remarkable. The writing for the left hand is particularly good, developing different kinds of independent motion without compromising the melodies. Their quality and variety is matched by Chisholm's treatments. Practically every kind of technique of variation is involved – in structure, extension, register, key, harmony, cadence, part-writing, texture, articulation and so on. These are classics of their kind and should be standard issue for all young pianists, Scottish or otherwise; but they remain unpublished.

Airs from the Patrick MacDonald Collection

These thirty-five pieces are naturally technically and harmonically much more demanding than the *Scottish Airs for Children*, but in amongst them are one or two which are not only simple, but have been fingered (in what appears to be Chisholm's hand) where no fingering was called for, unless for a learner. Sometimes the harmonies are pulled about almost outrageously. No. vi provides an example, but wittier still is the *a tempo* in No. xi, which hints at an utterly conventional dominant seventh and foils its resolution. The final cadence of this piece of impudence still manages to hold on to the fundamental modality.

On another occasion (No. x), virtually the entire harmonic substructure is written in smaller notes as though to be played as a background coming from a different part of the landscape. It requires considerable control of tone and dynamic to achieve the right effect, which, in part, mirrors the alternations between solo and chorus in the original, which Chisholm has restructured. This variety is evident from start to finish. The very first tune – a waulking song with chorus – enters with splendid aggression, only to find its energies dispersed into something almost poetic in its final quiescence – all within the space of twenty-four bars. The set ends with a splendid rendition of 'Prince Albert's March', invigorated by quasi-ostinato, octave displacements and cross-rhythms. This piece does not appear to come from the Patrick MacDonald airs and its title also places it much later.

One might, like Perdita, have been tempted to describe the freedom of treatment in these pieces as producing 'nature's bastards'. But, as Polixenes points out in reply, the art itself is nature – and it was certainly second nature to Chisholm. These have gone beyond being 'settings' or 'arrangements', and yet they are not wholly independent pieces. Without the tunes embedded within them, and frequently quite clearly stated, they could not exist. They might best be thought of as Scottish musical orchids, propagated in the fertile greenhouse of Chisholm's musical mind – quixotic native exotica – if the oxymoron may be permitted.

The six movements of the *Petite Suite* were also titled *Highland Sketches Book II*. They are described individually in volume 2 of the CD series referred to above.

■ Scottish Airs

Much of what has been said of the *Airs from the Patrick Macdonald Collection* could be said of the *Scottish Airs*, which are really part and parcel of the same compositional group. The *Lento* (No. viii) marries the Scottish tonal idiom with a quasi-chromatic one without any sense of dislocation and with no hint of self-conscious devices such as all too frequently mar arrangements of traditional material.

The opening piece, marked *poco pesante*, has nothing to do with the character of the Gaelic title – *A bhanarach dhonn a' chruidh* ('The Brown-haired Milk-maid') – but finds a determined strength in the melody with its wide stride. This wide range with seventh or octave leaps is a common feature of Gaelic airs, and one is tempted to relate it to the varied and dramatic contours of the landscape. For those who inhabit that landscape, such features are not unusual; but seen by an incomer, the drama is almost daunting, and what is an obvious path to a local is invisible to the stranger. Chisholm is not a stranger in this musical landscape; but he is not a local, either. He was basically an urban man, and he hears in these airs what he chooses to hear. But his instincts are good. It would be a mistake to create too many typologies of Gaelic airs and then criticise Chisholm for trans-gressing their distinctions. There are indeed types, but many tunes cross bounda-ries, and traditional musicians will turn an air into a march and think nothing of it. Chisholm's skill, as well as his nationality, earns him the right to join their company and play with the material as he pleases.

If the first air has little connection with its title, the opposite is true of the second – *Ceud soraidh nam do'n Ailleagan* ('A Thousand Blessings to the Lovely Youth'). The tenderness of this setting – and it is a setting in this case – reflects exquisitely the sense of a blessing imparted from a girl to her lover, with its sweetly enriched harmonies and gently spread chords.

The next two airs take us into a mood of 'pawky humour', as Chisholm writes as an instruction, and the fifth returns to a gentler mood, providing a lull before the assertiveness of the proud hero, Ossian – the sixth bard in Chisholm's *Night Song of the Bards*. Chisholm knew this widespread legend of the return of Ossian from *Tir-nan-og* (The Land of Youth), only to find that centuries have passed in his absence and there are none left to remember the great days. It is for this reason that the piece is not a lament, but a powerful statement, with full chords, harmonically relatively straightforward and ending with a determined heroic flourish.

The following piece is entitled *Aisling*, which more truly translates as 'vision' rather than 'dream', as MacDonald has it. In either event, the experience is any-thing but spooky, and Chisholm treats it accordingly – *poco scherzando*, and as chirpy in the left hand as is the tune in the right.

The *Lament for McGriogair of Roro* is, however, a different matter. This is an old tune, nowadays played by pipers as a Retreat,[22] and Chisholm treats it with due respect, but using the left-hand decorations and a descending arabesque to fill spaces where at this tempo the piano cannot, like the pipes, sustain the sound on the main melody notes or lead it into the next phrase. The group concludes with a spirited jig featuring splendid cross-rhythms.

Sixty pieces based upon the Patrick MacDonald airs were used by Chisholm in the groups referred to above – the remaining three probably come from other sources. One might think that would have satisfied Chisholm's desire to bring this treasure trove to public light. It did not. He returned to them in other works such as *The Forsaken Mermaid* and the *Celtic Song Book*. Most of the pieces are relatively short. Some are miniatures. What is astonishing about them, however, is that within what might be thought severe limitations, Chisholm has found a world of expression, of wonderful variety of mood, technique and texture. There is not one of these pieces that lacks interest, not one that overstays its welcome. They have the potential to appeal to all ages and abilities, and they bring to new life much of the melodic and rhythmic vocabulary of Scottish tradition, from whose deep well they spring, and their water is clean and good.

◼ Chisholm and *Piobaireachd*

In a press interview with Thomson Newspapers dated 16 March 1964, in response to the question what was the chief turning-point in his career, the second of the three Chisholm listed was '[W]hen I first became acquainted with "Piobaireachd" bagpipe music – later with the instrumental art music of India.'[23]

The uses to which Chisholm put his knowledge of *piobaireachd* are discussed below and in the Centre-piece. Many readers, however, will not know what the term refers to, never mind attempt a pronunciation, so there follows here a brief introduction to the form and an account of its influence on Scottish composers writing for a different medium.

The word *piobaireachd* simply means 'pipe music'. In the past it referred primarily to one particular form of pipe music, known today also as *ceol mór*. The older usage is retained throughout this book. It refers to a theme with variations. The theme is called an *ùrlar*, which means 'ground', but has little in common with the same term in sixteenth-century classical music. The *ùrlar* is a carefully structured melody, often with repeated or slightly varied units, which are gradually varied and embellished, often culminating in virtuosic display before returning to the initial material. The character of the *ùrlar* is determined by the choice of mode and how that mode relates to the drones, which constitute the unchanging bass. In this, the ground of a *piobaireachd* has nothing whatever in common with a ground bass, which necessarily changes pitch.

Piobaireachd is one of the most extended instrumental forms to be found in European traditional music. Despite the restrictions of the bagpipe's nine-note scale and the ever-present drones, the variety of invention and expression is astonishing. The basic form itself is readily enough applied to classical music, but it is the influence of the drones and of the different styles of embellishment which have intrigued its imitators and produced some remarkable music. Notably, from the early eighteenth century, a number of *piobaireachd* survive both in manuscript and as published pieces, arranged for fiddle or piano.[24] Chisholm knew of at least four of these, which form the concluding pieces to Patrick MacDonald's *A Collection of Highland Vocal Airs*, which he had studied from childhood.

The first classical composer to have used the term 'pibroch' (in its English spelling) to describe an original composition seems to have been Alexander Mackenzie. His use of the term is loose, his piece being a set of classical variations on traditional tunes, rather than *piobaireachd*-style variations on an *ùrlar*. That said, the *Pibroch Suite* (1889) for violin and orchestra is a stunning piece of music in which Sarasate revelled, and it and Mackenzie's *Scottish Concerto* provided excellent and internationally successful precedents for the use of Scottish melody for Mackenzie's successors.

From Hamish MacCunn, William Wallace, Learmont Drysdale and Frederic Lamond there is not, to my knowledge, any serious engagement with *piobaireachd*. However, though McEwen's slow march in his Piano Sonata in E minor is not a *piobaireachd*, the slow pace of the melody, with its main notes richly embellished, has surely some echoes of the form.

One of the reasons for the lack of involvement in *piobaireachd* was that it is notoriously difficult to transcribe. Pipers for the most part prefer to have nothing to do with written versions, learning *piobaireachd* from the fingers and *canntaireachd* of their teachers – *canntaireachd* being a kind of non-centralised sol-fa in which the vowel sounds represent notes and the consonants the finger movements for the different 'cuttings' or embellishments.

There had been some research into *piobaireachd* – notably by Major General Thomason in 1900.[25] But Thomason's shorthand transcriptions, though efficient in terms of space, were not user-friendly. Other researchers such as Lucy Broadwood and Frances Tolmie devoted their efforts primarily to song – specifically Gaelic song. The latter's researches were extensively used (with Tolmie's willing co-operation) by Marjory Kennedy-Fraser, whose equivocal position as a folkmusic collector is still regarded with the utmost suspicion in the Gaelic-speaking areas of Scotland.[26]

Marjory Kennedy-Fraser never really approached *piobaireachd* – though it was traditionally sung, both in short and extended song form and in *canntaireachd*; but Granville Bantock (who owes as much to Kennedy-Fraser as she does to Frances Tolmie) did try his hand at the form. His 'Pibroch' from his *Scottish Scenes* was composed in 1917–18 and starts impressively. Unfortunately, his romanticised pianistic conclusion spoils the effect, but there is no denying it is a striking piece, which he dedicated to the Queen's Own Cameron Highlanders.

On the other hand, F. G. Scott's song 'St Brendan's Graveyard' has the direction 'Like a Pibroch – impersonal and without nuance', which is not really true of *piobaireachd*, although it is a magical song, timeless and perfect in its simplicity. 'F. G.', as he was familiarly known, did, however, publish an article on *piobaireachd*, in which he analysed the same piece used by Chisholm for the *Piobaireachd* Concerto.[27]

What this tells us is that Chisholm had practically no precedent to work from in his adaptation of *piobaireachd* to classical music, or vice versa. His contribution was unique, ground-breaking and musically thoroughly convincing, in particular in the *Sonatine Écossaise*, the *Piobaireachd* Concerto and the Sonata in A – *An Rioban Dearg*, which are considered below; but also in a number of interpretations of *piobaireachd* in a series of piano solos of that title.

Piobaireachd

Based on individual *piobaireachds*, these studies were well under way, if not complete, by 1933. Almost as important as the *ùrlar* or main melody in *piobaireachd* are the 'cuttings'. These groups of rapid fingering patterns cannot really be described as 'ornaments' or 'graces'. This is something of which Chisholm was acutely conscious. In the *Evening News of India*, in pointing out the functional parallels between *piobaireachd* and Hindustani music, he wrote:

> Grace is not just some unessential additions to a melody, as it is in the incomparably richer Western harmonic musical language, but is an integral and inseparable part of the whole.[28]

Some examples are reproduced in *Scotland's Music*,[29] but they represent only a fraction of the fingerings, many of which have to be rearranged depending upon which note they are emphasising. This is because the open chanter is always sounding, so notes cannot be repeated without some other note or notes being interpolated. This apparent limitation has been developed as a powerful and yet very subtle feature which allows the music to choose just how much emphasis is given to any one note.

The subtlety and complexity of the applications of these 'cuttings' partly explain why *piobaireachd* is not played rapidly. It is not that the players do not have the technique – the standards are phenomenally high – but that the pointing of the melody would be lost at too rapid a speed. Likewise, Gaelic psalm-singing, which is highly embellished, is performed at a very much slower pace than psalms elsewhere in Europe. With *piobaireachd*, the challenge for the piper is never to lose the flow of the melody and yet to address each note, understanding its place in the whole.

One can, to a limited degree, reproduce some of these effects on other instruments, but in the end, if the tradition is to be honoured in such a radically different context as a keyboard, then one must make use of the different opportunities it offers. Chisholm had the knowledge and the pianism to do just that and, right from the start of his *Failte Chlann Raonaill* (ex. 4), the drone is not only enlivened by grace-notes and by added fifths and octaves, but also by pitch displacement and many other devices which are used to suit the concept to the keyboard.

Ex. 4 *Failte Chlann Raonaill*, bars 1–9

When it comes to the variations, the drone may be transposed into the right hand with the melody line underneath; and the drone itself, instead of being a reiterated note or octave, becomes an oscillation between three notes. The drone element becomes increasingly dissonant as pitches are displaced by a semitone in a cumulative manner, until the upper drone evolves into the melody line, but with the left hand remaining liberated in what has developed into a three-part texture. Yet, overall, the *piobaireachd* impression is still powerful in the music – the patterned repetitions, the steadiness of the pace, the style of the 'cuttings' and the adherence to the underlying phrase-structure all leave one in no doubt as to the Highland bagpipe origins of the music.

Chisholm treats each *piobaireachd* in a different manner. 'The Lament for the Harp Tree' is presented with arpeggiated chords, suggestive of the harp and also suited to the song-like element of the tune, and it is only developed by a single variation; whereas 'The Salute for Clan Ranald' is an extended piece with a stunning pianissimo variation in racing semi-quaver octaves, followed by a 'March' variation, a return to the *ùrlar*, and a final 'Presto'. As for his treatment of *Cas air amhaich, a Thighearna Chola* or 'MacLean of Coll Putting His Foot on the Neck of His Enemy', Chisholm clearly revelled in the violent power of the image.[30] His shifting drone is approached with off-key cuttings and is reiterated at first in, and then out of synchronisation with the *ùrlar*, of which practically every note is given a cutting. The opening of *Cluig Pheairt* shows him using a similar technique to that of 'MacLean of Coll' but, by placing the right hand in the upper register of the piano and keeping the left-hand drone reiterations clearer harmonically, he achieves the effect of bells – the title translates as 'The Bells of Perth'.

Further detail and discussion of these pieces can be found in the liner notes for *Erik Chisholm, Music for Piano*, vols. 3–5, Dunelm Records, DRD0224–6.

■ The Sonatine Écossaise

Chisholm's heart was undoubtedly firmly lodged in Scotland, but his assertion of his Scottishness is no simple matter. If we take the *Sonatine Écossaise* as an example, we should start by noting that its final title is in French. Why? Because this is not a piece of cultural revivalism or an attempt at authenticity – in which case the title should have been in Scots or Gaelic and the idiom uncompromised by polytonality – but rather it is a distillation of characteristics expressed through an idiom derived from an intimate feel for the tradition and an equally intimate feel for the cosmopolitan sophistication of French culture in the period preceding its composition.

This is not to say that Scottish traditional music is not sophisticated – it would have been an uneasy bed-fellow in such a situation were that the case. It is merely to indicate that Chisholm has found a place for it in a culture which was at the time extremely 'knowing' and which was borrowing from Javanese, Russian, Spanish and Blues sources simultaneously, in the works of Debussy, Stravinsky and Ravel. Chisholm's genius is to have found a place for the Scottish idiom within this broad context, retaining the native vitality in an international setting. It is extraordinary that this stylistic achievement, which has produced beautiful music, clearly structured, coherent and individualistic, has not made more of an impact.

At the level of British response to its traditional music, if we listen to Chisholm's own 'March, Strathspey and Reel', forming the third movement of the *Sonatine Écossaise*, we are in an altogether different world from that of Kennedy-Fraser and Bantock. It is the difference between active, participating virility and leisured imitation. She distorted her originals and occasionally sentimentalised them. Her 'Benbecula Bridal Procession' is a typical example of how the tradition can be charmingly emasculated. The words speak of 'rap of reel-step' and 'thrill of piping' – but of these there is no real sensation; nor is there anything of the sense of a procession. In fact the tune and words do not belong together. Kennedy-Fraser and her Gaelic amanuensis, Kenneth MacLeod (who should take equal share of the blame), made them up.

It would be unfair to Kennedy-Fraser not to acknowledge that she herself was a remarkable innovator in song arrangements. Compare her settings with any of the standard productions from the likes of Oxford University Press (*The Scottish*

Song Book) or Mainstream's *Songs of Scotland*, both decades later, and one real-ises that she is idiomatically at least as advanced. She took on board not only the modalism, but a degree of rhythmic and metric flexibility, and coupled these with textural adventure in her piano and clarsach writing. Her arrangements exhibit some of the recent stylistic developments in classical music – the influence of Debussy (who was profoundly enamoured of Celtic mist) is often apparent. But neither Debussy nor Kennedy-Fraser ever successfully engaged with the virility of traditional music, though Debussy's *Marche Écossaise*, based on the 'Earl of Ross's March', has its charms.

Chisholm's *Sonatine Écossaise*, on the other hand, displays understanding and daring simultaneously. Though revised in 1951, it was initially completed as early as 1929 with the title Pibroch Sonatina, when Chisholm was a mere twenty-five years old, and it already shows mastery of Scottish idioms.

The first movement – *Allegro con energia* – is in simple ABA form. It opens with a chromatically enriched version of *Ha-da-lolal-O* (MacDonald 15), later transposed up an octave and with polytonal harmonies. It is followed by *A Robaidh, tha thu gòrach* (MacDonald 152). This is a melody of great beauty, which Chisholm surrounds with Highland bagpipe filigree, but keeping the sweep of the melody ever to the fore.

The 'Lento' is a lament based upon the famous *piobaireachd Cha Till Mac-Cruimean* – 'MacCrimmon Will Never Return'. The basic story is that Domhnall Ban MacCrimmon composed the piece when leaving Skye, the chorus of the song predicting that he will never return.[31] In fact he was the only person killed at the rout of Moy in 1745, travelling with the MacLeods and Lord Loudon in the hope of capturing the Prince – the MacLeods did not support the Jacobite cause. MacCrimmon's death was foreseen by Patrick MacAskill, whose account was recorded in 1763. He had had a sudden vision of the six-foot-tall piper leav-ing for his last march, as no bigger than a boy of five years of age.[32] Many older Scots will recollect the song version as one traditionally sung at the quayside when people are emigrating, and it is quite possible that Chisholm not only knew the story behind this *piobaireachd*, but had also heard it sung on the quays of the Broomielaw, or further down the River Clyde; for his compatriots were still leav-ing for new lives in Canada and Australia well into the twentieth century. There is no bravura to be had in these circumstances, rather an aching nostalgia and, as a piece of pianistic texture, it is unique in the quality of its delicacy (ex. 5).

The concentrated riches of the final *Allegretto* are full of wit as well as poetry. It fulfils Chisholm's desire for a march – strathspey – reel set,[33] but it does so in under four minutes, with economy and a marvellous opening of a couple of exploratory drum-taps and a brilliant exploitation of piano texture, using the dif-ferent registers in a kind of *Klangfarbenmelodie* effect. The tune is MacDonald No. 9, treated as a 6/8 march with pointing of the rhythm so instinctively right that the forward drive becomes irresistible. The beat is accented with chords of two superimposed fifths and, once the pace is firmly established, with off-beat

Ex. 5 *Sonatine Écossaise*, second movement, bars 1–8

accents of the kind that musicians and dancers and hand-clappers will usually introduce as a tune settles in. The gentle refinement of the strathspey – 'Conon House' – takes a fresh approach to the Scotch snaps and dotted rhythms typical of the dance. This is a slow strathspey, elegant and beautiful, which Chisholm probably found in Logan's collection of 1924. The reel – 'Sleepy Maggie' – is characterised by the free movement of the left hand. Chisholm is a master at keeping his bass lines alive in forms which are inherently harmonically relatively static and which too often bind composers to a drone or the ubiquitous double-tonic. The leading American Scots fiddler, Bonnie Rideout (to whom I am indebted for identifying the tune as 'Sleepy Maggie'), wrote of it: 'And wow is Sleepy Maggie cheeky (must have swigged a few belts of something).' If only more musicology were expressed in such terms!

Taken as a whole, the structure of the sonata could scarcely be simpler, and this too is significant. It is in ABA form and the outer movements are also each in ABA form. Within each section, the thematic material is simply laid out. The tunes are stated and that is it. Within the tradition itself, the building up of a 'set' – a sequence of tunes – is an art of its own, but it rarely employs transitions. The skill is to find tunes which naturally run into each other, and this is a skill that is centuries old and readily observed even in early publications such as Oswald's *Caledonian Pocket Companion*.[34] In this movement, it is more within that tradition that Chisholm operates structurally, than within the European classical tradition. It is a method that cannot be readily described, never mind analysed. It relies upon sheer musical instinct and, in live performance, upon the mood of the moment.

▧ The *Piobaireachd* Concerto

Chisholm was also prepared to use this approach in larger-scale works. The Symphony No. 1 was built out of Cornish character pieces, no doubt collected during his stay there with the Pouishnoffs. As for Chisholm's Piano Concerto No. 1, the *Piobaireachd*, its individual movements are constructed on very similar lines to the *Sonatine Écossaise*.

An early version of the *Piobaireachd* Concerto was completed in 1932.[35] By 1936, it was revised and, in 1938, first performed in a broadcast from Edinburgh with Chisholm as soloist and Ian Whyte conducting. The first public performance, however, was in the St Andrew's Halls in Glasgow on 20 January 1940 with Chisholm again as soloist and Aylmer Buesst conducting the Scottish Orchestra.[36]

The *piobaireachd* on which the first movement is based is *Maol Donn*, now known as 'MacCrimmon's Sweetheart'. *Maol Donn* is in fact a lament for the death of a favourite cow and it has an associated *piobaireachd* song. Songs in praise of individual animals are common in the Gaelic-speaking world, and with good reason. Since his mother was a MacLeod, Chisholm would have welcomed the association of this tune with the MacCrimmons, who were the MacLeods' hereditary pipers. This may be a lament for a favourite cow, and such passions may seem ridiculous to some readers in an orchestral context, but we are dealing here with a culture which has retained much of its closeness to nature and which, at least at the time this *piobaireachd* was composed, still retained a degree of veneration for cattle, as is the case to this day in the East.

Barnaby Brown convincingly classes the *ùrlar* as an AABA BBAB or 'tail-woven' structure.[37] Chisholm's treatment is, however, entirely his own. At an early stage, the *ùrlar* is accompanied by sympathetic echoes of itself. The high A, used in the first and second variations of the original, appears (but not in the same way) at the end of the opening section of the concerto, heard in the upper woodwind, and the first and second variations are much more energetic affairs than would be the case in a normal *piobaireachd*, the piano stamping out the rhythm in the bass, with the tune in the violins and upper wind. These two variations form a pair, in much the same way as *piobaireachd* use what are known as 'singlings' and 'doublings' of a variation. In the 'doubling', the usual main difference is that cadential notes are also decorated, so the effect is of a slight increase in pace. There follows a return to the opening mood. This, though rarely if ever done in modern *piobaireachd* playing, used to be an integral part of the tradition in the eighteenth century.[38]

The ensuing variation (an 'Allegretto scherzando') is in jig tempo and brings out a totally different character in the tune. This is followed by a thoroughly joyful variation leading to the cadenza which runs the jig to ground and, via a ruminative passage, prepares us for a return to the opening, but in different guise. This is no conventional recapitulation of the main theme or, as would also occur in the tradition, the *ùrlar*. Instead, before we are back with the oboe and the drone on A, it is cloaked in a cloak of magnificence, a tone lower, on G. This upswell of feeling – it is marked *appassionato* – is more in the classical than in the traditional mould, technically speaking. But in terms of its emotional effect, it captures and extends that moment which, in a great performance of a *piobaireachd*, hovers between the elaborate and the simple as the *ùrlar* returns.

The 'Allegro Scherzando' is a wonderfully energetic Scottish dance, delivered with a splendid mix of Stravinskian neo-classical techniques and more volatile Bartókian twists, twice grounding itself in a slow powerful passage in the lower register which, on its second appearance, is summarily dismissed with the last gesture of the movement. The tune itself is a lively variation on the *piobaireachd Fàilte Uilleim Dhuibh Mhic Coinnich*, 'The Earl of Seaforth's Salute'.

The slow movement is based upon the famous *piobaireachd*, *Cumha Dhomhnuil Bhain Mhic Cruimein*, 'The Lament for Duncan Bàn MacCrimmon', for which Chisholm has marked the solo piano to be played 'very distant and impersonal'. This *piobaireachd* is reputed to have been composed by Malcolm MacCrimmon on the death, in 1746, of his younger brother, Donald Bàn. Donald Bàn is also the subject of *Cha Till MacCruimean* (see the discussion of the *Sonatine Écossaise* above). Even if it is not by his brother, we know that when Donald Bàn was previously captured, the pipers on the opposing side refused to play until their own leaders released him, which was duly done.[39] So it is anything but an impersonal *piobaireachd*. It is written of the famous piper John MacDonald that it 'was almost sacred to him'.[40]

If it was sacred to Chisholm, it was in a very different way. He has enshrined

it as though it were indeed a sacred object from the past, announced and concluded by a stroke on a gong, and veiled in mysterious textures. Low flutes set the
tone, over which the piano leads in with the *ùrlar*, like a bird in the night, utter-
ing high, complex cries, brief but haunting, and derived from the *piobaireachd*
and taken up by the oboe.

The sense of mystery is continued in the first variation, with the veiled tonal
wash of the piano and horn, against which a solo violin, followed by solo clarinet, draws out a long, thin line of sound from another world. The harmonic and
orchestral textures here are rich and strange – sometimes coming like waves of
water or light. Throughout it all, phrases from the *ùrlar* emerge and sink back
into the texture. As the music gathers strength, the trumpet sings its own lament
against rising arpeggios from the soloist, and the inherent riches of the whole
burgeon into a glorious climax which suggests a vastness beyond. There is a
close similarity between this movement and the latent and sometimes terrifying
power of the *Night Song of the Bards* (See Centre-piece).

The 'Allegro con Brio' starts as a reel – a quintessentially Scottish dance form –
which has traditionally involved rhythmic twists as part of its repertoire of tricks,
and which Chisholm is quick to exploit, with syncopations and notes picked out
by additional emphasis, here achieved through declamatory orchestral chords,
where the traditional fiddler would use bow attack or double-stopping. Into
this repertoire of standard tricks, Chisholm throws chromatic displacement of
chords and spirited orchestration, tossing fragments of rhythm around from section to section – and 'rhythm' is the operative word.

'Does melody or rhythm come first in your music?'

'I rather think the rhythmic impulse is strongest; a definite body stimulus which,
   by its continued reiteration induces a feeling of magnetic attraction (or sheer
   monotony) is a characteristic of the Piobaireachd, and also in my music.'[41]

The tune is number 16* in the MacDonald collection, and demonstrates that even
a quite uniform pattern, when related to pitch with skill, becomes wonderfully
provocative, rhythmically.

A more lyrical section follows, and triple time breaks the patterns until the
piece gathers energy and (perhaps anticipating Bartók's Third Piano Concerto
on its way back to the reel) now stamping a foot, now swirling and turning until,
with a final fusillade of off-centre chords, it ends anything but exhausted, but
with a flourish as much as to say, that is enough for now. It was not often that
Chisholm ran out of energy, and when asked, 'If you could make one wish, knowing it would come true, what would it be?' he ended his reply 'otherwise, more
talent or less energy!'.[42] Many would say he was a driven man, and this is certainly
a driven movement and rejoices in that fact.

Taken as a whole, this four-movement concerto not only introduces a new
idiom into the world of the concerto, but also a new type of virtuosity. The piano

concerto as a form is riddled with cliché, but the twentieth century, particularly in the concertos of Bartók, broke through to a new kind of pianism. Chisholm had played the solo part of Bartók's first concerto in Glasgow, but Bartók had only just completed his second concerto on his second visit to Glasgow in November 1933 (see Chapter 2). Chisholm's piano writing is totally different from both of these works. If there is a Bartók concerto which might be placed alongside the Chisholm, it is the third – composed after Bartók had met Chisholm and travelled home with *piobaireachd* under his arm. It was also after Chisholm had composed the first version of the *Piobaireachd* Concerto, which dates from 1930 and also precedes Bartók's second.[43] One would not want to assert that there was any proven connection between Bartók's experiences in Glasgow and the composition of the Third Piano Concerto but, given the fame of Bartók and relative obscurity of Chisholm and that Bartók stayed with the Chisholms, it is worth pointing out that Chisholm would have been able to play his own *Piobaireachd* Concerto to Bartók and that any influences might easily have gone either way.

Moreover, in the lengthy history of Scottish composers adapting traditional music to their own ends, even to the present day, Chisholm himself excepted, there is nothing more radical than this to be found. Composers such as Edward McGuire, John Geddes, William Sweeney and I thought we were breaking new ground in the 1970s and 80s. Little did we know. In this context, the fact that Maxwell Davies's *Orkney Wedding with Sunrise* should have become the work most closely associated with bagpipes in the public mind is hard to bear. The *Piobaireachd* studies, the *Sonatine Écossaise* and the *Piobaireachd* Concerto were not Chisholm's only radical treatments of *piobaireachd*, and he extended his ambitions in this direction still further, notably in the sonata *An Rioban Dearg*, but also in the orchestral work *Pictures from Dante*. Many who break new ground do not sow much seed therein. Chisholm, however, sowed good seed and his successors would do well to pay far more attention to the quality of his crop before considering ploughing it back into the soil to fertilise their own.

The Sonata in A – *An Rioban Dearg* is in four movements: *Molto moderato*; *Scherzo, Allegretto con moto*; Lament: HMS *Thetis*, 3 June 1939; *Allegro moderato*. It was premièred by Wight Henderson in Glasgow, November 1939, but subsequently lay unidentified in the University of Cape Town Archives in disparate manuscripts. Happily, research by the composer's daughter Morag led to its rediscovery and reconstruction. Henderson's performance was praised, and he was indeed a very fine and commanding performer. It was, on the whole, intelligently received.[44]

The sonata, unrevised as it is, and reconstituted from two sources, is occasionally prolix. Murray McLachlan has introduced some cuts into his second recording of the work and these are mostly judicious.[45] Nothing like this extraordinary adventure in pianism has been penned before or since, Chisholm himself excepted. Not even the extravagances of a Sorabji or the bravura textures of a Busoni can account for the pianistic colour in this work, derived almost entirely from Scottish sources – drones transposed, double tonics, complex decorative turns based on bagpipe fingerings and large structures built from small repetitive units. The uncut version is the one referred to here.

The first movement is a set of variations on *An Rioban Dearg*. The title translates as 'The Red Ribbon' and the *piobaireachd* is also known as *Spaidsearachd Mhic na Cearda* or 'The Sinclairs' March'. The Gaelic identifies the branch of the clan as the Western Sinclairs, the name being derived from the word 'ceàrd' meaning a craftsman – specifically a gold- or tin-smith. Chisholm's brother Jack had Sinclair as a middle name, but whether that is relevant has yet to be discovered. One connection that might have occurred to the family was that the Chisholms were master painters, and this will certainly have included gilding. It is, in any event, an interesting choice, for this is a rarely played *piobaireachd* which appears in only two published collections, based on only two manuscript sources. Chisholm would have had to seek this piece out.

The 'Red Ribbon' of the title refers to the ribbon worn (usually in the bonnet) by the supporters of the Duke of Montrose and the Royalist cause during the seventeenth-century Covenanting wars. The Covenanters wore a blue ribbon, and there is, of course, a *piobaireachd* of that name.[46] Chisholm starts with what is almost an exact transcription from the bagpipe notation of 'The Red Ribbon', except that the drone fifths and octaves on the standard bagpipe A (the key of the sonata as a whole) are not static. Instead they move in parallel, sometimes contracting or expanding the intervals, and leading into an early indication of the virtuosity which is to follow, and which is part of the tradition of *piobaireachd*.

Where Chisholm takes this *ùrlar* is a place far from the world of the bagpipes. Indeed, so arresting is this work that, after its recent performance by Murray McLachlan at Wigmore Hall, it was described as 'this giant among piano sonatas'[47], and Martin Anderson in the *Scotsman* found it dark, powerful and electrifying.[48] It is indeed all of these things, as well as being technically incredibly demanding. There is a parallel here between the technical bravura of Chisholm as a pianist (he performed Liszt's Piano Concerto No. 1 in public at the age of seventeen) and the *piobaireachd* player as virtuoso piper. Chisholm's virtuosity is no more for vulgar display than is a *crunluath a-mach* (the most complex and final variation) in a *piobaireachd*. Such demonstrations of skill are ultimately in the service of a greater conception than that attaching to showmanship – hence not every *piobaireachd* calls for a *crunluath* or an *a-mach* based upon it. But there is none the less a very real power and pride that attaches to such skill when it is properly used, and Chisholm does due honour to that aspect of music-making.

The *piobaireachd* is one of the most basic, using only four main melody notes – A, B, D, E – for the *ùrlar*, and these remain unchanged for the variations. The sixteen-bar structure is patterned AABA BBAB or 'tail-woven'.[49] In this analysis the sections can be seen to be inversions of each other. Chisholm's whole movement is held together by this basic structural link, although some of the eight variations are extended by codas. The first features repeated notes and, within

Ex. 6 Sonata, *An Rioban Dearg*, first movement, bars 3–11

a few bars of the start of the work, we are impelled into a world of power and drama (ex. 6).

The arabesques of the second variation are of obvious bagpipe provenance, expanded over three staves in the third variation. The fourth is a varied return of the opening *ùrlar*; and the fifth begins a process of increasing virtuosity and elaboration carried on through the sixth variation, which commences with deep rumbling arpeggios in the bass. The seventh takes up from this but gradually subsides into a grumbling conclusion which only hints at its origins in the initial tune.

The 'Scherzo' is exuberantly driven by a 3+3+2 rhythm sustained throughout in both hands. The main theme emerges from the texture just over a minute from the start of the piece, punched out in parallel intervals, also by both hands. It is based on *The Prince's Salute*, a *piobaireachd* welcoming the Old Pretender, James VIII, to Scotland. The bagpipe mood is sustained in a gentler ensuing episode, but its brief calm fails to restrain the incredible energy with which the music stamps and cascades towards a bravura finish. However, it is one thing to be carried along by irrepressible energy; it is another to be driven into retreat by it, and substantial cuts would probably have been made by Chisholm had he resumed his career as a virtuoso pianist after the war and revisited this work.

The slow movement laments the loss of the submarine *Thetis*, which foundered on her first diving trials on 1 June 1939. Out of 103 on board, there were only four survivors, who were rescued the next day. Chisholm gives the date as 3 June, presumably when full reports of the disaster reached the press. The dark watery textures evoke the situation without attempting anything programmatic, unless the repeated-note figure be taken for tapping on the hull. This figure forms the climactic gestures of the piece, marked *Grandioso*, in which the immensity of the tragedy, both in terms of the loss and the environment in which it took place, finds full expression. The troubled calm of the opening returns, with its whole-tone theme again encrusted with decorations derived from bagpipe fingerings; and the movement closes with an E minor chord with a major third in it that suggests pity more than consolation.

The final 'Allegro moderato' with its Scotch snaps and modal themes leaves us in no doubt as to the nationality of this sonata (ex. 7).

A succession of loosely related tunes, surrounded with virtuoso figurations and with echoes of the *piobaireachd Macintosh's Lament*, is treated with fiery exuberance and not a hint of sorrow. The return to the opening of the movement is managed beautifully as it slides in over written-out trills, to lead to a conclusion of explosive virtuosity. Indeed, the whole movement is a wonderful celebration of Chisholm as a Scot, Chisholm as a composer and Chisholm as a virtuoso pianist; coming from him, there are no holds barred.

What all these works demonstrate is the increasing confidence with which Chisholm treats his material, including his ability to adopt different approaches according to the nature of the work. Although the *Preludes from the True Edge*

Ex. 7 *Rioban Dearg*, fourth movement, bars 1–12

of the Great World post-date the *Piobaireachd* and *An Rioban Dearg*, they are stylistically less demanding, being preludes rather than studies and not having to form the basis of large structures. Chisholm was an ambitious modernist, but he never lost touch with his sources and, even later in his life, adopted the simplest of styles for some of his deepest emotions.

An Rioban Dearg, however, represents one of the high points of his ambitions in piano music, the *Night Song of the Bards* excepted, and I can do no better than conclude with extracts from Martin Anderson's finely written review in *Tempo*.

> The musical language is dark and intense … the first movement … develops into a proud and fierce fantasy of craggy strength … the Scherzo … is a quicksilver Bartókian toccata, superimposing hobgoblin anger over a boogie-woogie bass … the 'Lament' … extends a terse, fragmented right-hand threnody over aqueous chords … the Finale dances with a defiant humour … lyrical consolation suffuses one episode, but the grim jollity comes stomping back, ending the work in a mood of triumphant, splenetic optimism.[50]

The Love of Sorabji[1]

Kaikhosru Shapurji Sorabji (the birth certificate's 'Leon Dudley Sorabji' did not satisfy him) was extraordinary. Extra extraordinary. Patrick Shannon (Chisholm's partner in musical crime) advertised him as the 'greatest musical enigma of all time', an '*astonishing phenomenon*' and declared that 'The Greatest Virtuosi in the world are helpless as babes in handling his music – music which he himself executes without turning a hair.'[2] This was to advertise an open meeting of the Faculty of Arts in the National Academy of Music on Tuesday 25 March 1930, at which Sorabji played his recently composed Pianoforte Sonata No. IV.

The critic A. M. Henderson protested at the vulgarity of this flyer: 'Such publicity may well do more harm than good to the cause, and it cheapens both the promoters and the artists concerned.' Chisholm agreed,

> but the tone of his letter, which was pious and condescending, infuriated me. It is a weakness of mine that I do not take kindly to personal criticism, neither then nor now. So by return of post Mr. Henderson received a nitro-glycerine letter from me which, I was told later, knocked the kindly well-meaning old gentleman out for six. So Mr. Henderson's name was added to the growing list of my enemies.[3]

As for Sorabji, Diana was prejudiced against him before they even met. She resented his view that Erik should quit Glasgow for London (a view he must subsequently have totally reversed) and that in any case no ambitious composer should saddle himself with a wife, and also she was jealous of his jet-black naturally wavy hair.[4] All these prejudices she was soon to drop, but there may have been some instinctive awareness in her that Sorabji's interest in her husband-to-be was not entirely focused on music. The evidence for this cannot have escaped her even when Sorabji was not in Glasgow, for he commenced a correspondence in 1930, initially sending lengthy letters at a rate of more than one a week, though it would seem that Chisholm only rarely replied – alas, his side of the correspondence does not survive. Chisholm undoubtedly admired Sorabji and published an essay about him (illus. 7).[5]

The relationship between Chisholm and Sorabji – or perhaps better stated as between Sorabji and Chisholm – is not easily understood. That it was effusive to the point of passion on Sorabji's side cannot be doubted. The flood of letters and the flood of words and thoughts they contain would alone argue for a relationship of remarkable intensity, never mind their highly charged emotional and intellectual content and the fact that Sorabji sent Chisholm a substantial lock of his black hair.[6]

KAIKHOSRU SORABJI

An essay by Erik Chisholm, with a
descriptive catalogue of his works

7 Cover of *Kaikhosru Sorabji* – An essay by Erik Chisholm, *c.* 1938

I can only go on repeating that I am completely dazed and utterly bowled over by that which has come to pass for both of us – I say 'both of us' though perhaps for fear of offending you I ought to say what has come to pass for <u>me</u> where <u>you</u> are concerned – But, most dear one – I ask you – what could you expect? You attack me from so many quarters at once – weakened as I was already by the instantaneous sympathy that sprang up between us – first by your wondrous appreciation and understanding of my work as a creative artist, (and the equal of <u>that</u> I have never met in any human being) and then by showing me an ever increasing (Oh! <u>May it please God that it goes on increasing, even as mine does and will</u>) personal affection – how did you expect all my emotions not to go rushing towards you at once? How did you expect that <u>I</u> could be unmoved by all that from <u>you</u>? <u>I</u> with <u>my</u> temperament and <u>my</u> racial inheritance on top of it? …

    Oh! Erik dearest you <u>must</u> come to Corfe! <u>Don't</u> refuse … if 'a certain thing' is the obstacle won't you consent to be my guest as I asked you at first? – Surely you needn't allow any tender spots of personal pride to make you refuse <u>on that score</u> … Goodnight once again carissimo et amatissimo.[7]

The 'certain thing' is money, as later passages in the letter make clear. None the less, it would be easy enough to use this material to suggest that there was a physical relationship between the two men, even although we have none of Chisholm's side of the correspondence, which (it is clear from Sorabji's own letters) was very much less frequent. It is also important to point out that Sorabji's writing style is so exaggerated on practically every topic that to deduce anything about others from it would not be merely incautious, but almost ridiculous. However, the answer to these matters is contained in an undated letter (probably June or July 1930), in which he unequivocally admits his own passion and acknowledges that the last thing he would wish would be to impose an unwanted sexual advance upon Erik, who, it is clearly implied, had no desire for such an expression of their feelings for one another.[8]

I swear to you that never never NEVER has there been in me the smallest subterranean hankering for sexual relations between us … The mere thought that anything I do should be repellent or go against the grain with you makes me shrivel up inside and you cannot imagine my shrinking <u>dread</u> of it!

The letter continues to confess to feelings which do seem to transgress Sorabji's reassurances to Chisholm, and he was clearly deeply in love with Erik and had to come to terms with the fact that Erik's feelings were nothing like as intense.

Virginia Fortescue recalled a visit to Corfe Castle many years later, which makes Chisholm's own position reasonably clear:

He read his treatise on Homosexuality which was so brilliant, it was almost vicious … 'Wozzeck' was music of the utmost subtlety and brilliance set to gutter grand guignol. The ladies next door suffered from ingrowing virginity. He told most movingly and well the love story of his cousin and Stephen Mannering. I was really touched, but could not help a violent repugnance to the whole thing. Sorabji's argument, as Erik said, wholly collapses when he said that procreation is not the primary reason for the sexual act.[9]

But in those early days of their encounters, Sorabji was going through the kind of emotional experiences that are not uncommon to people in love, including irrational fears for the safety of the beloved:

> A curious thing happened tonight – Wednesday 15th October 1930 at 7.30 p.m. Sitting at the piano playing bits of Clavicem [*Opus Clavicembalisticum*] a sudden wave of apprehension and anxiety came over me with such intensity that I had to stop I could not go on. I started thinking about you at once (with greater intensity than usual, for I never stop doing that!) … is anything wrong: are you all right?[10]

But perhaps it is possible to find additional reasons for this sudden and scarcely inhibited devotion. Sorabji had suffered much humiliation at the hands of racist and social snobs in England and perhaps found in the aficionados of the Active Society, and specifically in Chisholm's company, an acceptance and a respect which had nothing to do with the colour of his skin or hair and which evoked in him a particularly effusive gratitude. He certainly expresses his preference for Glaswegians over Londoners in no uncertain terms:

> You know these Londoners are a foul crowd after your nice Glasgow people – brutal callous bestial in looks hog-like in manners, swinish in outlook and soulless – so below beasts – that it is an insult to the animal creation to compare them with them.[11]

The passage continues in similar vein for several more sentences, and underlines the degree of isolation which he must have felt, and which accounts to a high degree for his hermit-like behaviour. Many years later, in a letter to Erik, Sorabji recalled a seminal moment:

> My own experiences in THIS country as a child and a boy were APPALLING … I was once insulted with my mother in a first class railway carriage by a gaitered 'dignitary' (????!!!!) of the Church of England … I was in my early teens at the time, and rather timid … This cod-fishmouthed old reptile stared offensively at me and Ma for a long time then turning to the old faggot with him roared in a loud voice 'A BLACK BOY' … Ma turned LIVID … She wasn't a Sicilian for nothing … She went over to him and said, in that wonderful clear speaking voice of hers which could carry ever so far when she spoke in a perfectly normal tone of voice … 'YOU ODIOUS OLD CREATURE … MY SON IS NOT A BLACK BOY … BUT EVEN IF HE WERE IF HE WERE A GORILLA OR A BABOON I SHOULD THANK GOD FOR IT RATHER THAN THAT HE SHOULD BELONG TO ANYBODY THAT PRODUCES PEOPLE LIKE YOU!!!!'[12]

Chisholm never entertained such prejudices and, when apartheid loomed, even thought of leaving South Africa, so disgusted was he with the regime (see Chapter 8). Although Chisholm acknowledged Sorabji's influence on the *Hindustani* Piano Concerto, it was the *Pictures from Dante* which were dedicated to him. When Chisholm himself wrote admiringly about Sorabji, he did so with an element of dispassionate observation, backed up by Diana's wonderfully humorous description of Sorabji's performance of the *Opus Clavicembalisticum*, which Chisholm was nothing loath to use in his own lecture on Sorabji.

> Now that I come to think of it, it seems odd that the very first composer I should invite to perform at the Active Society concerts, should be the most remote, the most un-get-at-able of all my contemporaries. I like to think that this choice was determined by my audacious courage, unheard-of enterprise. The fact is, however, that Sorabji was 'news' around 1927.
>
> He had sent some of his manuscripts to the great English critic, Ernest Newman, who had returned them with a printed card, which stated that 'Mr. Newman does not review musical manuscripts'. Sorabji argued that music was music, whether published or not, starting a controversy which roped in many noted musicians resulting in heated arguments on both sides. ...
>
> I had followed the Newman–Sorabji controversy with interest and read the articles with the result that I wrote a letter to Sorabji, via *The Sackbut*, asking if he would consider coming to Glasgow and play one of his works. Contrary to my expectations I received a reply – a very courteous and charming letter saying he would be delighted to do so and suggested playing his new Fourth piano sonata. This was in 1928.[13]
>
> He came again in 1930 to play his famous or notorious (whichever word you like to use) *Opus Clavicembalisticum* – and in 1936 performed the nine movements of his second Toccata. We became good friends, and I visited him at his London flat and spent some holidays with him, in Bournemouth and at Corfe Castle. By this time I had become extremely interested in his music, and wrote a brochure on him published by the Oxford University Press.

Chisholm went on to describe some of Sorabji's French Impressionist-style works, writing of *Gulistan*:

> At a first impression, without access to a score, this music may seem to be formless, to have no memorable themes, to be without direction, dreamily vague; an unending stream of beautiful sounds. Following the music with a score will correct this mis-impression for then one can see the composer's intentions. I am afraid, too, one is forced to conclude that for all his finger dexterity and considered in toto, these intentions are beyond the performer's ability to convey convincingly to his listeners.
>
> When Sorabji played his works in Glasgow, he spent many months practising them. Even then, his performance fell far short of his own interpretative demands

on paper – I know, because I turned the pages for him. On this point he used to say; 'I am not a pianist and all I can hope to do is to give you a general impression of my work.'[14]

These almost detached thoughts of Chisholm's were penned decades after their first rich encounters, though Chisholm knew that his old friend was still very much alive and was happy to tell him that he was reading 'some of your swash-buckling letters.'[15]

Whatever the truth behind this extraordinary and sadly one-sided corre-spondence, Chisholm secured for the Active Society one of its most memorable concerts – the only performance Sorabji himself ever gave of the *Opus Clavi-cembalisticum*. There are those who worship at the shrine of this work and, as Chisholm has indicated, there is more to it than meets the ear. Diana did her best with what met her ears.

> On the night of the concert Sorabji came dressed in a typical Parsi suit of deep purple silk (it may have been satin). The unusual oriental style made him look somewhat like a Chinese Mandarin, to those as ignorant of Eastern modes of dress as were myself and the majority of the audience. Writing later, in the Glas-gow University Student Magazine an irrepressible critic said he thought Sorabji had come out in his pyjamas.
>
> But don't misunderstand me! This amazing little man had all the majesty, dignity and presence of his proud and honoured race and if some of us found his style of dress rather peculiar for a concert platform, no one would have dreamt of saying that he was other than outstanding in character and manner, with a power-ful (indeed over-powerful) and dynamic personality.
>
> As president, Erik, as usual at these concerts, was turning the pages. I knew he was rather anxious about the turning this time because of the terrific speed with which Sorabji skipped over the keyboard, and the almost illegible manuscript he had to follow.
>
> Sorabji had arranged with him to give a nod of his head when he was nearly ready to have the pages turned, in case of accidents. The first 10 minutes of that recital was a nerve-racking experience for Erik, (so he told me later) before he realised that Sorabji was entirely oblivious of the fact that he was nodding his head practically all the time, sometimes with such ferocity that I thought he would crack his skull on the piano keyboard.
>
> Chisholm was jumping up and down in his seat like a Jack-in-the-box, Yes, he was to turn. No: he shouldn't, but somehow or other always managing to get the page over at the psychological moment.
>
> The music, so unlike anything I had ever heard before, was literally terrifying. … Floods of notes, cascades of arpeggios, fugal subjects a mile long, yet all conjuring up the most fantastic pictures in my mind. But there was nothing I could under-stand.
>
> After about 10 minutes of this, I found myself sitting twisting my fingers in

sheer misery, hoping against hope that each crescendo was the final one so that I could get out of the hall for a breath of air. But it went on and on. The whole audience was spellbound. Never have I known such absorbed listening. I really believe that, if the work had continued for 15 hours no one would have dared to leave the hall before the end. Sorabji had his audience mesmerised. …

The second part seemed to be a complete repetition of the first! My musical friends however assured me afterwards that I was quite wrong. 'Well' I said, exasperated, 'I bet there were a lot of other people in the hall who couldn't tell the difference either.'

By the time the performance had been in progress for two hours and five minutes (never have I looked at my watch so assiduously) even Sorabji was beginning to show signs of wear and tear. By now, I was beyond showing any reaction, whatever, except an occasional wistful look at the door, and praying that I would soon be at the other side of it. The old proverb 'It is always darkest before the dawn' was definitely proved to me on that memorable evening. The last 10 minutes were almost unbearable; the perspiration was pouring down Sorabji's face. It was pouring down mine too if he had but known it, only in some mysterious way I seemed to be crying at the same time, filled with a strange sense of fear and frustration. In some ways I think it must have been the same sensation you would expect to feel if a snake had you hypnotised and you were completely unable to break the spell.

Up and down with tremendous crescendos, down and up with beautiful diminuendos (I did like the diminuendos) each crescendo raising my hopes, each following diminuendo flattening them till at last with one mighty cataclysmic sweep Sorabji finished playing his first and only performance of 'Opus Clavicembalisticum', which by the way, in simple language means 'a piece for the piano'.

There was an utter stillness in the hall and then a tremendous applause broke out. Whatever one thought of the music one could not fail to admire the virtuosity of the performance.

Slowly, so very slowly, Sorabji took out his pocket-handkerchief and wiped his face. Slowly inch by inch he lifted himself out of the piano stool and holding on to the piano lid supported himself to give an enfeebled bow and left the platform to return many times.

Slowly, so very, _very_ slowly I managed (without the aid of anything) to get out of my chair – I stood up, and at my feet fell a veritable bag of confetti! Unconsciously during the performance I had been tearing my programme into little bits![16]

As for the press, their opinions were not far different from Diana's, though less entertainingly expressed. The music was found to be too much of a good thing, but Sorabji's pianism undoubtedly created a sensation. Chisholm flew to the defence of Sorabji,[17] but his ready acceptance of Diana's assessment shows that he could understand why many people found the music hard to swallow. That, of course, did not prevent him from attempting to feed them with it and, in March

1931, he and Pat Shannon rehearsed the Sorabji Organ Symphony of 1925 in St Matthew's Church, whose elders must, on occasion, have wondered whether the devil had not come among them 'having great wrath', given the previous shenanigans of Erik and Pat (see Chapter 2). But there is no hint of dissent on their part, which goes to show that it is wise always to expect the unexpected.

Chisholm went on to perform Sorabji's *Djâmî* in April of 1931, along with a repeat of *Façade* and a Respighi violin sonata.[18] After that, there was a lull until 1936, when Sorabji returned to Glasgow to perform his Second Toccata. The start of the concert in which he appeared was given over to melodrama – a nice piece of programming if ever there was – and then came the Toccata. It consisted of a Preludio-Toccata; Preludio-Corale; Scherzo; Aria; Ostinato (at this point an interval intervened, mercifully, no doubt, for some); Notturno; Interludio; Cadenza; and a Fuga Libera a Cinque Voci to sum up and conclude. Many years later, Ernest Boden wrote to Chisholm, recalling the evening:

> The Hall was in complete darkness but for 2 candles on the piano. He was dressed in a heavy black robe. He played his own works including one which had a fugue in 9 parts, the subject being eleven bars long. There was supposed to be a reference to 'God Save the King' in some part of the work, but I don't think anyone picked it up! By 11 p.m. most of the audience had gone home.[19]

The critics were again astounded by Sorabji's technique, though one had the temerity to write that '[I]t is fairly safe to say that only Sorabji knew if the right notes were being struck.'[20] Montague Smith maintained that 'With few exceptions, the music – if it can be called music, as we know it – rushes along without, so far as one could judge, rhyme or reason. One marvels at the torrent of sound without being moved.'[21] These reactions are not merely the product of a lack of sophistication or open-mindedness among the music critics: they are experienced by many today. Even Ronald Stevenson, whom one might consider a likely candidate for placing candles on the Sorabji piano, if not quite the altar, expressed strong reservations:

> I don't agree with Erik about Sorabji. Sorabji was an auto-didact. He could not orchestrate – he didn't know the tessitura of instruments, and he certainly was not a great fugalist – very amateurish.[22]

Perhaps it is better to try and understand Sorabji, and his relationship with Chisholm, in the context of the modernist movement, of which Sorabji was in some strange way an eccentric exemplar, not least in Scotland. His own seventieth birthday tribute to that icon of Scottish modernism, MacDiarmid – the *Fantasiettina sul nome illustre dell'Egregio poeta Hugh MacDiarmid ossia Christopher Grieve MCMLXI* – is one of his best pieces. It is concise, varied, energetic, unruly and wastes no time getting to the heart of its assertive matter; yet it finds a place for that lyrical mystery which perhaps most truly links the Celtic modernist with the Far Eastern. The fact that, out of all Sorabji's works, Chisholm chose to perform *Djâmî* would support such a suggestion. It is perhaps the most beautiful and unpretentious of Sorabji's compositions, and it is inspired by a mysticism which Chisholm to some extent shared. He was no Christian, but he was interested in the spirit world and even took part in séances.[23] In this nocturnal dream, inspired by the fifteenth-century Persian mystic Jami, one might be hearing some pre-echoes of Chisholm's own *Night Song of the Bards*, though the latter inhabits a much more violent and less dreamy world (see Centre-piece: Night Song of the Bards).

Sorabji's place in that world is best described by Hugh MacDiarmid in *The Company I've Kept*, in which, thinking of Sorabji, he quotes from his own poem 'On a Raised Beach':

> It will be ever increasingly necessary to find
> > In the interests of all mankind
> > Men capable of rejecting all that all other men
> > > Think, as a stone remains
> > Essential to the world, inseparable from it
> > And rejects all other life yet.
> > Great work cannot be combined with surrender to the crowd.[24]

CHAPTER 4

A Trojan Horse in Glasgow

Berlioz, Mozart and Gluck

AS IF THE ACTIVITIES OF THE ACTIVE SOCIETY WERE NOT ENOUGH, Chisholm was planning in his head performances of little-known operas. That *Idomeneo* should have been one of these seems strange to us now, but it had yet to be heard in the British Isles. During 1927 or 1928, Chisholm was in correspondence with Maisie Radford about the edition of *Idomeneo*. She had seen a Munich production and appears from the correspondence to have been involved in the preparation of one of Chisholm's Berlioz revivals.[1] But the real opportunity to bring these schemes to fruition only came with Chisholm's appointment as conductor of the Glasgow Grand Opera Society.

OPERA SOCIETY.
New Conductor Appointed.
Mr Erik Chisholm to Wield Baton.
(Exclusive Interview.)

'I would like to see Glasgow Amateur enthusiasts,' said Mr Chisholm in an interview today, 'attempting fresh fields of operatic music, and escaping from the
convention that has tied them down to a narrow repertoire. To begin with, the
Glasgow Grand Opera Society, I am glad to say, has decided to produce next season "The Bartered Bride," ... my feeling is that amateurs could do some splendid
work in bringing before the public pieces that the professional companies have
not given here, such as those by de Falla, Granada, and Hugo Wolf.'[2]

Apparently, even *The Bartered Bride* was a novelty; but in opening its portals to Chisholm, did the Glasgow Grand Opera Society realise just how 'Grand' he expected it to be? He was himself almost a Trojan horse, and the Society was nearly brought to its knees, partly through his ambitions. But before launching into Chisholm's operatic ventures, never mind the continuing heroic efforts of the Active Society, it is time to catch up with everyday life, if such a thing ever existed in the Chisholm household, not forgetting his continuing output as a composer.

In 1931, Chisholm received his B.Mus. degree from the University of Edin-burgh, and no doubt he immediately turned his mind towards obtaining his doc-torate, but he had also turned his mind towards Diana Brodie, who had in fact prompted him to apply.[3]

Diana and Erik first met in St Matthew's Church, where she sang in the choir and he was organist.[4] She was good-looking and had a well-pitched dramatic soprano voice, and was also capable of accompanying herself at the piano by

8 Diana Brodie

ear, although she had had none of Erik's formal training. He admired her skill and, as with many formally trained musicians, wished he had the same kind of facility.[5] They often played and sang together and were clearly very well matched, socially, educationally and in terms of their complementary skills. On the social front, she made an excellent hostess to the many distinguished visiting musicians, whom she was able to put at ease; and, like Erik, she had a well developed sense of humour. Her secretarial skills must also have greatly assisted him.

Their eldest daughter, Morag, recalls them being very loving towards each other whenever Erik returned from touring, remembering her innocence in knocking on the locked door of their bedroom in the middle of the day.

Years later, differences were to develop and they were eventually divorced (see Chapter 10). In any event, on 22 November 1932, a leap year, Erik Chisholm, musician, bachelor, and Diana Brodie, university clerk, spinster, were married. He was twenty-eight and she twenty-one. Her father, William, had been a whisky exporter and the company had its own blend; but he was dead, so Diana was given away by Erik's friend and fellow composer, Francis George Scott. Archie Chisholm was best man, Betty Brodie (Diana's sister) the only bridesmaid, and the bride wore 'nigger brown' and mention was made of the fact that she was a member of Glasgow University Orchestra.[6] The colour of the dress is explained by the fact that Diana Morag was born on 11 June 1933, six and a half months later. Many years afterwards, when she asked her mother if her arrival was premature, she was quietly told it was not.

As for Chisholm, he recalled a story of his Glaswegian predecessor, Eugen d'Albert, having had feelings of delicacy on a much more important matter:

> When I was registering the birth of my eldest daughter at Prospect Hill Road Registry Office, Glasgow, in 1933, the clerk handed me a form to fill in. One query was 'Father's occupation?' I wrote 'Professional musician' and handed it back to the clerk, who looked at it a trifle suspiciously. 'Whit kin' o' musician would ye be, anyway, mister?' he asked me. 'Ye dinna look as if ye played a cornet in the streets.'
>
> 'Indeed no,' I replied laughingly, 'I teach and play the piano – but leave it at Professional musician.' 'Weel,' said the clerk, 'Ye're nothing like so perticular as a wee red-heeded fella who kept comin' back here; he had a kinda queer name – whit was it noo? Albert something? Dalbert. That's it Dalbert. You-gene Dalbert. He was a pee-anist, too, and every time he wis playing in Glesca he came up here tae see if we would change his birth certificate. He didna' want his fether's profession to be jest "Dancin'" but "Maitre de Ballet".'[7]

By 1933 Erik and Diana had moved to 118 University Avenue; a good location in the West End of Glasgow, and Erik's compositions were beginning to make a wider impact. The Double Trio for Clarinet in A, Bassoon, Trumpet in C, Violin, Violoncello and Double Bass was composed in 1931[8] and first performed, with a favourable reception, at an International Society for Contemporary Music (ISCM) concert in London in February 1933.[9]

In the spring of 1932 he had completed the *Piobaireachd* Piano Concerto (in its first version) and it drew favourable attention from William Saunders in an article in the *Scots Magazine*.[10] Barbirolli conducted the Scottish Orchestra in the 'March', 'Urlar' and 'Reel' from Chisholm's *Dance Suite*, and the complete suite was performed at the concluding orchestral concert of the tenth ISCM Festival in Amsterdam on 12 June 1933.[11]

Along with his new appointment as conductor of the Glasgow Grand Opera Society, Chisholm was still steering the Active Society's concert series. March 1932 saw performances of the Delius Sonata No. 2 for Violin and Piano; Mittler and Langstroth songs; a Lopatnikoff Sonata for Violin, Piano and Tambour Militaire; a Schoeck Sonata for Bassoon and Piano; and the Sibelius Sonatina for Violin and Piano Op. 80. 'Jock' Fairbairn was accompanied by Chisholm, A. T. Wood played the bassoon and M. Feggans the tambour. Angela Pallas (she whose admittance into the country had caused such a storm, for which see Chapter 2) sang.[12]

The following month, John Ireland gave a programme of his own music, accompanying James Reid in a group of songs and partnering the irrepressible Gasparini in the *Cello Sonata in G minor*, which one reviewer felt was too rhapsodic. The *Glasgow Herald* described his style quite aptly as one of 'finely finished virility'.[13] Chisholm had already met Ireland (see Chapter 1):

> In the car, which drove him from the station to Moore's Hotel, our favourite place to house distinguished guests (if for some reason it was not policy to offer them private hospitality), I said how much I admired his celebrated second violin sonata. 'Truly,' I said, 'one of the finest examples of recent British Chamber Music.'
>
> 'No, no,' he replied testily, 'it isn't all that good, believe me; and please don't say flowery things about my music to me, for I am sure you don't believe them, and neither do I.' He had a pretty bad cold all the time he was in Glasgow, which, if it affected his temper, had no ill effect on his playing. Both his compositions and piano playing made a deep impression ... The novelty was the unfamiliar Cello Sonata (1923) played by the Society's cellist, Luigi Gasparini.
>
> Ireland's early *Phantasie Trio* opened the programme, and ended with the familiar second violin sonata which all-in-all is his most satisfying work – tuneful, virile and with a wide range of expression.[14]

The series continued with an F. G. Scott recital which also included the Mackenzie Piano Quartet – a work of great beauty, which should stand proud in the piano quartet repertoire. Chisholm played the piano part, and one wonders whether old Mackenzie, by then on the last lap of the race, knew that his young firebrand of a musical successor had paid due homage to his predecessor.[15] Next came a collaborative venture with the Glasgow Grand Opera Society, which included excerpts from Hamish MacCunn's sadly neglected opera *Diarmid*, and a Florent Schmitt programme with the composer at the piano. Schmitt proved to be a difficult customer. He and the violinist, Edward Dennis, did not get on and

Chisholm offered to play the piano part of the *Sonate Libre* himself, leaving Schmitt to play in the other works.[16] However, the reviews indicate that Chisholm fell ill (strategically?) and the sonata was omitted.[17] Schmitt also had a mistress in tow who 'looked like a cross between a prison warden and a female Maigret'. This lady was never introduced, but as the London train was about to pull out of Waverley Station, Schmitt leaned out of the window and in a confidential whisper to Guy McCrone said: 'Monsieur Crone, when you come to Paris to see me, please do not mention to my wife anything about my English girl friend.'[18] Guy McCrone was a popular novelist whose *Wax Fruit* is a minor classic of Scottish Victorian life. A fluent French-speaker, he took the part of Aeneas in *The Trojans*.

Later that spring, the Society put on a repeat of Florent Schmitt's Piano Quintet, which is conceived on an enormous scale and lasts about an hour. This time Chisholm himself played the piano, along with his own arrangement of the last movement of Mahler's Fourth Symphony with Sally Thomson singing.[19] Mahler was rarely performed in those days, but such minor difficulties as the absence of a willing orchestra were not going to prevent Chisholm from letting the world know about what it ought to know.

A Cyril Scott programme, with Scott himself at the piano, concluded the season. Chisholm was long acquainted with his music:

> As a boy, I admired and played many of Scott's piano works, and when I was 15 or 16, gave the first and probably the only Scottish performance of his big piano sonata which I have already mentioned in connection with Grainger's claim for its influence on Stravinsky. I also publicly performed his two Pierrot pieces (*Pierrot triste, Pierrot gai*), *The Jungle Book* (after Kipling) and some of the 'Poems' where the unusual and delicate harmonic colouring of the chords, the abandoning of tonality, the bell tones, striking rhythms, oriental effects and other original features of his music held great fascination for me.[20]

Scott had brought the pianist Esther Fisher with him and she and Scott played a set of Scott's variations on an original theme. Grove (1954) dated this composition to 1947, but it was played in Glasgow in 1933.

On 10 May of that year, Chisholm accepted the post of organist/choirmaster at the Barony Church in central Glasgow, at £100 a year,[21] resigning his position at St Matthew's. The Barony was a prestigious appointment, but the organ left a lot to be desired. 'It is a disgrace that a musician of Dr Chisholm's ability be asked to play on such a wheezy asthmatic affair as the Barony organ.'[22]

It was that autumn that Bartók returned to Glasgow, with a programme of his own transcriptions of Purcell and others (see Chapter 2), and this was followed by a warmly received recital by Yvonne Arnaud, which featured Fauré and Enescu violin sonatas with Bessie Spence as a violinist worthy of her partner.[23] The accent of the concerts seems to have been shifting slightly from composer-performers towards well-known performers with an interest in enterprising repertoire; for instance the Barbirolli quartet (with John Barbirolli as cellist) took part in a programme which included the Bax Quintet for Oboe and Strings, a Glinka Violin Sonata, the Poulenc Trio for Piano, Oboe and Bassoon, Chisholm playing his own *Straloch Suite* and the Lennox Berkeley Suite for Oboe and Cello. The whole was rounded off by the Haydn Quartet in E♭ Op. 76, No. 6.[24] In the next concert, Tatiana Makushina sang a varied programme of Debussy, Medtner and Milhaud songs, among others.[25]

In 1934, Erik obtained his Edinburgh Mus.D. within the minimum period, as he was later proudly to record in a draft curriculum vitae.[26] In the same document he quotes Tovey's comment to the *Daily Record* that 'Edinburgh did not always agree with Glasgow but that both cities were proud of Glasgow's young Doctor of Music'. Chisholm gives an entertaining description of his final oral examination for his doctorate, imagining the vast range of questions that might be thrown at him, only to be offered a cigarette and to realise that, in his case at any rate, it was a formality. Sir Hugh P. Allen, Professor of Music at Oxford

9 Donald Tovey

and Principal of the Royal College of Music, was his external examiner, and they ended up talking about Walton, the conducting of whose *Façade* Chisholm had taken over in mid-stream (see Chapter 2).

According to Diana Chisholm, Tovey had said to Erik, 'My boy, I am giving you your pass on your composition – but I don't understand a word of it!' She couldn't recall which work (or works) was submitted, but speculated that it was one of the *piobaireachd* works.[27] (See also Interlude: The Love of Janáček.)

The new season of the Active Society opened once more with a great composer-performer – Karl Szymanowski. But one might say that there were two such present, for Chisholm performed Szymanowski's demanding Piano Sonata No. 2 Op. 20, in the presence of the composer himself, Szymanowski contenting himself with performing his own Violin Sonata in D minor (with Bessie Spence) and three Mazurkas. *Musical Opinion* was particularly impressed with Chisholm's playing.[28]

December produced the Busch Trio, performing Adolf Busch's Violin Sonata Op. 21, Piano Trio Op. 49 (its first public performance) and Piano Sonata Op. 25.[29] Rudolf Serkin, Adolf Busch's son-in-law, was the pianist, and Adolf and his brother Fritz were given honorary degrees by Edinburgh University, a year after Adolf had voluntarily renounced his German citizenship, in protest at Hitler's policies in Germany. Years later, Chisholm made his own assessment of the concert.

> Adolf and Max Reger had been close friends and associates since about 1907, and undoubtedly the earlier compositions of Busch were influenced by Reger's close contrapuntal texture and great compression of detail, although he later developed individual characteristics of his own. Perhaps, too, there was a touch of Busoni in the violin sonata Op. 21.
>
> Re-reading the notice of this concert in the *Glasgow Evening Times*, written by Stewart Deas (one-time music professor at Cape Town) I find that Deas thought the contrary. He felt that the new trio showed a tightening up of the structure as compared to the earlier sonatas. 'These,' wrote Deas 'had a certain luxuriousness which gave them a charm of their own.'
>
> The piano sonata is a very powerful work. Even 30 years later, I still recalled the great impression it made on me. After a strong first movement came an *andante and variations*, at first of a quiet meditative nature, and later, brilliant and lively. The *finale* is a gigantic fugue, which was played by Rudolf Serkin, with most striking effect.[30]

There were two further concerts with interesting programming that season (see Appendix 1), but 1935 will chiefly be remembered as the year of the first complete performance (the two parts on consecutive nights) of Berlioz's *Les Troyens* in the British Isles, and it was Chisholm and the amateur Glasgow Grand Opera Society who achieved it. There must have been an enormous amount of preparation involved, not merely of the musicians and soloists, sets and costumes, but also of the libretto and score themselves, which had been much mangled in the past.

In Glasgow the two halves were presented on alternate nights during the week and, at the end of the run, on Saturday 23 March, a matinée performance of *The Capture of Troy* was followed by *The Trojans in Carthage* in the evening, with only a one-hour gap.[31] It was performed complete with the ballet scenes, including the 'Chasse royale et orage', and with two brass bands and hidden chorus, for the moment when the wooden horse passed across the stage.[32] The opera was given in a new English translation by Dent, and among the guests were Hamilton Harty, Donald Francis Tovey, and Ernest Newman who wrote of 'Glasgow's brave effort', concluding 'Dr. Erik Chisholm, who conducted, had orchestra and stage well in hand: there were some ticklish moments, but his resource never failed him.'[33] In fact there was a standing ovation at the end of the first part.[34] Sir Thomas Beecham did not attend. He refused Chisholm's invitation, saying 'How does a little whipper-snapper like you think you can do the Trojans? I am going to do the Trojans'[35] – which indeed he did, many years later. Some time after Beecham's death in 1961, Chisholm wrote an essay on him in which he forgave Beecham's impudence: 'When Sir Thomas visited Cape Town a few years ago [he] invited me to dine with him, after we had amicably settled that little difference about "Les Troyens".'[36]

Previously the work had been ruthlessly cut, given in concert performances and/or divided across different days. The complete performance in Germany in the late nineteenth century, mentioned in a prominent preview of the production in the *Glasgow Herald*, had the two halves on consecutive nights,[37] and in France the first performance the work in its entirety in one evening came as late as 1921.

For an amateur opera company to have put on even one half of *Les Troyens* would have been daring enough. To put on both halves, include the ballet scenes, and run them in tandem for a week was quite simply heroic. Nor were the soloists necessarily bought in: local stalwart Guy McCrone, for example, taking the part of Aeneas, although he was a writer by profession. Of course voices tired, some singers were a bit static on stage, not all the scenery was deemed to do justice to Berlioz's conception, though much was praised – and so on.[38] But the thing was done, and, for many, a neglected masterpiece was, for the first time, vindicated, and practically every opera company in the world made to look mean and timid by a relatively small industrial city and a group of amateurs drawing everything out of their own meagre resources for the love of the thing. Diana Chisholm recalled that:

> It was not done for self-glorification. He wasn't writing up so many first performances because of credit. It was an inner striving, an inner drive. He said to Sir Thomas, I want to hear it in my lifetime – live, and when we came out and people were saying, 'oh you know, a little orchestra, well it's not – we're used to the Berlin

Great Scot!—CCXXIII.

ERIK CHISHOLM, *Mus.Doc.*

A' music's moderns he mak's known
To Scots wha think a tone's a tone;
An' ancient heroes loup an' skirl
When his wee baton starts to whirl.

10 Cartoon by WN of Erik Chisholm conducting Berlioz' *The Trojans*

Philharmonic' – there were a lot of Jewish refugees at that time – they were all a bit snooty, I don't mind saying, about having come from overseas – and Erik was very angry about it, because he said – he believed that a live performance, even if it wasn't perfect, even if it wasn't good, was better to have experienced than a no performance at all or something that came out completely smoothed out and ironed. It was strivings of people, and that was the value.[39]

Some of the performers were professionals, such as Margaret Dick, who sang the part of Anna and was later to teach singing at the Royal Scottish Academy of Music and Drama. The tenor Steuart Wilson, who was living in London, was approached as early as July 1934, and was eager to do it 'unless the Tenor part is one of Berlioz tearing high tenors'.[40]

After this momentous production, the following March the Society put on Berlioz's *Benvenuto Cellini* and *Beatrice and Benedict*, the latter in a double bill with Schubert's *The Faithful Warrior* in an arrangement by Tovey.[41] But Chisholm was soon back giving recitals for the Active Society, including Bartók, Bax, Bloch, Delius and Hindemith sonatas – testimony not only to his catholicity of taste but to his phenomenal energy and motivation in learning so much repertoire.[42] By October of that year he had learnt the Shostakovich Twenty-four Preludes and gave them their first British performance, and threw in the Busoni Violin Sonata Op. 29 and the Hindemith Violin Sonata Op. 11, No. 1;[43] and in November he was writing,[44] lecturing about and accompanying a programme of excerpts from Busoni operas.[45] January heard him accompanying an all-Shostakovich programme, including the Cello Sonata Op. 40, the Concerto for Piano, Trumpet and Strings Op. 35 and the fourth act of *Lady Macbeth of Mzensk* transcribed for piano by Chisholm. Shostakovich was as yet scarcely understood in the West, and a degree of puzzlement was expressed in the reviews.[46] His strange mixture of wit, cynicism, intellect, heart-felt emotion and monumentalism is not easy to tie down in any review.

For the fourth concert in the series, Chisholm took a back seat, and the ubiquitous Wight Henderson, along with Harold Thomson, did the honours at the piano in an all-Austrian recital that included songs by Schoenberg, Berg and Webern, sung by Hanna Schwarz, plus the Berg Piano Sonata in B minor Op. 1, and the Wellesz Sonata for Solo Cello Op. 31, played by Norah Sandeman.[47] How many comparable cities in Britain, and perhaps even Europe, came close to this incredible variety, which by April of 1936 had been going on for almost six years? And how many musicians could have sustained such a range of activities, including organisational skills, transcribing of scores, performing taxing new works and continuing to compose, for Chisholm was still at work with the pen, completing the ballet *The Forsaken Mermaid* in its two-piano version in 1936 and composing his Symphony No. 1.

Nor were the Scots forgotten, the 1936–7 season opening in November with F. G. Scott songs, Cedric Thorpe Davie's ballad 'Christ and the Sinner' and songs, and excerpts from W. B. Moonie's opera *The Weird of Colbar*, which Chisholm was planning to mount in a full production.

The following month, Sorabji returned to Scotland for the Active Society, performing his Second Toccata with 'unbelievable speed' in some passages (See Interlude: The Love of Sorabji). Of equal interest was the rare offering of melodramas by Schumann, Strauss, Sibelius and Grieg, with Patrick Shannon as reciter.

The new year saw the Active Society present a memorial concert for Berg and Van Dieren.[48] It was charitable of them to include the latter, considering his earlier behaviour (see Chapter 2); but Chisholm was above the meaner actions of life, and the Sonata for Solo Violin and four songs were performed, alongside Kilpinen and Berg songs, a Bloch Suite for Viola and Piano, the Hindemith Viola Sonata Op. 11 No. 4 and Debussy's *La Boîte à joujoux*, with William Lambie narrating.[49]

The season's fourth concert was an all-Hungarian one, with the pianist Maria Zöldesi and the violinist Horace Fellowes performing works by Szabó, Kadosa, Bartók, Reschofsky, Yemnitz, Weiner, Veress and Hammerschlag – in fact the usual run-of-the-mill fare for the Active Society![50]

On the opera front, *The Weird of Colbar* was duly put on, with sets and lighting by William Henry and with an orchestra of fifty, of whom thirty-five were engaged from the Scottish Orchestra. The production cost about £1,000[51] and scored a reasonable success.[52] Chisholm and the Glasgow Grand Opera Society did their best to give it a good launch. They held a luncheon for Moonie, at which Chisholm told a reporter that he had also hoped to stage Hamish MacCunn's *Diarmid* but could find no trace of the score.[53] He claimed that, unlike many operas since Wagner, the main interest in *The Weird of Colbar* was in the vocal parts, but 'At the same time he considers the orchestration remarkably good.'[54]

The following spring the GGOS (as they were familiarly known) put on *Aida*. It was to cost them dearly. The intended sets could not be used, and the consequence was a less than adequate staging and hesitant lighting, although the music went well enough.[55] *Aida* put the Society heavily into debt, and various schemes from concerts to whist drives were proposed and to a degree succeeded in helping them to survive. But Chisholm had to write at length to a benefactor, justifying his own position on a yearly salary of £60 (he offered to accept only £30 for 1939) and explaining that many of his proposals had been turned down by the Society.[56] Perhaps the Society had begun to realise just how many and how doughty were the operatic warriors Chisholm had concealed in his Trojan horse.

The Barony Musical Association, however, gave Chisholm alternative opportunities and was ambitious enough to mount rarely heard operas. They produced Gluck's *Iphigenia in Tauris* and *Armida*, on 20 and 21 January 1937, and 14 and 15 April 1939 respectively. Both productions were at the Lyric Theatre, Glasgow. In between, they mounted Mozart's *Titus* on 8 and 9 April 1938 at the Athenaeum Theatre,[57] where the rumble of the underground trains from Buchanan Street

Station would add a certain frisson on the rare occasions when their timing was dramatically appropriate.

Morag Martin produced *Iphigenia*, and the performances were in aid of the Barony Organ Restoration Fund.[58] Production and performances went well, though (judging from the press photographs) the costumes were a little strange. But it must be remembered that while this opera had had more than 2,000 performances, it had never been heard in Scotland, and this was a performance by a church music society. None the less, no doubt enlisted by the stop-at-nothing Chisholm, some notable figures contributed to the performance of *Titus*. The composer Cedric Thorpe Davie was second horn, Horace Fellowes was the leader and, in the chorus, was the composer John McQuaid, singing bass. The family was represented by Diana Chisholm and Betty Brodie (sopranos).[59] Sadly, the association with the Barony was to be ended during the war by a mean action of the Kirk Session (see Chapter 5).

If it might have seemed that the Active Society was beginning to run out of steam, it did not mean that the same thing was happening to Chisholm. He shifted the focus from composers from furth of Scotland to Scottish composers themselves, and was persuaded by Janey Drysdale to resurrect the Dunedin Association.

Chisholm and the Dunedin Association

It would be a mistake, however, to assume that Chisholm regarded it as incumbent upon himself or his colleagues to compose exclusively using some kind of identifiable Scottish idiom, and no such agenda was proposed when he revived the Dunedin Association.

Having invested an enormous amount of time and energy in bringing leading modernist (and not-so-modernist) composers to Glasgow, learning their music and performing and lecturing and writing about it, Chisholm must have felt the time was ripe to find a little room in the world of music for the active propagation of Scottish contemporary music. Giving the toast at a dinner held in Frederic Lamond's honour,[60] Chisholm referred to the fact that Lamond had had to leave his own country, as there was no demand for his services. Chisholm regarded this lack of interest by Scots in their own composers as typical.[61] Lamond (colour plate 1) is primarily remembered as a pianist, and rightly so. But he was no mean composer and his symphony and concert overture,[62] never mind some fine piano solos and chamber music, deserve a place in the repertoire.

The day following the dinner for Lamond, the sister of the deceased Scottish composer Learmont Drysdale wrote to Chisholm suggesting that he revive the Dunedin Association as its aims were essentially those that Chisholm had himself identified in his toast. The Association had been founded in 1911 and Janey Drysdale was its Vice-President, having formerly been its Secretary. Chisholm was happy to take up the reins, and the Association was duly revived.[63]

Needless to say, it was revived with wide-ranging ambitions. Exchange concerts with composers of other nations were proposed, a composition competition was set up[64] and a scheme of publication set in motion.[65]

> Every encouragement, however, must be given to our composers, if they are to
> form a school of composition equal to that of the great English and Continental
> Schools. The publication of their works must be accounted a powerful stimulant
> in achieving such an end. ...
>
> However difficult the times are in which to raise money for something other
> than a war objective, it must be realised that it is as much our duty to preserve and
> develop our cultural life as it is to retain our territorial independence.[66]

For once, Chisholm was a direct beneficiary of these activities. It gave him the opportunity to première his Sonata in A – *An Rioban Dearg* (see Chapter 3) and to enter the composition competition under a pseudonym.

The programme for the first concert of the Dunedin Association was a memorable one, not only for its inclusion of Chisholm's *An Rioban Dearg*, but with two other first performances of works completed in that year. They were Cedric Thorpe Davie's Violin Sonata and songs from F. G. Scott's *Scottish Lyrics, Book V*. It had also been intended that the Lamond Piano Trio be performed, perhaps in the hope that Lamond himself would play the piano. In the event, McEwen's *Improvisations Provençals* for violin and piano were given in its place. Press response was positive, not least for the Chisholm.[67]

As for the competition, the judges were Bax, Tovey and Aylmer Buesst and Chisholm's (pseudonymous) entry won. It was a symphony in four movements, which must be the Second, as the First had already been broadcast. Second prize went to Riddell Hunter, a Glaswegian living in London, for his *Clyde Symphony*.

Chisholm gave his £25 prize money to the Dunedin Fund for the Publication of Scottish Music.[68] From this too, he benefited, for the two-piano score of his ballet *The Forsaken Mermaid* was published by Dunedin Publications,[69] under the wing of William MacLellan. How typical of Scotland, indeed of any nation where resources come nowhere close to the proper calls upon them, that this should have caused friction between Chisholm and Scott, as Maurice Lindsay recounts:

> Scott, however, had the notion (rightly as it turned out) 'that Chisholm hopes
> to push through some symphony of his own, eating up a good £150 of the fund,
> and is prepared to spend a paltry £50 on me as a blind. He is a real snake in the
> grass, is Erik, and I get on guard whenever he makes a move in my direction.' The
> Chisholm volume eventually published in piano score was his ballet *The Forsaken
> Messiah*, [*sic!!*] and the Dunedin Society had, indeed, no funds thereafter to publish the promised volume of Scott's songs.[70]

This cannot be allowed to pass without comment. Chisholm (whose £25 prize money had gone into the fund) had championed Scott's music in print and in the programmes of both the Active Society and the Dunedin Association (see also Chapter 2). He had had little enough of his own music in print by 1940, whereas

Scott had already published five volumes of songs with Bayley & Ferguson. Scott was perhaps smarting a little, following the results of the Dunedin composition competition. In the second category thereof, he had come third (with his *Overture Renaissance*) to Stewart Findlay's Violin Sonata and Malcolm MacDonald's *Overture to Youth*. In the song category, where he might reasonably have expected to do well, neither Bax, Tovey nor Buesst thought any entry merited the prize, though Scott's 'Guid E'en to You Kimmer' got an honourable mention.[71] One wonders whether Lindsay's extraordinary alteration of the title of *The Forsaken Mermaid* to *The Forsaken Messiah* was not a Freudian slip, favouring his own champion. It is worth pointing out that in 1962 Chisholm 'caused Scott's entire archive to be photostatted'[72] for the Mitchell Library, as Lindsay himself admits. Not the work of a snake.

The Dunedin Association's second concert was devoted entirely to Russian music. Vera Vinogradova performed a number of her own piano pieces and accompanied Tatiana Makushina in songs by Mussorgsky. Chisholm's interest in Russia never waned. It had started with the concert for the Russo-Scottish Society (see Chapter 1), was pursued in articles in the *Weekly Herald*[73] and culminated in visits to Russia after the war (see Chapter 9).

For the third concert, it had been hoped that Lamond would play the piano in his own Piano Trio (rescheduled from November) but 'owing to unavoidable circumstances', Chisholm had to take over.[74] Friskin's early Piano Quintet Op. 1 made quite an impression, and Noreen Cargill sang Marjory Kennedy-Fraser arrangements of Gaelic song and songs by Drysdale, MacCunn and William Wallace, whose *Freebooter Songs* still enjoyed quite a vogue.[75] The concert started with a 'Funeral March on a Ground Bass' composed by Chisholm, and performed by him as a tribute to the memory of John Buchan (Lord Tweedsmuir), who had been a Vice-President of the Dunedin Association since 1916.[76] In the absence of any other work designated as a funeral march, never mind on a ground bass, it seems most likely that this was the 'Funeral March' which comprised the third movement of Chisholm's First Symphony, dated 1938 and originally intended to commemorate W. Wigham Parker, D.Mus., who died in 1937.[77]

No notices survive in the various Chisholm papers for the fourth concert, planned for St Patrick's Day 1940 and intended to feature a Scottish Exchange Programme and works by the successful competitors in the Dunedin composition competition. The evidence in Chisholm's papers suggests that the Dunedin Association never managed more than the four concerts initially advertised, which, given the effects of the Second World War, was no shame on anyone.[78]

As for the Dunedin Association itself, how long it survived in realistic terms, as opposed to the dreams dreamt by William MacLellan for many years thereafter, is not clear (but see Chapter 8). It had already survived an extended period of ghostly existence and its work was partly taken on by the Saltire Society, in conjunction with which the concert series was mounted and which remains highly active to this day.

For Chisholm, Scotland was soon going to have to be experienced only in dream and memory – but that did not prevent him from starting on yet another venture, the Scottish Ballet. It was succeeded by the Celtic Ballet, which had the temerity to set out its stall knowingly on the very edge of war.

CHAPTER 5

The Ballet & the Baton as Weapons of War

Dr Chisholm has called a meeting at Cuthbertson's on Thursday at eight of all those interested in the formation of a Scottish Ballet Society … the desire is to produce ballets in style similar to 'Job,' but based for the most part on Scottish themes and 'grafting a semi-classical foundation on to Scottish dances.' It is hoped to provide annual performances of ballet in Glasgow on parallel lines to the Grand Opera Society's productions of opera. Several native composers are already engaged on the composition of ballet music.[1]

THE SCOTTISH BALLET SOCIETY WAS DULY FORMED IN THE SPRING of 1937, with Erik as one of a temporary committee of five. He told a *Daily Mail* reporter:

It will be our object to evolve a new and national type of ballet expressive of the spirit and sentiment of Scotland. Purely classical and operatic themes will be avoided. There is every hope for the society's success because Scots people are great lovers of good dancing. There is a great advantage in the fact that Scotland has definite dancing traditions. A search has been made for suitable folk tunes and folk stories. Musicians, artists, dancers, and art students are among the new society's members.[2]

Scotland and ballet were not regarded as natural companions, but the Scots love to dance and have contributed to the world a number of dance forms – the reel, strathspey, and possibly the hornpipe,[3] and have certainly had a huge input into the jig from at least as early as the sixteenth century – so Scotland and ballet should feel no distrust, as Anna Pavlova commented when in Glasgow:

The news that a Scottish ballet company is to be started by amateurs in Glasgow reminds me of an interview I had with Madame Anna Pavlova on her last visit to this town. The famous dancer seemed a timid creature off the stage. But she became quite animated when she started to talk about Highland dancing.

She told me that she had been studying it carefully and had come to the conclusion that Highland and ballet dancing had the same base. She even demonstrated ballet movements to me and showed the corresponding movement in the Highland fling. With a heritage like that, she said, the Scots ought to be good ballet dancers. It will be interesting to see whether the new Scottish ballet can come up to her opinion.[4]

By a nice coincidence, Pavlova had danced in what was to become William Crosbie's studio (illus. 11), which served as the dining-room annexe of a hotel for a spell. The tables were cleared during the day for Pavlova and her *corps de ballet*

11   William Crosbie in his studio

to practise, as the floor was good. The studio was originally designed as such by Mackintosh for Sir D. Y. Cameron.[5] Crosbie was the designer of both sets and costumes for Chisholm's ballet *The Earth Shapers* (see below).

Chisholm must have worked rapidly to complete his ballet *The Pied Piper of Hamelin* in time for Christmas 1937. The ballet is based on the famous Browning poem and begins and ends with extracts from it. Marjory Middleton was the choreographer, though the original programme makes no mention of a designer. The whole was a Pat Sandeman production under the auspices of the Choral and Orchestral Union of Glasgow 'and on behalf of the Endowment Fund of the Scottish Orchestra'. The Pied Piper's tune was given to Chisholm by Marjory Middleton, who had evidently composed it herself and wrote to Chisholm suggesting that he might make use of 'my wee tune for piper'.[6]

In the nineteenth century, rats were often emblematic of Jews and gypsies, something which would scarcely have appealed to Chisholm, who was decidedly left wing. Perhaps he was unaware of such earlier connotations, although in 1930s Europe, racist oppression against Jews and gypsies was very much to the fore. But this is a children's ballet and shares in the same innocence with which Chisholm later told the story of Babar, although it too is not without its imperialist ironies.

Whether or not Chisholm realised that war was impending, he can scarcely have imagined that his experience as a ballet promoter and conductor was to provide him with an outlet for his own personal views on war and employment with ENSA – the Entertainments National Service Association. Instead he thought of applying for the Chair in Music at Glasgow. Had he been successful, his and Scotland's musical lives would have been very different. The musicologist Edward Dent wondered why he should want such a post:

> I rather wonder at your applying for it. I do not know the exact reasons why Whittaker resigned, but I gathered from common report that he found it impossible to work with his authorities. I suppose they wanted a slave and not an artist – least of all, a man of learning. I should have thought that you would have found the situation more difficult than he did, except that possibly you, being a native, would understand the native psychology better than he did and know how to manage it. … Any way, I enclose a sheet on which I have tried to put down my very sincere admiration for your activities … I hope Donald Tovey will also support you: he always spoke to me about you with the greatest cordiality.[7]

Hamilton Harty felt unable to recommend Chisholm for the Chair, having insufficient knowledge of his attainments, though not doubting he was qualified and full of admiration for the production of *Les Troyens*.[8] The Chair was taken by Sir Ernest Bullock, who occupied it without distinction.

On the compositional as opposed to the employment front, 6 January 1939 saw the 'successful' performance by the BBC Orchestra (Section D) of Chisholm's Symphony No. 1 in C minor, sometimes known as the 'Tragic'.[9] The symphony originated in a 'Funeral March' composed the previous year for the funeral of Dr Wigham Parker. Chisholm then added a Scherzo and Finale, composing the first movement last of all, and completing the orchestration on 11 December 1938.[10] It was substantially based on the *Cornish Dance Sonata*, and he must have felt some satisfaction that this work, so comprehensively rejected by his old teacher, Pouishnoff (see Chapter 1), had finally got an airing on national radio as his Symphony No. 1, especially as even as early as 1926 he had intended to turn it into a Symphony – *In Cornwall*.[11]

The 'Allegro agitato', with dramatic syncopations and chromatic passages, is firmly fixed in C minor and relatively conventional in its development, with a fine sweeping second subject in A♭ minor. The 'Scherzo' is an energetic 9/8 affair which prances along, derived, somewhat obliquely, from *Blown Spume*. The following 'Funeral March' is surprisingly conventional and may well also have been resurrected from some earlier piece. The C minor 'Finale' races along in 11/8, alternating 5/8 and 6/8 in what might be thought of as a Bartókian manner, but this movement is a combined reworking of 'Chin and Tongue Waggle' and 'The Wet Scythes', so its folk origins are Cornish and more in the Philip Heseltine manner.

Much more impressive is Chisholm's Symphony No. 2, *Ossian*, completed in 1939 but first performed as such for the recording made in 2007.[12] Chisholm arranged it almost immediately for the ballet *The Earth Shapers*, and in that form it is discussed below.[13]

Chisholm was also apparently planning an opera on Kafka's *The Trial* in 1939.[14] It was a subject which he would have handled superbly, and which would also have been all too relevant to the growing fascism in Europe, but it appears to have come to nothing. War's alarums had, however, galvanised the outstanding Scottish painter J. D. Fergusson and his wife, the dancer Margaret Morris, to return to Scotland from France.[15]

Chisholm claims that it was in 1938 that he was appointed musical director of the Celtic Ballet,[16] founded by Margaret Morris, whose own reminiscences[17] seem to suggest that it was founded in Glasgow in 1939 as the Celtic Ballet Club, based at 299 West George Street.[18] It was the Glasgow publisher William MacLellan who introduced Chisholm to Margaret Morris, and the dates are therefore further confused, as MacLellan states that he first met her in 1940.[19] Louise Annand follows Margaret Morris in her dating,[20] and it seems likely that Chisholm's date of 1938 is wrong, and that planning began in 1939 and came to fruition in 1940.

> One of the lucky things the war has done for me was to send M. Morris to Glasgow. Previous to the war she had been settled in Paris but she is now permanently in Glasgow and doing work here that no one else has ever done for us before.[21]

It was to be a brief but fruitful partnership, asserting through the arts not only the continuing validity of such activities even in wartime, but also something of an alternative world view, as seen through Celtic eyes. Whether such a view was in reality obscured by Celtic mist is discussed below, but it goes without saying that such ventures, misty or otherwise, carried with them more financial liabilities than they did rewards, and it is doubtful if Chisholm earned a single penny as a consequence of his association with the Margaret Morris movement.

Sometime in the first part of 1939, Erik's father had bought the house at 3 Carment Drive for Erik and Diana,[22] and this might have signalled the start of a period of some security for them, but the declaration of war at the beginning of September changed everything. Well, not quite everything. An exchange concert was held in Berlin of works by Scottish composers, 'while we, in Glasgow, gave a very successful evening of works by German Contemporary composers.'[23]

Chisholm was no doubt aware that he was not very likely to pass a medical examination for call-up, but he none the less sought support from Edward Dent to avoid recruitment, and Dent replied:

> I would gladly do anything I could to help you, but I can't think that a testimonial from me as to your abilities as a composer w'd have any influence whatever with War Office authorities, especially with subordinates.
>
> I should have thought your health, and especially your eye-troubles – would have been enough to obtain you complete exemption from military service ... Arthur Bliss has established himself at Cambridge, Mass: with his wife and children, I suppose. Hugh Ross is here too & not likely to move.[24]

Sir John Blackwood McEwen also wrote sympathetically:

> I have considered your suggestion with the greatest care and thought but I do not
> think that it would help you if I were to act upon it – rather, it might raise preju-
> dice against you. The artist, at the present time, is entirely superfluous, & he will
> only be treated with sympathy when the authorities realize that he can fill a useful
> role by carrying on his own work. But that won't be by composing!
>
> I should suggest that you associate yourself with some of the organisations
> which are being formed to supply entertainment to the fighting services. The Inc.
> Soc. of Musicians is engaged in organising such things, & you could be of use in
> this way.
>
> I feel very much for you & others of my musical friends who dread the future so
> much. Personally, I think that the most horrible of all the horrible things in store
> for us is the promiscuity of all kinds into which we shall be forced – but that is
> only because much is so foreign to my life & habits. Those of the younger people,
> like yourself, who pass through it, will get accustomed to all such disruptions of
> life. Few of us older people will survive a long period of stress and strain.
>
> All good wishes, yours
>
> J. B. McEwen[25]

McEwen did in fact survive the war, dying in 1948. Unknown to them all, an
attempt had been made to protect the lives of a select group of young creative
painters, musicians and writers, including Chisholm. Sculptors, architects, sci-
entists, scholars and re-creative artists were excluded, and the whole moral and
judgmental basis of this extraordinary, if not ludicrous idea, was most gently and
kindly questioned by Oliver Stanley, then Secretary of State for War. The panel
selecting the creative musicians consisted of Sir Hugh Allen, Malcolm Sargent
and Lord Berners. None of those selected was aware of the process, but it is
significant that they chose to include Erik Chisholm alongside Britten, Berkeley,
Walton, Rawsthorne, Rubbra and eight others.[26]

The outbreak of the Second World War not only carried with it the likelihood
of recruitment, it also created havoc with employment for creative artists. Diana
helped out by working in a fish market during the war years,[27] but Erik initially
found himself without sufficient work, as F. G. Scott records:

> I've had an appeal from Erik Chisholm asking me to try and have him recognised
> as a teacher of music at the schools: he's lost all his private pupils and is retired
> with wife and family to Innerleithen.[28]

There the family were visited by exiled Polish officers, to one of whom, apparently,
Diana took a shine.[29] A. F. Hyslop wrote to try and arrange the necessary recommendation for Chisholm to be able to teach music in schools, adding that he had
recently moved to Peeblesshire.[30]

One reason for his loss of employment was his apparent support of William Crosbie at a tribunal to assess Crosbie's conscientious objections. In 1939,

Crosbie, living in Paris, had offered his services to the Ministry of War. His offer was noted but not taken up. He objected to fighting on someone else's terms and 'would not kill under orders'.[31] Crosbie ended up serving with the Merchant Navy and drove ambulances in Liverpool, but was invalided out as he had tuberculosis.[32] Following the tribunal, Chisholm was asked to speak at a peace meeting which he happily did. The group in question was accused of being a thinly veiled communist organisation, and Chisholm was, initially, no longer given work by the BBC or any other official body.[33] Many years later, he recalled his attitudes, including in his horror of bloodshed his more recently acquired vegetarianism.

> I have always been a Socialist – that is ever since about the age of 12 when I read the proceedings of the Fabian Society and the brilliant reasoned expositions of that philosophy by Shaw, Wells and others: that the wealth of a country should be spread around the people with some degree of fairness to the majority of the inhabitants. ... My own, personal credo can be summed up something like this:

> 1) I refuse to accept any service whatsoever from any person or any government or any state, which I myself would not be prepared to give in return. At a pinch I would sweep streets and clean lavatories, but under no circumstances would I –

> (a) take a live pig and cut its throat with a knife or twist the neck of a chicken. Therefore, I do not eat bacon or chicken, or meat or fish or fowl, for I ask no one to do these murderous deeds for me.

> (b) Still less would I take the life of any human being or ask anyone to do this horrible business for me, so I am a fanatical hater of blood and violence whether it be in the butcher shop, the battlefield or in a prison cell.[34]

He ended up not far off sweeping streets and cleaning lavatories, as the script for an undated BBC children's broadcast he gave reveals:

> I am sure all of you must have noticed that large quantities of paint have been splashed about our streets and shops and windows since this war started. Those of you who are evacuated in the country can see miles and miles of white lines painted along the centre of the roads, and you've probably all noticed that a lot of black paint has been used as well – round the edges of windows – on roof lights, glass doors and so on, to prevent light from showing through the glass.
>
> Well, this is my war-time job – painting – and I think you'll agree that in war-time painting is very important. When we go home in the dark we're glad that things like lamp-posts and railings are painted white for it helps us to see them and saves us always bumping into them; and in the first month of the war, before the white paint on kerbs and pavements had been worn off, it was easier to get that extra pint of milk home to mother without spilling it than it is now that hundreds of muddy boots have walked over the paint. ...
>
> Well, in this painting business I don't think that my musical training is altogether wasted. When painting lines on steps and along the edge of pavements I

lay on the paint as a musical stave – in five lines with four spaces between – and this gives me an advantage over the man who lives as it were only from line to line, doing what must be one of the most monotonous jobs in the world. Looked at in this way, our gang must have ruled enough five lines and four spaces to write the complete works of Bach and Beethoven![35]

He put a brave face on it:

Some of my friends express their sympathy for me in my war-time job – they think it ... well ... a change for the worse. But I just remind them that ONE house-painter – from Austria – has managed to create quite a stir in the world recently! Nor can I complain that my life lacks variety – this morning, for instance, I was helping in blacking-out 1200 large windows in a large building & now I am going off to rehearse my piano concerto with the Scottish Orchestra.[36]

Of course he had all along been trying to keep himself going as a professional musician, but without success.

When I left Glasgow in 1940 to conduct for the Carl Rosa, I was trying to keep my growing family on £100 p.a. as organist of the Barony and a £3 a week job in a painter's shop. The records of the Scottish National Academy of Music can tell how often my application for a part-time teaching job was turned down – not to mention similar attempts to gain employment with the B.B.C. and at Edinburgh and other Scottish Universities.[37]

Chisholm himself attributed these difficulties to other causes than his political proclivities:

The contemporary music concerts I ran and financed almost single-handed for about 10 years in Glasgow (at which – among other noted composers – Bartok, Hindemith, Szymanowski, Sorabji, Medtner, were performers) brought me in no income. On the contrary, they resulted in well nigh wrecking my own private practice as a music teacher, it being whispered around – 'if we send our children to Chisholm for music, they will get nothing but the music of Bartok and Schön-berg to play'.[38]

It would seem, however, that the BBC was prepared to forgive Chisholm his pacifist and communist leanings, for in 1940 or 1941 they commissioned *The Adventures of Babar*, for narrator and orchestra.[39] Chisholm wrote the script, which was a humorous, rhyming résumé of the Babar books by Jean de Brun-hoff.[40] He described the work as 'introducing several French folk songs – if you like a cross between 'Peter and the Wolf' and 'Hary Janos'!.[41] It was composed for children and dedicated to his middle daughter, Sheila,[42] whose personal copy of *Babar* he dismembered in order to decorate the score therewith.[43] It was first performed by the BBC London (Symphony) Orchestra under Adrian Boult.

After a marvellous orchestral imitation of air-raid sirens, enemy aircraft and a bomb dropping on the original *Babar* drawings, many apparently thus destroyed, the work continues with a musical pun on the name, using the tune of 'Ba-ba Black Sheep'. It concludes with the sirens sounding the all-clear.

Apart from the air-raid, Chisholm's *Babar* also portrayed the war between the elephants and the rhinoceroses – a war won by the simple ruse of duping the enemy – so, at least for children, there was a happy ending for the goodies, headed by their king, in front of whom there is a celebratory procession. Such patriotism is not without its ironies in the original de Brunhoff text and illustrations, particularly as the war is provoked by the mischief of young Arthur, the elephant. Matching this, the score develops into a kind of medley of fragments of tunes one ought to recognise and which were probably included for Chisholm's personal amusement. The whole is imbued with a sense of mischief and irreverence which Tovey would have thoroughly enjoyed.

> I find that some German musicians object to Tovey's irrepressible sense of humour getting, they say, in the way of brilliant analytical writings. However after Tovey's death, Artur Schnabel sent me a letter in which he said, 'They just don't make musicians of Tovey's calibre any more.'[44]

If the BBC had forgiven Chisholm, they were less charitable to Sir Hugh Roberton's pacifism. He refused to have his famous Orpheus Choir sing the national anthem (something they had never done), and in 1940 the BBC banned all broadcasts of the choir. A lively correspondence in the *Glasgow Herald* from 2–12 December argued the pros and cons of the ban, most correspondents, as well as the *Glasgow Herald* leader writer, regarding it as heavy-handed.[45] It is worth noting that although the *Glasgow Herald* was a somewhat right-of-centre newspaper, its reporting of the hearings of conscientious objectors showed no unreasonable bias. Sir Hugh himself gives an account of the affair in which, it would appear, the ultimate blame for the ban lay with the authorities in London.[46]

Chisholm had made an unsuccessful bid for the University of Cape Town (UCT) Chair in Music in 1939. The reason for his failure is revealed in a comment on his later, successful application – 'The organizing ability he had displayed in this post [for ENSA in Singapore] overrode the reservations about his personality which had scotched his first bid for the UCT chair in 1939.'[47] In fact a large number of highly qualified musicians applied, many seeking to 'escape', recognising the inevitability of war. Among them were Dr Hans Gál, Roger Fiske, P. P. Sainton and, from Glasgow, Harold Thomson.[48] Chisholm's application was supported by Edward J. Dent, William Walton, Sir Arnold Bax, Paul Pisk (who had performed the Double Trio in Vienna) and Donald Tovey, in a letter worthy of reproduction:

> I hope that the high praise which is the least that I find due to Dr. Erik Chisholm may not be discounted as the language of 'testimoniolese'. Some of the most important terms of that language have sunk to the level of libel and slander; and

it is high time that you were taken literally. Accordingly I am ready to testify on oath that Dr. Chisholm is conscientious, means well, and makes the best use of his resources. His own musical resources are very extensive and of a high order. His enterprises in producing new and rare music have been Quixotic in their generosity and have exposed him to unfair criticism from persons with a more selfish care for their own reputation. But they have been carried through by a commonsense, which has usually resulted in something like triumph, and which assures me that he will be eminently practical and dignified occupant of any post to which he is elected.

I have not met any person who dislikes him, and my own acquaintance with him entitles me to form a poor opinion of any such person.[49]

Walton wrote:

[T]o recommend Dr. Erik Chisholm for the Chair of Music at Cape Town Univer-sity. I consider that he would fill the post with honour and distinction and greatly benefit those who came under his tuition. It is, I think, hardly necessary to say he is an excellent composer and that he combines a modernistic outlook with schol-arly foundations. He is also most enterprising in other branches of music being a good conductor, and having been concerned with various operatic productions. In fact, I think he would bring many qualities and exert much stimulus if he was to occupy such a position in the University.[50]

Bax, in his testimonial, described him as 'probably the most progressive com-poser that Scotland has produced'.[51]

He seems also to have asked his fellow Scot, the pianist and composer Frederic Lamond, for support.[52] But none of this was good enough to override the impres-sion that he was 'personally unsuitable, nervous and might be very difficult'.[53] Professor Eric Grant (a Fellow of the Royal Academy of Music in London) was appointed Director, but at no time was he Dean of the Faculty, nor is he ever actually named as Professor of Music.[54]

Chisholm was not the only musician in financial trouble. A touching letter from W. B. Moonie, whose opera Chisholm had mounted, thanks Erik for the gift of £10 and refers to Erik's own work street-painting.[55]

Despite his employment setbacks, 1940 was a good year for Chisholm. He premièred his revised Concerto for Pianoforte and Orchestra (the *Piobaire-achd*, see Chapter 3) on 20 January 1940 in the St Andrew's Halls, Glasgow, with Aylmer Buesst conducting the Scottish Orchestra (as it was then known). The concerto was very well received. The extensive programme note by W. C. L.[56] no doubt helped give it a boost; but it would seem that there was a readiness on the part of the critics to acknowledge the relevance of what Chisholm was attempt-ing as well as the skill with which it was achieved.

Also in 1940, on 6 and 7 December *The Forsaken Mermaid* was given at Glas-gow's Lyric Theatre.[57] It was the Celtic Ballet's first production, with choreography by Margaret Morris and decor by Andrew Taylor Elder. *The Forsaken Mermaid*, originally intended for the Scottish Ballet Society, was completed in 1936 for two pianos, the pianists being Chisholm himself and Jack Wight Henderson. Orchestral selections from it were performed by the Scottish Orchestra on 11 December 1937, with Chisholm conducting (George Szell conducted the rest of the programme). It was reasonably well received,[58] but in 1940 it was going to be impossible to recruit and pay for an orchestra, so Chisholm made the two-piano version published by MacLellan (colour plate 2). (See Chapter 4 for the bad feeling surrounding this.)

Stylistically, *The Forsaken Mermaid* is a much simpler and more direct work than *An Rioban Dearg* or, more significantly, the *Piobaireachd* Piano Concerto. No doubt Chisholm was conscious that he was composing for a ballet audience and for dancers, not all of whom were fully professional and who might have had difficulty following a complex score.

> He had composed several ballets on Celtic legends, and he played one of these to me, 'The Forsaken Mermaid'. I was enchanted by it, and saw that it was entirely suitable for presentation by my Celtic Ballet amateurs, most of the cast being fisher folk, so that the dances would have to be quite simple to be in character, and could thus be kept within the capacity of amateurs.[59]

The story itself is eminently suited to ballet. The contrasts of motion inherent in a tale which takes place partly on or under water and partly on land actively demand ballet treatment. Originally Chisholm had composed the work without the Prologue and Epilogue, so that all the action was on land, but Margaret Morris was not one to miss the opportunity of an underwater scene in a ballet. Chisholm also wanted a sad ending, but bowed to pressure by producing one which was bitter-sweet.[60] The music is largely – and very appealingly – based on airs from Patrick MacDonald's *A Collection of Highland Vocal Airs*.

Scene I is a Prologue – an underwater scene, in which a Mermaid wishes to play on the surface with her older sisters. It is the Mermaid's birthday and she will now be allowed to find out what it is like for herself. The two pianos produce a constant flow of movement, through which Chisholm has threaded a *piobaireachd*-like melody. In comparison with the slow movement of *An Rioban Dearg*, one might be tempted to suggest that this music is simplistic. But Chisholm knew what he was doing when it came to the theatre, and the whole of the music for this ballet must be understood in the light of that knowledge.

In Scene II, the young women of a Skye fishing village are dancing a Harris Dance (MacDonald 41). The men return and find the Little Mermaid caught in their nets and the air is appropriately *U-gu-vi-u, U-gu-vi-u, Port na maighdinn Chuain* – 'The Mermaid Song' (MacDonald 77). The Mermaid's fear is overcome by the people's kindness, who regard her presence as a sign of good luck. One fisherman – Alan – falls in love with her, forgetting his first love, Morag, and he and the Mermaid are married. Number V – 'The Wooing' – makes use of a Skye

Air, *Alasdair m' ansachd* (MacDonald 159) which, according to Bill MacLellan, everybody in the cast ended up singing.[61] Scene III takes place at Halloween, some months later, but Alan has grown tired of the Mermaid and forsakes her for Morag. In despair the Mermaid returns to the sea. Her music is an expanded version of *'S neonach le Clann dònail mi*, an appropriate choice as the title means 'Clan Donald Thinks Me Strange'. In Scene IV the people of the sea take revenge by conjuring up a storm in which two fishermen are drowned. Alan is held responsible, and when he sees the Mermaid, he plunges into the sea to join her. The Epilogue returns us to the scene of the Prologue and Alan is restored to life under the waves with the Mermaid.

Since Chisholm was writing for specifically Scottish and Celtic ballet companies, he chose scenarios based loosely on Gaelic material. Unfortunately, in outlining them in words, he aped the style of English used by the generation before him, such as Kenneth MacLeod and Marjory Kennedy-Fraser. Their prose and verse reads as a literal rather than an idiomatic translation of the originals. The effect is fanciful, even arch, and is evident in Chisholm's adaptation of James Stephens's *The Land of Youth* for the opera *Isle of Youth (The Feast of Samhain)*, whose libretto was published by MacLellan.[62] For Scene III of *The Forsaken Mermaid* Chisholm invites us to visualise the opening thus: 'The sea-folk are wroth, and no more is there the fair wind and the full net for the people of Skye.' Likewise, in the Epilogue, a sentence such as 'And herself with the broken heart looking on too, shame on you, ye callous lassies!' seems affected. Similar problems arise with the scenario for his ballet entitled *Piobaireachd*; but if the scenarios were to be rewritten and attention focused on the action and the music, the problem would simply be bypassed. It is worth noting that, as far as the music was concerned, Chisholm was appreciated as a modernist rather than a member of the Celtic Mist school:

> [T]he score by its clear-cut and metallic nature seemed admirably fitted to the treatment of its Celtic theme. Indeed, the contemporary composer is better fitted than his immediate predecessors to deal with the Celtic world not as a sad twilight place but as a bright hard heroic place, owing some kinship, say, to the archaic Greek.[63]

Besides his involvement with ballet, Chisholm was also still trying to mount operas, seeking funding for a proposal to put on Weber's *Euryanthe* in the autumn of 1940, and proposing Rimsky-Korsakov's *Matchie the Immortal* for the following year. He had already managed to put on *The Bartered Bride* by combining the Glasgow Grand Opera Society, the Barony Musical Association, the Regent Male Voice Choir and recruits from the Lyric Club and Barr and Stroud Male Voice Choir.[64] War had, of course, reduced the activities of these societies to zero, and it says a lot for Chisholm's organisational abilities and general persuasiveness that he was able to put on an opera at all. He felt it almost as a duty, and it was this sense of service in his work which was to lead to his parting company with

12 Erik Chisholm and Sheila, both in uniform

the Barony Church (see below). He had been rejected for the forces, having failed his medical.[65] However, in 1940 he took up the conductorship of the Carl Rosa opera company in two of their tours[66] before 'ENSA claimed him then for Army Adult Education to the British Forces, after which he toured the inner camps of the British Isles with lecture-recitals on symphony, opera and ballet. More tours followed for the International and Anglo-Polish Ballets.'[67]

Meanwhile Chisholm was putting together another ballet – *The Earth Shapers*. He used the music of his Symphony No. 2 for the work, whether out of despair of its performance in its original form or in order to supply Margaret Morris with a ballet in a hurry at a time when he was busy touring and lecturing for ENSA, is not known. The second movement also had a separate existence as *A Celtic Wonder Tale*. It comes as no surprise, then, that he described the work on the programme as 'A Symphonic Ballet', or that the symphony itself, named after the Celtic hero Ossian, is dramatic, if not exactly programmatic.

The Earth Shapers was the company's second production. The scenario was 'Adapted from various Celtic legends' by Chisholm himself,[68] and the ballet was premiered in the Lyric Theatre, Glasgow, in the autumn of 1941. It was an adventurous, but a small world. Chisholm's eldest daughter, Morag, aged eight, was one of the Animals, and his second daughter, Sheila Elesaid, aged six (and later to become a ballet dancer), was the Pooka. Chisholm used their names for characters in his ballet *The Forsaken Mermaid*. The publisher William MacLellan took the part of Ogma the Wise, Ian Clegg danced the part of Midyir and Margaret Morris that of the Earth Spirit, as well as being choreographer and producer. The costumes and decor were by William Crosbie. Chisholm and Wight Henderson played the music, which was arranged for two pianos.

Crosbie's watercolour sketches for the sets survive (colour plates 4 & 5), as do photographs of the dancers in costume. Both are striking in their bold semi-abstraction, not least the cover for the *Clàr-Cuimhneachais*. This Gaelic title, which means 'Souvenir Programme', is printed on the cover, asserting (albeit in a small gesture) the debt to the language and culture upon which the scenario is ultimately based. Crosbie's cover combines stylised tree, harp, stone circle, cup-and-ring mark, pin, a snake-like figure and a mask. Its lack of either historical or archaeological accuracy merely reflects the standard confusions as to what constitutes 'Celticity', and does little or no damage to the artistic integrity of Crosbie's work. His costumes and scenes are clean-cut – not so much Celtic mist as engaging deeply in the unique combination of observation and abstraction that defines much Celtic art.

The ballet is in four scenes, corresponding to the Second Symphony's four movements.[69] In the Prelude 'Tir-na-Moe, the Land of the Living Heart', the Earth Spirit pleads successfully for help from 'The Shining Ones' – Brigit, Midyir the Mighty, Ogma the Wise and Angus the Ever-young – to rid the world of the Fomors under their king, Balor of the Evil Eye. The second scene is entitled 'Sonata Movement "The Earth under the Fomors"' and also served for *A Celtic*

Wonder Tale. In it, the deformed race of Fomors sacrifice some of the Irish people to their sea-gods. The third scene is a Scherzo-Toccata – 'The Gods Descend to Battle', in which 'The Shining Ones' defeat the Fomors. In the Finale, 'The Gods Refashion the Earth', with the Spear of Victory, the Stone of Destiny and the sound of Angus's magic harp promising peace and plenty in Eire.

Interesting, this. In the dark days of the Second World War, we have a ballet company in one of the combatant nations suggesting that regeneration will start in a country which was neutral, and much criticised for being so. That it is the Irish Free State that is necessarily implied is indicated by the fact that at the end Brigit calls it 'the White Island, the Island of Destiny – Eire'.[70] The name Eire was used only by the Irish Free State, although (being an ancient name) it applied to the whole island. It remained the wish of most citizens of what was effectively a republic that the country should be unified, but the people of Northern Ireland would never have associated the name Eire with their own part of the island. It seems clear, then, that something approaching a neutral, if not pacifist agenda, could reasonably be detected in this work, although the Fomorian enemy would naturally be associated with Hitler and the Germans. But the ballet invokes Celtic, not Christian, Roman, Greek or British gods, to see off the evil with which the world is confronted.

The work opens with an impressive, almost cinematic Prelude. The sacrifice scene follows. In its existence as an independent piece in 1949, it was fairly well received,[71] and with its broad melody, parallel chords and hypnotically repeated figurations, it is a powerful piece, but there is not much variety of pace or rhythm for the dancers to respond to, which was pointed out in a review of the ballet performance.[72]

The same might be said of the remaining sections of the ballet, in which there seems to be no trace of the magic harp. Whether, in its full orchestral dress, it could be revived as a ballet is doubtful. Certainly as a symphony it has its own independent strength, and Lewis Foreman is right to suggest that its dark and thoughtful ending seems to take the form of a tragic funeral march rather than a victorious restoration, concluding, as it does, with a mystical question mark.[73]

There was another aspect to this assertion of Scoto-Celtic values, which Chisholm referred to trenchantly in a paper given to an unidentified club in Glasgow shortly before the performances of *The Earth Shapers*, although he made it clear that this was no personal grouse, as he had been doing well for performances:

> Scotland is one of the least national-minded races in the world: it likes its music German and Italian and its performers with unpronounceable names if possible. We've all laughed and joked at this for years but I believe it to be as fundamentally true for the vast majority of Scotsmen now as it was 20 years ago. Glasgow natives will support the so-called International Ballet, enthuse over a 2nd-rate Polish ballet but stay away from an English ballet altho the latter is incomparably

better than either of them. If our natives can't have foreign music and musicians then they'll put up with something out of London. Someone said to me the other day that if a successful German invasion of these Isles had taken place in 1939 and the Germans had been in charge of musical Scotland last year, their programmes could not have been more pro-German or anti-British.

I ask you what chance have we of _ever_ producing a school of native composers if this hostile attitude by our musical purveyors is allowed to persist?[74]

As usual, however, the Scottish composers themselves continued to plough their lonely furrows, though occasionally finding time to help drive each other's teams. Chisholm, for instance, appears to have been working on a proposed opera, _The Making of the Tartan_, with Arthur Geddes, who wrote to him in April 1942: 'Here, at last, are a series of airs from the "Tartan". I've begun with the last Act.'

A month later, in May, he sent another instalment of the music:

I'm sorry and disappointed it's so little, but I'm slow at coordinating music and words, being out of practice. And of course the 3rd term is the busy one. But I hope to send you more by taking the time next Sunday.

I hope practices of your own opera are going well or as well as can be hoped in a world imperfect musically as – alas in other arts, that of peace to start with![75]

How Chisholm found time to collaborate on any opera is hard to understand, given that he was not only Conductor and Music Director to the Royal Carl Rosa Opera Company, but was organising concerts and entertainments for the forces wherever the Company toured.

In the last six months I have given nearly 200 such entertainments to R.A.F., British Sailors Societies, Army and Y.M.C.A. Centres in every part of England and Wales. I have done this work without receiving any payment for it, often at great personal inconvenience, and more than once when enemy action was in progress.

The enthusiasm and appreciation of the forces for these efforts of mine have been ample reward and have convinced me that my employment with a touring company gives me a unique opportunity of giving service in my own particular way. …

On several occasions (at Brighton, Portsmouth, Plymouth, Keighley, Exeter, Cardiff, Croydon and Nottingham), I have toured remote gun sites, soldiers' camps etc., at the invitation of the Y.M.C.A., in their entertainment and supply vans, and the Lecture-entertainments I have given have been particularly welcomed in these isolated spots.[76]

His freely given work, however, landed him in trouble with the Kirk Session of the Barony church, where he had appointed a deputy. Many churches in Glasgow had given their organists leave of absence for the duration of the war, but not the Barony. The Kirk Session had called a special meeting to discuss a letter of protest from Chisholm; had instructed Sanderson to 'Express their sense of dissatisfaction' at Chisholm's conduct; had called Chisholm to a special meeting of censure; and had suspended him from his duties as organist until they had passed judgment on him. Chisholm felt he had no option but to resign, while recalling with pleasure the loyalty of the choir and collaboration with the ministers and others.[77]

Chisholm later broadcast a fascinating account of his work during these years, which included the hazards of lecturing, which he sensibly omitted from his protest to the Kirk Session:

> Mostly my lectures were received with interest. Question time at the end of course was always the most enjoyable part of the show for me. The sort of questions asked were mostly of a very elementary nature; 'What do you think of jazz?' 'Why is so much classical music tuneless?' or others of equal naivity [sic]. Some questioners displayed an uncommon facility in leading the discussion no matter what it was into matters political; – from 'Why is the "Messiah" the greatest oratorio?' to 'Should the Government encourage clay pigeon shooting in the U.S.S.R?' – in two moves! Once however I got a surprise after giving a talk of a very popular nature on opera illustrated with sugar plums from 'Trovatore', 'Faust' and 'Carmen'. A bespectacled youth asked me if I considered the 'Schönbergian sange-spracht' method as evidenced in 'Wosseck' & 'Pierrot Lunaire' 'an improvement in the Wagnerian voice line as a means of dramatic expression'.

> My most dismal failure to hold the interest of a soldier audience occurred somewhere in Yorkshire. They were a pretty tough bunch of privates, who I learned later, had been detained for the afternoon in camp for some misdemeanour or other, while their pals were off enjoying themselves at an important local football match – not, you will admit, the most receptive of audiences for a lecture on the evolution of opera. Shuffling of feet, blowing of noses. ...[78]

But at this delicate point, there is a page missing from the typescript.

Chisholm's contract with the Royal Carl Rosa Opera Company expired on 31 October, and it is presumably around this time that he took up the baton for the Anglo-Polish Ballet (colour plate 6). By November of 1943 they appear to have been in Southsea, and they were on tour, with Chisholm conducting, from 1943–4. They visited Chatham, Stockport, Kingston, Plymouth, Torquay, Lewisham, Bristol, Hull, Grimsby, Dundee, Aberdeen, Edinburgh and Glasgow,[79] as well as giving 'several London seasons', Chisholm occasionally orchestrating some of their ballets.[80]

Despite this heavy schedule, in May of that year he was completing some of his piano preludes, *From the True Edge of the Great World*, which he composed for Agnes Walker:

> He arrived one Sunday morning at my home in Whitecraigs dressed in pyjamas and overcoat; threw a parcel of music at my father who had opened the door and

said 'give those to Agnes. I've just finished them' and dashed back to a waiting taxi. They were the piano preludes from 'The true edge of the great world' ... I have played the preludes since both in Scotland and abroad.[81]

It was thus that the Scottish pianist Agnes Walker recalled the arrival of this group of preludes. Their title refers to the Hebridean islands which are thought by some to represent Ultima Thule, or the edge of the world. That the Americas are to be found beyond them seems a matter of small relevance to anyone who has stood on the Atlantic coastline of the Hebrides. They have captured the romantics, and with good reason. Their wild beauty and the antiquity and depth of their Gaelic-speaking culture, which today learns to co-exist with the internet and the mobile phone, makes such a title reasonable rather than fanciful. That it is tough out there is, of course, only alluded to by the romantics in an adoring kind of way, but that does not invalidate the strength of their response.

Chisholm very probably got the idea for this whole group of pieces from just such a romantic – Amy Murray, an American from whose *Father Allan's Island* he got all of the tunes except that of *Rudha Ban*, though its title refers to a placename in her book. In it she published Gaelic songs she collected in Eriskay, and she refers to the Hebrides as the 'True Edge of the World' and likens the songs themselves to something from music's own edge. Orchestrated versions of nine of the preludes of *From the True Edge of the Great World* (completed in 1943) were first performed by the BBC Scottish Orchestra in 1949, conducted by Chisholm himself.[82]

These are much more than simple settings of traditional melodies. As the description 'Preludes' implies, they are more in the form of meditations or improvisations on some aspect of a melody which may only appear in full once in the whole piece. Only nine of these preludes exist, although the numbering in his manuscripts suggests that twenty-four were planned.[83]

The first, *Port a Beul*, literally means 'mouth music' and refers to the continuing practice of singing dance music, often using nonsensical words and tongue-twisters to emphasise the rhythmic drive of the music. On no account may the rhythm be broken for the intake of breath, which has to be managed by subtle omission of a note or two. *Port a Beul* is often danced to, but is also sung simply for the fun of it. Chisholm's piece is in the form of a reel and enjoys the same breathless and almost relentless drive, the test of stamina being also part of the fun. This one is a wooing song. It is followed by 'The Song of the Mavis' – *Oran na Smeoraich* – which imitates the thrush and is well known in Gaelic tradition as a children's song describing the parent bird calling its young to dinner with characteristic repetitions. Chisholm has turned this homely piece into an idyllic ripple of birdsong. 'Sea-sorrow' is a song sung by a Gaelic-speaking sailor unable to follow English instructions in threatening weather. The original expresses a mock anxiety and, in the Gaelic-speaking world, the song would normally provoke amusement, but Chisholm has taken what is undoubtedly a dark tune and given it ominous undercurrents. 'The Shieling Lullaby', on the other hand, refers to the temporary houses on higher pastures that were used for managing the summer grazing of cattle and sheep. Cheese and butter were made, but as the work was often done by teenagers, shieling life presented an opportunity for love-making. Chisholm sets up a gently rocking introduction derived from the melody, which he treats with dreamy luxuriance, finally bringing introduction and melody together, as content as lovers.

Of the remaining six preludes, one is based upon a strange little incantation, another is a spinning song and the seventh is an 'Ossianic Lay'. This is a rhetorical piece in that its repeated notes suggest incantation – at one point it is marked 'quasi recitative'. Ossianic lays are rooted in ancient material, but have scarcely survived in the tradition. This one was collected by Amy Murray and the words are ascribed to Ossian, who recalls the heroic days with Oscar, Douglas and Fionn. Chisholm treats it with simplicity and respect, maintaining a drone and scarcely developing the harmony beyond octave doublings, with a few chords that colour rather than impel the music. He concludes his setting with a hushed, mystical scattering of notes.

The final prelude, 'The Hour of the Sluagh', is partly explained by the quotation from *Father Allan's Island* which Chisholm has placed at the top of the music – 'In the mouth of the night is the hour of the Sluagh, the host of the Dead, whose feet never touch on earth as they go drifting on the wind till Day of Burning. The light that is shadowless, colourless, softer than moonlight, is ever the light of their liking'. The tune, referred to briefly, is that of a song sung by the mythical water-horse enticing his human lover to come to him. The treatment is impressionistic and seductive.

Also completed in 1943 were the *Ceol Mór Dances* for orchestra, though they had to wait five years for their first performance in Cape Town in a reduced version.[84] But Chisholm can have had little time for composition and little enough time at home, although this was the common lot and at least he was nowhere near the firing line. The mail, at any rate, seems to have gone on functioning perfectly well, and Morag wrote to him after her confirmation, having been out for a Sunday walk with her grandfather to Rouken Glen, accompanied by Husky, 'an elkhound of tender (he could be a dashed sight more tender for my liking) years'.[85] Dogs were always a part of the Chisholm household and might well have merited a chapter on their own, had not music made prior claims. One of those claims on Erik was the arranging of 'El Alamein', a bagpipe march by Pipe-Major William Denholm, for piano, for at last there was something to celebrate in the conduct of the war (colour plate 7). Erik probably wrote it when the ballet company included Glasgow in one of its tours in 1944.[86]

It was for that Christmas that Sheila was given an autograph album by her parents in which she placed photos of members of the Anglo-Polish Ballet, gathered sometime earlier that year. All very nice for her, but her poor father was suffering:

At one time the Anglo-Polish might have been a possible force in the English ballet world but, owing to the incredible stupidity of its director (a one-time sausage maker), Jan Cobel allowed several of our best English dancers to slip through his hands.

It appears to have been an experience bordering on the farcical:

> We never knew what instruments would form our orchestra or how well their owners would play. I shall never forget Erik stamping out the rhythm quite desperately for the she-devil's dance in 'Pan Twardowsky' (or 'Polish Faust') on his rostrum, the nervous timpanist having completely dried up. Night after night, I filled in the gaps … Things were pretty fraught at times, being made more complicated by Erik declaring his devotion to me, while I was absurdly in love with the director, Janek Cobel, who in turn had another girlfriend more glamorous than I.[87]

Chisholm himself savages *Pan Twardowsky* in equally expressive prose:

> This horrible abortion, this balletic monstrosity, this unspeakable concoction of bits and pieces (set to the most blatantly plagiaristic and dully pretentious music it has ever been my misfortune to hear – by one Vladimir Launitz) has been dragging its slimy trail across England and Scotland for three interminable years, purporting, if you please, to be an example of Polish artistic endeavour at its finest.[88]

But as the Allies gradually turned the tide against the Germans, Chisholm and the ballet company were soon able to carry on their work abroad, and that story is taken up in the next chapter. Whether *Pan Twardowsky* travelled with them to Italy, I do not know, but, for the sake of Chisholm and the Italians, I sincerely hope not.

Pictures from Dante & Night Song of the Bards

A Journey from West to East

AMONG THE MAJOR MUSICAL FRUITS OF CHISHOLM'S WARTIME experiences are the two works which give this Centre-piece its title.

The orchestral work, *Pictures from Dante*, was substantially based upon a ballet he wrote during the war and, since it moves from *Inferno* to *Paradiso*, can be said to extricate itself from the horrors of human depravity which war entails. *Night Song of the Bards* also progresses from darkness to light, its ending anticipating the inevitability of dawn. It draws on Chisholm's experiences of Hindustani music during his brief stay in northern India towards the end of the Second World War, but is equally rooted in Celtic tradition.

Pictures from Dante is in two movements and was completed in South Africa in 1948 and dedicated to Sorabji (See Interlude: The Love of Sorabji). It received its first performance in 1952 from the Vienna Radio Orchestra under Kurt Woess.[1] The original full score and parts are in Cape Town. The first South African performance was on 30 August 1960, as part of the final concert for the South African College of Music jubilee celebrations (see Chapter 9).[2]

The inclusion of *Pictures from Dante* among the Scottish works requires explanation. Was Chisholm aware that Dante's *Inferno* and *Paradiso* had their origins in part in Celtic Christian visionary poetry? C. S. Boswell's *Irish Precursors of Dante* had been published in London in 1908 along with a translation of the tenth/eleventh-century *Fis Adamnáin* with which the work of Dante has several significant parallels, although these were probably transmitted indirectly. Whatever the case, Chisholm had a more obvious reason for describing the work as 'Scottish', and that is that the first movement is derived directly from Scene III of his ballet *Piobaireachd* and the first part of the second movement from Scene II. According to what he wrote on the score, the ballet was composed in 1940–1. I know of no performance of the ballet, and am also unaware of anyone else's involvement in its conception or possible execution. Perhaps its length was daunting, and since Chisholm intended that it should be based in part on scenes from Dante's *Inferno* as illustrated by Gustave Doré, it may be that Morris and others felt that this was depriving them of a Celtic design input. Also, *Piobaireachd* is a comic work, not without its darker moments, but there is an element of farce which renders the scenario implausible to the point of being merely ridiculous. It commences with a Highland Games in which a young fiddler jealously kills a respected piper by hitting him on the head with his fiddle. The scene moves to Heaven, where the angels are descending a golden staircase, making obeisance to St Cecilia. The music for this scene is used for the opening of the *Paradiso* movement of *Pictures from Dante*.

Next, the clarsairs (Celtic harpists) play Chisholm's version of the *piobaireachd* 'Lament for the Harp Tree' – which he had set in the series of piano pieces also entitled *Piobaireachd*. The angels admit the clarsairs with their harps. They are followed by a swing trio on saxophone, trumpet with wa-wa mute and piano accordion; but an angel replaces the saxophone with a clarinet, the mute is removed from the trumpet and the accordionist is given a harp. The angels also reject the piper, who chooses rather to go to Hell. It is at this point that the *piobaireachd* connection between the two works is made. The scenario actually describes Scene III as being 'after Doré', and it is clear that the engraving referred to in *Pictures from Dante* is the basis of the action.

Gustav Doré is famous for his book illustrations, and especially for his engravings for Cary's English verse translation of Dante. Both are as impressive today as they were when published at the turn of the twentieth century. Chisholm identifies the pictures by notes in the full score of *Pictures from Dante*, but his selection does not follow Dante's narrative sequence. Typically, he has planned his own journey, and under his own guidance.

In transferring this material from ballet to symphonic score, Chisholm has taken advantage of – indeed gloried in – the new opportunities afforded him in Cape Town. For the ballet, he had only a chamber ensemble. For *Pictures from Dante* he had triple wind, the usual brass, two harps, organ, piano, timpani and percussion (including tubular bells, celesta, xylophone and glockenspiel), and of course a large string section.

The opening music – described by Chisholm as a 'theme with variations (*Piobaireachd*)'[3] – is a version of *Fàilte Sheorais Oig* – 'Young George's Salute'. It is not known to whom this *piobaireachd* refers – the suggestion that it was George III has no real support, and the choice of this *piobaireachd* remains a mystery to me. In Chisholm's version, the *ùrlar* is given three variations: a *Siubhal* (literally, a travelling variation), a *Taorluath* and a *Crunluath*. Only the latter two are identified as such, and only in the full score of the ballet. Chisholm's *Inferno* movement is first inspired by the lines in Canto XXVI, lines 46–9 (picture no. 55 in Cary – see illus. 13):

> The guide, who mark'd
> How I did gaze attentive, thus began.
> 'Within these ardours are the spirits, each
> Swathed in confining fire.'

Dante and his guide look down into a chasm lit by fire. The image accents darkness and depth. The only source of light is from below, and it is not comforting. Chisholm expresses this by using divisi cellos and double-basses (including basses which must be fitted with the low C extension) on a drone that shifts ominously between D♭ and C. The remaining cellos play a chromatically altered

13 Gustav Doré's engraving for Canto XXVI of Dante's *Inferno*

version of the *ùrlar*. This was a technique he used on many occasions. Here, he does not take the original notes of the *piobaireachd* literally, but follows the melodic shapes which the eight notes per group produce. He has doubled the length of the note values so that he can express his equivalent of the cuttings, not as grace-notes, but as parts of the rhythmic structure.

The First Variation (*Poco più mosso*, score p. 10) also follows the structure, except that section D has a full four bars. The tune is given to the first violins, all to be played on the G string to give a rich, dark quality to the tone.

The Second Variation is marked *Vivo* and, in the ballet score, *Taorluth*. The spelling and translation of this term vary; but the finger movements to which it refers are well understood and follow a fairly rigorous pattern. It is a pattern which heightens the sense of activity and forward motion. Chisholm has reflected the character, but not the technique, of a *Taorluth*. The cuttings are replaced by repeated notes and trills. As for the accompanying image, here we see real torment. We hear it, too: in the quickened pace of the music, and the stabbing dotted rhythms exchanged between brass and lower strings and wind. The pain of 'dilated flakes of fire', searing the naked bodies of the damned, is rhythmically unrelieved, and the interchange between brass and strings ends up with their agonised defensive gestures coming together, as though trying to defend themselves from all sides at once.

> Unceasing was the play of wretched hands,
> Now this, now that way glancing, to shake off
> The heat, still falling fresh.

> Canto XIV, lines 37–9 (picture no. 38, score p. 19)

The Third Variation is marked *Grave e pesante* and changes pace and mood. In days gone by, something similar would have happened in the normal performance of a *piobaireachd*, the *ùrlar* being returned to, following the *taorluth*. The scene depicted is the punishment for the avaricious, pushing vast sacks of coin around in circles, in constant collision and deprived of its use, as they deprived others. They are anonymous – and there are yet thousands like them, in the exchanges of the world, queuing to join them. This was also the image that Chisholm had in mind for the ballet.

> Not all the gold that is beneath the moon,
> Or ever hath been, of these toil-worn souls,
> Might purchase rest for one.

> Canto VII, lines 65–7 (picture no. 22, score p. 23)

The scene is powerfully described in the music by trundling semi-quavers in the lower strings, and a deep rolling bass line on trombones, tuba and organ. Above this ponderous, grinding texture, the woodwind Scotch snaps push in vain.

The Fourth and Final Variation is a *crunluath* – again the spelling and meaning of this word are much debated. 'Crowning' variation is the translation most often used. It represents something approaching a culmination of finger dexterity in a series of standardised cuttings. However, there are different types of crunluath – *fosgailte*, *breabach*, *a-mach* – each of which has its own powerfully dramatising rhythmic and emphatic influence upon the basic note sequence. Chisholm does not attempt to imitate these finger movements orchestrally, though a stab at them can be made on the piano and on woodwind instruments. Instead he imitates their character, and unleashes a march, marked *Tempestuoso – Alla marcia* (score, p. 30) The high woodwind trills scream out their pain, the side-drum rattles out an inexorable 12/8 march rhythm, the horns pull the rhythm this way and that in a competing 4/4, and the strings lash the bodies of sinners, among whom is one Venedico, who prostituted his sister.

Ah! How they made them bound at the first stripe

Canto xviii, line 38 (picture no. 42, score p. 29)

The movement comes to a close with a recapitulation of the *ùrlar*, subsiding into darkness over a long-held bottom C on the double basses and organ pedals. A last high major chord, in harmonics and *tremolando* on the strings, is played simultaneously with a conflicting chord on the flutes and clarinet. It acts as a kind of disembodied enigma, subtly altering the mood to prepare for the next movement. Chisholm used a similar technique to effect such a transition between the second and last movements of the *Sonatine Écossaise*.

The second movement of *Pictures from Dante* is entitled *Paradiso*. The ballet scenario suggests that Chisholm had the same Doré engraving in mind as for the opening section of this movement, except that in the ballet, the angels are worshipping St Cecilia. The image is from Dante's Canto xxi, lines 28–31 (picture no. 55 – see illus. 14):

Down whose steps
I saw the splendours in such multitude
Descending, every light in heaven, methought,
Was shed thence.

The music itself is a cross between medieval plainchant, Gaelic pentatonicism and Lutheran chorale. I have been unable to find a source for it, but believe there is one. Here, the drone is in the treble, high and unwavering on D and A. The stately movement is in three beats to the bar, but with typical two-beat bars at cadential pauses.

Gradually, Chisholm draws away from the near-parallelism of the initial harmonies, towards a more contrapuntal texture, with an isomelodic bass – the equivalent of an isorhythmic line, except that the pitch pattern is repeated and the rhythm altered. Chisholm marks it ostinato. Above this, the chorale-like theme pauses on different chords in root position. As the counterpoint develops, the music sometimes cadences with typical medieval *tierce di Picardie* – a major third in what would be otherwise a minor mode (ex. 8).

The harmonic movement is further enriched by alternating two-bar sections in an alien key, with the basic mode of the music. The free passing dissonances of this style are exploited here (and later in the Chaucer operas) and the effect is often of the vibrancy of a bell. Coupled with this are the rising declamatory phrases which extend their pentatonicism into something more akin to medieval trumpet calls, until the whole expands into a wonderful climax, powerful and

14 Gustav Doré's engraving for Canto xxi of Dante's *Paradiso*

dignified. It finally resolves in D major and, as the music subsides, the ostinato makes its last ascent and descent into the second section, which follows without any break.

From here, to the best of my knowledge, the music is newly composed. The sketches appear to be largely related to this and the ensuing section.[4] Although the Canto and etching number are given at the beginning of the section, in the draft, Chisholm has written part of the quotation under a later passage when the piano joins the texture. Above an initial pedal D, the flutes and, soon, the

Ex. 8 *Pictures from Dante*, second movement, bars 1–22

clarinets share a simple flowing line of quavers. The quaver movement, passed from instrument to instrument and, later, section to section is uninterrupted by a single pause, and unbroken by so much as a crotchet, for ninety-three bars. The hypnotic effect is never allowed to dull. What is created is a magical sense of the mystery of flight as Chisholm evokes the extraordinary image in Dante and Doré, of angels rising like a flock of birds into the silver light of Jupiter. As they fly, they sing; and the letters their flight forms spell out *Diligite justitiam qui judicatis terram* – 'Love righteousness, ye that be judges of the earth' – which is a quotation from the first sentence of the Apocryphal Wisdom of Solomon.

> So, within the lights,
> The saintly creatures, flying, sang; and made
> Now D, now I, now L, figured i' the air.
>
> Canto XVIII, lines 70–2 (picture no. 50, score p. 14)

The beauty of this passage in the music is hard to explain. It appears to be utterly simple and almost devoid of content – nothing more than scales in contrary and parallel motion. But of course it is far from being so. The subtlety with which Chisholm shifts the harmonic and contrapuntal hints, touching on dissonance, touching on gentle consonance so delicately as the flow progresses, does not show on the page, and this music is sustained for pages. It commences on wind instruments only, in the softest of their registers. Only a large orchestra with triple wind allows Chisholm this luxury, otherwise it would be impossible to breathe it. It is hard also to select a music example, for the effect is only really understood through far more time and space than can be used here. Nevertheless, here is a brief sample (ex. 9); but it cannot convey the shifting perspectives given by the effect of one clarinet passing on the line to another, or to a flute or oboe, and, on keyboard, the harmonic texture and melodic flow lose much.

This is music of the utmost daring: but let no one confuse it with the mindless meanderings of minimalism, where change is effected mechanically within a texture, as often as not, composed in direct opposition to the natural bent of the instruments employed. Compare any such passage (I shall name no names) with this of Chisholm's and you are comparing a child at idle play with a master. Simplicity is the hardest thing of all to manage perfectly, and too often fools step in where angels fear to tread. Here we have angels.

The movement progresses in its stately way until the chorale-like theme returns, binding the two sections together, and leading to a concluding *Maestoso Gloria*.

> Then 'Glory to the Father, to the Son,
> And to the Holy Spirit,' rang aloud
> Throughout all Paradise; that with the song
> My spirit reel'd, so passing sweet the strain.
>
> Canto XXVII, lines 1–4 (picture no. 57, score p. 32)

Ex. 9 'Paradiso'

Chisholm has written the words of the Gloria into the score in the standard church formula used in Scotland (as opposed to Cary's translation), and continues it beyond what Dante has used. It comes in a broad hymn-like melody passed from the trumpets calling out 'Glory to the Father', to the organ on 'And to the Son and to the Holy Ghost' and continuing 'As it was in the beginning, is now and ever shall be, world without end'. Chisholm has not written in an 'Amen', but it is implicit in the concluding bars.

The Epilogue (so designated in the sketches), ripples with harps, celeste, high violins and muted solo cellos, leading into the beatific vision of the *Lento*. The work ends with a simple A major chord: two fifths on clarinets and two solo violins providing the major third.

> About us thus,
> Of sempiternal roses, bending, wreathed
> Those garlands twain; and to the innermost
> E'en thus the external anwer'd. ...

Canto XII, lines 16–19 (picture no. 46, score p. 32)

One could say of this work that indeed 'the innermost e'en to the external answered', for it should speak very directly to its audience. I write 'should' because there is no commercial recording of this work, and it has only been performed twice in public. But I am prepared to assert that, along with Wallace's symphonic tone poem *The Passing of Beatrice*, it brings us into the world of Dante with more vision and less bombast than Liszt, and does honour to Dante and Doré in full measure, earning its own garland of sempiternal roses, bending.

Night Song of the Bards

Night Song of the Bards – Six Nocturnes for Piano (after an anonymous Gaelic poem), was composed between 1944 and 1951[5] and is of pivotal importance. If the date of commencement is correct, it was started before Chisholm had been to the Far East. It basically precedes the main Hindustani-influenced works, the Second Piano Concerto, composed in 1948–9, the Violin Concerto (1951), and the *Van Riebeeck* Concerto (1950–1), for which see Chapter 7.[6] While its subject-matter is Celtic, its style is heavily influenced by Far Eastern music, particularly in its use of a chromatic unit of six notes which Chisholm wrote out at the front of one of the draft scores and which relates closely to *Râg Sohani* (see below).

The chronology would suggest that this was a piece in which Chisholm began to work out his ideas on the relationship between Celtic and Far Eastern ways of thinking and expression, no longer starting from the diatonic or pentatonic modal basis of Scottish tradition and then chromaticising it, but using chromaticism from the outset. It was dedicated to Harold Reubens [*sic*], briefly teaching piano at UCT under Chisholm. In programmes, the pianist's name appears as

Rubens. It is interesting that, despite its title, Chisholm did not include it in his handwritten list of 'Scottish works'.[7]

Nowhere does Chisholm identify the 'anonymous Gaelic poem', but in an uncatalogued manuscript in the Chisholm papers, the first two 'Songs' are given sub-titles: (i) 'Night is dull and dark' and (ii) 'The wind is up, the shower descends'. This sub-title also appears as a quotation above a sketch for the same bard in a separate uncatalogued manuscript in the same folder as the dedication. These provided the necessary stylistic clue for identification. The use of direct observational statements and short sentences, coupled with the higher-register 'descends', in place of 'falls', was suggestive of James Macpherson (illus. 15) – and so it proved. The *Night Song of the Bards* (the title is Chisholm's) forms an extended footnote to Macpherson's *Croma: A Poem*, and in an introduction Macpherson asserts that this was the only extempore Gaelic bardic composition which he had found worthy of translation. He continues:

> The story of it is this. Five bards, passing the night in the house of a chief, who was a poet himself, went severally to make their observations on, and returned with an extempore description of, night. The night happened to be one in [Oc]tober, as appears from the poem, and in the north of Scotland, it has all that variety which the bards ascribe to it, in their descriptions.[8]

The authenticity or otherwise of Macpherson's work is the object of much scholarly debate, as well as a good deal of ignorant opinion. Samuel Johnson's is perhaps the worst example of this ignorance, asserting that 'the Earse never was a written language' and that there 'is not in the world an Earse manuscript a hundred years old'.[9] His ignorance is unforgivable, for not only were such manuscripts already being gathered, but also much information derived from them had already been published in Ireland and London by such leading figures as Archbishop Ussher and John Toland.[10] Indeed a scribal tradition going back to the earliest vernacular writings in Western Europe was uniquely theirs, and not alone in Ireland, for the early sixteenth-century *Book of the Dean of Lismore* provides a direct Scottish Gaelic link, known to Macpherson himself.[11] It was Johnson who came from the younger literary culture. Let not the reader, then, dismiss out of hand the very real significance of Macpherson's work, or the even greater significance of that upon which it purported to be, and was in part, based.

However, in this instance, Macpherson's source has yet to be discovered, and his content and style indicate that he did not restrict himself to a direct translation, if indeed there is an original source.[12] Chisholm himself is very unlikely to have known anything more about it than what Macpherson declares, having almost certainly found it in a 1932 anthology of Celtic poetry.[13] There is, however, a traditional tale which has some parallels, for three of the Celtic heroes, Ossian's servants and a servant-maid, give different reports of the night to their blind master. It may well be that Macpherson heard a variant of this tale.[14]

It is possible to trace the relationship between the music and the different

15 James Macpherson

visions of night offered by each bard. But it is also true that these bards return from the same night each with a different vision, and Chisholm, in venturing into the dark, brings back his own response also.

Quite apart from the literary source for *Night Song of the Bards*, Chisholm, on one loose sheet, has laid out in ink a sequence of six notes in the bass clef, and below them the same sequence with the first note displaced down an octave. Both staves are marked with a figure '1' across the lines and a 'v' under it, seemingly indicating an octave below. This sequence of notes bears a close resemblance to the *Râg Sohani*, examples of which are found in Fox Strangways's book, which was known to Chisholm at least as early as 1945.[15]

Râg Sohani would be an appropriate choice for *Night Song of the Bards*, as it too is associated with the night. That Chisholm used Strangways's own presentation of it is confirmed by its re-emergence as the basis of the third movement of the Violin Concerto, in which Chisholm has attached Upendrakisor Ray's translation of the Tagore original, as the râg and the poem appear in Strangways. The poem is also relevant to the bardic theme:

Thy power is from all time; from all time is thy supreme radiance in the skies. Thine is the first word. Thy joy lives in each new year fresh in the heart. In the firmament of thy mind glisten the sun and the moon and the stars. The wave of life vibrates in the atmosphere. Thou art the first poet; the master of poems art thou. Thy deep-voiced utterances find voice in praise and prayer which ascend from all the world.[16]

The *Râg Sohani* (here described using Chisholm's transposition) has two augmented seconds (C–D♯ and F–G♯), and a diminished third (G♯–B♭) as well as having the F potentially exchanged with E. Of course, on the equally tempered piano for which Chisholm was writing, these equivalents (whether expressed enharmonically or no) do not match the subtleties of the Hindustani tradition. On a piano, whether a G♯ is called an A♭ is a matter of musical semantics, not acoustic reality, though it may well have a psychological impact on the player. But whether the use of an equally tempered instrument is to negate the whole meaning of a râg is a matter pointless to pursue here. Suffice it to say that the version of the râg chosen by Chisholm, for Western ears, immediately brings out characteristics perceived as Eastern and which are alien to Celtic tradition, and are heard as chromaticisms.

The choice might be thought to facilitate a wished-for chromaticisation of the harmonies, as Chisholm could easily have used a râg more obviously in tune with pentatonic and hexatonic modalism. But he did not need melodic chromaticism as a liberating force, for he had already applied chromatic procedures to *piobaireachd* in such works as *An Rioban Dearg* and in his various *piobaireachd* settings for piano, which play fast and loose with the harmonic implications of the basic material.

The title, *Night Song of the Bards*, is also taken seriously with respect to the word 'song', references to which are ever-present in the continuities of line, sustained even through the most violent explosions of temperament: but violent they are – chords savaged by major sevenths and separated by angry contrary-motion; and, throughout, passages of great rhythmic complexity.

And yet these are not nightmares, for they are totally controlled. The nocturnes of John Field and Frédéric Chopin, or Szymanowski's *Song of the Night*, are here translated to a world where nature dominates man, and where the bards, who, druid-like, might seek to control it, must be prepared to face mighty forces. But only the Chief approaches anything like a command: 'Let clouds rest on hills: spirits fly and travelers fear. Let the winds of the wood arise …' and this is not so much a command as a preparation for the assertions that the new day will always overcome night, whatever the other bards' visions of night may have described, and that the bards themselves will pass away.

Here may be felt Chisholm's response to Sorabji's densely textured music, with its orgies of embellishment and its Eastern mysticism, such as one finds in the nocturne *Djâmî*, which Chisholm himself performed (see Interlude: The Love of Sorabji). But where Sorabji's night in *Djâmî* is ritualistic and sensual, with textures based on spread octaves, Chisholm's is more often one of storm and tempest, and the octaves shrink and stretch into sevenths and ninths. And Chisholm's textures, complex though they are in these pieces, are more lucid, and his bards are also more disciplined in their relatively terse visions. Chisholm knew his Scotland, and that no man can survive for long in such weather. None the less, the music has much in common with Sorabji's quasi-Eastern school – a fact underlined by Diana's comment:

> If they travel to the North of Scotland and make contact with the Gaelic-speaking population, see our tartans, Celtic Crosses, and hear our piobaireachd music, they may realise that we have certain Asiatic qualities which are not shared by the Sassenach.[17]

No direct connections have yet been proven as regards Middle Eastern and/or Asian connections with Scottish traditional music; but that there are parallels is beyond doubt, and these parallels were noticed long before Chisholm's day. For instance, Fox Strangways, commenting that the Scottish bagpipe scale was 'similar to, but not the same as, the Indian', goes on to draw a comparison between the emphatic function of grace-notes in Highland and Indian music, as opposed to their transitional function in classical music.[18]

Other parallels are not hard to find. First and foremost is the ever-present implication and/or reality of the drone. Chisholm is undoubtedly radical in his handling of this fundamental element, but it is a presence which has to be handled and which is never denied, though often subverted in his music.

Second is the pre-eminence of melody which, in its treatment of time and pace, does not seek to travel at speed from one point to the next, but which works subtly upon the relationship between melody notes and the drone, and upon small changes of rhythmic emphasis, often involving embellishment which, in the *piobaireachd* tradition, almost certainly used also to be improvised. It is for these reasons that many familiar only with Western music find *piobaireachd* and Hindu music monotonous or narcotic in effect. The slower evolution of their forms calls for the equivalent mental adjustment required of the child who at first more readily grasps the excitement of the birth of an animal than that of a plant.

Third is the strong sense of what is appropriate for the time of day, season or human circumstance. The music is no mere entertainment, though it fulfils that function also; it is an experience which has spiritual and elemental associations which cannot readily be divorced from nature. The same applies with respect to the appropriate performance space and time for certain kinds of western classical music: the *St Matthew Passion* is more meaningful in a baroque church at Easter than in a modern concert hall at Hallowe'en. But whereas much Western music can be divorced from such considerations without loss, the same cannot so readily be said of Hindustani or of Celtic music. It is true that in modern times *piobaireachd* has been subverted by competition and formal performance; but in the hearts of the best pipers, it still only finds its true place and function in the right context. The 'Lament for Mary Macleod' is too gentle for use at the funeral of a young woman killed in a car crash. 'McNeill is Lord There' is too harsh and assertive to welcome a guest, and *Cha Till MacCruimean* cannot be played without bringing emigration to mind and would be a terrible way to start the day. As for 'The Flowers of the Forest', which commemorates the dead of the Battle of Flodden (1514), and is played at funerals and Remembrance Day services to this day, there is a virtual taboo on its performance in an inappropriate context. *Râg Sohani* is appropriate after midnight and before dawn, and that is why Chisholm chose it.

In writing out the six-note cell on the opening page of the draft for the First Bard, Chisholm has started on a B, a semitone lower than the usual notation, and has essentially mirrored the tuning of the instrument rather than the ascending and descending versions of the râg. He has then transposed the whole into E, with the First Bard's 'song' ending on an E major chord. The pervasive character of Chisholm's use of aspects of *Râg Sohani* is not to be ignored: in particular, the three adjacent semitones in the middle of the cell appear frequently (ex. 10).

The râg itself features two such groups and also employs different versions for ascent and descent – as in the Western melodic minor scales. Chisholm, likewise, uses two versions in the opening bars for the Second Bard. The correspondence

Ex 10 (a) Chisholm, six-note cell; (b) *Râg Sohani* tuning; (c) First Bard, bars 1–4

is not exact. Chisholm claims the freedom to touch briefly on notes that are not in the scale or normally associated with movement in the other direction. He is not writing Hindustani music, but music inspired by Hindustani models.

The broader correspondences between the Macpherson source and Chisholm's music are also of interest. Chisholm uses Macpherson's description of the Sixth Bard as 'The Chief', which suggests that he was following the sequence, but it seems from the internal evidence that at some point Chisholm changed the position of the Third Bard with that of the Fourth. Whether he swapped the two for musical reasons or because at some point their texts became confused is not known. Certainly any match between Chisholm's and Macpherson's Third and Fourth Bards is utterly implausible unless they are swapped.

The tempo and expression indications for each bard give a good idea of what is to follow: *Andante sostenuto* for the First Bard: *Allegro tempestuoso* for the Second: the Third, *Adagio, dolce e poco cant(abile)*. The Fourth is marked *Appassionato e dramatico*, the Fifth *Lento tranquillo* and the Chief, simply *Adagio*.

Each Bard concludes with a request to his fellow bards for admittance, with the exceptions of the Chief and the Third Bard, whose 'Receive me not, my friends, for lovely is the night' matches the languorous seduction of his experience. Chisholm manages the cadences of their requests with beautiful simplicity, even the Second Bard's account of a night of ghosts and storms being concluded with a modest submission in an enriched C major chord. All make their submissions *pianissimo* and in a mood of calm, with the exception of the Fourth Bard, whose opening *Apassionato e dramatico* delivery erupts unexpectedly from the quiet of falling snow into an urgent and hurried demand at the end. Fuller notes on the music for each bard will be found in the liner notes for *Erik Chisholm, Music for Piano*, vol. 6 (see Discography).

The dark mystery of the opening cell – semitone, minor third, major third – worms through the texture in an *Andante sostenuto* which reaches its way upwards from the depths.

> Night is dull and dark. The clouds rest on the hills. No star with green trembling beam; no moon looks from the sky.

The cell is repeated over and over like the parts of a complex organism forming itself in at least three different strata with controlled power, even menace. The centre-point is reached with an A major chord and the music quickly builds to a turbulent climax. Finally, the opening mood returns, and the First Bard asks for admittance.

> Dark, dusky, howling is night, cloudy, windy, and full of ghosts! The dead are abroad! my friends, receive me from the night.

Although the tonal structure of this movement is conventionally balanced between tonic and sub-dominant, there is no sense of triumphant formality; and the apparent innocence of the concluding cadence, settling on a major chord, should not delude us. This is no resolution, but a completely separate and mini-mal concluding formality, requesting admission into the hall and making polite way for the Second Bard.

That the Second Bard understands this passing on of the right of utterance is made clear by his use of the same basic musical germ, the potential violence of which he instantly declares, while retaining some passages of brooding danger. This music, marked *Allegro tempestuoso*, is stormy in mood and in its demanding physicality.

If the First bard promises a disturbing future, and the Second realises it in the present, Chisholm's Third Bard introduces a completely new element – a sense of history, nostalgia and reflection. The movement is an 'Adagio' marked *dolce e poco cant(abile)*, reasserting the song aspect of the title, and it progresses from an underlying E♭ minor to a final D major. The central *quasi cadenza* leads back into the opening tempo, but with the addition of a personally evocative request in a quasi-recitative, reiterating a single note (ex.11).

His final submission of his statement consists only of a D major chord for, unlike all the others, he does not seek admittance:

> Night is settled, calm, blue, starry, bright with the moon. Receive me not, my friends, for lovely is the night.

Chisholm's Fourth Bard takes something akin to the mood of the Second as his starting-point (ex.12).

At the climax, the opening motif of the râg is powerfully in evidence, and is followed by insistent trills – but they lay claim to a different rhetoric.

> Her lover promised to come. She saw his boat, when yet it was light on the lake. Is this his broken boat on the shore? Are these his groans on the wind?

This is not the rhetoric of nature, but of man, as introduced by the Third Bard, whose relative calm is also accepted towards the end, albeit with a defiant and

Ex. 11 *Night Song of the Bards*, Third Bard

Ex. 12 *Night Song of the Bards*, Fourth Bard

dramatic final statement. The progression so far seems to be from the impersonal to the personal: from mystery through violence to reflection, and then the
acceptance of their necessary co-existence. What then will the Fifth Bard sing of
the night?

Here the gaze is upward, to a higher register of sound, marked *lento tranquillo*.
But the Fifth Bard's stellar vision knows that it is so because seen from earth, the
lower register of which forms the central section, again with the three adjacent
semitones stirring in the midst of the texture, passing from left to right hand.

The return of the *Lento tranquillo* is much varied and leads to a wonderfully
imaginative ending, in which the depth of feeling is allowed a brief rhetorical
moment, with a climax that dies away in trills and *tremolando* chords to a final F
minor with added second. The thoughtfulness of this music and the refinement
of its textures, with the complex mix of sustained notes and minimal use of the
pedal, takes one into a world wholly apart. These are inner experiences of a vast
outer world; but is this enormous range of vision of the untameable forces of

night realisable as a coherent world-view? It is for the Chief Bard to bring to our ken an embracing vision of the obscure.

The Finale, delivered by the Sixth Bard, the Chief, never moves away from his sombre *adagio*, often asserting the fundamental drone element. He is measured and stern in his pace, the steady crotchet motion scarcely broken, the rhetoric the more telling for its comparative restraint. The broken chords of the left hand suggest a *clàrsach* accompaniment, and the demisemiquaver turns reiterate the motif from which so much of this music grows (ex. 13).

> They shall ask of the aged, 'Where stood the walls of our fathers?'
>   Raise the song, and strike the harp; send round the shells of joy. Suspend a hundred tapers on high. Youths and maids begin the dance. Let some gray bard be near me to tell the deeds of other times: of kings renowned in our land, of chiefs we behold no more.

When Chisholm used exactly the same passage in his opera *The Inland Woman*, he scored it for harp, with horn, double-bass harmonics, timpani and bass drum. The vocal part was simply added in.[19] The passage is used to accompany an old woman expressing a relief, equally sombre, that a drowned man's body has been recovered from 'the green grave' – by which she means the sea, not the land. The scene is also in the dark just before dawn. The opera was completed in the same year as *Night Song of the Bards*.[20]

The Chief's impressive peroration ends with bare fourths and fifths, and the old, dark mystery of a final minor second, left hovering unresolved; as is the tonality, which is left floating out into its own night air. Yet there is an element of line here more obvious than in all the previous pronouncements, save that of the Third Bard, as though the certainty of daybreak were sure to bring back the flow of movement and life.

Chisholm's bards are not simply reflective poets or professional musicians,

Ex. 13 *Night Song of the Bards*, Sixth Bard

and, heard outwith their literary context, they inhabit a more powerful environment of thought than Macpherson dared. Behind the enriched chords and chromatic progressions, there is the remembrance of tonal securities. They are not brushed aside, but surface occasionally, often at critical moments – climaxes, conclusions – asserting the truth of their own simplicity in the midst of complex events.

The term 'bard' has, in modern times, come to include many of the duties and powers that were originally ascribed and assigned to the *filidh* and the druids, the bards in ancient time being practitioners, but not theorists, magicians or philosophers. Chisholm's bards, however, are all of these things, not merely because the term has come potentially to include them, but because of the character of the music itself. Each bard has his own particular mystery to expound: each, after almost tortuous legerdemain and displays of power and restraint, reaches a conclusion of near-resolution. But these are night songs indeed, probing the darkness in texture, melody, rhythm and harmony. Here reflective thought and deep intuition are hand in hand. The result is one of the most remarkable groups of piano works of the twentieth century; but the conviction of these pieces, and the astonishing and imaginative world which they occupy, still lurk in the repertoire with their dark challenge, for few have dared them. So dramatically convincing are the textures of this music that the fact that it is a piano through which they are realised seems almost to miss the point: as Lamond recalled Liszt addressing a student playing the Chopin Polonaise in A♭:[21]

> I don't want to listen to how fast you can play octaves. What I wish to hear is the canter of the horses of the Polish cavalry before they gather force and destroy the enemy!

One could analyse these amazing piano textures, dissecting their mechanisms, naming their parts: but to what end, if one no longer hears the voice of the bard?

In aesthetic terms, Chisholm here shows a mastery of a true sense of poetry – one which Wordsworth would have appreciated for 'it is the spontaneous overflow of powerful feelings; it takes its origin from emotion recollected in tranquility.'[22] We can go further, for if we accept these night songs as representing different world-views, and consider them as a whole, then we have something approaching a philosophy arrived at through a discussion which has taken the form of musical action. Each bard has given a kind of delivery which is not so much a character description as a statement of each individual's emotional and philosophical disposition. Ultimately, then, it is reflection that must master experience, however harsh or intimidating that experience may be, and in bringing the intuitive and emotional response of the musician to this material, Chisholm has rescued Macpherson's overwrought prose and grasped the very heart of his intentions, bringing Eastern and Western mysticism together in an astonishing visionary *tour de force*.

CHAPTER 6

From Italy to India and Singapore

It seems likely that it was in 1944 that the Anglo-Polish Ballet toured Italy for ENSA – the Entertainments National Service Association. The tour included Rome, Perugia, Naples, Bari and Ancona.[1] Chisholm was at the helm. The date has been given as 1943,[2] but the tour extended well into the following year, as Rome was not liberated until June 1944. However, the tour must have been following reasonably closely on the action for, on one occasion, Chisholm narrowly escaped being killed, the two lorries in front of his being hit by land-mines.[3]

> This was at the time when cigarettes were the most powerful weapon of barter between army personnel & the civilian population. Italians, and therefore Italian orchestras were zoned. They could only travel within a very restricted area it being impossible, for instance, to take an orchestra from Rome to Naples or vice versa. This meant that I had dealings with a large number of Italian orchestral musicians. They were very fine fellows although one had to keep a wary eye out to avoid being waylayed in the street with the constant cry of 'Bon jouro [sic] Maestro – cigaretto please? – molto grazie, maestro.' On the other hand I got several extra orchestral rehearsals by giving each member of the orchestra 5 cigarettes at the end. I need hardly say that the Italian Musicians Union did not function very efficiently in '43 and '44.[4]

It was when they were at Rome's Argentinia Theatre that he took the opportunity to look up Casella, with whom he had performed at the Active Society Concerts (see Chapter 2). Casella, who lived nearby on the banks of the Tiber, was ill and depressed by the war. He was a fascist and a great Mussolini supporter, facts which did not prevent the left-wing Chisholm from arranging for food-parcels to be sent to the Casellas from ENSA stores.

> Towards the end of World War II, when British and American forces occupied Italy as far north as Ravenna, I called on Casella ... His wife opened the door and told me she was doubtful if her husband could see me as he had been ill, on and off, for the past two years. While waiting in the music room which was all but filled by two concert grand pianos, I noticed on one of them a large photograph of Mussolini signed by the Duce with the inscription 'To my dear, devoted and loyal friend, Alfredo Casella.'
>
> On the other piano was an equally large photograph of Roosevelt (signed by the President) and inscribed in words to the same effect, 'To my dear, devoted and loyal friend, Alfredo Casella.'
>
> Casella was propped up in bed, looking very pale and thin. He spoke in a low,

almost inaudible voice, of his illness, of the terrible war, of his work. On a table near the bed were some volumes of classical piano music (I forget what composers) – music which he had been editing. He still had that slight air of stiffness about him – but Casella's days of heel clicking were over. He never left his bed. I took a sad leave of him, and as his wife showed me to the door, she told me something of the great difficulties they were having in getting decent food.

'Everything can be had on the Black Market, but we just can't afford it. Perhaps, Mr. Chisholm, you through ENSA might be able to do something?' Under ENSA's auspices, I was conducting the Anglo Polish Ballet at Rome's Argentinia Theatre so with a little influence I did manage to make up some food parcels from their stores and sent them to the Casellas.

Apparently Chisholm had filmed Casella, amongst others, at an ISCM festival in Oxford in 1931, using 9.5 mm film, for he goes on to confess:

Sometimes when in sentimental mood, I will take out the little Pathe-Baby projector from its stained and dusty brown box, rig up the tiny Pathe-Baby screen and as I turn the little twisted handle which sets the mechanism in action, I see – promenading across the screen – the ghosts of Dr Jehovah Hertzog, Professor Edward Dent, Eugene Goossens and Alfredo Casella. All of them dead, dead, dead![5]

The ballet's last performance in Italy was in Naples, and Chisholm estimated that he had conducted the national Polish divertissement ballet *Crackow Wedding* nearly a thousand times. He thought it high time to look out for something else to do.[6] On 24 May 1945, he wrote to Henry George Farmer:

I have now returned from my tour of Italy. Working under excellent conditions there with symphony orchestras seldom less than 60 strong. I cannot now bring myself to continue touring with the Ballet using these wretched theatre orchestras in this country.

In any case I very much wish to settle down in Glasgow again if only to have the opportunity to continue my activities on behalf of Scottish music.

I see from an advertisement in the Glasgow 'Herald' that the Cramb University Trusts are establishing a full-time lectureship in music and I wonder if you would be so kind as to use your influence with the University authorities on my behalf.[7]

Farmer must have replied, suggesting Chisholm get in touch with Ernest Bullock, who was both Professor of Music and Principal of the Academy of Music in Glasgow. Chisholm replied:

I have never had anything but pleasant relations with him [Bullock] on the few occasions I have met him. The position, however, is rather curious. When I returned from Italy a month or so ago I met him for a few minutes & he suggested I should apply for the chair of music at Cape Town.

I have a letter from him today very kindly drawing my attention to a similar position in Sydney & a lectureship in Auckland – which are as far away from

Glasgow as is possible! – but no mention of the Cramb lectureship, which would look as if ...![8]

That same year, ENSA appointed him Musical Director in India.[9] Sir Hector Hetherington (Principal of Glasgow University) wrote to assure him that his absence would not prejudice his application for the Cramb music lectureship, but Chisholm did not get it.[10] Instead he was flown out by sea-plane to Bombay to conduct a series of orchestral concerts for Services entertainment in various centres throughout India.[11] Sheila (his ten-year-old second daughter) wrote to him at Greens Hotel, signing her name in kisses and wondering 'how do you feel in your new uniform & helmet (the white one).'[12]

However he felt in his uniform, he was in sprightly mood in his series of articles for the *Evening News of India*. A review of a concert by the Bombay String Quartet begins encouragingly and proceeds to dissect the performances and the individual players in a manner more suited to a private letter or master-class, than to a publication. Likewise, a generous and light-hearted review of the amateur Bombay Symphony Orchestral Society[13] was sufficiently uncompromising to raise a furore (as well as local support), and he was fortunate in having an editor who was willing to give him his head. That said, it is clear that he was having to cope with music-making at a much lower level than he was used to, and when, on 6 October 1945, he was authorised to recruit a symphony orchestra,[14] the character of many of the applications he received make one groan in sympathy, for the task he faced was truly daunting.[15]

While in Bombay he worked at ENSA headquarters in Green's hotel and had a single room at the Taj Mahal hotel, accorded to him on medical advice on account of his sight. For this, and the consumption of mineral water, he was later obliged to account, which goes to show that the blight of over-supervision of small sums in the midst of unchecked expenditure of vast ones is not a sign of degeneration in our time, but merely a continuance of established follies which survive just as happily in war as in peacetime.[16] Unfortunately the problems were not confined to mineral water. The ENSA authorities had omitted

the trifling detail of finding out if there <u>were</u> any suitable orchestras in India to conduct. There weren't – and I spent the next six months flying up and down India as far north as the Himalayas searching for and auditioning orchestral musicians for our proposed Indian E.N.S.A. Orchestra. After innumerable Kafka-like frustrations I eventually collected some fifty odd players only to find that with V.J. day the centre of Forces concentration had now drifted to the Far East and the great expense of touring a Symphony Orchestra around India was now considered no longer to be justified. That was the official explanation anyway. I felt pretty wild about it at the time (especially as I had a shrewd suspicion that there had been bungling and personal intrigues going on in the upper strata of E.N.S.A. High Command, which had somehow involved me and the proposed Indian Orchestra in the mesh.) Promises had been made to local musicians in Bombay, Calcutta,

Delhi, Madras and other centres; a whole batch of excellent Italian P.O.W. instrumentalists looked to me as the sole means of escape from the tedium of prison confinement. I had to let them all down, and a timely request that I should go to Malaya and start a symphony orchestra in Singapore was a welcome 'ootgang' from a situation which grew hourly more embarrassing.[17]

There were heart-lifting moments, just the same, as when he visited the Italian POW camp in Yohl in northern India, which had access to a university college complete with library and other facilities, in affiliation with the University of Rome.

The camp possessed an effective, if uneven symphony orchestra of sixty players with a first-class leader Umberto Spironelli whose string quartet was even allowed to undertake a tour of India and, incidentally, supplied a high-light in good music entertainment. They also had several theatres in the camp and I saw them do a Modern Revue, which for sets, lighting and costumes would have done credit to a London West End production.[18]

But the real pleasure for him was the opportunity to experience the music of the sub-continent.

Music of Hindustan gripped me from the first moment I arrived in Karachi: during my six months stay in India I was fortunate enough to make friends with some high-up Indians who allowed me to attend private concerts in homes, for public concerts, as we know them, hardly exist in that Continent. My ear soon became as familiar and fond of the Sitar, as of the violin: I love the sounds of the Veena, the Tambura, the Sarangi and their other beautiful and fascinating instruments.[19]

It is possible that one of these 'high-up' Indians was the Maharana Vijayadevji of Dharampur, the second volume of whose beautifully produced *Sangit Bhâva*, published in Bombay in 1939, is in the University of Cape Town Music Library, probably brought there by Chisholm himself. It is listed among the books which were in his estate.[20] It contains the music of a small selection of râgas in Eastern and Western notations and is apparently rare even in India (illus. 16). Copies of the Maharana's *Music Magazine* from its first issue in November 1935 to October 1936 are also held in Cape Town.

Chisholm did, however, engender controversy with his opinions on Hindustani music,[21] and was delighted to recall that this occasioned a substantial rise in sales of the newspaper he was writing for.[22] However, his stay was brief,[23] and the 'The Bombay Man's Diary' in the *Evening News of India* of Monday, 5 November 1945 bemoans his departure for Singapore the previous weekend. He wrote to Colonel White expressing strong misgivings about his transfer to Singapore, based upon the 'fanciful unreality which constituted the basis of my "two orchestras" in India'.[24] But the Bombay musicians themselves seem to have

16 Chisholm's marked copy of *Râg Shree* from *Sangit Bhâva*

shown a remarkable and humble acceptance of his many strictures, for which he is warmly thanked by the Joint Honorary Secretary of the Bombay Choral & Philharmonic Society.[25] Part of the trouble seems to have been occasioned by what Chisholm described as the 'dog in the manger' attitude of Colonels White and Hawkins,[26] who had made insufficient use of his talents and had apparently objected to his having published any articles on the grounds that they breached his ENSA contract – an assertion vigorously contested by Chisholm.[27]

In Singapore, he set to at once to provide entertainment by whatever means possible, including personally presenting 'Recorded Music Recitals' in the Victoria Hall, under the auspices of the NAAFI (Navy, Army and Air Force Institutes) and ENSA.[28] He founded the Singapore Symphony Orchestra as ENSA Musical Director for SEAC (South East Asia Command), based at Victoria Memorial Hall, Singapore, though some letters to potential orchestral members are headed 'ENSA H.Q. No. 2 Area, Singapore'.[29]

> I found on arriving in Singapore that the authorities really wanted an orchestra there and were prepared to give me carte-blanche to get it. The Japs had just vacated Singapore and the Allied Authorities moving in had little enough transport for their own official business, so in rickshaws and tongas I started to search the entire neighbourhood for orchestral musicians; within a week we had our first rehearsal and within a fortnight of my arrival in the country our first concert. I doubt if any such cosmopolitan orchestra has ever been assembled before or since.[30]

Chisholm advertised widely for musicians, including on entertainment forces' news-sheets, and received written enquiries which, in some cases, were followed by an audition. Players were also drawn from the Sikh Police Band[31] and the Royal Air Force Band.[32] An undated list of orchestral members shows they were paid £15, £12 or £10 per week and that there were roughly six first violins, eight seconds, six violas, five cellos and two basses, two flutes, two oboes, two clarinets, three horns, two trumpets, three trombones, one tuba and one percussion. The list contains adjustments – changes of principals and moves from first to second violins, and so on. Robert Pikler was the leader.

Acquiring music for the orchestra to play was no simple matter. On 19 January Chisholm wrote to the 'Officer in Charge, Music Department, British Council, London', acknowledging receipt of British music sent out on 18 June, 1945, intended, but too late for use, in India, and regretting that the Bax symphonies were too large for his fifty players. Music was borrowed from the Royal Air Force Band and the Viceregal Library at Delhi, as requested in a letter from Chisholm to Admiral Lord Mountbatten at Singapore, dated 9 February, in which he also refers to musical activities at ENSA Garrison Theatre. The next day he was protesting to Lieut.-Col. E. Dennis, ENSA Singapore, that the musicians from Java had had cigarette, sweet and wine rations stopped by Lieut. Manley, and requesting their restoration as they had been interned for three and a half years and had been receiving rations up to a week or so before.[33]

Chisholm never let up. He chased up Mountbatten again, writing on 23 February, in response to a letter from Mountbatten of the 19th, asking him to ask the Viceroy and Lady Wavell to send music from the Viceregal Lodge.[34] Mountbatten was a fan:

> Lord Louis Mountbatten and General Sir Miles Dempsey, (Commander-in-Chief, Allied Forces in the Far East) are not only distinguished patrons and regular

attenders at our concerts, but have placed at our disposal facilities for improving the standards of our performances.[35]

An example of the full extent of his administrative work is the letter he wrote to Sgt. Maj. Simpson on 20 February 1946:

> My dear Simmie,
>
> I wonder if you could please make me as soon as possible fifty boxes as per sample to hold our gramophone records? We need these very urgently in order to run our library with any degree of efficiency. Also, later, I should be grateful if you could let me have the sister-cabinet of the one you have already made for our music library. This one is for the purpose of storing the gramophone records.
>
> I appreciate very much the efforts and imagination in the specimens of your craft you have already presented to me.[36]

On another occasion he had to ask Air Chief Marshal Sir Keith Park to delay the transport of RAF Regiment Band members playing in the Singapore Orchestra who were required in Burma for the RAF exhibition.[37]

By 25 February he was writing to a Dr Sandre:

> It is very kind of you sending me the orchestral material for three Violin Concertos. I can assure you that every care will be taken of the material which will be returned to you as soon as we have performed the works.
>
> I now have a very good orchestra at my disposal. We give two different programmes weekly, hence it requires a constant supply of music to do this. Fortunately I brought about 200 scores with me and have an army of Chinese copyists making parts, but it is a difficult job as the parts require revising and I envy you having a well-stocked library. However, the orchestra plays very well and we always [have] large and enthusiastic audiences.
>
> It is very kind of you to suggest that I give a concert with the Calcutta Symphony Orchestra, and if I am coming there within the next six months I shall certainly take the opportunity.[38]

And on the same day he was thanking Major Demetriade, 'Bge: Major, Hd.Qrs. 4th British W.F. Brigade, SEAC, Singapore', for the loan of miniature scores from which he could get parts created. Music was even borrowed from the Raffles hotel music library.[39]

An undated typescript headed 'Lieut. Col. E. Dennis' states that the orchestra 'has been in existence for nearly three months and during that period has given 25 concerts playing to approximately 50,000 people'. Dennis noted that among leading soloists who came to play with them was Szymon Goldberg, 'who speaks with approval of the rapid improvement in the standard of performance achieved by the orchestra under its conductor and Musical Director, Dr. Erik Chisholm'.[40] Dennis was later to join Chisholm's staff at the University of Cape Town (see Chapter 7).

In Surabaya, Szymon Goldberg had trained an orchestra of Dutch, Hungarian and Russian POWs under Japanese domination. He had successfully hidden his precious Stradivarius up a chimney in the prison camp for three and a half years,[41] and later joined Chisholm in Cape Town and there gave the first performance of Chisholm's Violin Concerto.

Many of those in the camp were European musicians who had fled Nazi Germany for Batavia. They were gathered in Singapore by Eric Taylor, who was Chisholm's able administrative supporter.[42] What Chisholm had achieved in his few weeks in Singapore would have taken others many months and, decades later, his influence and energy were remembered by one of the orchestra members, Paul Abisheganaden:

> I was thrilled to be able to observe … a fine conductor at work. His technique at rehearsals, his style at concerts. It was also fortunate and important for me in trying to learn as much as I could, that Dr. Chisholm was not the 'show-man' type … Dr. Chisholm's chief attribute was his academic and scholarly approach to his interpretations.[43]

Of course, in achieving all this, Chisholm had practically no spare time, though he managed to hear Chinese and Malayan opera, but he never assimilated these styles in the same way as he did Hindustani music. Alan Gordon described him as 'the hardest working man in Singapore' (illus. 17):

> There must be huge numbers of servicemen and women, who, like myself, have felt a gnawing want for live music … and who will wish me to express their deep gratitude to Dr. Erik Chisholm … It has been my privilege to have many talks with Dr. Chisholm, but he never has time merely to converse; he will talk most interestingly about opera while sitting at a desk orchestrating a symphony from a piano score, or will discuss Shostakovich's 'Lady MacBeth' while bowing the string parts of a Mozart concerto.
>
> When (or whether) he sleeps or eats I simply don't know, for at any time of the day or night you will find him at the Memorial Hall either rehearsing the Symphony Orchestra (which he does for 3 or 4 hours every day of the week), conducting a concert (of which he does two a week in Singapore as well as giving Symphony concerts at Seletar and other outstations) … In him Singapore has a man in a million, and for all his modest and unassuming manner he is a tremendous force and is of the stuff of which true greatness is made.[44]

In the end South Africa had the good sense to grab him while he was free, and he proceeded directly from Singapore to Cape Town. Chisholm had applied in May and was recommended by Dr Ernest Bullock.[45] The competition was not that impressive, most potential applicants having been caught up in the war in one way or another. Among those who did apply were Walter Kaufmann, Cameron Taylor and Kenneth Barritt. Arnold Goldsborough, who had been seriously considered for the chair in 1938/9 was approached, but declined and suggested

17 'The Hardest Working Man in Singapore', illustration to Alan Gordon's article

Arnold Foster, adding, 'Erik Chisholm I do not know but I admire his work'.[46] In the event, Chisholm was unanimously recommended by a committee of five, convened by George Dyson and including Bullock, meeting in South Africa House, London; and he was duly appointed on 29 August 1945 on a 'salary scale one thousand by annual increments of twenty five to maximum eleven hundred and fifty pounds'.[47]

Chisholm accepted on 26 September,[48] having held off on the advice of Jashf Dolotine, in the hope of obtaining a directorship in the music department at the BBC in Scotland.[49] Communications were slow, however. A letter from Professor J. T. Irving of 26 November 1945, only reached Chisholm in Singapore the week before 18 January. Chisholm, replying,[50] recommends Mr George Eric Taylor (with whom he worked successfully in Singapore) as Assistant Director at the College. The Board of the Faculty of Music was not, however, 'in a position to submit any recommendation in regard to the post of assistant director'.[51]

There appears to have been a possibility that Chisholm would return to Scotland before proceeding to South Africa,[52] but in the end he flew out in April 1946, stopping only to change planes in Cairo on the 30th. He had a baggage allowance of 65 pounds.[53] Music is heavy so it is unlikely he had brought any quantity of his own to the Far East, never mind onward to Cape Town, and it is also unlikely that

18 Erik Chisholm taking a rehearsal break in Singapore

he managed much composition during this period. But his musical experiences undoubtedly bore fruit in several of his major works (see Centre-piece), and it could reasonably be asserted that, despite their difficulties, his wartime experiences were of major and positive significance in his development as a composer and administrator.

1   Frederick Lamond with the Scottish Orchestra, by William Crosbie

2   *The Forsaken Mermaid*, cover by Taylor Elder

3 Seaweed Maidens, costume design by Taylor Elder

4 *The Earth Shapers*, costume design by William Crosbie

5   *The Earth Shapers*, set design by William Crosbie

Jan Cobel's ANGLO-POLISH BALLET

Evenings 6-30   Programme, Week of March 22nd   Matinees Wed. & Sat. 2-30

Monday, 22nd March	**Wednesday, 24th.** (Matinee)	**Thursday, 25th.**	**Saturday, 27th.** (Matinee)
Lac Des Cygnes Grand Divertissment Spectre De La Rose Polish Faust	Cracow Wedding Lac Des Cygnes Spectre De La Rose Polish Faust	Les Sylphides Grand Divertissment Umarl Maciek Umarl Cracow Wedding	Cracow Wedding Les Sylphides Grand Divertissment Polish Faust
Tuesday, 23rd.	**Wednesday, 24th** (Evening)	**Friday, 26th.**	**Saturday, 27th.** (Evening)
Les Sylphides Grand Divertissment Umarl Maciek Umarl Cracow Wedding	Lac Des Cygnes Grand Divertissment Spectre De La Rose Polish Faust	Lac Des Cygnes Grand Divertissment Spectre De La Rose Polish Faust	Lac Des Cygnes Grand Divertissment Umarl Maciek Umarl Spectre De La Rose Cracow Wedding

"This performance was admirable."—SCOTT GODDARD, "News Chronicle."

6   Programme for Jan Cobel's Polish Ballet

7 Cover for *El Alamein*,
arranged by Erik Chisholm

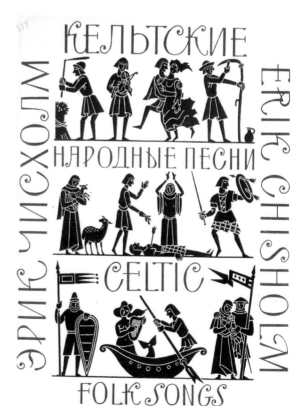

8 *Celtic Songbook* cover

CHAPTER 7

Under Table Mountain

CHISHOLM ARRIVED IN CAPE TOWN, VIA DURBAN, SOME TIME IN April or May of 1946,[1] having come by flying boat from Cairo and, before that, from Singapore. He was wearing only his tropical khaki suit which, according to the *Cape Argus*, was all he was allowed on his flight.[2] Perhaps he had been unable to take up the 65-pound baggage allowance itemised on his Cairo to Cape Town air ticket.[3]

He must have been going through a complex of emotions. He had been in environments and climates he had never experienced before, and performing in Italy must have widened Chisholm's horizons considerably. Apart from anything else, it was his first experience of a country where English was not spoken. In Singapore, he had been given virtually unconditional support by people operating under severe restrictions and had come into contact with musicians from many different countries who had spent months as prisoners of war. He had, in other words, been trusted, but also faced with extraordinary demands upon his administrative and personal skills – demands of a kind that had been thrust upon him previously only by his own ambitions.

He was now about to take up a triple responsibility at the University of Cape Town as Dean, Professor and Principal. As such, he was occupying in South Africa the same position held by Sir Ernest Bullock in Glasgow. The *University Calendar* shows nobody in charge for the years 1946–7, only registering Chisholm's presence in the 1948–9 edition. In this, however, he is duly credited as 'Professor of Music, Dean of the Faculty of Music, and Director of the College of Music'.[4] Chisholm must have felt some satisfaction – not least when he had the chance to compare climates! When asked what were the main turning-points in his career, the third and final one he listed was: 'when Dr. W. Gillies Whitaker told me in a Glasgow tramcar that they were looking for a music professor at Cape Town.'[5]

In succeeding Eric Grant, Chisholm was succeeding a man who was officially named neither as Dean of the Faculty nor Professor of Music, although he was personally styled as a professor.[6] Grant must, in fact, have disappeared from the scene, for Cameron Taylor wrote to Chisholm as Acting Director of the South African College of Music, outlining the immediate need for a violin teacher, a singing teacher ('male if possible') and someone to teach harmony and counterpoint in a manner that would lead on sensibly to Chisholm's lessons in composition.[7]

Chisholm had replied, apologising for his delay in going out to South Africa. The fact was that ENSA had pledged to carry on its work in the Far East at least until June and had approached South Africa House to request an extension of Chisholm's 'loan'. Chisholm felt morally and musically obliged to stay on:

> I took up this work in the first instance, as my contribution to National Service: it is unfortunate that my civilian commitments have overlapped with this work, and much as I desire to commence these [sic], I feel it is my duty to continue these until such services as I can offer to the Allied Forces are no longer required.[8]

His eagerness to take up the new post was undoubtedly genuine. Apart from anything else, Erik had also been away from his family for many months, and such time as he had had at home must have been so brief that it counted for nothing, for he added to the above a request for influence to be used to give them priority passages to South Africa:

> As I have been separated from them for nearly five years it is matter of great personal importance to me to have them in Cape Town when I commence my duties there.[9]

In the interim, he began to wrap up affairs in Singapore, with his usual attention to detail and to the courtesies that are often omitted by lesser administrators. In a letter thanking Mountbatten for the loan of music, duly returned, he also expressed a typical concern for the future of the orchestra:

> As you are aware certain memoranda were sent to you on your own instructions to be placed before the new Governor General. If there is any possibility of such a scheme coming to fruition no one would be more delighted than myself and even if I am so far away from Malaya as Cape Town, I think I could still supply you with suggestions for the orchestral personnel.[10]

He was proud of what he had achieved, but he did not achieve it for his own glory, rather for the sake of music. The muse was indeed restless, and he had worshipped her wearing tartan and in her costumes for opera, her tutu for ballet and her uniform for war. Now she was about to put on a gown and mortar-board. Nor was the colour of her skin of the slightest consequence, though he perhaps was particularly seduced by her in her Hindustani manifestations.

After some negotiation, Diana and the three girls were secured travel permits and berths to Cape Town. They were given little notice, having to pack and clear the house in two weeks and sell it, with the Beveridges, who were renting a room, still *in situ* (see Chapter 1). Morag was so stunned by the sudden plenty of South Africa that she kept pinching herself to believe it had really happened. It was a world of sun and flowers, fresh fruit and produce, with no rationing, and with the family lodged for the first months in a house with a view over the whole of Cape Town and the backdrop of Table Mountain, in all its magnificence, right behind them.[11]

While in the East, Erik had become attracted to vegetarianism, which he eventually adopted, though his refusal to eat the whites of eggs stemmed from a childhood prejudice.[12] His friend John Andrews took a dim view of it:

> Do you still cut off and throw away the white of your fried eggs? Not here you won't, with eggs at 5/6 a dozen.[13]

It must have been strange for them all, meeting up with a husband and father whom they had not seen for many months, and in totally new surroundings. Morag's innocently tactless comment as they met on the dockside was to say how old he looked.[14] There was also the fundamental fact that Chisholm now had, for the first time in his life, a position that offered financial security, professional dignity and enormous opportunity.

One of his first duties was to use his casting vote on behalf of John Joubert, who had applied for a Performing Rights Society scholarship to the Royal Academy of Music in London. The panel was evenly divided and the members decided to wait for Chisholm to arrive from Singapore and settle the matter. Years later he was to commission an opera from Joubert, which led to one of his most public and splendid controversies (see Chapter 9).

Meanwhile, back at the Edinburgh Festival, it took an English music critic to point out the scandal of Chisholm's absence from Scotland:

> If an outsider may be permitted to say so without offence, there seems to be something wrong somewhere when a musician of the all-round quality of Dr. Erik Chisholm has to go to South Africa to find full scope for his gifts.[15]

These early years in Cape Town have been described as ones of rapid turnover in the department, with several sackings and resignations, but it seems more noteworthy for its additions than its losses, the piano staff being increased from three to nine. However, by 1948, six long-serving, part-time teachers had been dismissed and the other four resigned in protest, though Cameron Taylor accepted the invitations to return.[16] Chisholm recruited from abroad: '[O]ur standard can only be maintained if we can attract musicians to the Union.'[17]

Robert Pikler must have come from Singapore at Chisholm's suggestion, to teach violin, but had left by the time the 1949–50 *University Calendar* was published. Also from his Far East friendships came the singer Ernest Dennis, Chisholm having heard that Dennis was based at Durban.[18] Lili Kraus, an outstanding concert pianist, joined the College staff for two years. Leonard Hall was added to the piano staff, and the composer Arnold Van Wyk was recruited. Chisholm added himself and Malcolm MacDonald to the harmony, counterpoint and composition staff, with Dr Gerstman Hamer leaving; the ballet staff received two additions, and otherwise most people remained in post. MacDonald, however, seems to have lasted only a year.[19]

The impact of Chisholm's arrival is entertainingly described by one of his former students, Désirée Talbot:

In mid-year of 1946 I was a third-year B.Mus student ... I was jogging my way peacefully through a rather ladylike music course ... generally life was leisurely and calm. There were some excellent teachers on the staff and also quite a bit of deadwood, but nobody minded ... Into this stagnant paradise Erik Chisholm erupted like a ball of fire.[20]

Even a more official assessment of his impact recognises his forcefulness:

The stagnation of the Deas-Grant decade did not survive into the post-war era, however, for everything that Grant's successor did was done at double speed. ... Within weeks, this pushful 'fireball of energy' (as one of his colleagues described him[21]) had secured a substantial special grant to purchase an array of new instruments, gramophones and records, had persuaded the University to let him build up the library's holding of scores and had won Council's support for a comprehensive reorganization of the College's establishment, involving the replacement of ten part-time teachers with four full-time appointees. It was his intention 'right from the start', he warned with characteristic forthrightness, 'to raise the standard of the teaching personnel in the College ... and to bring the University musical activities more in line with the (reasonably) advanced teaching methods now found in the best European, British and American Universities, i.e., more practical and artistic and less academically theoretical.'[22]

Chisholm's reasons for the staff changes were entirely valid academically, as there was a lack of coherence in the different teaching methods of the part-time staff which he wished to improve upon with a full-time appointment.[23] Even his successors looked back nostalgically to his regime. Writing in the late seventies, Michael Brimer, a former Professor of Music at the University of Cape Town, gave this assessment:

This human dynamo was a great force for both consolidation and expansion – but it was particularly in the field of opera and contemporary music that he pushed activities. In those wonderful days when nobody minded coming to South Africa, a great succession of 'stars' visited or taught in the college, and the UCT Opera Company even managed to tour Great Britain in 1956–7 – an undertaking unthinkable either economically or politically in 1979 ... Sir Adrian Boult stated that the University of Cape Town Music Department had 'the most go-ahead plan of any university in the world'. ... we could do with an injection of the enthusiasm, optimism, and genuine musical feeling of the fifties![24]

Such changes, however, were bound to lead to trouble and ill-feeling, and a complaint, dated 29 September 1947, was lodged with the Registrar, suggesting that excessive demands were being made of the students without sufficient consultation.[25] But the complaint, though starting 'We, the undersigned ...' was unsigned, and as far as is known there were no consequences. In any event, Chisholm was not the sort to bend under such pressure. He walked into a meeting of the dissident members of staff and in the end won the day, though at the price of acquiring some permanent enemies. Diana Chisholm recalled it as a difficult time both socially and professionally.[26]

Aside from reforming the staff and everyone's expectations of themselves and others, Chisholm insisted on a new emphasis on performance. To that end, he created two orchestras. One, the College of Music Orchestra, consisted solely of students:

> [P]upils, however inexperienced, become conversant with orchestral routine and get first-hand knowledge of the orchestral repertoire … [by being] thrown into the orchestra and forced to make some sort of noise on their instruments after only their first lessons.[27]

The other was a University Orchestra with more accomplished students, ex-students and local amateurs, which performed in public. In his first full year in charge, he conducted the University Orchestra in twelve concerts, as well as using it to provide accompaniment to an opera and a ballet. 'The College of Music, once a peaceful backwater, where one could listen to the gramophone and relax quietly, is now working at great pace.'[28]

It seems obvious to us today that musicians should be able to perform music. But the more old-fashioned university music departments of Chisholm's time were still primarily focused on theoretical and academic work. Keyboard skills were, of course, vital, but not necessarily to public performance levels.

> Chisholm also introduced classes in quick study and sight reading and a three-year course leading to a Performer's Certificate in Opera, thereby laying the foundation for a revitalized Opera Department. Opera at the College had languished in Paganelli's last years,[29] but Chisholm's brook-no-obstacle verve soon reversed this. Within six months of his arrival, he had mobilised the College's resources to stage its first opera in six years and by the end of 1948 had followed this with three more. The curtain was rising on a new act for opera at UCT.[30]

The productive collaboration of Professor William 'Daddy' Bell and Paganelli had ended with Bell's retirement in 1935, and the opera class at the College of Music, which had been subsumed into the Music Faculty of Cape Town University in 1923, came to an end in 1942. Bell's retirement was marked by a triple bill of two of his own operas flanking one of his ballets, and Chisholm wished to revive his opera *Hatsuyuki*, based on a fourteenth-century Japanese Noh play. Brief, lovely and delicate, and using seven female voices and a small orchestra, it deserves revival – something that Chisholm, for once, failed to achieve.

But Chisholm did inherit a beautiful little theatre, custom-renovated from the University's old Chemistry building in 1934 for opera production, with sunken orchestra pit and, later, comfortable seating, and which is in use to this day.[31] The first productions were of Gluck's *Iphigenia in Tauris* (1946), Mozart's *The Magic Flute* (1947) and Smetana's *The Bartered Bride* and Auber's *Fra Diavolo* (1948).

Chisholm was clearly making use of this new opportunity to carry on from where he had had to leave off in Glasgow. The Mozart performances achieved high standards and were generously reviewed.[32]

Chisholm must have made a considerable impression in other ways, quite apart from the memorable image of his riding to work on a lady's bicycle, wearing slippers and with the usual cigarette hanging from his lips.[33] One of the earliest concerts he put on included his own *Ceol Mór Dances* arranged for four pianos, timpani and percussion from their 1943 orchestral version. *Ceol Mór* is another name for *piobaireachd*, and nothing quite like it could have been heard in Cape Town before.[34] Confident in his own judgment, he even completely changed Désirée Talbot's career: from concert pianist to operatic singer.[35]

In 1947 he performed his *A Celtic Wonder Tale* with Stuart Findlay at the other piano, and a couple of months later the same duo performed *The Forsaken Mermaid*.[36] Meanwhile, in Glasgow, his ballet *The Hoodie Craw*, which he based on a Scottish folk-tale, was given as part of a mixed programme with Margaret Morris's own *Scottish Fantasia*. The pianists were Wight Henderson and June Mair.[37] *The Hoodie Craw* was later toured in France.[38] However, his use of Scottish material was as much an exploration of the past as the present, and his was a broad canvas and a broad kirk. He experimented in every field, and it was perhaps with an eye to some of his new academic responsibilities that he completed a group of six sonatinas with the overall title *E Praeterita*, meaning 'From the Past'.

These sonatinas are very far from being academic, and Chisholm has managed to inhabit their Renaissance idioms with felicity – an old-fashioned word which particularly suits these settings. Take, for instance, the magnificent bravura of the opening of the Third Sonatina. It is a prelude based on a ricercar for lute by Jounambrosio Dalza (*c.* 1500) and, like the *Adagio* second movement inspired by a ricercar for viola da gamba by Silbestro Ganassi (*b.* 1492), it demonstrates Chisholm's facility in an area of stylistic experiment which had its parallel in the neo-classical works of many European composers of the period. But it is one thing to ape a style, quite another to give it real meaning, especially in what appear to be its most banal manifestations. Yet this is what Chisholm achieves, notably in the beauty of the close of the *Adagio* movement, which depends upon its direct simplicity – a perfect cadence, enriched but utterly unspoilt. To make these little miracles happen requires tremendous subtlety of touch. The way the chords are spread; the context of richer harmonies from which they emerge, these are the bald explanations of how the end is achieved. But the truth is that the old, old things can only be said anew if the heart is with them.

One heart that had always been with Erik was that of his father, who died on 19 August 1949. His father was a delightful man – good fun and full of humour[39] – and he had been a life-long supporter of his son's, through thick and thin. He had allowed him to leave school at the age of thirteen and encouraged him as a musician and composer. He had bought a house for him and his wife, and seems never to have been anything other than practical and positive. The only letter from him to Erik that seems to survive is full of practical affairs and short sentences – mostly questions. It must be one of the last, for it is dated 1 May 1949. It would seem from a postscript that Erik was looking for a job 'at London music', though whether his father's 'even an assistant to them' would have satisfied Erik, one can only guess. Perhaps father and son were hoping for a way of being together again, but the postscript continues '– still you are happy at C.T.'[40]

Happy or no, Erik took himself into his study and cried, and he was a man who never cried.[41]

His father's death must also have had the effect of breaking some of his ties with his native Scotland, and Scotland itself did little to retain its ties with Chisholm. That winter, in a review of a performance of *A Celtic Wonder Tale*, Maurice Lindsay lamented his absence:

> This highly gifted man was first of all allowed to become lost to Scotland as an administrative musical organiser: and now his music is either absurdly over-praised or absurdly denigrated by folk who never hear it. But 'A Celtic Wonder Tale' is a skilful, delightful short excursion which should certainly find its way into Festival programmes, if the Festival Committee can, for once, bring itself to accept a recommendation from the West.[42]

As though to establish himself as a man of other continents, Chisholm embarked upon a series of works in Hindustani style – the Piano Concerto No. 2 (*The Hindustani*), the Violin Concerto and the Concerto for Orchestra – also known as the *Van Riebeeck* Concerto. This latter name was not Chisholm's preferred title for the work, which was not performed at the Van Riebeeck Festival, owing to lack of rehearsal. It is also likely enough that, with the rising tide of Afrikaans nationalism and apartheid, the celebration of the founding of the Dutch colony in South Africa would have lost whatever appeal it might once have had for Chisholm.

The other major Hindustani works are the *Night Song of the Bards* (see Centrepiece) and the operas *Simoon* and *Dark Sonnet*, which are considered in Chapter 8. Chisholm himself identified the two operas as being in the same style as the *Hindustani* Piano Concerto:

> I should very much like your opinion on the success – or otherwise – on this 'style', particularly as you are knowledgable on a hybrid mixture in the music of K. Sorabji. Do you see much of him these days now that he is settled in Dorset? I hear from him occasionally, and find he is as prolific in output as ever.[43]

Chisholm also published his own responses to Hindustani music in two articles in the *Bombay Evening News* and in a draft for a radio talk, part of which is reproduced here (see also Chapter 6).

> I got into some fierce arguments with their learned musicians and, to prove my point – that their music need not be one line of sound, but that they could develop

harmonically and contrapuntally along their own individual musical concepts – I wrote three concertos, one for piano, one for violin and one for orchestra, all based on Hindustani themes and rhythms. But – let's face it – the study of Hindustani music is a job for a life-time, and most Western musicians really don't know a thing about it.

Of course, our Western music took big strides ahead – it seems to us – when we started to use two and more sounds simultaneously, but it is as well to remember – in case we get big-headed about it – that the whole of Western culture – Art –Science – Religion – reached us from the East, and that the Indians and Chinese had a culture three or more thousand years ago when most of our Western races were just getting down from the tree-tops.[44]

In addition to a copy of the Maharana Vijayadevji of Dharampur's *Sangit Bhâva*, copies of Fox Strangways's *Music of Hindostan* and Captain Francis Day's *Music and Musical Instruments of India* of 1891 in the UCT Library were also probably donated by Chisholm.[45] *Sangit Bhâva* has Chisholm's pencil markings on relevant passages in the music.

The *Hindustani* Concerto was completed in 1949 and dedicated to Adolph Hallis.[46] It was first performed at an International Society of Contemporary Music concert in the University of Cape Town on 22 November 1949, with Hallis playing the solo part and Chisholm conducting.[47] The next day it was broadcast by the South Africa Broadcasting Company and, in 1950, by the BBC Scottish Orchestra, again with Hallis as soloist and Chisholm conducting.[48] Schott published a two-piano score in 1951, with several cuts following the 1950 performance;[49] and it was re-orchestrated in 1953 and other alterations made for a further broadcast that year.[50] There was also a disastrous London performance on 6 April 1953, in which the old and new versions got mixed up and the rehearsal time was used up sorting out the mess. The London Philharmonic only got the parts on the day of the concert, having underestimated the work's difficulty.[51]

Chisholm preferred this concerto to his *Piobaireachd* Concerto. Tony Baldwin had offered to play either or both of them, to which Chisholm replied:

> The second is by far the best (relative term) and is published by Schott's, so you will have no difficulty in getting a copy. I should love you to play it with Ian Whyte, but for several reasons it would not be 'politic' for me to suggest it to him.[52]

What those reasons were, I cannot say, unless the fact that Chisholm had conducted its première in Great Britain with Whyte's orchestra had irked Whyte.

Besides the use of Hindustani models, Chisholm wondered whether Gray-Fisk 'would see any of K's influence in the second piano concerto of mine?' – 'K' being Sorabji.[53] If there are any such influences, they are most probably in the middle movement, though no doubt it was before Chisholm's employment in India that Sorabji initiated his interest in Far Eastern music.

In relating Chisholm's music to any particular râga, it must be remembered that a râga is not so much a tune, as a melody type. Each râga has its appropriate season or time of day or night, and carries with it emotional and even ethical significance and may be associated with particular colours or symbolic pictorial associations. Each note has its own character in the context of the particular râga, and the sequence of notes is approached differently according to whether in *Aroha* (ascending) or *Avaroha* (descending) mode, and according to the mood of the player and the development of the improvisation. The improvisation itself follows fairly strict rules and makes use of important melodic, rhythmic and 'ornamental' formulae; but ultimately it is the player and none other who makes the music, who brings to the ancient formulae life, meaning and originality, as Asad Ali Khan has written:

> Each raga has its own character which must be understood and developed in presentation. But the raga itself is only a structure for musical discipline, and to come alive it must be steeped in rasa, the essence of emotion. An artiste can invest the notes with any rasa, and the true listener will understand and respond to the musician.[54]

In many of the characteristics listed above, râgas resemble *piobaireachd*, and to a composer such as Chisholm, who had studied *piobaireachd*, the transition from making use of the one to the other, in a Western classical context, was relatively easy. But there is one characteristic which, surprisingly and perhaps crucially, he rarely made use of and that was the drone. Just as in *piobaireachd*, so in râga, the notes speak their character and evoke emotion not just in relation to each other but in relation to the drone. In 'liberating' this material from its fundamental reference point, Chisholm ran the risk of depriving it of much of its potential emotional impact. Why did he do it? In his treatment of *piobaire-achd*, although he does indeed liberate himself from the drone, it is only a partial liberation, and he frequently evokes it with the use of fifths and octaves in the bass, albeit at different pitches, but nearly always reverting to the original pitch, usually of A, at some point or another, to keep that *terra firma* secure in the ear (see Chapter 3). The only explanation I can offer is that he sought in his Hindustani works to prove a point – to 'win' his argument with north India's 'learned musicians' and demonstrate that they could indeed 'develop harmonically and contrapuntally along their own individual musical concepts'.

The *Hindustani* Concerto makes use of three different râgas for each of its three movements, which are I, *Poco maestoso e con fuoco*, based on the late morning râga, *Asavari*; II, *Andante – Tema con variazione*, on the afternoon râga, *Shri*; and III, *Rondo burlesca* on the spring râga, *Vasantee*. The Hindustani singer Prakriti Dutta maintained that Chisholm's understanding of these râgs revealed that he had studied them intensively and with real appreciation of their structures and significances.[55]

The first movement is at times troubled and even aggressive in its passions; but there is also mystery, especially in the dialogue between the piano and the timpani. It is based upon *Râginee Âsâvaree*, which is usually played in the morning at about nine o'clock. The accompanying image is of Âsâvaree, adorned with peacock feathers, seated on top of Mount Malaygiri. Chisholm emphasises the darker aspects of this râga, the expression of which centres around such words as 'grave', 'dignified', 'melancholy', 'wise', 'sober', as well as 'very tender and loving'. Asad Ali Khan describes it as 'full of bhakti rasa, devotional and contemplative'.[56] Chisholm's own direction *con fuoco* – 'with fire' – cannot be easily reconciled with these traditional associations; but as the movement develops, so the music reveals both grave and melancholy aspects, especially in the second subject, enunciated by the piano, and also at the start of the recapitulation, in which the theme is given to the clarinet against a throbbing rhythm on the piano.

The piano's opening statement is derived directly from the version of *Râg Âsâvaree* in *Sangit Bhâva*,[57] but almost immediately breaks away into chromatic colouring of the material, which one might construe as Chisholm's way of suggesting the various microtonal inflections that would be part of the expressive technique of a Hindu musician (ex. 14).

Motifs from the *Sangit Bhâva* version of the râg appear in many guises, sometimes delicate, sometimes dramatic,[58] and the *Meno mosso* makes use of a transposed version of the *Aroha*, but it is part of a complex texture which uses the predominant intervals of the râg (semitones and major thirds) in different transpositions simultaneously. The central climax of the work is in a mood more of desperation than anger. As the storm passes, it leaves behind the rumblings of the timpani, and the soloist falls back in halting rhythms, as though emotionally drained. The music then settles on a pulsating drone in E♭, over which a solo clarinet returns to the opening theme. It is a moment of beauty and mystery which soon reveals that passions are anything but spent. The movement ends with an extended cadenza for the soloist and a brief orchestral coda.

The second movement is an *Andante*, a set of seven variations on a theme based on *Râg Shri* (see illus. 16, Chapter 6). It is associated with the months of December and January and with the early evening. The image that goes with it is of a youth of such beauty that women become infatuated, and anger is soothed. But it can also be spiritual in its effect, like a call to evening prayer.[59] In Chisholm's opening statement, the notes of the *Aroha* (ascent) and *Avaroha* (descent) are combined and accompany a melodic line similarly derived. The movement is a wonderfully compelling exploration of mystery, sensuousness and allure. In particular, the fifth variation draws close to the mood and the mode of *Râg Shri*, extruding a sinuous line against a rippling ostinato that breaks upon the shores of this exotic music in gentle but urgent waves. One critic found this overdone,[60] but its seduction is not for one moment overprolonged, and the beauty with which Chisholm embellishes the line, with subtle use of repeated notes and tremolo, would surely have created sensations down Sorabji's spine. Sorabji might well have preferred to receive the dedication of this work, rather than the heavenly purity of Beatrice as envisioned in *Pictures from Dante*; but Chisholm's

Ex. 14 (a) *Râg Asavari*, *Aroha* and *Avaroha*; (b) *Sangit Bhâva*, bars 1–10;
(c) Chisholm, *Hindustani* Concerto, first movement, bars 1–9

true musical homage is here, for it is in passages such as this that the scent-laden sensuality of Sorabji's own *Djâmî* drifts into the more austere world of Chisholm and, as the Song of Solomon would have it, steals like little foxes into the heart of the beloved (ex. 15).

In the following variation, the bass clarinet and strings release a rush of passion which, in the final variation (VII), relapses into a dialogue between solo cello and piano – a beautiful submission to, and admission of, irresistible desire.

The third movement, an *Allegretto* marked *Rondo burlesca*,[61] is capricious, even bird-like in places, mixing delicacy, wit and energy. *Râg Vasantee* itself celebrates the coming of spring and, in the concluding *Allegro barbaro*, Chisholm lets loose the orchestra in a riot of festivity.

It would have required only this work for Chisholm to have proved his point – that one could meaningfully adapt the Hindustani idiom to a contrapuntal Western one, but he had yet to tackle some of the wider formal issues involved. Rather than pursue the path he had done with *piobaireachd*, involving a gradual increase in elaboration and virtuosity, in the *Hindustani* Concerto he had reverted to classical sonata form for the first movement and rondo form for the last. Perhaps conscious of this, he moved further back in Western musical style, to the passacaglia form, for the first movement of the Violin Concerto. But it was to be with a difference – a *Passacaglia Telescopico (in modo Vasantee)*.

The Violin Concerto was completed in 1950. The work has four movements, but the second and fourth were exchanged at the first performance in Cape Town, though whether at soloist Szymon Goldberg's request or as a decision of Chisholm's is not clear. He must in any case have approved it, as he was present at the first performance in 1952 at the Van Riebeeck Festival.[62]

The Hindustani sources for two of the movements are declared by Chisholm: the first, a *Passacaglia Telescopico (in modo Vasantee)*, and the third, *Aria in modo Sohani*, based upon *Râg Sohani* (which he also used for *Night Song of the Bards*). For the opening statement, on muted cellos, Chisholm has done little more than transcribe the first thirteen bars of the version of *Râginee Vasantee* in *Sangit Bhâva*, in his copy of which his pencil marks and transpositions can be readily made out.[63] This is a râga of the spring, evoking the image of a woman whose hair is decorated by peacock feathers and her ears ornamented by mango blossoms.

The sequence of notes pervades the movement and has a hypnotic effect upon the whole. It is not only that the passacaglia theme itself is drawn from it, but that the entire melodic material is derived from its sinuous movement of semitones and augmented and diminished seconds and thirds. Even in the fast passages, the mysterious beauty of the note sequence is sustained, flowing like a great slow-moving river through the changing landscape of the variations, which have strong points of contact with the slow movement of the *Hindustani* Piano Concerto.

In the scherzo, *Râginee Vasantee* still dominates in on-rushing quavers, but

Ex. 15 *Hindustani* Concerto, second movement

the central section provides an atmospheric contrast. Two side-drums, one with, one without snares, are played with the fingernails, with the right hand 'always a little stronger than the left' and, for a few bars, are the sole accompaniment to the soloist, whose descending chromatic line, derived from the same râga, is first played high on the G string, then contrasted with A and D string tone, although basically in the same register. This sense of colour in the writing is a vital part of the work, without which it cannot be properly assessed, and it calls for outstanding performance.

The slow movement, *Aria in modo Sohani*, is a beauty and it is where the work should end. The finale – *Fuga senza tema* – is too clever for its own good, and it does not surprise me that it and the second movement were exchanged at the first performance. The *Aria* is inspired by Tagore's verses and music, using *Râg Sohani* in the form of a Brahmin Samāj hymn. Chisholm inserted this before the movement in the piano score, using Upendrakisor Ray's translation of the Tagore original, both music and verse appearing as in Strangways (for the relevant text, see Centrepiece).[64]

Chisholm was not a Christian and gave trenchant reasons for that position, but he was by no means indifferent to spiritual matters and was well aware of competing claims on the deity. The final reason given for his position in his incomplete typescript *Why I Am Not a Christian* was:

> I see no reason, other than geographical ones, why I should believe particularly in Christianity more than in any other of the 5 major contemporary religions, the multiple minor contemporary religions, or the great and little defunct religions. Last November I was standing in St. Peter's square when hundreds of thousands of Italian believers acclaimed Pope John XXIII as God's representative on earth, a moving example of the belief of millions of Catholics. I attended a most religious ceremony at the Swie Daron – the land of a thousand Buddhas in Rangoon, along with an enormous group of sincere Buddhists who testified their undying belief in the tenancy of Buddhism. I have also visited the tremendous Mosque in Delhi.[65]

We may take it from this that Chisholm was as likely to be sincere in his devotions to an Eastern as to a Western god; and it is quite possible that, in the Hindustani works, he was ready to acknowledge the extent to which music and spiritual awareness are combined in that culture.

The final composition in this group of Hindustani works was composed for the Van Riebeeck Festival of 1952, but never performed; nor has it been performed subsequently. A note on the cover states that Chisholm wanted it to be called 'Concerto for Orchestra' and not 'Van Riebeeck Concerto'. It was not performed at the Van Riebeeck Festival because of constraints on rehearsal, and no complete full score has been found, though there is a complete set of parts. It is in the same vein as its predecessors, but at first sight seems to be less charcterful.

If the Hindustani works were in part the fulfilment of the boast Chisholm made in Karachi (see above), they were also evidence of that restlessness which had always attended his muse and which was only to settle in old territory in his last years. Not that the people of Cape Town were going to get away without hearing something more of Scotland than Chisholm on two pianos. *The Freiris of Berwick* was conducted by Jorda with the Cape Town Municipal Orchestra, Chisholm describing it as a 'short comedy Overture … in compressed sonata-form … first performed by the B.B.C. Orchestra under Constant Lambert [sic]. It is based on a narrative poem by the Scottish poet Dunbar.'[66] Chisholm was also busy revising a number of his earlier Scottish piano works, apparently completing the revisions in 1951, including *Night Song of the Bards.*[67]

The College of Music was, meanwhile, expanding. In 1950 there were 430 students, 17 full-time staff and 27 part-time. The library issued 1,569 books, 11,684 music scores, 11,519 records and 288 periodicals.[68] By 1950, Chisholm had promoted Stuart Findlay from the piano staff to the post of Assistant to the Director, and had made one of the most stimulating appointments of his tenure – that of Gregorio Fiasconaro, affectionately known as 'Gigi', to the singing department. Fiasconaro's career had been cut short by the war. He had been shot down, seriously wounded and captured in the Sahara and then brought to South Africa, and Chisholm was quick to seize the opportunity to employ him. Fiasconaro's Italian temperament and Chisholm's Scottish one created what was known as 'the duelling duo'. Duelling or no, it produced some of the highest achievements in South Africa's musical history. Fiasconaro was employed as a singer and teacher of singing, but Chisholm asked if he had ever produced or directed. When Fiasconaro replied that he had not, Chisholm abruptly told him that he was starting now, with *Suor Angelica* and *La Serva Padrona*. It was an inspired piece of bullying and Fiasconaro's productions, as well as his subtle stage performances, are remembered to this day.[69] Whether he had to bully him into singing works by F. G. Scott is not known, but Fiasconaro included four Scott settings in a recital in September 1950.[70] The Puccini–Pergolesi double bill was performed as part of the UCT Arts Festival in September 1951. Chisholm conducted the Puccini and Ernest Fleischman the Pergolesi.[71] Years later, Fleischmann was to recall Chisholm as teacher and composer in the warmest possible terms:

> I had the singular privilege of conducting the first performances of his very powerful little opera, 'The Inland Woman'. I worked closely with him on many other interesting projects. He was such a remarkable man, and wonderfully encouraging and supportive of his students, whom he gave extraordinary opportunities of performance. It was he who was responsible for my appointment to manage the musical aspects of the 1952 Van Riebeeck Festival, which was the first step in a series of events that resulted in my being here [as Executive Vice-President and Managing Director of the Los Angeles Philharmonic Association] in one of the best musical administration positions in the United States, if not the world.[72]

Following the first performance of the *Hindustani* Concerto in late 1949, Chisholm was back in Glasgow conducting his *Nine Orchestral Preludes: From the True Edge of the Great World* with the BBC Scottish Orchestra.[73] 'It was really exciting and thrilling to be back again but I left your country without any regrets. For one thing the Scottish winter is quite intolerable to me now. (I seem to have got soft after so many years in tropical and semi-tropical countries).'[74]

Perhaps recalling the Dunedin Association's publishing venture in Glasgow (see Chapter 4) in 1951 Chisholm founded the South African National Music Press, 'which aims principally at publishing the works of young South African composers'.[75] As usual, he was hard at work promoting the music of others rather than his own, including promoting highly successful performances of the complete Bartók string quartets, using the ISCM and the University Music Society to that end,[76] though he kept trying to make a mark in Scotland, writing in gratitude to Christopher Grier of the *Scotsman* for an encouraging review:

> It is most comforting to know that there is at least one person in Scotland who has some sort of opinion of my compositions. I had given up all hope of ever breaking into the home ground.[77]

But a performance of the *Hindustani* Concerto had to be postponed, as Agnes Walker was ill.[78] In any case, it was a somewhat naïve hope that Scotland would make efforts on his behalf when there were already so few openings and opportunities for composers. It was simply not possible for a composer to make a living in Scotland at that time without access to alternative sources of income, and the music profession had few to offer beyond secondary-school teaching.

Nor was Chisholm the only Scottish composer obliged to work abroad. Iain Hamilton and Thea Musgrave both emigrated to the USA and London; and while F. G. Scott ran the music department for the teacher training college at Jordanhill, being essentially a song-writer, he had fewer demands to make on the profession. Ian Whyte, as Music Director and Conductor of the BBC Scottish Orchestra, had cornered one of the few real openings for a composer, which he undoubtedly used to his advantage, and Cedric Thorpe Davie ran the music department at St Andrews University and did well with film music. Tovey had been succeeded in the Reid Chair of Music at Edinburgh by another Englishman, Sidney Newman, who was instrumental in setting up the School of Scottish Studies; and, while the Gardiner Chair at Glasgow was held by Sir Ernest Bullock (also English), when the Royal Scottish Academy of Music and Drama eventually gained its own Principal, the post was taken by the splendid Henry Havergal, also from south of the border. Whether this tendency to appoint musicians from outwith Scotland had a beneficial or detrimental effect upon the nurturing of the profession within the country is a nice point. But without doubt, had Chisholm succeeded in obtaining a post in Scotland, the musical life of the country would have received a much-needed shot in the arm, not least in terms of a proper respect for the country's own musical traditions.

Scotland, at any rate, did give the British première of his Violin Concerto at the 1952 Edinburgh International Festival, with Max Rostal as the soloist, conducted by Ian Whyte. The world première was in Cape Town a little earlier, at the Van Riebeeck Festival, with Szymon Goldberg playing the solo part (and possibly requesting a change in the order of the movements). Goldberg was, of course, known to Chisholm from his time in the Far East, and there are happy photographs of him and Chisholm together in Cape Town, along with Chisholm's mother and his daughters (illus. 19, 20).

In August he sent a script of his ballet *Piobaireachd* to Dame Ninette de Valois, the formidable Irish Director of Sadlers Wells Ballet:

> I hear that the ballet Ian Whyte wrote for you has been successful: probably that ballet will supply all the Scottish contribution you require for a long time. On the other hand, it may stimulate interest. The music of the ballet is 'authentically Scottish' and uses the highly characteristic Scottish–Asiatic piobaireachd rhythms and tunes which gives the music an original colouring.[79]

19 Erik Chisholm
and Szymon
Goldberg,
Cape Town 1952

20 Erik Chisholm, his mother and three daughters
with Szymon Goldberg, Cape Town 1952

But despite the good liaison that existed between Sadlers Wells and the UCT Ballet School, the reply was typically blunt:

> I am afraid it would be out of the question for us to produce another Scottish work of this order. It is, frankly, too like the one already in our repertoire.[80]

It was part of this ballet which he had used for his orchestral work *Pictures from Dante* (see Centre-piece). In September and October of that year, Chisholm's approach to Chester Music Publishers to publish the Violin Concerto was turned down on economic grounds by R. D. Gibson, who advised making it available for hire, to which Chisholm replied 'I think you write me sound advice and good sense, and I am grateful to you for your considered and experienced opinion of this matter.'[81] It was, however, the *Hindustani* Piano Concerto to which Hindemith refers in a Christmas card, responding to a letter of Chisholm's seeking support for an application for a Carnegie grant:[82]

> Your concerto seems to be a very decent piece of music. Of course, I would like to hear it before uttering any definite appraisal. – From the Carnegie Foundation I have not heard so far. Your application will probably meander through all the burocratic [*sic*] channels, but be assured that it will have all my support whenever they ask me about your coming here.[83]

Some months later Chisholm replied with the news that, 'Thanks to your recommendation I have myself been awarded a Carnegie Corporation grant which will allow me to travel in the States for several months.'[84] In the meantime, he had ensured that Hindemith was given due honour in South Africa, using the combined efforts of the University Music Society and the South African Section of the ISCM to put on a series of three concerts of the complete cycle of Hinde-mith string quartets.[85]

That year (1952), his eldest daughter Morag was married. The wedding was a huge affair with five hundred guests and, of course, pipers. The reception was held at the College of Music, where Diana danced the Highland Fling on one of the tables.

> P.S. By the way, she whom you called Chops is now a fourth year medical student, and getting married to a fifth ditto in about 10 days time.[86]

Chisholm might very well have been pushing his own music in South Africa at this time, for example by giving piano recitals, but he seems to have backed off from that possibility.[87] But he did promote his own operas, *Dark Sonnet* being mounted in March and *The Inland Woman* (in a double bill with Martinu's *Comedy on the Bridge*) in October of 1953, in productions by Fiasconaro.[88] The singers disliked the Martinu[89] and, writing in *Opera* magazine, David Shepherd also preferred Chisholm to Martinu:

> Although somewhat lacking in action, this one-hour opera made a powerful emotional impact on the audience … a production of Martinu's *Comedy on the Bridge* … neither amused nor interested the audience.[90]

Chisholm was also forwarding his music abroad, writing to the music critic of *Musical Opinion*, informing him of the forthcoming Festival Hall performance of the *Hindustani* Piano Concerto, and wondering 'if you would see any of K's [Sor-abji's] influence in the second piano concerto of mine?'. It seems the performance was not a success: the parts required correction, Agnes Walker was not regarded as a good pianist by Gray-Fisk and the orchestra had inadequate rehearsal time.[91]

He also wrote (unsuccessfully) to Rafael Kubelik offering Andor Foldes as soloist for the *Hindustani* Piano Concerto: 'Mr Foldes wrote to me the other day: "I am tremendously interested in the concerto, and hope I can be given the first American performance of it some time next season." ' But Kubelik was leaving Chicago and the proposal came to nothing.[92]

On the domestic front, Chisholm's middle daughter, Sheila, had had an acci-dent to her back, which was to put paid to her career as a professional dancer, though not as a teacher of dance. It was hoped that a Mrs L. M. Gilbert, who lived in Salisbury and was proposing to pass through Cape Town on her way to England, would succeed where doctors had failed. She wrote advertising her skills: '[T]he first case must be to tend your daughter. I have a letter before me from a Gentleman in Umtali, who had five vertebrae out, says he hasn't felt so fit for years.'[93]

Chisholm replied, offering his own house as a *pied à terre* for Mrs Gilbert's stopover:

> If you would care to stay with my wife and me, we shall be delighted to have you: only our house is by no means 'quiet', and with 7 dogs running loose, an aviary and musical rehearsals taking place hourly, if you think this would be too noisy (and it is noisy!), please do not hesitate to say so.[94]

Mrs Gilbert was a faith-healer and presumably capable of putting spiritual distance between herself and noise, but the passing of hands over Sheila's spine did nothing for her condition.[95] Erik himself, though no Christian, explored the possibility of a life after death and took part in seances in the house, to which mediums were brought.[96] Diana took part in the seances, but was none the less a Christian, and when Morag, who was going through a deeply religious phase, publicly declared that she came from a non-Christian background, her mother was in tears.[97]

Erik naturally loved things of the spirit – he had, of course, been a church organist for many years, but perhaps his love of the stars, which was manifest in the *Cameos*, was a more consistent stimulus to such thoughts. He had watched them through a huge telescope as a young man[98] and he continued to watch them throughout his life, on occasion insisting that others share in observing the beauty of the heavens:

> We arrived in the morning late after a week of continuous performances and journeys, and Gigi [Fiasconaro] had immediately off-loaded, set up and done the lighting with his four 'stage-crew'. Then he had an hour's rest and went back to sing *Figaro*. Afterwards they packed up everything in readiness for the morrow's journey and at 2.00 a.m. he fell into bed completely exhausted.
>
> At 3.00 a.m. there was a thunderous knocking on his door and Dr Chisholm's voice summoned him from the depths of sleep, 'Cici, come quickly.' He staggered out of bed in a panic and opened the door. 'Whassamarrar?' 'Come, Cici, come onto the roof and look at the rings around Venus through my telescope' said the ebullient Chisholm.[99]

Sometimes the restless muse is not even earth-bound.

On Tour in the USA and Europe

Despite all his successes and opportunities in Cape Town, Chisholm must still have felt keenly the draw of home, and he appears to have shown interest in the Chair of Music at Queen's University, Belfast, in 1953, though whether he actually applied is not clear.[1] He was also not uncritical of his own productions, though confident enough to compare his work with British equivalents:

> Things keep very lively here in quantity, if not always in quality. I suppose we have as much music as provincial British towns like Manchester, Liverpool, and Glasgow get. The music school keeps bright and active too, and over the last holiday period we took six of our operas on a tour of Southern Rhodesia.[2]

The quantity, in this case, consisted of Puccini's *Gianni Schicchi,* Pergolesi's *La Serva Padrona,* Menotti's *The Telephone* and *The Medium,* Wolf-Ferrari's *Susanna's Secret* and Chisholm's *Dark Sonnet.* In setting up these tours in Africa (of which this was but one of several), Chisholm was going far beyond the call of duty. One could almost say that he was on a mission to African audiences on behalf of the operas themselves, and also on behalf of his singers and musicians, who were thereby gaining tremendous work experience. He too was gaining in experience as a composer of operas and, harking back, perhaps, to his youthful ploys in cinema 'noir' (see Chapter 1), planned a triptych of his own operas to be entitled *Murder in Three Keys.* The candidates for inclusion were *Dark Sonnet, Sweeney Agonistes* (which became *Black Roses*), *Simoon,* and *The Pardoner's Tale.* This latter was one of three operas based on Chaucer, in the original Middle English (see Chapter 9).

Dark Sonnet is a remarkable piece. With one of the most unrelenting and grim scenarios of any opera, it succeeded in becoming one of Chisholm's most successful compositions. A woman getting ready for work taunts her off-stage unfaithful husband until, at the very end of the opera, he commits suicide. The soprano, who has to carry the entire vocal and dramatic burden, has to be exceptional and, in Noreen Berry, Chisholm had such a singer and actress. Chisholm's music is intense and employs an idiom which is as dissonant as anything he produced. But voice and orchestra are superbly integrated, and the psychological insight with which the music reflects every biting turn of the script makes this a compelling work. In January 1954, *Dark Sonnet* was televised in the United Kingdom by the BBC and given a substantial and laudatory write-up in the *Radio Times.*[3]

Nearly all of Chisholm's operas are closely based on original dramas of high quality and *Dark Sonnet* is such a one. It was completed in 1952 and scored for solo soprano, single winds, trumpet, trombone, percussion, celesta, piano duet and strings. It is based on *Before Breakfast* by Eugene O'Neill, and its renaming was approved by O'Neill.[4] Expressionistic in style, its title aptly describes the music as well as the 'plot'. In fact this is a dramatic monologue that has as one of its finest precursors, in an equally macabre genre, the astonishing *Fra Giacomo* by Chisholm's compatriot Cecil Coles, though this work was not designed to be staged. Menotti's *The Medium* offers an operatic parallel, with a similarly disturbing dénouement, and Chisholm acknowledged the relationship.[5]

Stylistically, the Chisholm is a more integrated work than the Menotti, with a driving psychological insight that is powerfully sustained. It is also decidedly uncompromising. It may have its recitatives and arias marked in the score, but they are not that clearly distinguished, nor should they be, if the flow of invective is to achieve its final goal – the suicide of the husband.

The monologue takes place in the kitchen of a cheap New York apartment. Mrs Roland is making a breakfast of coffee, bread and butter – all she has – while her husband slowly gets up and shaves with a cut-throat razor. She taunts him with his failure to make a living out of his writing, which she despises. She finds a hidden letter, from which she discovers that her suspicions that he has a mistress are true, and that this woman is pregnant. Her and her husband's only child died as a baby. Her own sorrow is soon lost in her vindictiveness, as she taunts him about his mistress. Just as she is about to leave, she hears a sound from the bathroom which she cannot ignore. It is her husband, who has cut his own throat.

The sonnet form is associated with love, and in choosing to set the whole opera in the form of the Shakespearean sonnet, Chisholm adds ironic bitterness to the piece: 'I have worked it out on a plan of 14 movements, a parallel with sonnet form with the climax in the last movement.'[6]

Dark Sonnet is in dodecaphonic style, 'although without the Schönbergian "tone-rows" and other restrictions and devices of the Viennese school'.[7] Each of the first two bars contains all twelve semitones, but not without repetitions. More important is the presence of two symmetrical four-note motifs, one also in inversion, and which, in both forms, are identical with their own retrogrades. They could have been extracted just as readily from *Râginee Vasantee*, *Râg Sohani* or *Râg Shree*, each of which he used in his Hindustani works. (See ex. 16.)

The self-reflecting nature of both these motifs, with their emphasis on thirds and semitones, corresponds with the mental state of Mrs Roland, who is almost exclusively concerned with her own feelings and, disastrously, rarely stops to think what might be the feelings of her husband. The second of these motifs appears frequently throughout the opera, in chromatic passages, in cadential phrases and in the vocal line. The style might take its obsessiveness into monotony, were it not that Chisholm makes dramatic use of a variety of techniques, for example leaps of a seventh, and octave transpositions. In the example, we see the motif at the start of the opera and then subtly embedded in the orchestral part, with the vocal line more widely spaced, but the bass line binding the whole together with ordinary minor chords.

Ex. 16 *Dark Sonnet*, (a) piano reduction, bars 1–2;
(b) five bars before figure 27, with motifs bracketed

Dark as is this sonnet, it has its gentle moments, and it is impossible not to feel as much sympathy for Mrs Roland as for her husband. Her brief cavatina, as she wonders if her rival is pretty, and recalls that she herself was pretty once, is all the more touching for the rarity of its tenderness.

> The music, closely knit and intensely gripping, follows with vibrant harshness every outburst of the woman's ravings, except in an extraordinarily touching moment of beautiful sound when she soliloquizes over her past girlhood.[8]

But the dark returns as Mrs Roland describes her husband's mistress, Helen, as no better than a common street-walker (ex. 17). In this example we have reached the final line of the sonnet. Chisholm has marked the line divisions in the vocal score in roman numerals. Here, again, the opening motifs are hinted at and even stated overtly.

This level of concentration, matched with carefully devised variety, is sustained throughout the piece, as is proper in a sonnet. How well it matches the libretto (which is absolutely faithful to O'Neill's original script) can only be appreciated on hearing it performed. The orchestration matches the mood throughout. The colours are dark and, where actions are described orchestrally, it is the sound of the floor being swept, the razor being sharpened on the leather, or of blood dropping to the floor.

This is not a pretty work, but it is undoubtedly utterly compelling – something I can vouch for personally, having attended all the performances in Cape Town in February 2004, and discussed it with the audiences.

Chisholm's life-long attachment to German Expressionist cinema finds its

Ex. 17 *Dark Sonnet*, figure 128

best expression in this work and in *Simoon*, but there is no clear indication that *Simoon* was ever performed with orchestra.[9] This is a tragedy, for it is an intriguing piece, at once both fantastical and psychologically arresting. The play dates from 1889 and might, superficially, be classified as Grand Guignol. But in going deeper than mere sensationalism, and exploring the mental states of its characters, it anticipates the Modernists.

> I am now half-way through a second chamber opera on Strindberg's 'Simoon' which is to be the first part of a triptych 'Murder in Four Keys', the finale being Chaucer's 'The Pardoner's Tale' in James Bridie's dramatisation. The music style is roughly Wosseck-ish.[10]

Berg's seminal opera *Wozzeck* (as it is now usually spelt) was composed using dodecaphonic techniques which were being formulated not long after Strindberg wrote the play. The term implies atonality, if the system is adhered to strictly; but it rarely has been, and if Berg's *Wozzeck* was Chisholm's model, then there is plenty of tonal music to be found within it. Chisholm's own score is heavily influenced by dodecaphonic techniques, but the melodic material in *Simoon* comes, in part, from Hindustani sources, and, for all that the action is Arabian and set in Algeria, one could have included this opera with the Hindustani works.

Exotic *Simoon* may be, but in Strindberg's and Chisholm's hands, none of the comforts of the merely exotic are to be had. The work is also psychologically brutal, and its sensuality feeds upon death. Its religious and political motivation in the context of a foreign presence, and the refined torture which is used to lead the psychological prisoner to his death, yield a scenario which has many resonances half a century after the opera was composed and well over a century after the text was written. Algeria in the 1880s (the time specified by Strindberg) was undergoing a period of aggressive French colonisation, and it is in this context that the plot operates. It is a plot, not a story, and the plot is a native Arab one, to defeat the Franks. There are three characters: Biskra, an Arabian girl utterly consumed by a desire for revenge for the murder of a former lover; Yusuf, her present lover; and the Frank, Guimard, a lieutenant in the Zouaves. The Zouaves were a regiment, originally of native soldiers, fighting for the French. Guimard is therefore seen as an enemy. Biskra knows that Guimard is approaching the sepulchral chamber and will be already mentally exhausted by the simoon, a strong, sand-laden, suffocating desert wind. She intends to use her magical skills to reduce him to such a state that he dies of despair and wretchedness. In this she succeeds, with some help from Yusuf.

Chisholm has provided not only the characters, but also the subject-matter, with leitmotifs,[11] and the opera is divided into characterised movements – for example, in Scene II:

> 1st movement: 2nd movement (mad-dog): 3rd movement (Uncanny music): 4th movement (Ali, the guide): 5th movement (spring): 6th movement (Funerale): 7th movement (Impending Death): 8th movement (Battle): 9th movement (Skull).[12]

The opera is scored for small orchestra with additional colour provided by celesta, glockenspiel, xylophone, two tubular bells, gong, two pianos, wind machine and a harmonium. One only has to look at the first few pages of the full score to recognise that any performance of this work without the orchestra is going to be little short of a travesty. The Introduction ('Overture' in the vocal score) follows Strindberg's stage direction that the simoon can be heard whining outside. The uncanny chromatic scales, designed to produce multiple dissonances to such an extent that only the vaguest sense of pitch will emerge (the whole accompanied by wind machine), initiates the work in a mood of scarcely suppressed terror. In the vocal score, Chisholm added a third double-stave for the piano, just to let everyone know how much of the music was missing from the two-piano reduction.

Emerging from the simoon is the outline of part of the *Râga Lalitā*, which has a very similar outline to *Râginee Vasantee*. The latter Chisholm used in the first movement of the Violin Concerto (see Chapter 7). Here *Râga Lalitā* is the basis of Biskra's motif, and the dodecaphonic basis of the work is present from the outset:

Ex. 18 (a) *Râga Lalitā* (descending form);
(b) *Simoon*, Biskra's motif; (c) *Simoon*, 'simoon', bars 1–4.]

(a) Râga Lalitā
(Avaroha)

(b) Biskra's Motif ($\quad$ = 84)

(c) Misterioso ($\quad$ = 92)

However, Chisholm is far from rigorous in his application of the tone-row system. He allows for repetition, feels no obligation to complete the series (in the second phrase, above, the A♮ is only supplied in the *tremolando* accompaniment), and allows for duplication of notes in accompanying harmonies, or within the same phrase or harmonic sequence. Aside from its technicalities, the sounds in this work are intriguing.

The harmonium is not listed by Chisholm with the other instruments in the vocal score,[13] but it has a vital part to play, there being no real substitute for its strange sostenuto tone to accompany Biskra and Guimard's ecstatic 'There is only one God. There is no other God but He. The Merciful one, the compassionate one!' Then there is the extraordinary texture Chisholm produces to accompany the torturing of Guimard with visions of his son and of his wife with his friend's arm round her neck. It is at the start of the *Funerale*, and the first piano has tissue-paper placed between the dampers and the strings in the upper register; the violins, violas and cellos are plucking close to the bridge with the fingernails, producing a dry, dead sound; and the tubular bell is tolling, against a background of harmonium and double-bass and trombone. This is followed by a passage of *pianissimo spiccato* on the upper strings and woodwind.

A few bars later, Guimard is weeping – *dogliosissimo* – at the vision of his son's coffin, bearing a wreath from himself upon it. In the piano score, it looks like many another passage, but the sound is that of three solo cellos, the first with undulating sobs, the others with *pianissimo tremolando sul ponte* – a thin, shivering veil of sound. With them is the harmonium building a soft chord on the descending melodic outline derived from the 'Love' motif; and in the middle of this texture, the cor anglais weeps and echoes the harmonium. Its line is simply omitted from the vocal score.

If the colouring of the orchestration is vital, so too is the colouring of the voices. The contrast between Eastern and Western could and should be made clear; and, within any one part, there are to be found violent extremes of mood, calling for vocal flexibility and a huge variety of tone – something too often in short supply from singers. When Yusuf sings the 'Love' motif, we are clearly in the sensual world of the râgas, with the vocal line echoed in doubled note values on the violins, accompanied by pizzicati, hinting at a lute (ex. 19).

Chisholm (following Strindberg's instruction) actually forces the singer to change voice by making Biskra sing a passage holding a piece of palm leaf between her teeth. The sensuality of the line is accentuated by the narrowing and focusing of the tone created by singing with clenched teeth, and the effect is made the more subversive by Yusuf imitating the same line from a position below the stage (ex. 20).[14]

As part of Chisholm's *Murder in Three Keys, Simoon* was performed in New York by Punch Opera, but without an orchestra. Opera was frequently performed in the USA with piano only, and Chisholm boasted to Christopher Grier that whereas Columbia University did opera with piano, Cape Town was doing better.[15] The production took place the year after Erik and Diana took a trip to the USA in the summer recess of 1953. They visited all the major music schools and departments, and, besides setting up eventual performances of his operas, Chisholm was approached by Cleveland University about a possible teaching exchange.[16]

We have had a simply wonderful time in Nth America – everything said about the hospitality & kindness & generosity of the Americans turned out to be true. Of course we had our ups and downs but with the former far outweighing the latter. I managed to visit more than 30 universities. I – having the luck to attend

Ex. 19 *Simoon*, 'Love' motif

Ex. 20 *Simoon*, Trio

a nation-wide conference on my particular subjects at Chicago – met & talked to representatives from as many more universities again. The equipment at some of the music schools is entirely fabulous – Eastman (Rochester) Bloomington (Indiana) Julliard (N. York) for example but frequently much in advance of the teaching quality. I found, too, unique features about our own little school in C.T. without parallel in the U.S.

I heard all the major Symphony Orchestras throughout the country & met practically everyone I wanted to meet: I've also managed to create some interest in my own compositions with the promise of quite a few performances in the near future.[17]

In New York, Erik met Copland in a tea-shop, though when is not clear.[18] He and Diana returned from there to Southampton on the Cunard Line RMS *Queen Mary*, built on the River Clyde, which flowed through the city of his birth.

On the way back to South Africa, Chisholm had three dates conducting the London Philharmonic Orchestra and hoped to be back in time for Freshers' Week in Cape Town.[19] He must also have made a trip back to Scotland, for he gave lecture-recitals in Edinburgh and Glasgow, illustrated with tape recordings of *Dark Sonnet* and *The Inland Woman*.[20] On both journeys, he was composing the music for his opera *Black Roses*, to be based on T. S. Eliot's *Sweeney Agonistes*. The occasion for this was the suggestion of Nelson Sykes (artistic director of Punch Opera in New York) that the proposed triptych of *Murder in Three Keys* was 'somewhat overpowering'. Chisholm concurred, and started work on the Eliot script while trying to get permission from Eliot.[21] It turned out to be a difficult task, but he finally caught up with him in Cape Town, where Eliot was on holiday. Eliot did not like the idea and eventually turned it down flat, on the grounds that

> 'Sweeney' consisted of two almost disconnected fragments the final outcome of which he had himself never really imagined, and that my permanent and conclusive version of them – necessary in any operatic treatment – would inevitably go beyond the intention and invention of his own 'Sweeney'.[22]

Chisholm could see Eliot's point and set about writing a completely new libretto to match the existing music as nearly as possible. He seems at first to have been pleased with it,[23] but a few years afterwards confessed that it was 'no good'.[24]

It was in 1954 also that Bartók's *Bluebeard's Castle* was produced, on 2–4 September. Fiasconaro and Talbot were to take the parts of Bluebeard and Judith. Both singers were in a state of consternation, never having tackled anything that, to their ears, was so modern. In addition, Judith has to sing a top C absolutely 'cold' and without any lead-in. Chisholm coached them.

> It was a revelation. Not only did he play our parts but also added all the orchestral parts missing in the vocal score reduction. He built it up for us harmonically and melodically so that in the end it became easy. It also taught me a lesson I

never forgot. From then on I learnt every piece of music I sang from the bass clef upwards.[25]

The performance, with an augmented College Orchestra, was a first for South Africa, and made a powerful impression. These sets were by Cecil Pym, and the costumes were by Doreen Graves.

All of these achievements would have satisfied most people, but in a letter to Professor Clark at McGill University, Chisholm's inherent restlessness is revealed:

> I confess that I found your music department at McGill particularly attractive.
>
> You may remember saying to me that you were due to retire in about two years time, and 'you are welcome to have my job after that if you feel like it'. I know that the latter part of your remark was said by way of a joke: nevertheless I feel very much like taking you up on this, and should be grateful if you could send me some particulars about the appointment.
>
> The fact is that I came to Capetown [sic] seven years ago to re-organise the music department here. The job is now done and consolidated, and I am feeling a bit bored: during this period things have gone – politically – from bad to worse, and with the recent change of premier and the narrow racialism of the present government, many of us fear that what we know as liberal education will very soon – in this part of the world – be a thing of the past! Besides, ever since I spent a year or so in Canada 1927–8, I have had a great liking for the country, and Montreal as a centre of activity appeals to me enormously.
>
> Do let me know if you are retiring shortly, and whether you think an application from me would be at all welcomed.[26]

The new premier was J. G. Strijdom, who altered the nature of the Appeal Court and enlarged and packed the Senate via the infamous Senate Act of 1955, so that 'in February, 1956, the Cape Coloured voters were finally removed from the common roll and South Africa took another stride away from the Western conception of shared government and government by consent.'[27]

While the worsening political situation was turning Chisholm's thoughts away from South Africa, there was also, and always, the call of his native land. Writing to Agnes Duncan in 1954 about the fate of the original score of *A Dune of Barra*, which she had thought of performing, he said, 'Diana and I love it out here, but occasionally feel homesick for our old friends in Scotland.'[28]

On the other hand, in September of that same year, he wrote to Farmer explaining why he was unlikely to return to Scotland, extolling the virtues of his situation in Cape Town and suggesting that Ross's 'Alas, poor country – almost afraid to know itself! It cannot be called our mother but our grave' was probably truer at that moment than in the eleventh century.[29]

Chisholm's assessment was entirely justified. Farmer, who was and remains one of the great international scholars of Middle Eastern music and who was the first to write a comprehensive history of the music of Scotland, had nothing better than a minor post in the University Library. In order to hear what the *a cappella* music of the great Scottish composer Robert Carver sounded like, Farmer had to arrange it to be played by his theatre band during entr'actes. The Professor of Music at that time was a Scot, Robin Orr, and he told me this story without any apparent awareness that it might have been incumbent upon the music department, with its chapel choir, to do something about this music itself. As we have seen, Scottish composers of the stature of Iain Hamilton and Thea Musgrave also sought opportunity and employment abroad. Talking to a *Daily Mail* reporter back in 1950, Chisholm had given his own reason for the failure of Scotland to produce national symphonic music as being 'the lack of a school of musicians, because there is no co-operation between young composers. "Everybody's an individualist," he said.'[30]

In Cape Town, however, he was in a position to dictate, and he had, for the most part, willing and admiring co-operation. He sent Percy Grainger a syllabus of the musical activities for the year at UCT, and got back this reply:

> What an immense undertaking & what a truly universalist attitude in the selection of music!
>
> That is indeed the only way to present the world's music, but most musicians lack the catholicity of taste & breadth of vision to be able to compass it.
>
> A thousand congratulations![31]

On 6 November 1955, Erik's mother died. She remains something of an enigma. Her grandchildren found her severe, and Chisholm himself makes little reference to her. She and her husband had come out to join the family in Cape Town for a few weeks in the late 40s. But it was she who had been the singer, she who noted his first essay in composition and she who made the best strawberry ice-cream and who was prepared to sit in the front of the Harley-Davidson sidecar, with her baby on her knee. And it was she, perhaps most important of all in Chisholm's mind, who was a MacLeod and therefore gave him a link to the traditions of *piobaireachd* and to that ancient culture which was the *fons et origo* of practically everything he did (see Chapter 1).

Deeply sensitive to the universality of life, Chisholm, a few months later, launched into a heartfelt attack upon the effects of modern weaponry – effects which for him included everything from the simplest forms of life to the entire creation:

> An explosion in a Welsh mine in which twelve men lost their lives recently, was described by the English press as 'terrific'. If this explosion is 'terrific', what word would one use to describe the one at Hiroshima which destroyed 300,000 people? And to go on from these little pops to the real Mackay, what shall we call the collision between a globular and spiral galaxy in N.G.C. 5128, whose pulsating radio waves were broadcast on New Year's night?
>
> If a baboon is an 'aggressive brute' because it claws a woman's arm and tears

her cardigan, shift one or two arcs of time down the evolutionary scale and try and find words to describe the more recent outrages of modern man; for example, the deliberate and unwarranted attacks (homo sapiens thinks it more decent to call them nuclear-atom 'tests') by the Americans and the British on the maritime population of the Pacific – killing 'innocent' fish by the millions! – or find a word to describe the depth of moral degradation in men who hope and aspire to a 5,000 mile-an-hour guided missile to liquidate a continent.[32]

Chisholm followed this up with a further letter to the editor of the *Cape Times*, describing the horror of animal slaughter for consumption and declaring that he had severed his connections with the animal corpse factories ever since seeing an animal parade in Singapore with notices reading 'LOVE YOUR ANIMALS BY NOT EATING THEM'.[33] However, according to his daughter Morag he was not refusing food from animal sources during his earlier years in Cape Town, so the above statement is perhaps a little exaggerated.

Happier human affairs arrived that year when the fine young Scottish pianist Virginia Fortescue joined the UCT staff as a lecturer. Chisholm had been in love with her during his ENSA days in Britain (see Chapter 5) and wrote to her most sympathetically on hearing of her husband's death in Burma less than three months after they were married.[34]

1956 was also the year of his second daughter, Sheila's, marriage. Chisholm gave a speech of sufficient silliness and with enough bad jokes to act as an exemplar of the genre, stating that:

> Sheila has not only inherited her father's grace, charm and beauty, which is pretty obvious – but seems also to have his gift of making enemies. Fiona, who is taking first year Biology at the University, says that it is something to do with the shape or size, or is it the colour, of the chromosomes!
>
> I remember the playwright James Bridie once consoling me in a bad moment by saying that 'A man's strength of character and personality can be determined by counting the number of his enemies.'

It would be surprising if Chisholm did not, for a moment at least, make an enemy of his own daughter with such a pronouncement, even if meant more as an affectionate compliment than a criticism, and what really pleased him about the day was the sense he had of the union of the two worlds which he perforce inhabited:

> If you look around the walls to the delightful decorations of George Jaholkowski, you will find that he also has blended the Protea and the Thistle; and that is what today's marriage really means.
>
> I am delighted that a daughter of mine has married into a pukka Afrikaner family, although if this sort of thing is encouraged, political life in South Africa will become intolerably dull.[35]

That autumn, the effects of the new apartheid policy began to kick in. At the last minute, the Town Clerk had suddenly forbidden six of the regular members of the University Orchestra, who were drawn from the Municipal Orchestra, to appear, but the substitute players rose to the challenge and indeed one could say that the entire music department rose to yet another challenge, this time imposed by Chisholm in the form of a tour in Europe. To get a feel for the significance of this, one must put oneself into the mind of a colonial society in a relatively small city, thousands of miles from the cultural centres to which it still owed much allegiance. One did not expect London or Amsterdam to pay much attention to what went on in Cape Town. Even less did one expect that if one went to these centres with student performers, there would be anything other than a thoroughly condescending attitude to such a venture. None the less, Chisholm persuaded the University Council to make a loan of £400 towards costs of getting students to London, the loan being at 5 per cent per annum, to be repaid by the end of 1958 and secured by Chisholm's own salary, as he had suggested.[36]

They had the sense not to bring easy favourites. Instead, on 9 January 1957, they gave the British première of Bartók's *Bluebeard's Castle*, Chisholm's *Inland Woman* and Van Wyk's song-cycle *Of Love and Forsakenness*, which was featured in a programme of music by South African composers, including Joubert and Du Plessis.[37] They also featured works by Janáček, whose music was little known even in London in those days.[38] Chisholm's own developing work on the *Celtic Song Book* was given a hearing, the critic approving the choice of words but not the accompaniments[39] – an opinion I would choose to reverse. They followed this up with a mixed programme of South African pieces, all set alongside Granados, Berg and Szymanowski. The *Times* review is as good as one could expect from London critics who were not without their own colonial bias:

> The series of concerts has brought forward much interesting music: the performers have been well prepared in works, some of which are extremely difficult: it is the standard of sheer execution which seems to lag behind musical enthusiasm at Cape Town.[40]

The tour was much more of a success than this would suggest. Roy McNab, the cultural attaché at South Africa House, wrote:

> This venture must be accounted the greatest success of its kind ever undertaken by an oversea [*sic*] Commonwealth country in London.
>
> I would suggest that no cultural incursion into this country has made a greater impression since the visit of the Russian Bolshoi ballet.
>
> 500 column inches of Press publicity have so far appeared. Favourable comment came from journals 'normally unfriendly to South Africa', and a television recital reached some 4,000,000 viewers, while an appearance in the top radio programme 'In Town To-night' reached millions more.[41]

Mosco Carner wrote in *Time and Tide*:

Two things stand out from these performances. One, that the young forces under Dr. Chisholm's energetic command are inspired by a spirit of adventure that is sorely lacking in our own London music schools; the other, that they contain artistic material potentially as good as we turn out ourselves, and in one or two instances, superior. They offered us fare which it would be difficult to match for variety and scope.[42]

George Jaholkowski's outstanding set was used again,[43] but the orchestra had to be severely reduced because of inadequate space at Rudolf Steiner Hall. Approval had, however, been given by Bartók's son, Peter, writing from the New York offices of Bartók Records, who had themselves issued what might well be described as the definitive recording:

Dear Dr. Chisholm:

I am delighted to receive your letter stating the plans for your forthcoming pro-duction of BLUEBEARD'S CASTLE in London during December and January.

Although the facilities of the theatres you mentioned do not permit use of a large orchestra, nevertheless I am sure there are some gains to be made through a more intimate production.[44]

They also gave *Bluebeard's Castle* in the Stevenson Hall, Glasgow, on 28 and 29 January 1957,[45] and the Glasgow Arts Centre hosted a 'Recital of songs and piano music from Erik Chisholm's *A Celtic Song Book*', under the aegis of the

21 Erik Chisholm at the piano, by Margaret Morris, 1957

Dunedin Society; so the Society was still ticking over, though described by one commentator at the time as 'somewhat shadowy.'[46] The singers were Kathleen Nesbit, William Noble, Sally Thomson and Hilda Stewart.[47] Apparently Désirée Talbot and Albie Louw were also there. Erik Chisholm was at the piano, and Margaret Morris was in the audience sketching (illus. 21, 22), clearly delighted to be in the company of her old colleague of Celtic Ballet days (see Chapter 5).

22 Erik Chisholm with cat, by Margaret Morris, 1957

Maurice Lindsay wrote a lengthy and intelligent review of the *Celtic Song Book* for the *Glasgow Bulletin*, finding much to praise, but also much to criticise.[48] *A Celtic Song Book* brought together traditional Highland melodies from the Patrick MacDonald collection and verses culled from a' the airts: but the lyrics were already fixed and had to be fitted to tunes already fixed. Sometimes they make a tight squeeze.

That year, Chisholm gave the Cramb Lectures for the University of Glasgow, devoting them to *A Celtic Song Book*. The draft scripts speak of his serendipitously coming across a library of Celtic material which provided him with many potential texts for the collection. The lectures contain interesting points of analysis – notably of Patrick MacDonald's No. 6, *O chiadain an lò*. Chisholm understands the form of the melody perfectly and maintains it would be nigh impossible to set words to it. But being unfamiliar with Gaelic verse forms and speech rhythms, he was in no position to judge the matter. He wrote: 'I had no earthly idea where one might look for the original words; and besides were there not quite enough Gaelic and Lowland songs in circulation as it was?[49]

This is not a strong argument, as some of the songs to which these tunes belong are crying out for resurrection, and others are very well known in the Gaelic world and would be regarded as among the classics of seventeenth- and eighteenth-century song, with lyrics by some of the greatest Gaelic poets of postmedieval times. The endnote lists the most famous corresponding poets and the appropriate titles of the verses.[50]

As for the accompaniments, Chisholm maintained:

> [M]y belief is that folk-songs should be performed without any accompaniments. If for practical performing conditions today you <u>must</u> write an accompaniment I see no reason why it should necessarily be written in so-called traditional or classical harmony. Accompaniments, like song and opera translations, follow a style or fashion for a certain period, but require to be re-written every so often in a style more in keeping with contemporary literary and musical thought.[51]

What Chisholm achieves in *A Celtic Song Book* is a later twentieth-century version of Marjory Kennedy-Fraser. His accompaniments are more varied, imaginative and, occasionally, intrusive, though, for the most part, the skill is easily a match for his earlier purely instrumental arrangements of the Patrick MacDonald airs. That said, no amount of ingenuity can circumvent the awkwardness that inevitably arises from combining lyrics and tunes that were never intended for each other.

CHAPTER 9

Soviet Ambassador

Chisholm behind the Iron Curtain

IN JULY AND AUGUST OF 1957, ERIK AND DIANA WERE GUESTS OF THE USSR. They travelled via Helsinki, where Diana had the utmost trouble preventing Erik from ringing Sibelius at 2.15 a.m., having looked him up in the telephone book.[1] Since Chisholm was going to conduct and required rehearsal time, they were part of an advance guard from Britain and found themselves in the company of John Osborne and his troupe, on their way to perform *Look Back in Anger*.

When they arrived in Moscow, Kabalevsky greeted them. They were given a suite in the Ukrainia hotel and a chauffeur-driven car, which was frequently mobbed, and both were showered with flowers and kisses. They met Bulganin and Khrushchev at a reception in the Kremlin, and on his last appearance conducting the State Orchestra in the Bolshoi Hall, Erik was given an ovation and was embraced by every single member of the orchestra. He also served on a jury, judging 200 different works under the chairmanship of Shostakovich,[2] gave a series of lectures, and the Minister of Culture offered to publish the entire 200 songs in the *Celtic Song Book* – a proposal which, though only partly realised, put his own and his adopted countries to shame.[3] He was impressed by the student residences and grant system, and he noted the Russians' love of classical music and the excellent supply of it in record shops, and himself bought over seventy LPs. He also visited the Lenin Library, the Scriabin Museum (which he was able to present with a rare recording of Scriabin playing some of his preludes) and watched Obraztsov's puppets.[4]

Of course, Chisholm was always well to the left of centre in his political views and was ready to find the best in the Soviet world, even commenting with apparent approval on the crowded attendances in the churches, despite not being a Christian.[5]

Agnes Walker was with them, to perform Chisholm's *Hindustani* Piano Concerto: 'Had my first concert last night: which went with a bang, even if Agnes Walker made a hell of a mess of the solo piano part.'[6] The reason for this was her mistaken attempt to perform it from memory, having been told this was expected in Russia. But she had also performed it in 1954 and, according to the Russian singer Oda Slobodskaya, had done so 'magnificently. She made a striking impression with her assurance and musi[ci]anly playing. She held my attention from the beginning to the last note.'[7] Slobodskaya appears to have been a fan of Chisholm's, addressing him as 'My dearest Erik', to which he replied with 'Darling Oda.'[8]

The trip to Russia did not cure Chisholm of itchy feet, and it would seem that,

23 Chisholm and Shostakovich

later that year, he had shown interest in a position at the Peabody Conservatory in Baltimore, for Nicolas Slonimsky wrote to him suggesting he apply direct to the board of trustees.

> Since you have had educational and administrative experience, they ought to be interested. Besides, you are a 'name' and that counts, too, and you are not involved in any intramural American teaching situations. It would be swell if you would get it![9]

He also got support from Henry Cowell, who wrote:

> Delighted to hear from you. We have thought of you so often as we spent last year going around the world – alas! – only in the north temperate zone.
>
> Your activities, as usual, read like a fairy tale. They are wonderfully impressive, and I am sending your material with my recommendation to the Peabody Conservatory. I am not there now, but am on excellent terms with them there. It would be splendid if you were there – I'd enjoy having you nearby. Hearty greetings
>
> Henry
>
> P.S. Yesterday I finished my 13th symphony![10]

24 Erik Chisholm conducting in Moscow

Whether Chisholm applied has yet to be determined, but if he did, nothing came of it. Instead, there was a call to Czechoslovakia, for Erik and Morag (recruited at the last minute as an assistant and five months pregnant) were invited by the Minister of Culture to Brno for the Janáček festival.[11] Leave of absence was granted, as well it might be, since in that year Chisholm was awarded a Fellowship by UCT 'in recognition of your distinguished work'.[12] But the Fellowship was only for five years, was not renewed and resulted in a drop in salary. Fellowship and salary were shortly afterwards reinstated.[13] Such are the ways of universities.

The trip was to prove a revelatory experience, with performances of many Janáček works, including all the major operas. It was a time when there was little interest in Janáček's music in the West, and any journey behind the Iron Curtain was regarded as fraught with dangers. Upon their safe return, Morag's young husband wept with relief, something she saw him do only on two other occasions.[14]

Meanwhile, her father was true to form, firing off his own broadsides to the newspapers, which, though without the venom of a Sorabji, had their own uncompromising critical penetration.

> As always I enjoyed your letter in the newspaper ... It must be embarrassing to argue in public with you – you're always so squashingly right![15]

The letter in question was probably like the following, of which only a portion is reproduced here:

> My point in hauling up B. G. for her juvenile and perky criticism of Johanson's excellent sonata in dodecaphonic idiom was not conditioned by whether she, or anyone else, liked or disliked the work (a matter of complete indifference to me), but because she condemned the sonata on the grounds that the music was 'a lot of nonsense' and possesses 'no logical sequence'.
>
> One notes that in her reply she makes no attempt to justify her use of the phrase 'no logical sequence': indeed, the subject is not even touched upon. On the contrary, what could be more <u>logical</u> than a system, which in B. G.'s own words is 'arranging one tone after the other in a certain order and keeping that order incessantly'. If her ear fails to acknowledge the inherent logic of the musical sounds which her eyes can see to be logical on the music paper, then it is her ear and not the music which is at fault: the ear only 'hears' what the brain will accept, a state of reception conditioned by such matters as environment, education, experience, development, etc. For this reason, the 'primitive' Bantu, with a physical auditory apparatus the equal to our own, will make as little sense of a Beethoven symphony as apparently B. G. does of Johanson's music: both ears are uneducated in a particular direction. And, of course, we cannot hear the music of the Bantu with his own appreciation of its particular qualities, any more than we can now hear the music of Palestrina as it sounded to the ears of audiences in the 16th Century.[16]

The year ended with performances of *The Marriage of Figaro, Falstaff* and Arne's one-act comic opera of 1772 *The Cooper*, in a revision by Joseph Horowitz.[17]

The year 1959 saw the completion of Chisholm's 'rhythmical bacchanalia' or 'Ballad Opera', *The Midnight Court*, which is a wonderful battle in the Fairy Court between the women and the men of late eighteenth-century Ireland. Bryan Merryman's poem is an undervalued classic, and Chisholm's treatment of it more than worthy of performance. But 1959 was also a year of battles of another sort. The university had felled a couple of pine trees near the Music School, pine trees being an 'alien species' and the subject of righteous indignation on the part of conservationists, who are paid to have very strange versions of the proper history of the migration of plants. Chisholm, recognising, like most sensible Cape-dwellers, that the pines were just about their most reliable source of shade in a burning landscape, refused to provide music for the Graduation Ceremony.

The pressure on him to carry out his proper functions, was, however, enormous, and understandably so, and 'appeals from tearful graduates urged him to change his mind.' He finally appeared to capitulate, but no sooner had the students processed into the hall to the appropriate strains of *Gaudeamus Igitur* than the programme changed to 'McDowell's *In Deep Woods* and *To an Old White Pine*, sylvan arias by Handel, and concluded with *March of the Tree Planters*'. There were more than enough people aware of the controversy and the music to appreciate that their unrepentant professor had balanced the score.[18]

But far more serious than this controversy was that surrounding the proposed commissioning of the South African composer John Joubert to write an opera for the 1960 Union Festival. Joubert owed it to Chisholm that he had won a scholarship to London, and Chisholm was more than ready to find an opening for a leading composer of South African birth (see Chapter 7). The Bloemfontein Committee, possibly influenced by the South African Broadcasting Company, which held the musical reins of power, refused to commission it, proposing instead a festival overture, which was quite properly turned down by Joubert, who had already commenced work on *Silas Marner*. A letter to Joubert from Chisholm found its way into the hands of the press, and parts of it were quoted:

> What's behind it all? Goodness knows. Most probably sheer stupidity ... Could it be that you are not one hundred per cent Afrikaner and the opera is not about those crushing Voortrekker bores?

The letter went on to describe the Bloemfontein Committee as 'operatic boneheads', for which his apology was 'Surely I am letting them down lightly.'[19]

Let his daughter Fiona (herself a distinguished journalist) take up the story:

> Probably his most famous controversy was over 'The Bloemfontein Boneheads'. ... My father roared into battle with his usual white-hot enthusiasm. He

called the committee a bunch of 'operatic boneheads' and because they were in Bloemfontein, well, they soon became known as the 'Bloemfontein Boneheads'.

In an article in the Sunday Times on July 5, 1959, he had another crack at the 'BBs' (as they then were called) blaming them for being unable to distinguish between creative work and recreative work.

'Thus they are selecting operas merely to give big fancy parts to over-publicised South African singers such as Mimi Coertse.'

He got away with the slight on *Onse* [Afrikaans for 'our'] Mimi but was forced to apologise for his remarks about the 'worthy Voortrekkers'.

'I mean of course,' he hurriedly explained, 'that so diffuse a movement as the Voortrekkers is not a suitable subject for concentrated operatic treatment.'

Eventually *Silas Marner* was given its world premiere in Cape Town by the UCT Opera School, with Albie Louw in the title role and my father conducting.[20]

Joubert came out for the production (which was by Fiasconaro) in May 1961:

I thought the performance was splendid, especially considering the forces available. It was very stimulating – very well attended and well received. Chisholm had to move heaven and earth to get it put on. He was a workaholic – he had tremendous drive and enthusiasm and was extremely professional. He wrote a very good essay about the opera. It was generous of him.[21]

On such occasions the true mettle of a man is discovered, and Chisholm was made of the right stuff; for what was ultimately behind all of this was the sad and rising tide of Afrikaans nationalism which gave birth to apartheid.

But this was a time to celebrate as 1960 was not only the year of the Union Festival but also the Golden Jubilee year of the UCT South African College of Music. Chisholm's Foreword in the *Souvenir Programme* is a proud one, but full of generous acknowledgment of his predecessors:

Since its inception in 1910, the College has gained a reputation for being very much 'alive': it has always been much more than just an institution for training teachers and performers. Its extra-mural activities in concert and theatre arts (drama, opera and ballet) beginning in Cape Town, have now extended by extensive tours through the whole of South Africa, the Rhodesias, Belgian Congo, Kenya and (in 1957) even to Europe.

In the fullest sense this is an International College: students of all races can study here and there is no bias towards any one race in recruiting staff (our present teachers come from S.A., England, Scotland, Germany, Austria, Holland, Russia and Israeli [*sic*]). Music of all periods and nationalities is studied, including folk-music and jazz.

He followed this review with a look at the requirements of the next fifty years. These included close co-operation with the Municipality of Cape Town (something which never really came about) and he declared:

There should be a department of African Native Music Studies and both Europeans and Africans should be trained to collect, classify and study African Native music.[22]

Throughout 1959 he had been attempting to bring in leading musicians from Europe. In the case of Hindemith, travel and remuneration issues, conducted via Mrs Hindemith, were never resolved, although Hindemith seems to have been willing enough.[23] He also attempted to bring Shostakovitch to South Africa, but was told by the Ministry of Culture that 'Shostakovitch has never conducted a Symphony Orchestra, besides, his health does not allow him to leave Russia.'[24] Kabalevsky, on the other hand, replied personally and was apparently ready to make a serious contribution as a lecturer and conductor, declaring that 'such a trip to your country sounds to me most interesting.'[25] Approaches to Gilels and Ivanoff were, however, quite openly turned down by the Minister of Culture:

[T]hey are not allowed out of the country without special permit from the Minister of Culture and therefore both artists are not able to accept your kind offer to come to South Africa for the season 1960–61.

With respect

L. Soupagin.[26]

However, a little later, Chisholm having guaranteed entry permits for both artists, the negotiations were reopened. The correspondence is almost entirely from Chisholm, seeking clarification and confirmation. In the end, he had to write on 18 May 1960, stating that South Africa was in a state of emergency and suggesting that if any letters had been mislaid, the Ministry should send duplicates via William MacLellan in Glasgow, presumably in the hope of avoiding South African censorship of incoming mail from the Soviet Union. Finally, Soupagin wrote on 15 July cancelling all visits.[27] On the other side of the world, Copland was also approached, but seems not to have managed a reply. Such are the trials of those who, like Chisholm, attempt to do anything ambitious, particularly when dealing with countries which, though believing themselves to be politically diametrically opposed, are in fact eating and voiding each other's swill.

Chisholm made little of his own works during the festival, which ended up featuring Matyas Seiber and John Joubert,[28] but he did allow himself to end the whole event with a performance of his own *Pictures from Dante* and Mahler's *Das Lied von der Erde*, both of which he conducted.[29] The preparations involved a huge amount of organisation, in which Stanley Glasser, the Assistant Director, did much to galvanise the various artists, not to mention the committees to which the music department had to give progress reports.[30] The operas mounted that year were Arne's *The Cooper*, Pergolesi's *La Serva Padrona* – a real stalwart, not too taxing on younger voices – Telemann's *Pimpinone*, the second in Puccini's *Il Trittico – Suor Angelica* and Mozart's *Il Seraglio*.

The previous year they had toured with *Tosca* and *Falstaff*. The casts for this outstanding series of productions were, of course, a mixture of staff and students, but the energies employed to sustain such a varied and demanding repertoire, for which everyone was doubling up on costumes, scenery, lighting, shifting sets, catering and transport, speak for themselves. There can be few comparable musical institutions that have come close to such an output.

As if the music programme for the Jubilee were not enough, Chisholm was also trying to have films of ballet and opera sent out by the British Film Institute, for his own interest in cinema remained undiminished.[31] It was he who established the UCT Staff Film Society, which met on Sunday evenings at the College of Music.[32]

One small incident, however, left a sour taste in the mouth and provoked Chisholm into a response. Chisholm was not frightened of controversy, but his controversies were almost entirely conducted in the defence of others. Rarely, if ever, did he protest at criticisms of himself or his music. This episode arose in the columns of the UCT student magazine, *Varsity*, when their music critic, 'Pizzicato', wrote scathingly about Lawrence Leonard's conducting style, describing him as 'an apoplectic penguin'. Chisholm wrote to protest that the remarks were 'offensive' and to make it clear that 'Pizzicato'

> is not a music student nor in any way connected with the UCT Music Faculty. If he likes to enrol, in time we might possibly be able to substitute some knowledge for merely grimy gimmicks.

'Pizzicato' replied in the same issue that Chisholm, as well as Leonard, 'would benefit from a few lessons from Sargent. Perhaps in this way the learned Professor would acquire some of the knowledge about conducting which he thinks I lack.' This monumental piece of impudence was both defended and attacked by other correspondents, but Chisholm's final reply displays a winning combination of good humour and dignity without yielding an inch on the matter:

> Sir, – one expects criticism in an under-graduate newspaper to be bright, snappy, vital, imaginative and impressionable; if you like, uninformed, naïve and gauche, but **not**, I hope, nasty, spiteful, insulting and personally offensive.
>
> It was because some remarks of your contributor 'Pizzicato' appeared to me to belong to the latter category that I bothered to write to you: remarks, by the way, which, printed in one of our daily newspapers, would probably have landed both author and editor in a lawsuit for libel.
>
> I only wanted Mr. Leonard and readers of 'Varsity' to know that this display of pompous charlatanism did not proceed from anyone connected with the Music Faculty.
>
> So, Mr. Editor, for the reputation of yourself and your otherwise excellent paper, keep 'Pizzicato' well plucked, and at the foot of the bin – with the lid on.
>
> Erik Chisholm

P.S. – Sir Malcolm Sargent is not a '*model of dignity and restraint*'; on the contrary, he is a fine showman (as well as a fine musician) and on that account has been known to audiences for the past 25 years as 'Flash Harry'.

P.P.S. – The physical side of conducting can be mastered in a fortnight: a life-time is too short to master the mental – artistic – interpretative side of conducting – the side that *really* counts.

Leonard himself brought the whole matter to a dignified and charitable close the following week.[33]

Chisholm was still pursuing his interest in Eastern music and intended to visit India to work on a proposed opera on Kailidas's *Shakuntula*;[34] and he was as active as ever bringing unfamiliar music to public notice, writing proudly to William MacLellan in February:

For the last month or so I have been conducting the City Orchestra – will send you some programmes. I managed to work in some pieces by Chinese and U.S.S.R. contemporary composers – not to mention Scottish – the 'Dowie Dens o' Yarrow' (a stirring Overture by Hamish MacCunn) and my own 'Celtic Wonder Tale'.[35]

But the next time he wrote to MacLellan, it was to tell him that a state of emergency had been declared in South Africa and, believing his mail from Communist countries was being interfered with, to ask MacLellan to post an enclosed letter to Moscow and to act as 'go-between'.

Not that the censorship was all one way, for the *Celtic Song Book* had to be modified to satisfy the Russian musical censors:

One of the concert programmes [for a proposed tour by UCT musicians] will be A Thousand years of Celtic Story and Song (see enclosed) developed, of course, from my old Celtic Song Book, but I think a much more attractive proposition this time, with a narrator and all objectionable dissonances in the accompaniments now fully Sovietised.[36]

It is a measure of Chisholm's socialist leanings that even this totally unjustifiable intrusion upon his artistic integrity did not call forth from him an explosion of righteous indignation. Instead 1962 found him again in the USSR and renewing an old acquaintance:

In 1962 when I was in Moscow in the office of Mrs Lewtonowa of the USSR State Music Publishers, who looked after my interests and made Russian translations of the first volume of my *Celtic Song Book,* she said there was someone in Moscow who was anxious to meet me. Someone I had last met in Glasgow 31 years previously.

'It is a very old lady, and you will be doing her a pleasant little service if you would come with me right now and talk with her for a little.' I agreed if only because I was curious to see inside a private house in Russia and this was the first time I had ever been invited.

Mrs Lewtanowa took me in her car to one of those large blocks of flats, which were springing up all round Moscow. We went up in an elevator to the third floor, I think it was, walked along a rather dark corridor and rang the bell. The door was opened by a plumpish little woman, who looked at me with lively twinkling eyes before extending her hand, saying, 'Welcome to Moscow, Mr. Chisholm. We meet again after so long a time.'

Thirty-one years had made surprising little change in Mrs Medtner. She told me she had come to Moscow to edit a definitive edition of her husband's works. 'The two previous editors both died before finishing the task and they asked me to complete the editing before I died,' she said, with a pout and a smile.

I asked her how she remembered the Glasgow concert and me after all this time, when she must have accompanied her husband on hundreds of other concerts. She laughed gaily. 'Yes indeed, but there was something rather special about that concert,' she said looking warily at me. I caught her eye, and we both burst out laughing.

'Ah, that Mr. Henderson', she said, 'he was so jealous of you, so very jealous. He just would not let you come near my poor dear husband. We saw through it all, of course, but well (a Russian shrug of her shoulder) Mr. Henderson had been very kind to Mr. Medtner in London, and he did not wish to offend him.'[37]

The trip had started off in Riga, but it was not only Chisholm who went on tour to Latvia in September. Cedric Thorpe Davie and Frederick Rimmer were with him.[38] In Riga he was lionized. He appeared on TV and radio and was even thinking about getting a job in the Soviet Union as a composer.[39] He mentioned in his speech to the Latvian Composers' Union:

> You might be interested to know that, of the 6000 students attending my university, 370 of them last year were Bantu or Coloured – that, in my own dept of 600 students 47 were <u>non</u>-European & we had ten such students taking a full-time diploma. C. Town University is the most liberal-minded of all the S.A. universities & Government legislation will soon put a stop to this mixing of races at our universities – & that is a major reason why I intend leaving S.A. in a year's time.
>
> It is only fair to say that the National Government in S.A. (which I detest) is providing separate University education for the non-European (non white) people of S.A.[40]

Chisholm followed up this introduction with a four-hour session with Latvian composers. No doubt exchanges were discussed, and there was considerable interest in mounting a production in Latvia of Chisholm's latest opera, *The Pardoner's Tale*.

▦ The Pardoner's Tale

This, one of Chisholm's finest scores, had been premièred at the Little Theatre in October 1961. Following on the modernist style of *Dark Sonnet* and *Simoon*, and the deliberately uneasy idiom of *Black Roses*, *The Pardoner's Tale* comes as quite a contrast. Here Chisholm's restless muse has not simply put on a medieval gown, for she sings in Middle English, and the rhythm and flow of her melody are medieval also.

The idea of setting Chaucer in the original Middle English seems to have been Chisholm's alone. Quite what prompted him is not clear. He was not insensitive to language, being one of the first to point out its importance in the work of Janáček (see Interlude: The Love of Janáček) and he used Scots in *Robert Burns*. But he never set any Scottish Gaelic to music, although he used its song melodies over and over again and certainly knew the original lyrics of several of them. At the time of composition of the Chaucer operas, he wrote an essay entitled *The Wonder of English*.[41] It is clearly prompted by his disgust with the rising tide of the Afrikaans language and nationalist movement. It endorses English as the best candidate for a universal tongue, welcoming the prospect of the demise of the Babel of tongues, which he regards as a cause of misunderstanding and strife. Only at the end of the essay does he curb his enthusiasm with a more realistic observation: 'Bi-lingualism seems to be the immediate answer: your native language and some universally understood tongue.'[42]

Chisholm's opera productions were generally in English, with specially commissioned translations if need be; so it is particularly striking that, when it came to his own composition, he should have stuck with the Middle English, although a parallel modern English text has been added to the vocal scores of *The Pardoner's Tale* and *The Nun's Priest's Tale*. The status of this modern English translation is not clear, but was possibly there to assist the conductor and singers in comprehension, if not intended for use in production. Perhaps the real reason for using Middle English was not so much one of communicability as musicality, and in this he had the endorsement of none other than Nevill Coghill, who was probably the leading Chaucer scholar of his day:

> So far as I know no one has ever set Chaucer in the real text; I think Dr Jacobs'
> Prologue is in a modernised version, but am not very sure – yes, now I remember,
> I think it is in mine. It was some time ago. The original text is incomparably more
> singable, if the singers know how to pronounce it![43]

It is its singability that is one of the best reasons for sticking to the original. So long as the metre is respected, Chaucer's Middle English can be read and sung, word for word, using pronunciation very close to the modern English of your choice, with far less damage to the original than the ghastly, mannered attempts at reproducing a putative medieval accent pedalled by some academics. Coghill, I fear, was of their number, but the fact is that Chaucer's text, whether read aloud or silently, would probably have had a variety of pronunciations, for there was no centralised norm in his day. Did Chaucer, in reading in English to a French-speaking Norman court, read with a French accent or in his own regional English accent? We do not know. So long as some artificial scholarly norm is not imposed, there need be no serious issue of comprehension, but, at the same time, the flavour of the original can be substantially retained without loss of spontaneity. This was the case in the 2004 production of *The Pardoner's Tale* in Cape Town, where a brief introduction to the work, and clever production, solved any problems of comprehension there might have been.

The Pardoner's Tale received its world première on 28 October 1961, in the Little Theatre, Cape Town, and was revived there on 5–7 February 2004. Chisholm set Chaucer's original Middle English, with a cast of eight singers plus two narrators, and the role of the Old Man – Death – was created by the first black student to enrol at the UCT Opera School.[44] The opera is scored for single wind and brass, timpani and percussion (including medieval-style tambour or a side-drum without snares), piano, organ, harmonium and strings.[45] A pencil note on the MS full score describes the stage setting:

> This opera requires a composite set for its short scenes: (a) at back stage slightly L. built on rostrums a room in a tavern, later the Apothecary's shop. (b) L. down stage a style with a path (through a wood) sweeping up to an oak tree R. beside which the treasure is found. There must be sufficient space in this area for the fight.

Chisholm sticks closely to the story as told by Chaucer at the heart of *The Pardoner's Tale*, but he omits the Pardoner's extended moralising that surrounds it, for the opera is not concerned with the Pardoner himself, and he does not appear, nor is he mentioned, unless the Narrator be cast as the Pardoner. The opera is in two parts, the first being divided into two scenes preceded by a brief introduction. The music is itself inspired by medieval rhythmic and melodic style, but given new vigour with the use of chromaticisms and polytonality.

> I drafted a libretto on Chaucer's Pardoner's Tale. Then did the voice parts & now started work on the orchestral accompaniment: this is difficult – to find a 20thc harmonic idiom not too remote from my consciously contrived 14thc vocal line. However by trial and error I may succeed.[46]

The opening figure in the bass line, descending step-wise in thirds, has a subtle suggestion of the *Dies Irae*, which is thoroughly appropriate for the subject of the tale. This motif appears at the end of the introduction and returns at the conclusion of the opera, and echoes of it are heard on other occasions when Chisholm wishes to remind us of death. But the theme is never quoted literally, and Chisholm slightly alters the intervallic values to ensure that it does not parade itself as crudely as it does in the works of many another composer. Another medieval echo occurs when the three Roisterers discover the gold under the oak tree and briefly sing 'Alleluia' in faux-bourdon, underlining the blaspheming of the men.

It is possible that Chisholm was aware of the beautiful medieval Scottish carol 'All Sons of Adam', in which the angels sing in the typical parallel chords of faux-bourdon to distinguish them from mankind. Later, the First Roisterer sings a brief section of the well-known opening to the early mediaeval *Lamento di Tristano* on the words 'and he that hath the cut, with herte blithe, Shal renne to the town and that ful swithe, And brynge us breed an wyn ful prively'. Angelo Gobbato, referring to the clashing of contrapuntal themes 'as so often happened in mediaeval music',[47] picks on another of its aspects which would have been particularly striking in the 1960s, when few audiences would have been familiar with medieval styles.

The story tells of three drunken Roisterers who set out to kill Death. Death, disguised as an Old Man, is its central figure. His song, *Allegro agitato e poco rubato*, accompanied by solo string quartet, is hauntingly weary and sad, its modal and rhythmic character based directly upon *Worldes blis*, a beautiful thirteenth-century Anglo-Saxon song which Chisholm might have gathered from Wooldridge's *Early English Harmony*.[48] The three rogues have abused the Old Man for living so long, but he replies that no one will exchange their youth for his old age, and even his mother, the earth, will not receive him (ex. 21).

He tells the three that Death, whom they seek to destroy, frequents the old tree nearby. There they find gold and wait until night to take it home with them, glorying in their wealth. One goes to fetch food and plots to poison the other two. They, meanwhile, plot to kill him. All three succeed. The Old Man reappears and reveals himself as the skeletal figure of Death, pronouncing the moral *Radix malorum est cupiditas*.

Comparing the different versions, it is clear that alterations to the score are of the type driven by experience in rehearsal or performance. Extra bars were added where the action was likely to require more time, for instance when the Old Man is first sighted, or when the three Roisterers discover the gold under the oak tree. But extra bars were also added simply to give breathing space to the music, particularly in winding down the opening scene and in the Old Man's song. On other occasions, the vocal parts were extended on top notes for increased dramatic effect, as when the Roisterers celebrate their 'riche tresor'.

Chisholm's colleague Pulvermacher wrote a review of it:[49]

In his music Erik Chisholm shows that he is highly sensitive to the poetic cadence of the 'heroic' decasyllabic metre of the richly inflective English language of the 14th century ... Chisholm's scholarly mind could not fail to notice the attraction of the supple syncopated rhythms, the bold treatment of dissonances and the free contrapuntal texture of the 'Ars Nova', elements of which he has used to add to his own, entirely contemporary music a special flavour, so to speak, superbly suited for Chaucer's expressive language.

Ex. 21 *Pardoner's Tale*

Dramatically and vocally, this is a highly effective opera, well contrasted between solo and ensemble passages, as well as by the speaking part of the Narrator. As usual with Chisholm, the orchestration is colourful without being exploited for its own sake. The accompaniment to the Old Man's aria, with its grim drumbeats and later dark wind and string tones, is uncanny, and Chisholm contrasts this with the crude interpolations of the three Rogues. Later, he gives a striking false brilliance to their delight in their apparent wealth, immediately set off by the Narrator followed by cor anglais and low clarinet and tremolo strings, for the scene in which one of the Rogues buys poison at an apothecary's. Echoes of this scene, with drum taps and triangle, are heard at the end between the celebratory cries of triumph of the two Rogues who have just murdered the third and are now, unwittingly, drinking poisoned wine. The C major I–V–I chord sequence, repeated over and over, creates powerful dramatic irony (ex. 22).

Chisholm had a recording made of the first production, as Coghill reveals:

I should love to hear your Pardoner's Tale recording; would it be possible for you to come and dine with me and spend the evening over your Chaucerian work? I am just out of hospital and not supposed to gad about too much, so you would be

Ex. 22 *Pardoner's Tale*

doing me a favour if you came to Merton. ... I used to play the fiddle a lot, but one can't keep one's standard, let alone improve, at less than 2 hours a day; and where am I to find them? So I have given up playing these ten or fifteen years, and now could hardly play an open note without an ugly noise. I can hope, however, to help over the W. of B. and look forward to hearing your problems.[50]

The Nun's Priest's Tale

Chisholm sometimes referred to this opera as 'my Chauntecleer the Cock opera' and had written quite a sizeable chunk of it by March 1961, staying with Sheila and her husband, Peter, at Durbanville. 'They have 4 hens & I bought myself a cock – to get his voice well into my bones. I love the country life, with hens, all the birds in the world & a moo-cow or two.'[51] On the back of the full score, Chisholm has written 'Music composed March – April 6, 1961 at ... Durbanville.'[52]

The vocal score was 'made Dec 23–31/1961 at 108 Westway Oxford at Morag & Ralph's place with Terry, Deirdre, Jennifer, Fiona & Aunt Hely', as Chisholm himself recorded.[53] The presence of the children is relevant, as this is, in many respects, a children's opera. He took the libretto directly from an off-print of the Chaucer, which he annotated in pencil, in particular putting in the accents,[54] presumably as advised by Coghill, whom he had visited in Oxford. The characters are Chauntecleer, the cock (baritone); Pertelote, his wife (soprano); the Fox (light tenor); the Widow (soprano); her two daughters (soprano); and a female chorus of Six Hens, Chaucer's seven being made up by Pertelote, who takes the place of each hen that has a solo.[55]

The story is no more than a moral fable in the manner of Aesop. Chauntecleer has had a bad dream of being caught by a fox, and his wife accuses him of cowardice and blames his digestion for the dream, which he should cure with a purgative. Her endless stream of advice finally provokes the cock into an equally lengthy defence of the significance of dreams, based upon classical authors. They agree to disagree and sing a Serenade and Hymn to Love. Chisholm gathered words for the latter from Chaucer's *Troilus and Criseyde* and the tune from Guillaume de Machaut's ballade, *Ma chère dame*. There follows a delightful Chorus of Hens and a rondel welcoming summer, with words taken from Chaucer's *The Parlament of Fowles*, and they all troop out of the hen-house into the yard.

At this point the Fox appears. He calms Chauntecleer's suspicions and praises his singing, inviting him to see if he can match his father's matchless crowing. Chauntecleer is deceived by the flattery and crows his loudest with his eyes tight shut. His vocal display is comically set against the dancing rhythm of the anticipatory glee of the Fox, by whom he is, of course, seized. Funnier still, is the exaggerated Latin Lament of the hens, led by Pertelote (ex. 23).

This alerts the Widow and her daughters, who give chase, the music involving the hens' frantic clucking. Meanwhile, Chauntecleer, having been dragged to the

23 *Nun's Priest's Tale*

continued overleaf

Illus. 23 *continued*

edge of the woods, appeals to the fox's own pride to turn and shout at his pursu-ers – which he does, thus releasing Chauntecleer, who flies up into the trees. A triumphal procession follows, with the moral, in the form of a vaudeville, sung by Chauntecleer, Pertelote and the Fox. They are all wiser after the event, and the Widow advises us not to ignore the moral just because it is a story of a cock, a hen and a fox.

Nor should we ignore this opera just because it is a simple story, told in rela-tively simple musical language. Perhaps new love (see below), young grand-children or a desire to move on from dodecaphonic techniques also took hold of Chisholm and prompted him to employ a much less dissonant and more direct style. It is, in any event, an absolutely delightful piece of fun – one which, if not produced with its Chaucer companions, would make an excellent foil to *Hansel and Gretel* in an operatic evening for children. It has never been performed.

◼ The Wyf of Bath's Tale

The remaining opera of the Chaucer triptych was *The Wyf of Bath's Tale* com-pleted in 1962,[56] during his sabbatical year in Britain and in the midst of his affair with Lillias Scott, for which see Chapter 10. If he was aware of any ironies in this connection, his correspondence does not suggest it. But the recipient, Diana, must have been acutely conscious of such things, and the following ending to a letter in which he asks her to release him to marry Lillias can only have been written in a moment of thoughtlessness, for the general tenor of his letters is mostly as thoughtful and as considerate as such a situation might allow.

I'm writing a passacaglia at the spot where the old wife insists in keeping the young knight to the bargain & he has no desire to wed someone 'foul, & ould & poore'. Don't think too badly of me, Diana, if you can. Love ever Erik x x[57]

Whatever Diana may have thought, Coghill was pleased that Chisholm was working on it:

Thank you very much for your letter; it is delightful for me to think that my little editions, which were aimed at a school audience, should have been of use at a so much higher level. I missed the review of your music as I was deep in the country, where the Times did not reach me. I am very glad to hear you are working on the W of B's Tale. Years ago I suggested this fable as a basis for the scenario of an opera to Christopher Fry, but it didn't 'take' with him. I am not thinking of doing an edition of her story.[58]

The characters are the Knight (baritone); the Old Wife (mezzo); King Arthur (tenor); the Queen (coloratura soprano); the Young Wife (lyric soprano); a Soldier (baritone); and a Clerk (baritone), plus chorus. The orchestra consists of strings, single wind plus cor anglais, piano, electric organ, celesta, glockenspiel and xylophone, but with vibraphone and mouth-organ thrown in, along with a wind machine and the usual percussion.

The plot revolves around a Knight who has to atone, with his death, for having committed rape. The Queen asks that he be judged by one who was once a maiden and offers him his life if he can, within a year, answer the question 'what is it that women most desire?' He receives so many contrary answers that he despairs, until he meets an old hag who gives him the answer, in return for his promise to undertake the first thing within his power when she requires it of him.

The answer is that women desire sovereignty over their husbands or lovers more than anything else, and this is agreed by the Queen, when he returns. He is duly granted his life. At this point the old hag appears and demands his hand in marriage. He is revolted at the idea, but on their wedding night is given the choice of her as an old woman and faithful or as a young beauty, taking his chances on her behaviour. He leaves the decision to her, and is rewarded with both beauty and the promise that she will be true.

The opera is divided into four scenes, with orchestral interludes at the ends of Scene I and Scene II. The word 'vaudeville' (which Chisholm used to describe a scene in The Pardoner's Tale) is not used here, but might reasonably be applied to the whole opera. It commences with a procession, the interludes are character pieces, there is a scene with off-stage voices to be heard through an echo-chamber and accompanied by wind machine, and there is a Dance and Song of the Fairies and a Rustic Dance of Clowns, Tumblers and Jugglers. The part for the Queen (which could be doubled with that of the Young Wife), being for a coloratura soprano, adds to the heightened colouring, as does the use of a mouth-organ and organ in the second interlude. It is as though Chisholm had rouged the cheeks of this *Wyf of Bath's Tale*, staging it as a variety act rather than a serious piece. It is an imaginative and entirely appropriate response to the character of both the Wyf of Bath and her fairy-tale, whose mixture of the down-to-earth and the fanciful still survives in British pantomime.

But in 1962, a much more serious muse was to come to him in the form of Lillias Scott, daughter of Chisholm's erstwhile colleague F. G. Scott, and in this form she was to see Erik to his rest.

The Love of Janáček

ERIK CHISHOLM WAS NOT THOUGHT OF AS A SCHOLAR. HIS BACHELOR of Music degree and his doctorate in music were undertaken in an unorthodox manner. In the catalogues of Edinburgh University there is no reference to any material relating to Chisholm's submission for his doctorate. There is nothing in the Senate Minutes, and the schedule for graduates in music 1898–1950, confirming his graduations in 1931 and 1934, has, under the heading 'Courses of Study in the University', nothing more than 'studied subjects privately'.[1]

What this means is that, whatever training Tovey put him through, we cannot demonstrate that he had studied the then current musicological methodologies, or that he had conducted any in-depth analysis of a genre of works or an individual work. What we do know (see Chapter 2) is that Tovey and Chisholm were close to each other, and that as a student of Tovey, spending hours with him each week, with no one else to bother them, Chisholm had a unique opportunity to learn from a man who was regarded as one of the greatest all-round musicians of his time. We also know in what high respect Tovey held Chisholm (see Chapter 5), and it is worth pointing out that Tovey could himself be thoroughly radical in his approach to the explication and teaching of music.

> Professor Tovey always maintained that the writing of strict counterpoint was an intellectual exercise on a par with trigonometry, and consequently should be taught to the adolescent of thirteen rather than to the undergraduate of eighteen – but perhaps nobody learns strict counterpoint these super-serial days![2]

None the less, on becoming Dean of the Faculty of Music, as well as Professor and Principal of the College in Cape Town, Chisholm must occasionally have felt the need to address himself to the kinds of things that musicologists do: analysing works, tracing manuscript traditions, detecting influences, correcting scribal and printing errors and, occasionally, expressing pleasure in the material they discuss. In preparing rare Berlioz, Gluck and Mozart operas for performance (see Chapter 4), he had already some experience of working on the production of a proper edition, but these were not prepared to scholarly standards, which require justification for each decision, accompanied by thorough annotation. Chisholm's were working editions and none the worse for that.

As part of his duties in Cape Town, Chisholm had to devise courses and, in so doing, he took on a pedagogic role. Choices have to be made between this or that approach, and in Chisholm's case his approach was decidedly radical for the time. He accepted jazz as an integral part of musical development long before many another institution, and he was as eager to explore unusual repertoire as ever. But, apart from his compositions and articles scattered here and there, mostly of a relatively popular nature, Chisholm had not produced, never mind published, any major work of analysis.

One could describe the many different approaches he took to Scottish traditional music as works of analysis in their own right, especially when coupled with the Cramb Lectures on *A Celtic Song Book*, but in terms of scholarship these are nothing like weighty enough to set him up as a scholar rather than a creative mind. Did he, then, take on the work of analysis of Janáček's operas from a desire to impress himself upon the academic world? I do not believe so, and it is for that reason that I have given this Interlude the title 'The Love of Janáček', just as I gave the title 'The Love of Sorabji' to the first Interlude. He studied Janáček closely because he loved the music, and this study resulted in the publication of Chisholm's only book, *The Operas of Leoš Janáček*, commissioned by the Pergamon Press in 1963 on the basis of that enthusiasm.[3] Writing in 1959, the year after his and Morag's trip to the Janáček festival (see Chapter 9), he named Janáček as one of his five favourite contemporary composers:

> The contemporary composers I like best are Bartók, Hindemith, Janáček, Schönberg and Sorabji: maybe because I knew personally three of these composers fairly well. I once gave concerts in the U.K. with Hindemith and Bartók, and had the honour of conducting the first performance in that country of the latter's 'Bluebeard's Castle'.
>
> Janáček ... ignores the classical procedure of musical development and substitutes something of his own: repetition of small pregnant musical ideas treated with endless variations. Up till November of last year I knew most of his operas only from scores, although I had seen 'Jenufa' – the most popular of them: it was only after seeing all nine operas on the stage of the Brno Janáček theatre in Czechoslovakia that I was, like most of the foreign visitors and critics present, completely captivated by the dramatic power, effectiveness and originality of this great modern Czechoslovakian composer, indeed the only great contemporary Czechoslovakian composer. I believe that, along with Strauss and Puccini, he represents the best for opera in this century.[4]

The writing of Chisholm's book was squeezed in between the composition of his last operas and his continuing teaching and organisational functions. He never managed to put on a Janáček opera, but with his long experience in opera and, in 1964 alone, conducting the UCT Opera Company in productions of *Otello*, *Don Giovanni*, *Don Pasquale*, *Pimpinone*, *The Telephone* and *Susanna's Secret* he was certainly keeping his hand in with respect to the medium.[5] Having attended the Janáček festival and, having been honoured by the Czechs with the Dvořák medal in 1956, he was, in many respects, ideally placed to undertake an appraisal of Janáček's operatic output. On the other hand, he had no knowledge of Czech itself, nor did he have access to all the vocal scores or libretti, as John Tyrrell was quick to point out in his damning review of the book.[6] Tyrrell was a student of Chisholm's at the time the book was being written, and Ronald Stevenson has suggested that much of the work was undertaken by Tyrrell himself.[7] Malcolm Rayment, on the other hand, reviewing it for the *Glasgow Herald*, was thoroughly enthusiastic, declaring that 'No more valuable book on opera has been published since Ernest Newman's "Wagner Nights".[8]

Chisholm completed the book shortly before his death, and it was published posthumously. He had no chance to revise it at even a basic level of response to his publishers, never mind proofread it in a final version, but Ken Wright edited it sympathetically, if not anything like as rigorously as it required:

> Knowing him as I did, I can hear his Scots voice speaking the text, with his homely but striking allusions, colloquial phrases, and always with humour and humanity peeping through. Therefore I have in the main left his copy as he sent it.[9]

Of particular interest to Chisholm was Janáček's relationship with the Czech language. Chisholm, as a Scot, was naturally aware of the significance of the cadences and tonal qualities of his own native Scots. No Scot can take his or her use of Scots for granted. It is commented upon by any foreigner who speaks English, and this of course includes the English themselves. It was Robert Burns who was the first poet of international status to assert the rights of his language as a vehicle for poetry of the highest ambition, and Chisholm was at work on an opera based upon Burns's lyrics and his letters. As we have seen, Chisholm's own Scots voice is commented upon by his editor.

It might be thought that the comparison of Scots with Czech is a false one, but in the world of vocal music this is not so. The use of any language other than Italian for opera was an act of cultural assertion even in the nineteenth century. Beethoven studied Italian because that was what a musician should do to complete his technical equipment. To this very day, Universal Edition have yet to publish a full study score of Bartók's *Cantata Profana* with Bartók's own original Hungarian – an example of cultural imperialism which almost beggars belief. Chisholm, having twice visited the Czechoslovak People's Republic, must have been conscious of the importance of this issue. But the fact remains that he himself did not speak or read Czech with any degree of fluency, and many of his comments must have arisen from an instinctive rather than an intellectual appreciation of Janáček's use of Czech.

> Certain musicologists have closely related the difference between traditional folk music of various countries to the different speech habits of the people in these countries. As early as 1906, Janáček was advocating a plan for a musical dictionary of the Czech language ... within the microscopic musical cells is to be found the secret of Janáček's great originality and genius, and his compositional technique, of continually varying and repeating these short pregnant motifs which is a basic feature of his style, is also rooted in his speech curve studies.[10]

Had Chisholm lived longer, he might have pursued such techniques with respect to his own native language, as he did to a degree in the Chaucer operas, but in the Burns opera he was using traditional melodies which already address the issue and he had yet to develop a consistent position on matters related to language use. But it is clear from his study of Janáček that he was deeply appreciative of the connections between language and expression, and his own humour and humanity are not merely 'peeping through' in Chisholm's writing (as Wright puts it), they are shining through. He retells the stories of the operas with instinctive sympathy for the characters, and his comments on the music are practically always directed towards its dramatic function. It is this deep inner sympathy that makes his commentary so valuable. Typical is his treatment of the opening of *Jenufa*:

> The very first sound in *Jenufa* is the dry crackling, cricket-like timbre of a xylophone repeating a low C flat note above a pizzicato falling octave in the bass: somehow, the resulting effect is sinister, even threatening, and when the violins bring in their infinitely poignant melody with its persistently agitated two-note counterpoint, the mood is set for a drama which already hints at unusual emotional depths and personal tragedy.[11]

This is not how such books are normally written. Musicologists fight shy of adjectives, unless they are part of the composer's musical instructions and, preferably, in another language. But unlike many a musicologist, as Chisholm writes, so he hears in his head, and as he hears in his head, so he responds in his heart. The technical knowledge necessary to explain how such results are achieved is always there, but it is not flaunted. Technique has little value *per se*: its function is to enable the expression of ideas and feelings, and if these are not a part of the musicologist's reckoning, then the resultant study becomes not only dry in the extreme but divorced from its proper function almost to the point of irrelevance. Tovey's no-nonsense style of analysis may have been, for a spell, deeply unfashionable, but Tovey's editions and analyses are still in print. Others, who have dissected the living music with such assiduity that they have almost made a corpse of it, are now themselves ignored and will hopefully remain so. Chisholm did, however, include as an appendix an extended thematic analysis of Siskov's Monologue in *From the House of the Dead*, but here too he uses phrases such as 'forceful and belligerent' or 'a coarse all top and bottom version of the Filka theme', which are splendidly descriptive, but scarcely analytical.

Sadly, one has to admit that Chisholm's approach, for all its virtues, is aimed at an audience unlikely to purchase the book. The musicologists do not need the story to be retold, nor do they necessarily want their emotions to be stirred by a book, when the operas are there waiting for them. What they seek is analytical insight with evidence, discussion and demonstration. These are indeed present in Chisholm's work, but not as consistently and rigorously as would be possible today. His was, after all, the first book about Janáček published in the English language. It was, as with so much else in his life, a ground-breaking exercise. On the other hand, those who might enjoy such a study are unlikely to wish to buy and read a whole book on Janáček operas. Even Ken Wright, in his Editorial Note, conceded that 'As an opera composer and conductor his analyses are unusually perceptive, even though some may find them occasionally pedantic.'[12] That is not my experience in reading the book, but it might well be that of a general rather than a specialist reader.

What Chisholm has written is more like a biography and, in many respects, might be more profitably read as such and as a reflection of his own enthusiastic approach to his subject-matter. Tyrrell is no doubt right in condemning aspects of the book on scholarly grounds, but he has also chosen to ignore much that is of value and that may well continue to be of use to scholars of Janáček, as well as to scholars of Chisholm himself.

CHAPTER 10

Chasing a Restless Muse
The Heart's Betrayal

MOST PEOPLE'S HEARTS BETRAY THEM AT SOME TIME OR ANOTHER, but whether they betray an inner truth or necessity by exposing it, or cheat their owners into a false situation, is a matter of fine judgment. Chisholm's heart was undoubtedly restless, and his muse was not of the sort to stroke the fevered brow. They betrayed him doubly. They led him away from a marriage which had in many ways been an excellent and fruitful match, into a new and undoubtedly rejuvenating love and then failed to stand up to the strain, physiologically. Diana also had lost heart and was setting up her own establishment by late June 1961,[1] while Erik was already suggesting the possibility of divorce.[2] He was frequently out in Durbanville (where Sheila was living), having had his own Bechstein piano moved there,[3] and found his time in Cape Town a hell by comparison.[4] In Durbanville, he worked on *The Nun's Priest's Tale*, sending Sheila out to find a suitable cockerel to bring home so that he could make use of its crowing – the plot of the tale concerns a cock, a hen and a fox (see Chapter 9).

But the award of a sabbatical for 1962 was, perhaps, the final catalyst in the breakup of his marriage.

> I spent a considerable part of 1962 living in Scotland and in touch with my old friend the distinguished and also honorary member of your Burns Fellowship Club, Christopher Grieve (Hugh MacDiarmid). We agreed to collaborate together in the writing of an opera and I have suggested as a tentative subject and title 'ROBERT BURNS, HIS LIFE, HIS LOVES, HIS SONGS'.[5]

It was a sadly appropriate time for Chisholm to be studying Burns's loves in particular. Diana, who had been his mainstay and had supported him loyally for so many years, had never quite matched the sexual energies of a man who knew himself he had been born with too much energy. She had been a brilliant hostess; was musically sensitive; had borne him three lovely daughters, though the lack of a son did touch them; had coped, whether efficiently or not, with periods of genuine financial hardship; had carried out many secretarial functions; drove him everywhere (he never troubled himself to drive); was a clever writer in her own right, and a naturally gifted singer and pianist; and in her youth had possessed real beauty. What more could he have asked for? But there were differences. Erik had a canny streak to him and often accused Diana of mismanaging the household finances; and Diana would, almost unfailingly, have lost her car keys at precisely the moment when Erik, keyed-up for a performance, had to leave to get to the concert hall on time.[6] Perhaps the fact that she struck out a little on her own and took on work for the Cape Town and District Association for the Deaf, often taking up her evenings, gave him an unpleasant taste of the medicine that workaholic husbands give their wives: perhaps the whole sixties mood caught up with him, for he was after all in the company of students, day in, day out.[7]

His one public pronouncement on the subject of sex speaks for itself:

Q. What is your attitude to money?

A. Rather like sex: you don't really notice it until you haven't any.[8]

Erik had a considerable appetite for sex and did not restrict its gratification to the marriage-bed, though at what point in the marriage this started, and how many others were involved over the years, is matter for conjecture. There had been affairs on his side,[9] but marriages survive such things, as had his for some time. Maybe it had been a 'mid-life crisis' which came to a head a little late in the day. Back in 1954 he had proposed marriage to a former pupil, having dragged her away from her husband into the next room – a story told me 'just to illustrate his impulsive nature'.[10] In any event, he was feeling strangely vulnerable, for sometime late in 1962 he had written to Fiasconaro, suggesting that nobody in the faculty liked him. The whereabouts of this letter is not known, but Gunter Pulvermacher wrote back kindly, sensitively and reassuringly, with a full account of how the academic year had worked out in Chisholm's absence and also making gentle reference to his personal problems: 'Is it possible that this groundless opinion of yours has been influenced by your domestic troubles? … whatever the ultimate solution of your domestic difficulties will be – our attitude to you (I speak here for myself and the staff) is definitely unchanged.'[11]

It was during 1962 that Chisholm and 'Lovey' (Lillias) Scott became involved. Lillias's father, F. G. Scott, had died in November, 1958. He had admired Erik's skill and expertise but was suspicious of his eclecticism.[12] However, that did not prevent Lovey from falling for Chisholm. She was teaching in Knightswood, Glasgow, which she described as 'not quite me', when Erik asked her out to *West Side Story*. They didn't go. Instead they ended up at the famous Rogano restaurant, not eating much. Lillias was a poet, a singer, an old family friend and a good few years younger than Erik. 'In fact he was looking for a wife', she recalled; but he clearly lost his heart to her in the process.[13]

Morag and her husband were also in Britain, and Erik, though mostly on the move, lived in their house in Oxford. Morag, by then a mature woman with children, remembers him as being very much in love. She felt she could not stand in his way and was kind and welcoming to Lillias.[14] Characteristically, Erik had made his decision without giving himself time to review it: 'I gave up smoking, eating meat and took other big decisions at the drop of a hat – even proposing to my wife within hours of first meeting her.'[15] In London, Erik stayed with friends, and Lillias lodged nearby, but they were regular guests at the

Solomons', where Erik would place a bottle of wine on the piano as a thank you, though it was he who drank most of it. 'He was so happy – he got a new lease of life.'[16]

He was, however, still writing regularly to Diana, chatty, pleasant, unstrained letters; but in February, 1962 he raised the issue of their marriage and proposed a separation,[17] only later raising the subject of Lillias.

Meanwhile, he was working, perhaps not inappropriately, if somewhat ironically, on his opera based on *The Wyf of Bath's Tale*. In furtherance of his Chaucer trilogy, he dined with Nevill Coghill, who was most impressed with Chisholm's rendering of *The Pardoner's Tale*.[18] A visit to Sorabji followed, Erik taking a tape recorder with him to capture Sorabji's playing.[19]

Later that year, Erik and Lillias performed together in Manchester, the programme including four of Chisholm's settings of her poems (see below) and some of Lillias's father's songs.[20] It seems that she was originally going to go out to Cape Town with Chisholm, for Bill MacLellan ends a hasty note, written in the midst of a mounting crisis of debt:

> So Lovey did not come! ... She told Ronald Stevenson it was all off, so I suppose it's a heave ho on the old net to catch the other 'good fish' in the sea. How damnably unlike fish the delightful creatures turn out to be! Yrs Bill[21]

Uncertain about his own personal future, Erik must have been looking for separate accommodation for himself, for Tom Price, professor of Roman-Dutch law, wrote to him in December offering him a room in his own house 'Roscranna'.[22] Meanwhile, Lillias wisely took her time to make up her mind. She had her life still before her, whereas Erik was married (although he declared it was all over), and he was very much older. But the force of his personality, his music and the new life he had to offer her must have been powerful inducements when coupled with new love. She came out to join him in the end.

Early the next year, Mona Glasser, with marital troubles of her own, thanked him for his 'warm note and offer of help' and wrote, 'I <u>have</u> heard of your problems and truly hope that all works out well for you without too much pain and strife.'[23] If Chisholm's troubles were bad, Stanley Glasser's were worse. He had been caught with a coloured woman, was liable to be prosecuted under the Immorality Act and had to flee the country. Adultery across racial frontiers was made a more serious offence by a stiffening of the Immorality Act in the 1950s and could carry a substantial prison sentence.[24] In reply to letters from Erik,[25] Fiasconaro wrote about the situation:

> I then went to see Mrs. Glasser – she had just received your letter – I found her calm and resigned – she was very mooved [*sic*] for your kindness & she asked me to tank [*sic*] you very much – she is not bitter against Stanley, she is only bitter at his stupidity ...

On top of all this, Fiasconaro had to report that Phyllis Brodie ('Aunt P'),

Diana's sister and long-time secretary at the South African Music College, had somehow got to know of the contents of Erik's letter to Mona:

> she told Sheilah [*sic*] in the office that had she known the contents of your letter before readdressing it she would have not forwarded it!! I ask you, what on earth has Mrs Glasser done to her!! By the way, she is again up in arms because she knows about you coming back with Miss Scott.[26]

The letter goes on to suggest Priaulx Rainier as a replacement for Glasser, to approve proposals for more co-operation with the Stellenbosch conservatoire, to request operatic material and express willingness to put on a Gilbert and Sullivan work – 'there is no "depth" that I can't reach – also we would give a little shock to the local G & S Society.'[27]

If Fiasconaro and Chisholm were not infrequently at daggers drawn (see Chapter 7), there is no sign of it here: rather one gets the impression of two men of energy, humour and adventure, supporting each other through thick and thin.[28] There was no shortage of either, as Fiasconaro's next letter to Chisholm, with its idiosyncratic spelling, reports:

> Before your departure I want to write you once more to answer your letter of the 20th January – I had to laugh about your 'inspiration' for 'School for Scandall'!! How right you are! As a matter of fact I want to put you wise, before you arrive, about the very latest 'NEWS' that has been referred to me. She [Phyllis Brodie] says that almost surely you are going to offer her the post of 'Assistant Director', the reason being that you are going to try your very best to be nice to her, because you know well that without her the College could not go on!!! – Of course she did not say this to me – Now, I am all for it that you should have an Assistant, actuely I think you realy must have one to help you in running the College & to give you more time to composition. But please not Miss Brodie – I don't know if Pulvermacher has told you, but more than once she has absolutely acted as Director, above his head & making him feel a full. – Do you know that she has 'appointed' G. Miller!
>
> 'School for Scandal' should make a good opera, I hope you'll do it – By the way, do you think Miss Scott could sing 'Miss Prim'? If you think vocally she is allright for the part I'll be glad to have her & also I'll be happy to help her in whatever I can – I take off my hat to your decision of running your own life as you please – I admire you – If people would be less hypocrites & have more courage of their own actions the world would be much better off – Well, 'bon voyage' enjoy the sun have a good rest – I'll be at the docks at about 7.30 a.m. & I shall wait for you –
>
> Love Gigi.[29]

In the same year, Virginia Fortescue wrote to Erik about her own separation.[30] Though Chisholm was not directly involved, they were close friends.[31] At about the same time, Erik received a delightfully playful letter from one of his students, full of innuendo and addressing him as 'Dr. Chis'. It includes mention of Stravinsky's visit, in which he is described as 'a nice old guy but rather plain'. News of Erik's relationship with Lillias Scott must have reached the College, as she asks about his falling for an opera singer – 'Singers are dumb people man, I can't understand you. Please clarify'.[32]

Erik and Diana's divorce was granted in the Supreme Court of South Africa, Cape of Good Hope Provincial Division, on 9 May 1963. The grounds were a refusal to restore conjugal rights in response to a request for their restitution;[33] but this was, in all probability, merely a form of words to achieve a reluctantly agreed end. Erik and Lillias were married almost immediately afterwards, but of his daughters, only Morag was ready to accept the new situation. He wrote to her on 3 June of his gratitude and happiness – a happiness which must have communicated itself to his students, for he declared that they were 'all delighted with the "new" professor'. He was missing Morag and her husband, Ralph, and trying to persuade them to return to South Africa – 'the country is as beautiful as ever – just WONDERFUL these days.' But the shadows of apartheid were growing longer, so he also writes to assure them that the country is likely to remain stable, should they think of returning.[34] By September, still very much in love, he was writing that Phyllis had been cutting Lillias dead since February. Erik was fearful that the embarrassment would force him to ask for her transfer to another department and commented on the irony of the fact that she herself was associated intimately with a man who was already twice divorced: 'Here's Phyllis with this Holier-than-thou attitude about me being divorced, while at the same time she was proposing herself to marry a divorcee!!!'[35] The heart's betrayal, indeed. Sometime later, Phyllis 'caved in' and made friends with Lovey.[36]

Meanwhile, the Burns opera project continued to form an appropriate backdrop to Chisholm's personal saga, though he appears to have had notions of a Burns opera from as early as 1957.[37] He had already composed a 'Ballad-opera in One Act', *The Midnight Court*, completed in 1959,[38] which he also described as 'a rhythmical bacchanalia'.[39] The libretto is based upon a brilliant translation by Frank O'Connor from the original Irish of Bryan Merryman's poem, written in 1780. It is a superbly witty Irish classic, depicting the impoverished and depressed state of the country and, in particular, the prudery of the men and their failure to marry until too late in life. The court itself is a Fairy Court, set up in opposition to the corrupt English courts, to hear the complaints of the people and especially those of the women. Despite the impressive diatribe against marriage from an old man (Snarly Gob), the court decides in favour of the women, and the author himself is about to be savagely beaten when he wakes up from his dream.

Chisholm wrote to Frank O'Connor on 12 December 1960, asking permission to use his translation:

I have known parts of Merryman's <u>Midnight Court</u> in Kenneth Jackson's translation for many years, but only recently did I make the acquaintance of your own
brilliant verse transcription of the whole thousand-line poem.

I have been working for a number of years at a Celtic Anthology in Song of
which Volume 1 (60 Songs) is shortly to be issued by the U.S.S.R. State Publishers,
Moscow. I hope to perform selections from this alternating with readings from
Celtic literature and would like your permission to allow parts of your translation
of the <u>Midnight Court</u> to be read.

I would also ask if you would allow me to make a play version of your poem
with a view to using it as an opera libretto. Incidentally, although we have never
met, your 'personality' is known to me not only through your writings, but pro-
jected quite positively in your 'Oedipus Complex' and 'The Drunkard' in the
Caedmon recording.[40]

Chisholm extracted the characters from the narrative of the text, and they
are Merryman, The Girl, A Police Woman, The Judge, Snarlygob, His Wife and
Women in the Court. He placed pages of the libretto before the numbers that
they correspond to, and scored it economically, if eccentrically, for flute/recorder,
viola, trombone and piano.[41]

The music of *The Midnight Court* is written in a neo-classical style, almost
pastiche, and entirely appropriate to its subject-matter, which was considered so
risqué that O'Connor's translation was banned in Ireland when it first appeared.[42]
There are certainly some juicy lines in it, and Chisholm was nothing loath to set
them in his own slightly off-beat version of the musical world of Henry Playford
and John Gay. Some of the tunes suggest links to Irish material of the kind published by Playford as, for instance, the aria, number 7, sung by the Wife, in which
the flute obligato provides the tune against which the vocal part is set.

However, where the incorporation of traditional material was peripheral in
The Midnight Court, it was central to *The Life and Loves of Robert Burns*. Writing
as the 271st member of the Robert Burns Friendship Club at the Pushkin School
in Moscow, Chisholm refers to his collaboration with MacDiarmid, who was an
honorary member of the club. In the letter he proposes a performance of the
completed work in Moscow:

> The first draft of the libretto is completed but awaits revision and approval by
> Christopher Grieve. Meanwhile, while waiting for these, I have written the music
> for about twenty numbers. … When you get this libretto, you will see:- 1) that
> the book of the opera is taken entirely from the writings of himself, his brother,
> Gilbert, and other of Burns' contemporaries, 2) that the music consists of simple
> arrangements of the songs traditionally associated with Burns' poems, so that the
> whole stage presentation will be entirely authentic. … Please note that the final
> libretto will be very much simpler than the first draft which I send you, as this is
> altogether too elaborate, too long, and too repetitive.[43]

Chisholm described it as a 'Folk Opera',[44] and it is somewhat in the style of Ramsay's *The Gentle Shepherd* or Gay's *The Beggar's Opera*. As the title page of the libretto states, it is 'A play with music in Three Acts for 6 narrators (3 men and 3 women) 2 solo voices (soprano and tenor) Chamber choir, Piano and string quartet'.[45] This description of the work is entirely accurate, for it is not really an opera, though referred to at times as such. So too is his suggestion that the libretto needs cutting. The piece does not attempt a full life of Burns – his death is not included – and it follows no strict chronology. Rather, it attempts to evoke his character and times and, with some help from a skilful dramatist, might be a success on the stage. However, when it comes to Burns, so many Scots have made their own versions of his life, using their own arrangements of his songs, that the chances of putting this work on are relatively slim. There would have to be an outstanding musical reason for so doing, and, while Chisholm's arrangements are good, they were never designed to call attention to themselves.

In addition to Chisholm's personal problems, on the administrative front the enforced resignation of Stanley Glasser left a serious staffing gap. Chisholm, on the look-out for a new lecturer while in Scotland, had asked MacDiarmid for suggestions. MacDiarmid proposed Ronald Stevenson, though when Chisholm arrived at the Stevensons' he found only Marjorie Stevenson in, and she told him that Ronald wouldn't thank him for an invitation to a 'fascist country'. But

25 Erik Chisholm at his desk, 1960s

Ronald was at a crossroads and decided to take up the offer.[46] He came out as a temporary lecturer but was successful in obtaining the senior lectureship. He and Marjorie arrived in 1963 and shared the Chisholms' house, 'Watersedge', in Rondebosch:

> 'Watersedge' is more symbolic than factual: true there is a dirty little stream appropriately called Blackwater 'river' entrenched at the foot of the garden: but to we explorers familiar with the aqua-tints of Victoria and Niagara, it is nothing very much to write an epic about really.
>
> The Stevensons arrived the day before Good Friday ... I get on fine with the lot of them – they lend an air of respectability to the house here.[47]

Ronald Stevenson ARMCM first appears in the 1964 *University Calendar* as a Senior Lecturer in Music, but he was highly active in the department from the start, premièring his *Passacaglia on DSCH*, at Erik's insistence. The performance was advertised as lasting one and a quarter hours, being preceded by the Bach–Busoni 'Chaconne'. Stevenson also gave six lectures on Busoni, as well as another recital on 13 August. Realising that Stevenson's work was based on the name of, and had been presented to, a great Soviet composer and knowing that Chisholm had been to and extolled the Soviet Union, the day after the première the secret police raided Erik's study in the university and emptied every drawer, leaving the room in chaos. They were looking for his address book. Undaunted, Chisholm arranged for publication of a double LP recording by Stevenson of the work in a limited edition of 100. When a set was sent to Walton, he enthused to his publisher OUP, who published it in 1967. 'In a way he [Chisholm] began my late career as a composer', said Stevenson, who commented that Chisholm possessed no jealousy at all and gave no indication of it.[48]

Meanwhile, Chisholm and Lillias Scott performed his settings of her poems in an all-Scottish programme, similar to that which they had given that summer at the Edinburgh Festival.[49] 'A.S.' (Antoinette Silvestri), writing in the *Cape Argus* on 28 August 1963, said Lillias 'interpreted these songs with temperament'.[50] No doubt, on such an occasion, there was a good deal of temperament to spare! On the domestic front, Lillias was getting to grips with her new status as wife and housewife, coping with Erik's culinary and other demands, Marjorie Stevenson finally beating Erik with a tea-towel to break up his amorous approaches to Lillias while she was at work in the kitchen.[51] Ronald had the use of Erik's music room and piano, and with Marjorie and their three young children sharing the same house with the newly-weds, it does not come as a surprise that things did not always run smoothly. At the same time, Erik's own eccentric sense of humour amused the Stevenson children, who called him by his Christian name and told him off if he misbehaved. When seven-year-old Gerda passed under his window, he would offer her a sweetie, command her to open her mouth and then put a rubber in it. 'He liked children, because he behaved like one', was Ronald's comment.[52]

By July 1963, the Stevensons had found a place to live, and Erik felt his own house empty without the three children rushing around. But Lillias made a good impression at her first formal meeting with all the staff, and they eventually got a house close to the music department, neither of them being able to drive.[53]

Aside from the Burns project, Chisholm had been busy at work on the vocal score of an opera on *The Importance of Being Earnest.* It was completed on 10 January 1963[54] and was drawn from Oscar Wilde's comedy, 'using additional lines from the original 4-Act version of the play recently published'.[55] Chisholm also wrote a number of lyrics for the set musical numbers. The opera is scored for a chamber orchestra and is dedicated to the leading musicologist, Sir Jack Westrup, who suggested it.[56] Westrup lived in Woodstock Road, Oxford, where Chisholm would have had plenty of opportunity to discuss the work with him during its composition at his daughter's house there. Permission from Vyvyan Holland (Oscar Wilde's son) for the use of the work was 'to be followed up'.[57] Whether permission was granted is not known.[58]

Ronald Stevenson recollects seeing the score on the music stand alongside a Britten opera score which Chisholm was using in part as a model – a method Stevenson maintained was Chisholm's common practice.[59] It should not be understood from this that Chisholm was borrowing from his model in the sense of plagiarism, but it is interesting that his methodology was as eclectic as his tastes in music.

Generally speaking, the vocal writing is as crisp as possible with a libretto which requires rapid-fire responses, and there are entertaining passages in the opera, not least the Bunbury blues for alto saxophone and piano which precedes the curtain for Act I.

Around this time Chisholm was showing an interest in native African music (see Chapter 9). Hugh Tracey was invited to lecture on the subject, although he was no liberal by comparison with Chisholm. He had made a very important film on the bushmen and on music and instruments of South Africa. Chisholm, in his impatience, managed to damage the film, much to Tracey's annoyance.[60] Chisholm also knew Percival Kirby, who was an expert on native African music and was a friend of many years' standing.[61]

In 1964 the Stevensons decided to leave. One of the reasons for their departure was to save their son from square-bashing for the South African army when youth call-up loomed – a precaution for which they had Erik himself to thank.[62] But there was a falling out, substantially occasioned by Chisholm's open proposal, at Leonard Hall's house, to give Humphrey Searle Ronald's job and demote Ronald to ordinary lecturer. Such impulsive and, on this occasion, thoughtless pronouncements were not untypical. Ronald wrote a letter of resignation and kept it in his drawer for some weeks before delivering it personally. They had also had a shouting match about the locking up of a piano studio, the student who had been denied access hiding in the bushes the while.[63] Writing to Sorabji in July, Chisholm mentioned: 'I have, too, on my staff another of your admirers Ronald

Stevenson: he's a grand chap, a bit dotty about Busoni though and he has decided to return to Scotland at the end of this year.'[64]

Ronald and Erik enjoyed each other's company, and Ronald came to realise the extent to which Erik had already covered the same ground that he himself was going over, but he could hardly be expected to accept an unjustified demotion.[65] Erik kept saying 'let's forget it' and wrote a conciliatory letter, ending with offers of recommendation and 'my sincere congratulations on DSCH – it's a great work greatly played and I am proud to have had a hand (however humble) in its making'.[66]

But reconciliation was not to be, and the Stevensons beat a retreat back to Britain – not to Hugh MacDiarmid's surprise, who wrote to them in typically pontificating manner, wise after many events and boasting that he had not replied to letters from Chisholm or Lillias: 'He had written me a shoal of letters suggesting I write libretti for him, give him songs of mine to set, etc., etc. – a host of suggestions that seemed to imply I had no purposes of my own and would naturally be free to devote myself to collaboration with him.' His final ludicrous thrust was to link Chisholm with Bill MacLellan, 'whom I never see nowadays anyhow. He and Chisholm are birds of a feather – destitute of spiritual integrity or any concern for or insight into the creative process.'[67]

Is it any wonder that Scots find it hard to succeed in their own country when leading figures such as MacDiarmid can allow themselves to write such ignorant and unjust nonsense about a man whose entire life was dedicated to the creative process for so many people besides himself? One might excuse this kind of polemicism as part of the social currency of their artistic circle, a currency which had included the famous flyting between MacDiarmid and Edwin Muir, but MacDiarmid became more personal, inveighing against Chisholm's and Lillias Scott's marriage: 'I am very sorry to hear she has marital troubles – sorry for Mrs Scott's sake too – but then I did not think that marriage should ever have taken place; it was enough to make F.G. [Scott] turn in his grave – and meant to me a repudiation by his widow and daughter of all he had stood for.'[68]

Whether his second marriage was in any trouble or no, his love for Lillias as expressed in his settings of her poems makes MacDiarmid's suggestion seem utterly inappropriate.

People in love see the world more brightly. Readers not currently in love can induce a similar sensation by looking at the world upside down, as one did in childhood. But does the ear in love hear with greater clarity? Love turned Chisholm upside down and, in his settings of Lillias Scott's lyrics, written in Scots, he went back almost to the bright and innocent vision of childhood. Spontaneity was all. He never wrote anything more simple, direct or beautiful. He came home. 'I have a hunch that I would like to end my musical days in Scotland.'[69]

The songs are redolent of traditional Scottish melody. It is a tradition that runs deep. 'Simple melody' is a phrase applied by the Scots themselves to their ideal,[70] but of all things in life, simplicity is the most dangerous. It is a kind of falling in love. That Chisholm was able to produce such melody himself was not a thing to be expected as natural to a Scottish composer. Conscious of that beauty which is as hard to grasp as the thin mist over a loch at dawn, a canny Scot will not make the attempt rashly. One cannot step into such a tradition with the authority of a classical, or even a traditional, music training. It can only, ultimately, be inhabited by the heart. Chisholm gave it his heart. 'He was so happy!', Neil Solomon recalled, himself happy in the recollection.[71]

Lillias's collection, *Poems of Love*, was published in 1966[72] and was dedicated retrospectively:

> To my husband
> Erik Chisholm
> Scottish Composer
> died 8th June 1965
> these poems are dedicated
>
> May the rare genius of his love
> yet find echo in their lines.

MacDiarmid had written a foreword to the poems in 1961, praising Lillias's 'natural, unassuming and spontaneous way' and her 'integrity'. By the time of their publication, his references to her were naturally changed by Lillias to her married name of Chisholm,[73] but it would be unrealistic to imagine that, had he ever heard Chisholm's settings of the poems, MacDiarmid would have been ready to modify what he wrote:

> The author of these poems is the younger daughter of the greatest Scottish composer (perhaps the only Scottish composer of any consequence whose work was based on, and developed, our native tradition), the late Francis George Scott.

Chisholm set seven of these with every bit as much skill as F. G. Scott might have done, but MacDiarmid had no time for Chisholm, and no amount of evidence – and we have seen throughout this book just how much evidence there was – would have persuaded him to concede a place for him in the same rank as Scott, even though Scott scarcely ventured beyond song writing.

The Lillias Scott settings were not Chisholm's last compositions, but if there had to be a swan-song, they could not have been more appropriate. His response to Lillias's poetry was practically instantaneous. He was visiting her at her mother's house and composed them there on various visits.[74] On the manuscript of 'Love's Reward' he wrote that she had dedicated the poem to him, and he his music to her, and the whole was dedicated by them both to them both. At the end of the last bar he added the date – '18 March '62 (1 hour after receiving the poem!)'.

The setting is to be performed 'Lovingly', and it deserves it. The song opens with a caressing gesture, repeated, almost as one might stroke someone's cheek. It is taken up by the voice, whose first two phrases, one unaccented note excepted, are pentatonic. Gone are the subtle chromaticisms of even his simplest settings in the *Scottish Airs for Children*. The accompaniment shadows the voice, and the harmonies scarcely shift from chords IV, V and I (ex. 24).

No intended order of the songs is known, and they are not a group in Lillias's book. One of them – 'Fragment' – is not even a love song, but a lament for the transitoriness of all things. The spread chords suggest clarsach accompaniment, and this is also a feature of 'Fragment', in which the last chord is spread downwards, as was often the style in Celtic harp playing.[75] The flattened sixths provide a touch of darkness to what is basically a pentatonic melody, but Chisholm does colour both melody and harmony chromatically for the words 'Sine, in the unkennt shade the doolin' o' daith comes doon' – 'Then in the unknown dark, the sorrowing of death comes down (ex. 25).'

'Johnnie Logie' is a deliciously frank love song. Chisholm has put a question mark after Lillias's name as author and two exclamation marks after his own name as composer. The reason for this was that he was wondering whether Lillias herself would follow the same unashamed course as the girl in the song. His setting is jaunty and full of Scotticisms – double tonic progressions, Scotch snaps, octave leaps, repeated crotchets at phrase ends and a basic pentatonicism. How could Lillias not follow her own and her lover's lead with such persuasive tactics employed?[76]

Ex. 24 'Love's Reward', bars 1–7

'Prayer' could almost be a hymn. It too is pentatonic, as is 'Skreigh O' Day' – a homage to the beauty of Ben Cruachan at dawn as a young man rises from his sleep. The music is still half-asleep, rocking gently, or softly spread, yet almost static.

'The White Blood of Innocence' (ex. 26) is perhaps the most beautiful of all these songs. 'Quiet' is the instruction. The melody is the simplest of things, gently urged by, and gently urging, the repeated rhythm of the sweet-sounding parallel sixths, moving into the most basic of modulations as though they were the loveliest things in the world. So they are in this context. Perhaps it is the settled harmony, with its drone D in the first few bars, that makes the move to the dominant and back seem so fresh. But there comes a time when analysis should be abandoned, and this is such a time. The poem begins with an image of defilement – 'Wi' love's ain lips ye filed me' – and much personal feeling must have passed between Erik and Lillias when they performed this song together. But there is no guilt, only a tenderness which truly creates its own innocence.

Innocent or not, the complexities of Chisholm's personal and professional life must have been taking their toll. He had pushed himself too far. In January of 1965 he was already beginning to complain of nervous tension and stress, 'my old complaint – but I think worse than usual'.[77] The next day, he wrote to Diana, suggesting that she return to Cape Town and sending her love 'whether you want it or not'.[78] Perhaps his illness had turned his thoughts back to the many years they had shared together so creatively. He was told he was suffering from depression and to expect it at his age, presumably implying the male menopause; and he

Ex. 25 'Fragment'

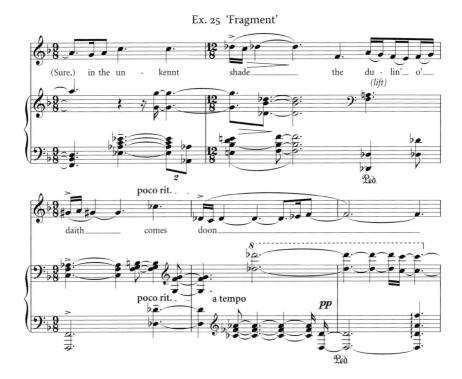

Ex. 26 'The White Blood of Innocence'

continued overleaf

Illus. 26 *continued*

was taking sleeping pills. 'I feel a lot of the time as though I was living an octave higher than I should.' He had all but finished the Janáček book, but his good secretary was away and her substitute 'ain't too bright'.[79]

Ernest Dennis noticed that he was leaning on the rostrum when he was conducting, and he had trouble with his right leg. After a visit to Dr Jacobs, Erik took to his bed for some weeks, but the damage was already done.[80] In April he had to turn down an invitation to conduct *The Bartered Bride* in Durban:

> He feels that he should not over-tax himself now, as he will be conducting the City Orchestra in Verdi's 'Otello' at the UCT Music Festival to be held during the last two weeks of August and the whole of September. In addition he will be visiting England in July on University business and wants his health to improve before then.[81]

The trip was to England to interview possible applicants for three lectureships in music, piano and organ, respectively, and he was to sail out in June and fly back via Rhodesia in July.[82]

In June he was ill again, despite having taken it relatively easy. He lost a lot of weight and became 'pale, transparent and weak'. Breathing was difficult, and he had to be helped even to wash. His vegetarian diet was abandoned, and he hoped to get to England and check in at the Radcliffe Infirmary, in Oxford, for the best treatment.

Professor Inskip told him he could have all the sick leave he needed. But it was too late. He died peacefully and without suffering on 8 June 1965, between Lillias talking to him and her going to the door to meet his brother Archie. Trying to put as positive a light upon it to her doctor sister as she could, Fiona suggested that had he gone to hospital he would have died of despair.[83] He might equally well have been saved. Cape Town was, after all, the leading centre in the world for treatment of diseases of the heart. The death certificate reads, 'Cardiac Decomposition with Terminal Coronary thrombosis – duration of disease + or – 2 months, [signed] R. W. Pickering'.[84]

The funeral took place at the Maitland Crematorium, the path lined by students wearing their gowns. The bearers were the acting principal, Professor Inskip, Professor Guelke, Chisholm's brother Archie, his son-in-law Dr Smit, Gregorio Fiasconaro and Ernest Dennis. Professor Price gave a eulogy.[85] There is no record of where his ashes were deposited.

He had received one or two honours in his life, for what such things are worth – The Dvořák Medal was certainly one he treasured. In 1952 he had been awarded the Van Riebeeck Medal for services to Dutch music, and he also received the Queen's Medal for services to South African music.[86]

There were telegrams and letters of sympathy from music departments and individuals,[87] and the whole family were, of course, devastated. In the obituary in the *Cape Times*, Dulcie Howes (head of ballet, and one who had not always seen eye-to-eye with Chisholm)[88] wrote:

I have always had a great admiration for his drive and enthusiasm. Many small operas would never have been seen in this country if it were not for his initiative. He took difficulties in his stride. He always insisted on constant performances of operas by his students. This was a great asset to them. He was a practical man of music, not just an academic.

Gregorio Fiasconaro tried to keep a dispassionate distance, but his last sentence tells the real story:

Professor Chisholm virtually changed the college, in the sense that from a little music department it became a real conservatoire on European lines.

He had a tremendous driving force, and if sometimes you disagreed with him you could not help admiring him. Everything he did was for the advancement of music. ... He was certainly a member of the modern school of music, an *avant garde*. And he was president of the UCT Jazz Appreciation Society for some years.

When teaching, his goal was that the student should have a broad knowledge of music, not just a mastery of his own particular sphere.

I have lost a very dear friend.[89]

Désirée Talbot gave an honest appraisal:

He was a difficult man, a belligerent man, who could cause one hurt and annoyance, but now he is dead I seem only able to remember the kindnesses he did throughout our long musical association. If one were in trouble of any kind one had only to go to him, and he would put all his tremendous energies into helping. ... Dr. Chisholm could make you flaming mad, but usually, when you calmed down, you found you were another rung up the ladder of progress. Anger is a great stimulant.[90]

Virginia Fortescue wrote touchingly of his influence upon her career, 'above all encouraging and helping me to aim higher, tempering criticism with belief in my abilities ... others have spoken of his unflagging energy, his enthusiasms and passionate convictions, his erudition and his talents. He could be sympathetic, generous and funny. I shall always think of him with gratitude and affection.[91]

The Times (London) gave him the lead obituary:

Chisholm was a man of vast energies, and he channelled many of them into the cause of promoting new music. He was a man with deep feelings about the social significance of his art ...[92]

That last remark is perceptive. In his sense of social responsibility, Chisholm was a quintessential Scot. It is a quality happily found still among his successors – MacMillan, Sweeney and McGuire immediately come to mind. But we have yet to realise to what a great extent Chisholm broke the ground we thought had lain fallow, or to appreciate just what fruitful seed he planted in it, whether in Scotland or South Africa.

Dave Galloway wrote a fine retrospective profile, outlining Chisholm's achievements in reorganising what was the only faculty of music (as opposed to department) on the African continent. Galloway was at one time a suitor for Erik's youngest daughter, Fiona, but had been told by Erik not to presume to such a status until he had held down a job for a year. He went on to other things, but this demand from a potential father-in-law did not dull his appreciation of the man, and I subscribe absolutely to his concluding comment:

> In closing, one is inclined to reflect that, no matter what **has** been written, and what **shall** be written about the man Erik Chisholm, both pro and con, the products of his own creativity will always tell the fullest story.[93]

Those products – the haunting piano works, the challenging operas, the native lyricism of the songs – are as wide-ranging and restless as was the man himself. We do not each choose our own muse but have to learn to live with the one assigned to us. His was indeed a restless muse, but he gave her all the love she could possibly have desired.

The last word, however, should be left to Diana Chisholm.

> He was a man who needed challenge. He got depressed if he wasn't almost fighting with his shadow. He needed something to get his teeth into. There was nothing greater than a challenge to bring out the best in him. Tell him he hadn't got any money – I don't mean money for me, I mean money for chores: he'd find ways and means. Tell him he couldn't get an orchestra: he'd find an orchestra. Tell him he couldn't get music: he'd sit and write it out. It was a challenge, and this is where he had such terrific reserve and – power. Because he did it.[94]

Envoi

OF ALL THE COMPOSERS SCOTLAND HAS PRODUCED, CHISHOLM HAS perhaps come closest to 'finding a nation's soul', as Vaughan Williams put it, for the Scots are adventurers as well as traditionalists. They have planted their seed, and their music with it, all over the globe, and they have embraced the new while honouring the old – historically most obviously in the field of technological development, but also in the arts. When Chisholm was born, Charles Rennie Mackintosh's Glasgow Art School was five years from completion. Building upon a profound knowledge of Scottish vernacular architecture, it none the less remains one of the world's great modernist structures.

In many respects, Chisholm's is a parallel achievement. His study of his own Scottish inheritance led him well beyond its traditional boundaries, while from childhood he was conversant with a vast repertoire of European music through the centuries. That repertoire he actively expanded through concert promotion and opera production, but it is as a composer that he should chiefly be remembered.

Looking at Chisholm's compositional development, it is easy to identify an increasing freedom with his handling of source material such as *piobaireachd*, in which both virtuosity and dissonance become more prevalent. From the *Sonatine Écossaise* to the sonata *An Rioban Dearg* is no great stylistic leap: the techniques applied in the former are simply taken a stage further. Nor is there any great distance between *An Rioban Dearg* and *Night Song of the Bards*, which picks up on the virtuosity and the complexity of texture but still retains something of the mood of Scotland in its more static passages. From *Night Song of the Bards* to the Hindustani works is scarcely a move at all, for all are based upon râgas of similar character, at least to Western ears.

From the Hindustani works to the modernist operas such as *Dark Sonnet* and *Simoon* is also a logical move, for the choice of chromatic râgas had already dictated a degree of movement away from tonal centres towards a freer and more dissonant style. There are, in any case, direct connections between these various pieces. *The Inland Woman* shares material with *Night Song of the Bards*, and *Simoon* is heavily influenced by Hindustani styles, although it is, to a fair degree, a dodecaphonic work.

In his last years, Chisholm turned to a style informed by older musical traditions, notably in the Chaucer operas, with their strong medieval characteristics. This was not a new departure. The sonatinas of *E Praeterita* had already explored the Renaissance, and the second movement of *Pictures from Dante* is thoroughly medieval in character, as befits its subject-matter.

It is a considerable and varied output. In Chisholm's case, the extraordinary

catholicity of his taste, and the vast extent of his knowledge as performer, conductor, concert, ballet and opera promoter, teacher and dean of a faculty of music
offered him many models. He was not shy of indicating the music, composers
and individual works which had influenced him, and these influences have been
traced throughout the book. Not to be overlooked is the significance of his having acted as *secondo* pianist for Casella and page-turner for Bartók, or of his performing Szymanowski in the presence of Szymanowski. In this, Chisholm was
not outside a movement and learning from it; he was in it and creating it along
with some of the greatest of his contemporaries – for he did not only sit beside
them: they too sat beside him. They too heard how he played and what he had
experienced, both in his native music and with the rest of that extraordinary mix
of composers, who did not necessarily know each other or each other's work. The
connecting factor was Chisholm himself, chasing his restless muse, that he might
embrace her loveliness once again, no matter what, if anything, she wore.

The Active Society for the Propagation of Contemporary Music

THE INFORMATION GATHERED HERE COMES FROM A VARIETY OF sources – chiefly the Mitchell Library, Glasgow; the University of Cape Town Manuscripts and Archives Department, the Chisholm Papers (mainly Box 10), and Morag Chisholm's Papers.

The caveat given in Chapter 2 is here repeated. Future researchers are warned that both contemporary and modern dates, whether typed, in Chisholm's own hand or pencilled in by others, are at odds with one other. For instance, a type-written statement announcing the formal constitution of the Active Society is dated '19 October 1931', but a printed leaflet for the Society declares it to have been founded in 1930 and other evidence (letters, reviews, programmes, etc.) makes it clear that 1930 is the correct date. But Chisholm himself, in later undated attempts to put together the Society's history, has taken 1931 as the start date (Chisholm Papers, Box 1, 8). The only certain guides are newspaper clippings which include the printed date or have been dated by a news clipping agency, or documents of similar provenance. In addition concerts were cancelled or moved to another date, programmes were altered and some concerts were repeated at other venues. What appears in a prospectus and perhaps even in a programme may very well not have occurred at the actual concert, especially as some of the programmes consulted are mock-ups made prior to printing. To collect a whole run of printed programmes and then correlate them with the reviews to establish what actually occurred would be a substantial, and possibly impossible, task. Nor have I included every single piece that was performed, or every performer. What follows here is therefore offered only as an initial sorting of partial evidence in the hope that some braver soul with more time decides to take on the search. Where information has been derived from a prospectus or a programme, this is indicated in bold type.

▓ Office Holders

PRESIDENT: Her Grace, The Duchess of Atholl (the first President was Professor
Donald Francis Tovey)

VICE-PRESIDENTS: Principal Robert S. Rait, Professor W. G. Whittaker,
Sir D. M. Stevenson, Bt.

HON. PRESIDENT: Erik Chisholm; HON. SECRETARY: Diana Brodie;
HON. TREASURER: A. M. Chisholm, CA, AIAC.

HON. VICE-PRESIDENTS: Béla Bartók, Arnold Bax, Lord Berners, Arthur
Bliss, Alfredo Casella, Frederick Delius, B. Van Dieren, Edwin Evans, Cecil
Gray, Paul Hindemith, Nicolas Medtner, Jean Sibelius, Ernst Toch, Donald F.
Tovey, William Walton

Karl Szymanowski was on the first list, as was Francis George Scott, the latter as
Hon. Vice-President.

The Executive Committee consisted of E. J. Boden, J. W. Henderson,
K. MacPherson and E. Reid. The General Committee was E. J. Boden, J. R.
Fraser, John Pullein, Guy McCrone, H. S. Reid, Helen Sandeman, J. H. Whyte
and H. K. Wood.

▓ The Concert Programmes

First
Wednesday 15 October 1930 – Whittaker: Quintet, 'Among Northumbrian Hills';
Sonatina for Violin and Piano; Songs. **Prospectus**

Second
Tuesday 28 October 1930 – Walton conducting *Façade*; Bax, Piano Quartet; Foss,
Shakespeare Songs. **Prospectus**

Third
Monday 10 November 1930 – Hindemith playing his own Sonata for Viola Op. 11
No. 4; Sonata for Viola d'amore Op. 25 No. 2; Music for Five Wind Instruments
Op. 24 No. 2; *We Build a Town* (1930), cantata for children, first performance,
given by the Junior Orpheus Choir, etc., with EC, piano. **Prospectus**

Fourth
Wednesday 18 November 1930 – F. G. Scott, songs; Henry Gibson, 'Scottish
Sketches'. **Prospectus**

Fifth
Monday 1 December 1930 – Sorabji giving the one and only performance of his
Opus Clavicembalisticum. **Prospectus**

Sixth

Wednesday 17 December 1930 – David Stephen, 'Fantasy' Quintet; Bartók, Rhapsody, 1930, for Cello and Piano; Kodaly, Solo Cello Sonata; Satie, *Embryons desséches*. EC, with Logan Annand as vocalist. **Prospectus**

> [In fact this was the date of the cancelled Van Dieren concert, for which no substitute was put on (see Chisholm Papers, Box 10, 48). The date of the David Stephen, etc., programme must therefore have been changed from that given in the Prospectus.]

Seventh

Monday 12 January 1931 – Pouishnoff recital: Glazunov, Sonata; Szymanowski, Rachmaninoff. **Prospectus**

Eighth

Wednesday 21 January 1931 – Gavin Gordon, 'Fantasia' Quintet; Chisholm, Second Piano Concerto [*sic*]; Ian Whyte, New Quintet for Strings. **Prospectus**

Ninth

Monday 2 February 1931 – Medtner, first performance of his Sonata Romantica. **Prospectus**

> [An advertisement in *The Scottish Musical Magazine*, XII (3), January 1931, p. 55, refers to the repeat of the programme in St Andrews University on Thursday 5 February 1931.]

Tenth

Monday 23 February 1931 – Casella: *Symphonia Burlesca*; Cello Sonata; Medieval songs.

> [The concert was repeated in part in St Andrews on Thursday 26 February 1931, Casella having had to leave.] **Prospectus**

Eleventh

Tuesday 17 March 1931 – Van Dieren, to include Marginalia in Musica to De Quincey's 'Murder'.

Twelfth

Tuesday 31 March 1931 – Sorabji, Organ Symphony, 1925, played by EC and P. Shannon in St Matthew's Church, Bath St (Charing Cross).

Thirteenth?

Wednesday 29 April 1931, Stevenson Hall – Respighi, Violin Sonata in B minor; Sorabji, *Djami* [INTERVAL] Walton, *Façade*, EC conducting, A. Parry Gunn, reciter.

SEASON 1931–2 (AUTUMN TO SPRING)

First
Friday 23 October 1931 – Tovey (piano) and Gasparini (cello) played Tovey, Sonata in F major and 'Elegiac Variations'; Röntgen, Sonata Op. 56; and Debussy, Sonata.

> [See reviews in Chisholm Papers, Box 10, 53.]

Second
Wednesday 11 November 1931 – Egon Petri played Busoni: 'Fantasie nach Bach' in F minor; Sonatina no. 1; 'All'Italia'; Mozaret; Giga, Bolero e Variazione II; Fantasia Contrappuntistica III; Indianisches Tagebuch. **Programme**

Third
Thursday 17 December 1931 – Hindemith Trio for Viola, Saxophone and Piano; Smyth, Trio for Violin, Horn and Piano; Schmitt, Legende for Saxophone and Piano; Scott, New songs.

> [In fact this concert was postponed to 23 December 1931. The Brahms Horn Trio was substituted for the Hindemith, and the Schmitt was not performed. EC played Bartók's Marche Funèbre and Allegro Barbaro.]

Fourth
Wednesday 20 January 1932 – Bax (piano) played his Viola Sonata; EC (piano) played the First Sonata in E for Violin and Piano, 1915–20; piano pieces; Cello Sonata, Bax and Ruth Waddell. **Programme**

Fifth
Monday 29 February 1932 – Bartók: Second Elegy, 1909; Three Burlesques; Village Scenes (with Angela Pallas); Rumanian Christmas Songs; Lassú; Sonatina; Rumanian Folk-Dances (with Bessie Spence, violin) [INTERVAL] Five Slovakian Folk-Songs; Preludio: all'Ungherese (no. 9 of 'Nine Small Piano Pieces'); Music of the Night; With Drums and Pipes (from Out of Doors suite); First Rumanian Dance, 1909. Bartók played the piano throughout. **Programme**

Sixth
Tuesday 15 March 1932 [NB the programme is for season 1931–2, but the year is misprinted as 1931] – Delius, Sonata no. 2 for Violin and Piano; Mittler, Songs; Lopatnikoff, Sonata Op. 9 for Violin, Piano and Tambour Militaire [INTERVAL] Schoeck, Sonata for Bassoon and Piano; Langstroth, Songs; Sibelius, Sonatina for Violin and Piano Op. 80. **Programme**

Seventh
Tuesday 12 April 1932 – John Ireland played piano for some of his songs and his 'Phantasie' Trio in A minor; songs; Sonata in G minor for Cello and Piano, 1923 (with Gasparini) [INTERVAL] Piano solos: 'The Island Spell', 'The Holy Boy' (Preludes, 1912), 'Chelsea Reach', 'Ragamuffin' (London Pieces 1917).

> [Among those invited to perform at the SPCM was Percy Grainger, who would have loved to come but was not free.] **Programme**

SEASON 1932–3 (AUTUMN TO SPRING)

First

Wednesday 23 November 1932 – Schumann, Violin Sonata, Ami; Smetana, Trio Op. 15; [INTERVAL] Bloch, Three Nocturnes (piano trio); Brahms, Piano Trio Op. 8 (revised version).

Second

Wednesday 14 December 1932 – Arnold Bax personal appearance. **Prospectus**

Third

Wednesday 11 January 1933 – Choral and orchestral concert, including scenes from MacCunn's *Diarmid*, excerpts from Smetana, *The Bartered Bride* and Vaughan Williams, *In Windsor Forest*. **Prospectus**

Fourth

Wednesday 8 February 1933 – Songs and choral works by F. G. Scott, and MacKenzie, Piano Quartet. Glasgow Select Choir conducted by Scott. EC played piano in the Piano Quartet.

Fifth

Tuesday 14 March 1933 – Schmitt, *Sonate Libre* was omitted as EC was unwell; Schmitt, Finale for Cello and Piano [INTERVAL] Quintet for Piano and Strings (Schmitt, piano, Mozart Allan, cello).

Sixth

Tuesday 28 March 1933 – Hindemith personal appearance. **Prospectus**

[Hindemith was unable to come.]

Seventh

2 May 1933 – Bloch and Schmitt, Quintets; Szymanowski, piano solos, performed by EC; Wight Henderson, a String Quartet, plus an arrangement by EC of the last movement of Mahler's Fourth Symphony, with Sally Thomson singing.

[Originally scheduled for Tuesday 25 April 1933.]

Eighth and final

Friday 26 May 1933 – Cyril Scott, Three Pieces for Two pianos; songs; Knorr Varns and Fugue on Russian Theme for Two pianos (Scott and Esther Fisher); Scott, Prelude, Sphinx, Caprice Chinoise, Ode Héroique [crossed out for Souvenir de Vienna? (in pencil)]. **Programme**

[The date of this concert is unclear. Chisholm himself has dated the reviews 1 May 1933 (Chisholm Papers, Box 10, 67).]

SEASON 1933–4

First
Thursday 2 November 1933 – St Andrew's Halls (Berkeley Hall). Bartók
recital: Purcell Preludes in G and C major; Marcello, Sonata in B♭ major in
four movements; Rossi, Toccata in A minor; della Ciaia, Canzone in C major
[INTERVAL] Kodály, Chant Hongrois; Rubato; Epitaphe (Op. 11); Allegretto,
"Quos Ego" (Op. 3); Bartók, Sonata in E (three movements); Three Rondos; Two
Dirges, nos 1and 2, Op. 8; Ballade; Dance-songs.

Second
Wednesday 20 December 1933 – Yvonne Arnaud recital: Fauré, Violin Sonata in
A major; Enesco, Violin Sonata Op. 6; Dowland, Four songs; Halstead, Bairstow,
Smetana, Glière. With Bessie Spence, violin, and William Noble, baritone.

Third
Friday 26 January 1934 – Bax, Quintet for Oboe and Strings; Glinka, Violin
Sonata; Poulenc, Trio for Piano, Oboe and Bassoon; Chisholm, *Straloch Suite*;
Two Canons by Dubois; Lennox Berkeley, Suite for Oboe and Cello; Haydn,
Quartet in E♭ Op. 76 No. 6. Performed by the Barbirolli Quartet and EC (piano),
Evelyn Rothwell (oboe) and A. T. Wood (bassoon).

Fourth and final
Thursday 12 April 1934 – Medtner, Debussy, Milhaud, Mussorgsky songs, plus
pieces for two pianos. Tatyana Makushina, singer.

SEASON 1934–5

First
Wednesday 31 October 1934 – Szymanowski: Violin Sonata in D minor; *Der
Hafis Liebeslieder* Op. 24; Second Sonata for Piano Solo Op. 21 (with EC, piano)
[INTERVAL] Four songs, two from *Mythes* Op. 30; Three Mazurkas Op. 50.
Szymanowski played in most items, but not the Piano Sonata. Bessie Spence
was the violinist. Miss Pugh sang.

Second
Friday 14 December 1934 – Adolf Busch: Violin Sonata Op. 21; Piano Trio
Op. 49 (first public performance); Piano Sonata Op. 25. Busch Trio (Adolf and
Hermann Busch, with Rudolf Serkin, piano).

Third?
Monday 11 March 1935 – Bloch, Sonata, 1920; Webern, Four Pieces, 1910; Delius,
Third Sonata, 1930 [INTERVAL] Bartók Second Sonata, 1923; Bossi, Momenti
Agresti, 1929. Edward Dennis, violin; EC, piano.

Fourth?

Thursday 2 April 1935 – Bax, Sonata; Kodaly, Sonata for Solo Cello; Bax, Moy Mell [INTERVAL] Hindemith, Cello Sonata; Bax, The Devil that Tempted St Antony; The Poisoned Fountain; Hardanger. Gasparini, cello, Harold Thomson and EC, piano.

SEASON 1935–6

First

Monday 28 October 1935 – Busoni, Violin Sonata Op. 29; Antheil, music from 'Fighting the Waves' (first performance); Shostakovich, Twenty-four Preludes (first British performance).

Second

Friday 29 November1935 – Scenes from Busoni operas, *Die Brautwahl*, Act 3, Part II; *Arlecchino*, excerpts from second and fourth scenes; *Doktor Faust*, the Duchess's aria; *Turandot*, from Act I, Parts I and II and Turandot's aria, and Finale from Act II. EC, piano and lecturer, with Dorothy Pugh, Retta McAllister, Harold Green, William Noble and the Rev. Robert Scott as narrator.

Third

Wednesday 29 January 1936 – Shostakovich: Cello Sonata Op. 40, 1934 (Peggie Sampson and EC); Excerpts from *Lady MacBeth of Mzensk* [INTERVAL] Concerto for Piano, Strings and Trumpet Op. 35, 1933 (EC, piano). **Programme**

Fourth

Thursday 9 April 1936 – Austrian composers: Pisk, Three Piano Pieces from Op. 7 and Three Songs; Kanitz, Three Dances; Schoenberg, three songs; Webern, two songs; Berg, Sonata in B minor Op. 1 (W. Henderson); Spitzmüller-Hamersbach, two songs, and Prelude and Double Fugue Op. 7; Wellesz, Sonata for Solo Cello Op. 31; Berg, Seven Early Songs; Brahms, Wolf, Marx, songs. Hanna Schwarz, soprano, Wight Henderson and Harold Thomson, pianists.

SEASON 1936–7

First

Thursday 19 November 1936 – Contemporary Scottish composers: F. G. Scott, songs; Cedric Thorpe Davie, Ballad 'Christ and the Sinner' and songs; excerpts from Moonie's opera *The Weird of Colbar*; piano pieces by Kodaly, Busoni and others played by EC.

Second

Wednesday 16 December 1936, Stevenson Hall – Patrick Shannon, reciter, EC, piano, Kaikhosru Sorabji, piano: melodrama for declamation with piano; Schumann; three ballads from *Fair Hedwig* Op. 106; *The Heather Boy*; *The Fugitives* Op. 122; Strauss, *The Castle by the Sea*; Sibelius, *The Lone Ski Trail*; Grieg, *Bergliot* Op. 42; Sorabji, Second Toccata (Preludio-Toccata; Preludio-Corale; Scherzo; Aria; Ostinato) [INTERVAL] Notturno; Interludio; Cadenza; Fuga Libera a Cinque Voci. **Programme**

Third

Wednesday 13 January 1937 – Bloch, Suite for Viola and Piano; Berg, songs; Van Dieren, Sonata for Violin Solo; songs; Debussy, *La boîte à joujoux* (Wm Lambie, narrator, EC, piano) [INTERVAL] Kilpinen, songs (Joan Alexander and Cedric Thorpe Davie); Hindemith, Viola Sonata Op. 11 No. 4 (not EC).

Fourth

Tuesday 23 February 1937 – Szabó, Toccata; Kadosa, Sonata in One Movement; Bartók, Etude; Reschofsky, Badinage (Maria Zöldesi); Yemnitz, Violin Sonata (with H. Fellowes) [INTERVAL] Weiner, Violin Sonata; Veress, Sonatina (M.S.S.) Hammerschlag Allegro con fuoco (all solo piano or piano and violin).

■ ■ ■

There seems to be contradictory evidence about both the date of the programme featuring Van Dieren and Berg and the existence of a further concert including excerpts from a Busoni opera. According to an unidentified Glasgow newspaper cutting (Morag Chisholm Papers, Press Cuttings, Scotland, 1939–40) dated in pencil 1 March 1937:

> The third concert will be in memory of Van Dieren and Alban Berg, with songs and piano works by the former and Berg's double concerto and piano sonata. In February there is a promised operatic evening with Wolf's unfinished opera 'Manuel Venegas', translated for the occasion by Mr Guy F. McCrone, and the Magic casket scene from Busoni's opera 'Die Brautwahl'.

Patrick Macdonald Sources for Chisholm's Piano Works

TRANSLATIONS IN SQUARE BRACKETS ARE THE AUTHOR'S. ASTERISKS indicate the second group of page numbers in the original MacDonald publication. The numbers given for items in MacDonald are those assigned by Chisholm himself.
(CSB: *A Celtic Song Book*.)

▪ Airs from the Patrick MacDonald Collection

  i   McD 81 (unnamed)
  ii McD 114 (unnamed)
  iii McD 158 *'S cianail m' aigne* – 'Tender Is My Affection'
  iv McD 147 *Tearlach Stiùbhart* – 'Charlie Stewart'
  v   Mcd 122 *Mànus* – 'An Ancient Air'
  vi McD 155 (unnamed)
  vii McD 151 *Faoileagan Scarba* – 'A Scarba Air' (Chisholm misspells this as *fadilengen*, which is not any kind of word at all)
  viii McD 23 *Gur bòidheach, bòidheach an cnocan* – 'Lovely, Lovely Is Yonder Mount [Hillock]'. (Chisholm transposes the chorus phrases up a semitone, and further transposes them when he places them in the bass)
  ix McD 91 *'S fad tha mi m'ònaran* – 'Long A[m] I in Solitude' (Chisholm misspells the Gaelic)
  x   McD 90 *Tha loingeas fo bréide* – 'A Nurse's Lamentation for the Loss of Her Foster Child'
  xi McD 129 *Nochd gur faoin mo chadal domh* ['Tonight My Sleep Is Lonely – Useless to Me']
  xii McD [from a *piobaireachd*?]
  xiii McD 60 *Mnathan Chrospuil is Bhaile Mhuirich* ['Women of Crossapol and BalaVurich']
  xiv McD 149 *Moch madainn chéitein* – ['Early One May Morning']
  xv McD 65 *Imir sein, a Choinnich chridhe* – 'Row Thou, Dearest Kenneth' (this is used for the 'Ness Rowing Song')
  xvi McD 30* (unnamed)
  xvii McD 5 *Si 'nàill fo dhuisg mi* ['It Is This Desire from Which I Awoke']
  xviii McD 140 *'Scian 'sgur fad mi m' thàmh* ['It Is Long Since I Was at My Ease']
  xix McD 76 *A do-ade-a do dh'fhalbh mi* ['A-do-ade-a-do I Left']
  xx McD 69 *The ceò mòr air Meall a' mhuirich* – 'Low Lies the Mist on Mallavurich' (this is the name of a mountain)
  xxi McD 141 (unnamed)
  xxii McD 162 *Oran an aoig* – 'The Song of Death'

xxiii McD 161 *'S toigh leam fein mo laochan* – 'Dear to Me Is My Little Hero'
xxiv McD 78 *Dh' eirich mi moch* ['I Awoke Early']
 xxv McD 68 (unnamed)
xxvi 'Prince Albert's March' (Chisholm probably got this from David Glen's *Highland Bagpipe Tutor*. It has not be identified in MacDonald)

Scottish Airs

At least seven of the nine airs are taken from the Patrick MacDonald Collection. They are:

   i McD 105 'The Brown-haired Milk-maid'
  ii McD 87 'A Thousand Blessings to the Lovely Youth'
 iii Source not yet found
 iv This is the tune used for the piper in *The Pied Piper of Hamelin* ballet, taken from Peacock's *Fifty Favourite Scotch Airs for a Violin*, London 1767
  v McD 95 *'S mi air cragan na sgurra*
 vi McD 117 'Ossian's Soliloquy on the Death of the Heroes'
 vii McD 169 *Aisling* – 'Dream'
viii McD 88 'Lament for McGriogair of Roro'
 ix McD 8* 9/8 jig

Scottish Airs for Children

i McD 27, ii McD 103, iii McD 22, iv McD 118, v McD 31, vi McD 82, vii McD 44, viii McD 13, ix Mcd 37, x McD p. 38, xi McD 126, xii McD 12, xiii McD 16, xiv McD 85, xv McD 5, xvi McD 125, xvii McD 119, xviii McD 58, xix McD 30*, xx McD 32, xxi McD 67, xxii McD 55

Highland Sketches

The numbers are as given in the MS.

BOOK I

  4 McD 129 Airs xi CSB 59 *Nochd gur faoin mo chadal domb*. Similar to, but not the same as 'Airs' xi
 III McD 92 CSB 157 *Nis o rinneadh ar taghadh*
  v McD 120 CSB 105 and 125 *Dàn Liughair*
 vi McD 123 CSB 168 *Gur muladach tha mi* – 'Sad Am I'
 vii McD 86 CSB 71 'Fair, Beautiful and Cheerful Maid' – *Ribhinn, alainn, aoibhinn òig*
viii McD 136 CSB 85 *Ho-rin-o-i-ri-o-ho, Nighean an àirich*
 ix McD 155 CSB 9 EC Airs vi. This seems to be a draft version of EC 'Airs' vi for all that the suggested cuts are not implemented in the latter.
  x Missing
 xi McD 110 CSB 150 *'S math an là fhuair m'eudail*

BOOK II

    I McD 29* 'Skye Dance'

Unnumbered starts p. 3 to p. 7 McD 21* ('North Highland Air')

    9 McD 130 *Leam is aithearr an t suain* – 'To Me Comfortable Is Repose'

   10 McD 21 CSB 106 *A' bhliadhna gus an aimsir so* (see less complete version in Book IV)

Unnumbered McD 151 CSB 172 EC Airs vii *Faoileagan Sgarba*

   12 McD 111 CSB 142

   13 McD 25* 'Western Isle Dance'

BOOK III

Unnumbered McD 105 CSB 119 'Scottish Airs I'

Unnumbered Thomason *Ceol Mór* p. 336 and Glen *A Collection of Ancient Piobaireachd*, Fourth Part, p. 124. *Piobaireachd Dùsgadh Fir na Bainnse* – 'The Waking of the Bridegroom'

BOOK IV

    i McD 40 CSB 66 *Tha fonn gun bhi trom* – 'I Am Disposed to Mirth'

   ii McD 81 CSB 161 EC 'Airs' No. 1

  iii McD 158 CSB 28 EC 'Airs' No. 3 *'S cianail m' aigne* – 'Tender Is My Affection'

   iv McD 95 CSB 3 'Scottish Airs' v (5) *'S mi air cragan na sgurra*. This is almost, but not quite identical with the version in 'Scottish Airs'

    v McD 97 *Bhliadhna dh'eirich an iomairt* – 'Lament for Clan Ronald'

   vi McD 63 CSB 14 *Cha bhi mi m'iasgair*: McD 61 CSB 91 *Keapach na Fasach* – 'The Vale of Keppoch is Become Desolate', first half: McD 63 again: McD 61 second half: McD 63 again

  vii Unidentified, crossed out by Chisholm and to be revised and simplified

IV Unidentified, unidentified, McD 3*, 'March, Strathspey and Reel'

    x McD 22* CSB 175, 'Strathspey'

   xi McD 21 CSB 106 *A' bhliadhna gus an aimsir so* (see more complete version in Book II)

  xii McD 147 CSB 164 EC 'Airs' No. iv, *Tearlach Stiubhart* – 'Charlie Stewart' (different setting from EC 'Airs')

Unnumbered p. 25 McD 41

   iv Unidentified

    I 'I Am Disposed to Mirth' – See i above – this is in a different hand with minor alterations

   II See ii above – this is in a different hand with minor alterations

   3 See iii above – this is in a different hand with minor alterations

Unnumbered Simon Fraser p. 53 No. 133 *Alastair m'ansachd* also in Book I No. 3 where it is incomplete

Gaelic Airs and Dances

4   McD 29* 'Skye Dance' (See HS Bk II 1 of which this is a slightly different version)

Unnumbered McD 21* ('North Highland Air') (See Book II unnumbered starts p. 3 to p. 7, of which this is a slightly different version)

McD 32 (See 'Scottish Airs for Children' xx). This is a very different version.

Notes

The four main sources referred to in the following notes are entitled 'Chisholm Papers', 'Chisholm Works List', 'Morag Chisholm Papers' and 'Chisholm – Men and Music'. The first two are housed in the Archives department of the University of Cape Town (UCT). The Morag Chisholm papers are in her personal possession. Chisholm's typescripts for *Men and Music* are in the Chisholm Papers. However, I have primarily used the versions of these edited by Morag and Fiona Chisholm which are in the Morag Chisholm Papers.

As this book was being prepared for the press, Michael Tuffin was nearing completion of a new *catalogue raisonné* of all the UCT Chisholm Papers (which include scores, correspondence and memorabilia). This catalogue has been accompanied by a rearrangement of the papers in a more coherent form than was the case when I examined them, and is to be thoroughly welcomed. However, visitors to the Archives at UCT will be able to cross-reference from the old system to the new catalogue.

The Chisholm Works List is a provisional catalogue of the scores and manuscripts made for the Archives department at UCT. As with the Chisholm Papers, it will be possible to cross-reference from the old to the new catalogue.

The Morag Chisholm Papers are not publicly availably, but some of the material in them is duplicated in the UCT Archives, and it is proposed to house the bulk of them in UCT in the near future.

CHAPTER 1 Glasgow: Kailyard or Coal Yard?

1 T. Royle (ed.), *The Mainstream Companion to Scottish Literature,* Edinburgh, 1993, entry under 'kailyard', and W. Donaldson, *Popular Literature in Victorian Scotland*, Aberdeen, 1986, chapter 5.

2 H. MacDiarmid, writing under the pseudonym 'Isobel Guthrie', 'Mr Scott and Scottish Music', *The Northern Review,* August 1924, reprinted in A. Calder, G. Murray and A. Riach (eds.), *Hugh MacDiarmid – The Raucle Tongue*, vol. I, Manchester, 1996, pp. 218–20.

3 E. Chisholm, 'Scottish Music in 1931', unidentified newspaper cutting; Morag Chisholm Papers.

4 E. Chisholm, 'The Mystery of Sir Thomas Beecham', undated, unpublished typescript; Morag Chisholm Papers.

5 A contributor to *The Scottish Musical Magazine* welcomes the idea of a Scottish National Academy of Music, but not the proposal to blend it with Chair of Music at Glasgow University, instead proposing the Athenaeum School as a good foundation. 'S', 'A Scottish National Academy of Music', *The Scottish Musical Magazine,* VII (4), 1 December 1925, pp. 65–6. Hugh MacDiarmid greeted the proposal with the deepest suspicion, suspecting that it would do nothing to foster Scottish music *per se* and would not employ Scots. H. MacDiarmid, 'Scottish Music', in A. Riach (ed.), *Hugh MacDiarmid – Albyn*, Manchester, 1996, pp. 40–58. That this turned out to be substantially correct until the end of the twentieth century was Chisholm's and this author's own experience.

6 Diana Chisholm, interview with S. S. Buis, 1979; Morag Chisholm Papers.

7 D. Talbot, *For the Love of Singing*, Cape Town: Oxford University Press, 1978, p. 21; and letter from Leff Pouishnoff, Kenway Cottage, Kenway Road, sw5, 24 September 1929, to the Secretary, Scottish University Entrance Board; Chisholm Papers, Correspondence G–Z, 220. Also Diana Chisholm, interview with S. S. Buis, 1979, Morag Chisholm Papers, in which she states that Erik held a sit-down strike to get off school.

8 E. Chisholm, *Men and Music – Alfredo Casella*, p. 3; Chisholm Papers, Box 15, 116.

9 Ibid.

10 Personal communication from Morag Chisholm.

11 Talbot, *For the Love of Singing*, p. 21.

12 Personal communication from Morag Chisholm.

13 Personal communications from Alex Beveridge, 16 January 2004, and Morag Chisholm.

14 Personal communication from Dr Basil Jaffe.

15 Chisholm, *Men and Music – Alfredo Casella*, p. 1; Chisholm Papers, Box 15, 116.

16 E. Chisholm, 'What Life Has Taught Me'. Interview with Cyril Watling, *Cape Times Weekend Magazine*, 16 May 1964, p. 1.

17 'His mother, still well known as a singer, listened last night as he conducted', 'Forgotten Scot Back As Leader', *Daily Mail*, 7 March 1950; Chisholm Papers, Writings about EC, Box 1, 22.

18 Ibid.

19 E. Chisholm, First Lecture on 'A Celtic Song Book', undated typescript with emendations in Chisholm's hand; Chisholm Papers, Box 9, 241.

20 Chisholm's copy of Patrick MacDonald, *A Collection of Highland Vocal Airs* is in its own folder in the Chisholm Papers, Uncatalogued Papers.

21 Chisholm, *Men and Music – Medtner*, original typescript; Chisholm Papers, Box 15, 119, p. 2.

22 Erik must, however, have retained some lingering affection for his old school, for in 1931 he preceded a Queen's Park Secondary School Choir concert with a short organ recital of works by Nesbit and Lemmens, which included Bach's D minor Toccata and Fugue. (See Corporation of Glasgow, Saturday Afternoon Musical Recitals, Concert programme, 28 November 1931, in Morag Chisholm's Papers.)

23 Diana Chisholm, interview with S. S. Buis, 1979; Morag Chisholm Papers.

24 Glasgow Athenaeum School of Music programme, 24 November 1917; Morag Chisholm Papers.

25 Carbon copy of typewritten programme,

Saturday, 9 March 1918; Chisholm Papers, Box 21, 156.

26 Chisholm, Typescript of a Curriculum Vitae; Chisholm Papers Box 16, 127; and 'The Baillie', 'The Man You Know', *Glasgow Weekly Herald*, 7 December 1935. Another of his teachers was Thomas Nesbitt. W. Saunders, 'Scottish Chiefs, no. XV. A Chief Composer', *The Scots Magazine*, 1933, pp. 17–20.

27 Chisholm, *Men and Music – John Ireland*, original typescript; Chisholm Papers, Box 15, 122, pp. 1–2.

28 Information from Morag Chisholm.

29 Personal conversation with David Tidboald, 1 February 2004.

30 'Forgotten Scot Back As Leader'.

31 Carbon copy of letter from Chisholm to Paul Hindemith, Music Department, Yale University, Newhaven, Connecticut, 21 August 1952; Chisholm Papers, BC 129, Correspondence G–Z, 220.

32 Chisholm, *Men and Music – John Ireland*, pp. 1–2.

33 Undated scrapbook containing reviews and concert programmes from *c.* 1917–28; Chisholm Papers, Box 21, 156.

34 Carbon copy typescripts of extracts from reviews; Chisholm Papers, Box 21, 156.

35 British Music Society Programme, 6 March 1922; Morag Chisholm Papers. The programme gives the movements as Lento–Adagio–Con brio, but someone has pencilled in a change from Lento to Allegretto-Allegro. The hand may be Chisholm's.

36 Reviews in the *Glasgow Herald*, 7 March 1922, and the *Evening Times* of the same date.

37 Letter from David Stephen to Chisholm, 13 February 1923; Chisholm Papers, Correspondence G–Z.

38 Letter to the author from Margaret S. May, 20 September 2004.

39 Chisholm, *Men and Music –Medtner*.

40 Chisholm, Typescript of a Curriculum Vitae; 'The Man You Know'; and Diana Chisholm, interview with S. S. Buis, 1979.

41 There are manuscript versions of these and several others which remained unpublished and some of which are only drafts. The titles are listed as follows in

the Chisholm Works List Q13 GMB 2–28:
1. 'A Jewel from the Siderial Casket';
2. 'Other Worlds'; 3. 'The Witch-Hare';
4. 'The Spring Lamb'; 5. 'The Blited Tulip';
6. 'The Seven Delicate Sisters'; 7. 'Moonlit
Apples'; 8. 'Cargoes'; 9. 'Drum Taps'; 10. 'Tall
Poplars'; 11. 'The Wagoner'; 12. 'Seumas
Beg'; 13. 'The Rainbow'; 14. 'The Mirror';
15. 'Polnesia's Lullaby'; 16. 'The Rolling
Stone'; 17. 'The Garden of Silence'; 18. 'Sleep';
19. 'Happiness – Laugh and Be Merry';
20. 'The Wet Scythes; 21. 'The Merry-go
Round'; 22. 'A Jolly Lor?'; 24. 'By Avon
Stream, the Sunken Garden'. 1. was also
titled 'Beta Cygnus'; 2. 'A Companion to
Sirius', and so on.

42 Chisholm *Men and Music – Casella*,
pp. 2–3; see also Chapter 2.

43 Carbon copy of letter from Chisholm
to Christopher Grier (music critic at the
Scotsman), 20 January 1951; Chisholm
Papers, Correspondence G–Z.

44 Incomplete manuscript A307, Chisholm
Works List; Chisholm Papers.

45 Unidentified article with 'article by
Watson Lyle – 1932' in ink in Chisholm's
hand, written beside it; Chisholm Papers,
Box 16, 126.

46 Russo-Scottish Society Recital
Programme, 16 February 1926, McLellan
Galleries; Chisholm Papers, Box 5, 26.

47 'Lorgnette', 'Talk of the Town', *Evening
News*, Glasgow, 13 February 1926; Morag
Chisholm Papers. The programme also
included a first British performance of
Godowsky's *Java Suite*.

48 Letter from Leigh Henry to Chisholm, 30
April 1927; Morag Chisholm Papers, Letters
from Musical Celebrities.

49 Concert Programme, UCT Music
Library, Concert Programmes, Overseas
7D 68/4.

50 Letter from Dunton Green to Chisholm,
26 November 1926; Morag Chisholm Papers.

51 'J.R.F.', 'Spanish Music'. Unidentified,
undated review in a Glasgow newspaper
(possibly the *Glasgow Herald*); Morag
Chisholm Papers.

52 Chisholm Papers, TPA 781.4 CHI 80/529.

53 Written on an early version of the
Cornish Dance Sonata; Chisholm Papers
TPA 781.4 CHI 80/529.

54 See Chisholm's own note on envelope
of sketches for the symphony; Chisholm
Papers TPA 782.7 CHI 79/512.

55 Letter from Leff Pouishnoff to Chisholm,
30 April 1927; Morag Chisholm Papers,
Letters from Musical Celebrities.

56 Letter from Sorabji to Chisholm, 22
January 1931; Morag Chisholm Papers,
Sorabji Letters.

57 Chisholm, Typescript of a Curriculum
Vitae, Morag Chisholm Papers.

58 Letter from Geo: Rbt: Chisholm, Norfolk
House, New Glasgow, Nova Scotia to Erik
Chisholm, 16 July 1931; Morag Chisholm
Papers. The letter sends best wishes also
from 'Aunt Jessie'. References to characters
mutually known to Erik and his uncle, and
general familiarity with the musical scene
in Nova Scotia would indicate that his uncle
had been living there for some years.

59 Carbon copy typescripts of extracts
from reviews, *Nova Scotia Evening News*, 31
February 1928; Chisholm Papers, Newspaper
Clippings, Box 21, 156.

60 Programme of recital, 16 February 1928;
Morag Chisholm Papers, and unidentified
newspaper clipping; Chisholm Papers,
Box 22, 159.

61 Programme of concert, 8 April 1928,
and extract from a review in the *Pictou
Advocate*, 11 May 1928; Morag Chisholm
Papers.

62 Diana Chisholm, interview with S. S.
Buis, 1979.

CHAPTER 2   The Active Society

1 In the following references to Chisholm's *Men and Music* I have used the edited versions of Chisholm's typescripts made by Morag and Fiona Chisholm. Most of the original typescripts can be accessed in the Chisholm Papers at the University of Cape Town, where they are in Box 8 (Bartók only) and Box 15.

2 Letter to the author from Margaret S. May, 20 September 2004.

3 Postcards from Gustav Holst at St Paul's Girls' School, to Chisholm at 27 Langland Rd., Newlands, Glasgow, dated 6 December [1928], 12 December [1928], 14 December 1928; Chisholm Papers, Correspondence G–Z.

4 Diana Chisholm, interview with S. S. Buis, 1979.

5 Letter from Leff Pouishnoff to the Secretary, Scottish University Entrance Board, 24 September 1929; Chisholm Papers, Correspondence G–Z, 220.

6 'Testimonial to Eric [*sic*] Chisholm from Hugh Roberton, 56 Queen Mary Avenue, Glasgow, S', 12 September 1929; Chisholm Papers, Correspondence G–Z, 220.

7 E. Chisholm, 'Scottish Music in 1931', unidentified newspaper cutting; Morag Chisholm Papers.

8 Typescript of lecture on D. F. Tovey, p. 3; Chisholm Papers, Lectures and Talks, Box 15, 117.

9 'J.W.', 'Music in Glasgow', *The Scottish Musical Magazine*, X (5), February–March 1929, p. 90.

10 Carbon copy of a typescript of a review by 'P.G.', music critic for Scotland, *Musical Opinion*, May 1929; Chisholm Papers, Box 29, 240.

11 Chisholm, 'Introduction' to *Men and Music*; Morag Chisholm Papers.

12 Chisholm writes that he became Bishop of Aberdeen, but this is not the case. My thanks to Ian Olson and the Very Rev. Richard Kilgour for this information; also to Stanley Flett of Aberdeen, a former member of the Youth Fellowship.

13 Ibid.

14 See J. Purser, *Is the Red Light On? – The Story of the BBC Scottish Symphony Orchestra*, Glasgow, 1987, chapter entitled 'The Ian Whyte Years'.

15 Chisholm, 'Introduction' to *Men and Music*.

16 The *Citizen* for 20 September 1930 states that it was 'founded some three months ago by Mr Erik Chisholm'. Press cutting in Chisholm Papers, Box 1, 8.

17 Future researchers are warned that both contemporary and modern dates, whether typed, in Chisholm's own hand or pencilled in by others, are at odds with one other. For instance, the typewritten statement announcing the formal constitution of the Active Society on the 13th is dated '19 October 1931', but a printed leaflet and notepaper for the Society declare it to have been founded in 1930, and other evidence (letters, reviews, programmes, etc.) makes it clear that 1930 is the correct date. But Chisholm himself, in undated later efforts to put together the Society's history, has taken 1931 as the start date (Chisholm Papers, Box 1, 8). The only certain guides are newspaper clippings which include the printed date or have been dated by a news clipping agency, or documents of similar provenance. In addition, concerts were cancelled or moved to a different date, programmes were altered and some concerts were repeated at other venues. An attempt to gather this information together in a coherent fashion is made in Appendix 1. What appears in a prospectus and perhaps even in a programme may very well not have occurred at the actual concert.

18 See Appendix 1.

19 Foreword on reverse of list of office-bearers, etc. of The Active Society for the Propagation of Contemporary Music; Chisholm Papers, Box 1, 7.

20 Letter from Neil Gunn at Larachan, Dochfour Drive, Inverness, to Chisholm, 4 October 1930; Chisholm Papers, Box 1, 8.

21 The display of scores does seem to have taken place, but there was no suitable lecture room, and a proposal that the Mitchell Library purchase published scores and commission copies of manuscripts by Scottish composers was 'not considered'. Correspondence between Chisholm and the City Librarian, 4 October 1930, 27 May 1931, 9 June 1931 and 1 July 1931 in Active Society Papers, Mitchell Library, Glasgow.

22 E. Chisholm, 'An Outstanding Work

by a Native Composer – Mr Ian Whyte's Quintet', *The Scottish Musical Magazine*, XI (10), August 1930, pp. 184–5.

E. Chisholm, 'The Active Society for the Propagation of Contemporary Music, Glasgow – First Concert', *The Scottish Musical Magazine*, XI (12), October 1930, pp. 222–3.

E. Chisholm, 'The Active Society for the Propagation of Contemporary Music, Glasgow – Second Concert', *The Scottish Musical Magazine*, XI (12), October 1930, pp. 229–30.

E. Chisholm, 'Third Concert of the Active Society', *The Scottish Musical Magazine*, XII (1), November 1930, pp. 5–10,

E. Chisholm, 'Active Society's Concert, January 21st', *The Scottish Musical Magazine*, XII (3), January 1931, pp. 44–7 and 52.

23 See Appendix 1.

24 Chisholm, 'Scottish Music in 1931'.

25 Hugh Roberton, 'Youth at the Prow', unidentified, undated cutting but probably the *Daily Record* and prior to 15 October 1930, when Whittaker was featured in the first concert.

26 H. MacDiarmid, 'Hugh Roberton and the Musical Festival Movement', *Contemporary Scottish Studies*, 6 November 1925, and 'Mrs Kennedy-Fraser and the Songs of the Hebrides', *Contemporary Scottish Studies*, 9 April 1926; both reproduced in A. Riach (ed.), *Hugh MacDiarmid – Contemporary Scottish Studies*, Manchester, 1995, pp. 164–71 and 314–21.

27 Letter from Chisholm to Dr Henry George Farmer, 30 September 1955, Glasgow University Library, Farmer Collection 888.

28 Typescript list of Chisholm's works; Morag Chisholm Papers.

29 Letter to Chisholm from Andre Sas of the ISCM, 10 December 1933; Morag Chisholm Papers.

30 'Glasgow Active Society', by our Music Critic, *Glasgow Herald*, 16 September 1930. 'Chamber Music Concert', *Daily Record*, 16 September 1930. 'Active Society's First Concert', *Evening Times*, 16 September 1930; Chisholm Papers, Box 10, 43.

31 Chisholm, *Men and Music – Donald Tovey*.

32 Programme, 11 November 1931 and reviews in Chisholm Papers, Box 10, 53.

33 The Tovey Piano Concerto is coupled with the Mackenzie *Scottish* Concerto on Hyperion CDA 67023, with liner notes by the present author; and the Symphony in D and prelude to *The Bride of Dionysus* are on Toccata Classics TOCC 0033.

34 Chisholm, *Men and Music – Donald Tovey*.

35 Letter from Walton to Chisholm, undated, 'Monday', probably the Monday before Saturday 25 October; Chisholm Papers, Box 10, 44.

36 Chisholm, *Men and Music – William Walton*.

37 Reviews, 'Unusual Musical Work' in a clipping identified separately as the *Evening Times*, 29 October 1930, and 'Music v. Verse', likewise identified, in the *Daily Express*, 29 October 1930. Further reviews in Chisholm Papers, Box 10, 44.

38 Letter from Walton to Chisholm, 4 November 1930; Chisholm Papers, Box 10, 44.

39 This refers to the music critic of the *Glasgow Herald*, whose review (undated, but probably 11 November 1930) is quoted by Chisholm later in italics.

40 Chisholm, *Men and Music – Hindemith*. Hindemith returned to Glasgow to perform his Viola Concerto on 14 December 1937, see *Glasgow Herald*, 11 December 1937, p. 7.

41 Chisholm, 'Scottish Music in 1931'.

42 Chisholm, 'Introduction' to *Men and Music*. Sorabji had a private income but it was not large, and his father was not a millionaire.

43 Press cuttings dated 20 November 1930 in Chisholm Papers Box 10, 46.

44 Chisholm, *Men and Music – Van Dieren*.

45 Correspondence from Van Dieren to Chisholm concerning the arrangements in the Chisholm Papers, Box 10, 48.

46 Diana Chisholm, 'Bernard Van Dieren'; Morag Chisholm Papers.

47 Chisholm, *Men and Music – Van Dieren*.

48 Diana Chisholm, 'Bernard Van Dieren'.

49 Ibid., and letter from Virginia Fortescue to the author, 30 July 2006. Virginia Fortescue was a student of Frida Kindler's, who gave her this information.

50 Letter from Sorabji to Chisholm, commenced 9 December 1930, this

quotation from 17 December 1930. Later letters (6 January 1931 and 8 January1932) after Sorabji had met Van Dieren, broadly sympathise with Erik's experiences at Van Dieren's hands; Morag Chisholm Papers, Sorabji Letters.

51 Unidentified and undated newspaper cuttings from the correspondence columns, presumably of the *Glasgow Herald*. The letters themselves are dated 17, 18 and 22 December and one from Van Dieren 5 January; Chisholm Papers, Box 10, 48.

52 See J. Purser, *Scotland's Music*, Edinburgh, 2007, pp. 336–7.

53 Programme and unidentified press cuttings; Chisholm Papers, Box 1, 6.

54 Letter from Medtner to Chisholm, 1 September 1931; Chisholm Papers, Box 10, 50.

55 Chisholm, *Men and Music – Medtner*. See also Interlude: The Love of Sorabji. A. M. Henderson's *Musical Memories*, Glasgow, 1938, is both interesting and modest, and adds considerably to our knowledge of music in Glasgow in the late nineteenth and early twentieth century.

56 See review in (Dundee) *Evening Telegraph*, 27 February 1931; Chisholm Papers, Box 10, 51.

57 Chisholm, *Men and Music – Casella*.

58 Chisholm, *Men and Music – Adolf Busch – A Bushel of Buschs*.

59 Busoni gave a Celebrity Concert in Glasgow in 1922. 'I was shocked to see him so changed; looking so prematurely old and ill', Henderson, *Musical Memories*, p. 37.

60 Chisholm, *Men and Music –Lamond* (Petri is a sub-heading).

61 For a programme and reviews, see Chisholm Papers, Box 10, 55.

62 See Purser, *Scotland's Music*, p. 300.

63 Letter from F. G. Scott to Chisholm, 25 November 1931; Chisholm Papers, Box 10, 55.

64 'Arnold Bax', unsigned review in *The Scotsman*, 15 December 1932; Chisholm Papers, Box 10, 62.

65 Reviews of this concert are in the Unidentified Newspaper Cuttings; Chisholm Papers, Box 1, 8. Further largely unidentified reviews are in Box 10, 62.

66 Correspondence between Erik Chisholm and Sergei Prokofiev, various dates between 1931 and 1935, the Serge Prokofiev Archive, Goldsmiths, University of London.

67 Unidentified newspaper cutting; Chisholm Papers, Box 10, 55.

68 Chisholm, *Men and Music – Arnold Bax*.

69 Chisholm, *Men and Music – Béla Bartók*. The following is from a letter from Bartók to Chisholm, in the Chisholm Papers, Correspondence, A–G: 'I am very glad to hear from you again. Now, I have a BBC engagement (Queens-Hall) for 8. Nov. 1933, so it would be possible for me to come to Glasgow after that day. There are only 2 questions to be settled: 1) What kind of programm? Could you not engage the Hungarian violinist Zoltán Székely ... Of course you know his name? We could play my 2 violin sonatas both. 2) As for the fee, could it be fixed at £15 for me?'

70 Unidentified newspaper cuttings, including the *Glasgow Herald*, presumably 1 or 2 March 1932; Chisholm Papers, Box 1, 6. Also Chisholm papers Box 10, 57.

71 Unidentified newspaper clippings dated February 1932, including letters from Tovey of 25 and 29 February, the latter in reply to letters from Professor Grierson and F. Eames (General Secretary of the ISM); Chisholm Papers BC 129, Box 14, 112.

72 Chisholm, *Men and Music – Béla Bartók*.

73 Diana Chisholm, typescript on Bartók; Morag Chisholm Papers.

74 Ibid. and Chisholm, *Men and Music – Béla Bartók*. Also letter from Ernest Boden (but not in his hand as he had Parkinson's disease) to Chisholm, 5 December 1963; Chisholm Papers Box 1, 8.

75 The scores and dedicated copy are in the Chisholm Papers, Box 8, 33.

76 Diana Chisholm, typescript on Bartók.

77 Ibid.

78 Ibid.

79 Review of piano recital, 'Bela Bartok in Glasgow', *Glasgow Herald*, 3? November 1933; Chisholm Papers, Miscellaneous, Box 1, 6.

80 Chisholm, *Men and Music – Béla Bartók*.

81 Ibid.

82 Ibid.

83 Ibid.

CHAPTER 3   Chisholm's Scottish Inheritance

1 See J. Purser, *Scotland's Music*, Edinburgh, 2007, 'Introduction – The Scottish Idiom', pp. 15–20.

2 The attitudes referred to here and below I have personally experienced over many years in Scotland. My musical education took place at the RSAMD and University of Glasgow. Neither institution paid the slightest attention to Scottish traditional music, outwith song, well into the 1970s, nor was the history of Scottish music of any kind studied in any depth, the vast majority of it being unpublished, unedited and unavailable. I am happy to report that the situation today is very different, though there is a fair distance to go yet before the effects of more than a century of musical racial discrimination are overcome.

3 E. Chisholm, 'The Composer in Scotland', manuscript notes in Chisholm Papers, Writings by EC, Box 16, 129. Paper given at a club in central Glasgow shortly before the performances of *The Earth Shapers* in November 1941. A further passage is quoted in Chapter 5. Quite a bit of the information in this talk seems to have been taken from letters from J. B. McEwen to Chisholm, dated 14 and 23 July 1939; Chisholm Papers, Correspondence G–Z.

4 H. MacDiarmid, 'Francis George Scott', in A. Riach (ed.), *Hugh MacDiarmid – Contemporary Scottish Studies*, Manchester, 1995, pp. 103–13. H. MacDiarmid, writing under the pseudonym 'Isobel Guthrie', 'Mr Scott and Scottish Music', *The Northern Review*, August 1924, reprinted in reprinted in A. Calder, G. Murray and A. Riach (eds.), *Hugh MacDiarmid – The Raucle Tongue*, vol. I, pp. 218–20.

5 Personal communications from George Bruce and Maurice Lindsay.

6 Chisholm, *Men and Music – Béla Bartók*, p. 11.

7 E. Chisholm, 'What Life Has Taught Me', interview with Cyril Watling, *Cape Times Weekend Magazine*, 16 May 1964.

8 'Scottish music 1929 – (onward) to 1940 (?)

Piano sonata: Piobaireachd piano concerto: Music for Children: Sonatina for piano: Petite Suite for piano: 4 Elegies for piano: Straloch Suite for piano (also for orchestra): 27 small piano pieces: Symphony No 2. (including 'Celtic Wonder Tale'): 9 Preludes for orchestra (also for piano): (Beyond the edge of the great world). Opera: The feast of Samhain (Stephens).

Piobaireachd (arr. of 20 odd for piano solo).

Ballets: The Forsaken Mermaid (Dunedin): The Earth Shapers: Piobaireachd: The Hoodie.

Various orchestral suites from ballets: Cantata 'St Mungo' (Boyd Scott): Dance Suite for piano and orchestra: Pictures from Dante for orch.: Overture – Frieris of Berwick: Ceol Mor Dance for orchestra.'

E. Chisholm, handwritten list; Morag Chisholm Papers.

9 See Purser, *Scotland's Music*, Edinburgh 2007, chapter 14.

10 Chisholm, 'Some Aspects of European and Hindustani Music', *Evening News of India*, 11 August 1945, p. 4; Chisholm Papers, Box 21, 158.

11 W. L. Manson, *The Highland Bagpipe*, Paisley, 1901, p. 228.

12 Unidentified newspaper article 'by Watson Lyle 1932' (written in Chisholm's hand in ink). No further details are given; Chisholm Papers, Box 16, 126.

13 Chisholm, *Celtic Folk Songs*, Moscow: State Music Publishers, 1964, and Eden Music Publishing, Glasgow, no date, pp. 3–6.

14 A list of these is kept in the Erik Chisholm Trust's copy of the present author's research work.

15 Chisholm, *Men and Music – Béla Bartók*, p. 11.

16 Uncatalogued folder containing transcriptions from Dauney, *Ancient Scottish Melodies*, 1837; Chisholm Papers.

17 Chisholm Papers, Celtic Song Book, Notes, etc., Box 9, 244.

18 Uncatalogued Papers; Chisholm Papers. Chisholm's annotated copy of Patrick MacDonald, e.g. No. 156.

19 For example, Malcolm MacFarlane's paper of 3 December 1908 in the *Transactions of the Gaelic Society of Inverness*; the entry under Scottish

National Music, in *Groves*, vol. IV; and Duncan MacIsaac's brief essay on Gaelic pronunciation; Chisholm Papers, Celtic Song Book, Notes, etc., Box 9, 244.

20 Letter from Granville Bantock to Chisholm, 14 February 1929; Chisholm Papers, Correspondence, A–K.

21 Chisholm's gradings for the *Scottish Airs for Children* are as follows:

Easy: Numbers 4, 3, 2, 7, 8, 9, 13, 15, 19.

Moderately Easy: Numbers 1, 6, 16, 11, 18, 21, 5.

Moderately Difficult: Numbers 10, 14, 17, 22, 20, 12.

22 R. Cannon, *The Highland Bagpipe and Its Music*, Edinburgh, 1988, p. 130.

23 Chisholm, 'What Life Has Taught Me'.

24 For instance the McFarlane Manuscripts, *c.* 1740, contain many bagpipe airs and include several *piobaireachd*. Of the three parts, Part I is missing, and unfortunately the accompanying Index is seriously inaccurate as regards tune numbers, and Part III suffers particularly badly from bleed-through of ink from the other sides of the pages, rendering much illegible. There is an editing job waiting there which would be worth a PhD. The Daniel Dow, Joseph, Patrick and Donald MacDonald publications, along with Oswald's *Caledonian Pocket Companion* and Campbell's *Albyn's Anthology*, all contain *piobaireachd* in alternative instrumental dress.

25 See Purser, *Scotland's Music*, p. 91.

26 See the relevant entries and attendant bibliographies in *The Biographical Dictionary of Scottish Women*, Edinburgh, 2006.

27 F. G. Scott, 'Pibroch', a lecture given to the Saltire Society, 23 November 1946, reproduced in M. Lindsay, *Francis George Scott and the Scottish Renaissance*, Edinburgh, 1980, pp. 173–83.

28 Chisholm, 'Some Aspects of European and Hindustani Music'.

29 Purser, *Scotland's Music*, pp. 22–3 and 157–63.

30 The *piobaireachd* is referred to in 'Fionn', *The Martial Music of the Clans*, Glasgow, 1904, p. 60.

31 Ibid., pp. 128–9.

32 V. S. Blankenhorn, 'Traditional and Bogus Elements in "MacCrimmon's Lament"', *Scottish Studies*, 22, 1978, pp. 45–67.

33 Chisholm, 'What Life Has Taught Me'.

34 J. Purser, James Oswald's *Caledonian Pocket Companion* – an annotated edition on CD-ROM from nickparkes@btinternet.com.

35 See Chapter 4 and W. Saunders, 'Scottish Chiefs, no. XV. A Chief Composer', *The Scots Magazine*, 1933, pp. 17–20. Also W. Saunders, 'A Front-Rank Scottish Composer', *The Sackbut*, September 1933, pp. 45–7; Chisholm Papers, Box 16, 126. Raymond Holden states that Chisholm was the soloist at its première in Amsterdam that year. R. Holden, 'Chisholm, Erik William', *Oxford DNB*, 2004. I am unaware of any such performance. The programme of the event shows that his *Dance Suite for Orchestra and Pianoforte* was performed on 14 June. The statement is possibly the result of a confused reading of the second of Saunders's articles, or an acceptance of the same assertion in A. Walker, 'Erik Chisholm', *Stretto*, Summer 1986, p. 9. Agnes Walker wrote this article specifically for that issue and was relying on her memory and may have used the Holden article as a source. The *Dance Suite* is listed as a separate work in a typescript of his compositions in the Morag Chisholm papers, and is referred to as a separate work in Saunders, 'Scottish Chiefs, no. XV. A Chief Composer'.

36 Concert programme note; Chisholm Papers, Box 5, 26, and review 'The Scottish Orchestra – Erik Chisholm's Piano Concerto', *Glasgow Herald*, 22 January 1940.

37 B. Brown, 'The Pibroch Repertory of the Eighteenth Century: A Musical Index and Key', unpublished, p. 26, but see B. Brown, 'The Whole Pibroch Repertory', handout for paper given to the Piobaireachd Society Conference, Bridge of Allan, 31 March 2001, p. 26.

38 Joseph MacDonald's treatise written in 1760 makes this clear. See Purser, *Scotland's Music*, p. 162.

39 'Fionn', *The Martial Music of the Clans*, pp. 135–6.

40 S. MacNeill and F. Richardson, *Piobaireachd and Its Interpretation*, Edinburgh, 1987, pp. 105–6.

41 Article 'by Watson Lyle, – 1932' (written in Chisholm's hand in ink). No further details are given; Chisholm Papers, Box 16, 126.

42 Typescript of interview with Thomson Newspapers in the 'What Life Has Taught Me' series, 16 March 1964, p. 1.

43 Chisholm Papers, TPA 782.7 CHI 80/586.

44 'By Our Music Critic', 'New Scottish Music', *Glasgow Herald*, 29 November 1939 and 'H. K. W', 'New Works Presented', *The Bulletin and Scots Pictorial*, 29 November 1939; Morag Chisholm Papers, Press Cuttings, Scotland 1939–40.

45 *Erik Chisholm*, Dunelm Records DRD0219 (full version), and *Erik Chisholm Music for Piano*, vol. 1, DRD0222 (abridged version).

46 B. Mackenzie, 'History and Folklore Surrounding the Music', CD liner notes, *Donald MacPherson – A Living Legend*, Siubhal, Glasgow, 2004, pp. 9–18.

47 D. H. Johnson, 'Chisholm Centenary Concert', *BMS News*, 101, March 2004, p. 142.

48 M. Anderson, 'Sonata Finally Given Its Place in Musical History', *The Scotsman*, 5 January 2004, p. 15.

49 Brown, '*The Whole Pibroch Repertory*', p. 1. But see also Brown, 'The Pibroch Repertory of the Eighteenth Century: A Musical Index and Key', p. 25.

50 M. Anderson, 'London, Wigmore Hall: Erik Chisholm and Ronald Stevenson', *Tempo*, 58 (228), April 2004, p. 75.

INTERLUDE   The Love of Sorabji

1 I am most grateful to the Sorabji Archive and Alistair Hinton for permission to quote extensively from Sorabji's letters.

2 Flyer in the form of a letter from Patrick Shannon (Secretary, Faculty of Music), 12 March 1930; Chisholm Papers, Box 10, 42.

3 E. Chisholm, *Men and Music – Medtner*; Morag Chisholm Papers.

4 Diana Chisholm, 'Kaikhosru Sorabji', unpublished typescript; Morag Chisholm Papers.

5 *Kaikhosru Sorabji – An Essay by Erik Chisholm, with a Descriptive Catalogue of His Works*, London, c. 1938, reprinted privately, c. 1964.

6 The Sorabji letters are in the Morag Chisholm Papers. Sorabji himself gave Morag Chisholm permission to publish their contents, in a letter to her dated 14 September 1985.

7 Letter from Sorabji to Chisholm, commenced 27 May 1930 and continued here on 28 May 1930; Morag Chisholm Papers, Sorabji Letters.

8 Undated letter from Sorabji to Chisholm; Morag Chisholm Papers, Sorabji Letters.

9 Entry from Virginia Fortescue's diary for 31 January 1954, with her kind permission.

10 Letter from Sorabji to Chisholm, 15 October 1930; Chisholm Papers, Correspondence G–Z, Box 6, 220.

11 Undated letter from Sorabji to Chisholm; Morag Chisholm Papers, Sorabji Letters.

12 Letter from Sorabji to Chisholm, 16 May 1960; Chisholm Papers, Correspondence G–Z, Box 6, 220. I am indebted to Lilli Savitz for urging upon me the significance of this letter.

13 Probably 1929, as a review in *The Bulletin* of 22 September 1930 refers to Sorabji's appearance 'last spring'. Likewise, an article by Hugh Roberton, 'Youth at the Prow', heralding the Active Society's prospectus for the season 1930–1, refers to Sorabji's recital 'last year'. Unidentified, undated cutting but probably the *Daily Record* and prior to 15 October, when Whittaker was featured in the first concert.

14 Chisholm *Men and Music – Sorabji*; Morag Chisholm Papers. Diana Chisholm's original typescripts, from which Erik drew substantially, are in the Chisholm Papers, Box 14, 106.

15 Copy of a letter from Chisholm to Sorabji, 31 July 1964; Morag Chisholm Papers, Sorabji Letters.

16 Diana Chisholm, quoted in Chisholm, *Men and Music – Sorabji*.

17 'Sorabji in Glasgow', *Glasgow Herald*, 2 December 1930. 'J.B', 'Glasgow "Active" Society', *Glasgow Daily Record and Mail* (?) ? December 1930, and subsequent correspondence.

18 Prospectus in Mitchell Library, Active Society Papers.

19 Letter from Ernest Boden (but not in his hand, as he had Parkinson's disease) to Chisholm, 5 December 1963; Chisholm Papers Box 1, 8.

20 R.E.A., 'Parsee Pianist's Puzzle', unidentified newspaper review; Chisholm Papers, Box 1, 6.

21 'Active Society's Concert', unidentified newspaper review; Chisholm Papers, Box 1, 6.

22 Ronald and Marjorie Stevenson, interview with the author, 21 May 2004.

23 Personal communication from Morag Chisholm.

24 H. MacDiarmid, *The Company I've Kept*, London, 1966, p. 63.

CHAPTER 4   A Trojan Horse in Glasgow

1 Letters from Maisie Radford to Chisholm, 5 May192?; 24 May 192?; 2 October 192?; 19 October 192?; 30 March 192?, congratulating Chisholm on the Glasgow performance of *Idomeneo* and thanking him for his kindness; and one undated, asking for the return of the *Idomeneo* score and of the *Titus* score if he is not going to use it – which he did. The folder is dated 1927–28; Morag Chisholm Papers.

2 Unidentified Glasgow newspaper cutting dated in ink, 1932 in Chisholm Papers, Box 14, 110.

3 Erik thought that his having left school without a Leaving Certificate would disqualify him, but Diana worked for Glasgow University and, when the subject came up with Professor Milligan (who was Clerk of the Senate), he advised her that, with good recommendations, he had every chance of success. Diana Chisholm, interview with S. S. Buis, 1979; Morag Chisholm Papers.

4 Ibid.

5 Morag Chisholm, personal communication.

6 Erik Chisholm and Diana Brodie's marriage certificate; and newspaper cuttings in the Chisholm Papers, Box 22, 159.

7 Chisholm *Men and Music – Lamond*; Morag Chisholm Papers.

8 1931 is the date according to a typescript of Chisholm's works, but, according to the title page, it is 1930.

9 Concert programme,17 February 1933, the Concert Hall, Broadcasting House, Concerts of Contemporary Music, Seventh Season, Fourth Concert; Chisholm Papers, Box 22, 163.

10 W. Saunders, 'Scottish Chiefs, no. XV. A Chief Composer', *The Scots Magazine*, 1933, pp. 17–20. Also W. Saunders, 'A Front-Rank Scottish Composer', *The Sackbut*, September 1933, pp. 45–7; Chisholm Papers, Box 16, 126.

11 Flyer for Amsterdam Festival; Morag Chisholm Papers.

12 Programmes and unidentified reviews, dated by hand 15 March 1932, in Chisholm Papers Box 10, 58. The programme is misdated 1931.

13 Unidentified review, 'Active Society' by Montague Smith, 13 April 1932, and 'Active Society', *Glasgow Herald*, 13 April 1932; Chisholm Papers, Box 10, 59.

14 Chisholm, *Men and Music – John Ireland*.

15 Programme in Chisholm Papers, Box 10, 64. The Mackenzie is at long last available on CD performed by the Ames Quartet, on *British Piano Quartets*, Albany Records, ALB 910.

16 Chisholm, *Men and Music – Schmitt*.

17 Unidentified, undated reviews in Chisholm Papers, Box 1, 6, with photograph of Schmitt and of the quintet of players. Also unidentified and pencil-dated reviews; Chisholm Papers, Box 10, 65 and 66.

18 Chisholm, *Men and Music – Schmitt*.

19 See note 17 above.

20 Chisholm, *Men and Music – Scott*.

21 Letter from Chisholm to Dr Henry George Farmer, 30 September 1955. Glasgow University Library, Farmer Collection 888.

22 Letter from 'Diapason', unidentified undated press cutting, probably *Glasgow Herald*; Chisholm Papers, Box 1, 2.

23 Programme and unidentified reviews; Chisholm Papers, Box 10, 69.

24 Programme and reviews in Chisholm Papers, Box 10, 70.

25 Programme and unidentified reviews; Chisholm Papers, Box 10, 71.

26 Carbon copy of a draft CV of Chisholm; Chisholm Papers, Box 1, 7.

27 Diana Chisholm, interview with S. S. Buis, 1979. In the interview, Diana speculates that he also submitted a thesis, but no thesis was submitted, the compositions serving the same function.

28 Programme and undated review in *Musical Opinion*; Chisholm Papers, Box 10, 72.

29 Flyer and unidentified reviews; Chisholm Papers, Box 10, 73.

30 Chisholm, *Men and Music – Busch*.

31 Diana Chisholm, interview with S. S. Buis, 1979.

32 '"The Trojans", by Our Music Critic', *Glasgow Herald*, 19 March 1935; and '"The Trojans at Carthage", by Our Music Critic', *Glasgow Herald*, 30 November 1935.

33 Ernest Newman, 'The Trojans – Glasgow's Brave Effort', *The Sunday Times*, 24 March 1935, p. 7; Chisholm Papers, Box 12, 91, containing a number of other reviews, mostly unidentified.

34 Diana Chisholm, interview with S. S. Buis, 1979.

35 Ibid.

36 E. Chisholm, 'The Mystery of Sir Thomas Beecham', undated typescript (but post-1961); Chisholm Papers.

37 The performance was conducted by Felix Mottl in Karlsruhe in 1890, according to an article '"The Trojans" of Berlioz, by Our Music Critic', *Glasgow Herald*, 15 March 1935. Mitchell Library Glasgow, Grand Opera Society Papers.

38 '"The Trojans", by Our Music Critic', *Glasgow Herald*, 19 March 1935; and '"The Trojans at Carthage", by Our Music Critic', *Glasgow Herald*, 30 November 1935.

39 Diana Chisholm, interview with S. S. Buis, 1979.

40 Steuart Wilson, letter to Chisholm from 23 Chepstow Villas, London W11, 27 July 1934.

41 Unidentified newspaper cutting, 'Berlioz Operas in Glasgow'; Chisholm Papers, Box 12, 92.

42 Programmes in Chisholm Papers, Box 10, 74.

43 Programmes and reviews in Chisholm Papers, Box 10, 75.

44 E. Chisholm, 'The Operas of Ferruccio Busoni', *Weekly Herald*, 30 November 1935. Also E. Chisholm, 'Busoni on the Possibilities of Music', *Weekly Herald*, 7 December 1935. Large scrapbook in Morag Chisholm Papers.

45 Programme in Chisholm Papers, Box 10, 76.

46 Programme in Mitchell Library, Active Society for the Propagation of Contemporary Music; and reviews in Chisholm Papers, Box 10, 77.

47 Programme in Chisholm Papers, Box 10, 78.

48 There is some uncertainty about the actual concerts given at this time. See Appendix 1.

49 Programme in Chisholm Papers, Box 10, 81.

50 Programme in Chisholm Papers, Box 10, 82.

51 Unidentified newspaper cutting, 'Lost Scottish Opera'; Chisholm Papers, Box 14, 109, dated February 1937 in pencil.

52 Unidentified newspaper cutting, 'Production of New Scottish Opera'; Chisholm Papers, Box 14, 109.

53 Both full and vocal scores of this work are in Glasgow University Library, Ms. MacCunn 27 and 27a (the latter a photographic reproduction of the manuscript score); and Ms. 28, which is a set of parts for Act I only, and not including trumpets, trombone, tuba and percussion. The original call number for both the full score and its copy was Ca. 15 – y.1-4. Ca. 15 – x.7. was the original call number for the parts. The call number for the vocal score is unchanged as Ca. 15 – w.32.

54 Unidentified newspaper cutting, 'Lost Scottish Opera'.

55 Undated and unidentified reviews for March 1938; Chisholm Papers, Box 1, 2.

56 Letter from Chisholm to a Mr Meighan, 10 July 1939; Chisholm Papers Box 1, 2. It is not clear whether this letter was actually sent. It is an original MS and is not signed.

57 Chisholm Papers, Programmes Box 5, 26.

58 Unidentified newspaper cutting, Mitchell Library, Glasgow Grand Opera Society.

59 Programme in Athenaeum programme box, Mitchell Library.

60 'Nation of Music Snobs', undated, unattributed notice, probably *Glasgow Herald*. The year is 1939, as the notice refers to the recent Jubilee celebrations for Sir Henry J. Wood, which began in October 1938; Chisholm Papers, Box 16, 136.

61 Anon., 'Cold Shoulder for Scots Composers', *The People's Journal*, no date, but the year can be more deduced from the fact that the article refers to Janey Drysdale as being 'now aged 78'. Janey Drysdale was born in 1861, so the year has to be 1939, as reviews of the Society's revived activities appear in November of that year; Morag Chisholm Papers, Press Cuttings, Scotland 1939–40.

62 A CD of these two works and Lamond's *Sword Dance* was issued on the Hyperion label, CDA67387.

63 A review in the *Evening Times* dated 14 November 1939 states that the Association 'was revived a year ago with headquarters in Glasgow'; Morag Chisholm Papers, Press Cuttings, Scotland 1939–40.

64 Notice in *The Bulletin and Scots Pictorial*, 8 January 1940; Morag Chisholm Papers, Press Cuttings, Scotland 1939–40.

65 Flyer, 'The Dunedin Fund for the Publication of Scottish Music'. The President was Lord Provost P. J. Dollan and the Vice-President Lady Dunedin; Morag Chisholm Papers, Press Cuttings, Scotland 1939–40.

66 Ibid.

67 Preview and reviews in *The Bulletin and Scots Pictorial*, 28 November 1939; the *Evening Times*, and *Evening News*, both 29 November 1939; Morag Chisholm Papers, Press Cuttings, Scotland 1939–40.

68 Anon., 'Scots Composers', *Evening Dispatch*, 20 March 1940; Anon., 'Scottish

Composers', *Weekly Scotsman*, 23 March 1940 and an unidentified article with sub-heading 'Miscalled' in *The Bulletin and Scots Pictorial*, 23 March 1940; Morag Chisholm Papers, Press Cuttings, Scotland 1939–40.

69 E. Chisholm, *The Forsaken Mermaid*, Dunedin Collection of Scottish Music, Mitchell Library, Glasgow, no date, but probably 1941 as the December 1940 production is referred to in the cast list in the publication.

70 M. Lindsay, *Francis George Scott and the Scottish Renaissance*, Edinburgh, 1980, p. 208.

71 Anon., 'Scots Composers'.

72 Quoted in Lindsay, *Francis George Scott and the Scottish Renaissance*, p. 152.

73 E. Chisholm, 'About Music – Music in Soviet Russia', parts I, II, and III, *Weekly Herald*, 9, 16 and 23 November 1935.

74 Letter from Alison Sheppard (Secretary of the Dunedin Association), to subscribers, etc., 12 February 1940. This letter makes it clear that the original proposed date of Sunday 18 February had been altered to the 20th.

75 Works of MacCunn and Wallace are available on the Hyperion label, CDA66815 (MacCunn) and CDA66848 and CDA66987 (Wallace), with extensive liner notes.

76 Undated review 'By Our Music Critic', *Glasgow Herald*, [21?] February 1940; Morag Chisholm Papers, Press Cuttings, Scotland 1939–40. Whether the Association had more than one Vice-President, or whether he had recently demitted office in favour of Janey Drysdale, is not known.

77 The relevant press notice simply reads 'a Funeral March on a Ground Bass (composed by himself)' and does not suggest it was written for the occasion. Undated review 'By Our Music Critic', *Glasgow Herald*, [21?] February 1940.

78 Schedule for 'Dunedin Association Concerts (supported by the Saltire Society) Season 1939–40'; Morag Chisholm Papers, Press Cuttings, Scotland 1939–40.

CHAPTER 5   The Ballet & the Baton as Weapons of War

1 Unidentified Glasgow newspaper cutting, dated in pencil [1 March 1937]; Chisholm Papers Box 14, 109.

2 Unidentified newspaper cutting 'Folk Songs Theme for Ballet', *Daily Mail* no date, probably January 1937; Chisholm Papers, Box 16, 129.

3 See J. Purser, *Scotland's Music*, Edinburgh 2007, 'Introduction' and notes.

4 Unidentified Glasgow newspaper cutting; Chisholm Papers, Box 14, 109.

5 Personal communication between William Crosbie and the author.

6 Letter from Marjory Middleton to Chisholm, 26 September 193? (probably 1937); Morag Chisholm Papers, Ballet Box.

7 Letter to Chisholm from Edward Dent, 13 February 1938; Chisholm Papers, Correspondence A–I.

8 Letter to Chisholm from Hamilton Harty, 7 March 1938; Chisholm Papers, Correspondence G–Z.

9 Letter to Chisholm from J. Gibson at J. & W. Chester Ltd., 7 January 1939; Chisholm Papers, BC 129, Correspondence A–I 219.

10 Concert programme for Concerts of Contemporary Music, Thirteenth Season, Fourth Concert, Friday, 6 January 1939; Chisholm Papers, Box 1, Folder 7. Two versions of the full score (October 1937 and June 1938) are in the Chisholm Papers TPA 782.7 CHI 79/371 (with 79/354, which is a photostat full score of the Violin Concerto) and TPA 782.7 CHI 80/314 (with 80/630 and 631 being parts of *The Wolfings*, an unfinished opera and numbered as 80/360 on the folder spine). Drafts of the work are in Chisholm Papers, TPA 782.7 CHI 79/512.

11 Chisholm papers, Symphony in Cornwall, uncatalogued incomplete manuscript, of which there is only one full page.

12 Erik Chisholm, Symphony No. 2, *Ossian*, Epoch Dutton CDLX 7196, tracks 1–6.

13 On a copy of the Souvenir Programme for *The Earth Shapers*, 28, 29 November 1941 (Chisholm Papers Box 5, 26), the title has '(SYMPHONY NO 2)' written in ink beneath it. Chisholm has also written on the front page of the full score of Symphony No. 2, 'used for ballet "The Earth Shapers"' underneath his signature and the year, 1939.

14 Letter to Chisholm from Dr H. F. Koenigsgarten, 15 June 1939; Chisholm Papers, Correspondence G–Z.

15 L. Annand, *J. D. Fergusson in Glasgow 1939–1961*, Abingdon, 2003, p. 7.

16 E. Chisholm, Curriculum vitae compiled by Chisholm, Chisholm Papers T780.941 CHI 55/131 from M/A file p. 1.

17 M. Morris, *My Life in Movement*, London, 1969, and The International Association of MMM Ltd., Garelochhead, 2003, pp. 98–9.

18 W. MacLellan, 'Reminiscences of the Celtic Ballet', in *Margaret Morris Drawings and Designs and the Glasgow Years*, Glasgow, 1985, p. 19.

19 Ibid.

20 Annand, *J. D. Fergusson in Glasgow 1939–1961*, pp. 7–8, 13.

21 E. Chisholm, 'The Composer in Scotland', MS notes in Chisholm Papers, Box 16, 129, paper given at a club in central Glasgow shortly before the performances of *The Earth Shapers* in November 1941, see pp. 3 and 4 of the typescript.

22 Personal communication from Sheila and Morag Chisholm, and letter to Chisholm at that address from Dr Koenigsgarten, 15 June 1939.

23 Carbon copy of letter from Diana Chisholm to the editor, 'OPUS', Johannesburg, 12 August 1966; Morag Chisholm Papers.

24 Letter to Chisholm from Edward Dent, Hotel New Weston, New York, 18 September 1939; Chisholm Papers, Correspondence A–I.

25 Letter from J. B. McEwen to Chisholm, 26 September 1939; Chisholm Papers, Correspondence A–I.

26 L. Esher, 'The Plot to Save the Artists', *Times Literary Supplement*, 2 January 1987.

27 Personal communication from Morag Chisholm.

28 Quoted in M. Lindsay, *Francis George Scott and the Scottish Renaissance*, Edinburgh, 1980, p. 204.

29 Personal communication from Morag Chisholm.

30 Letter from A. M. Hyslop to Mr Scott, 26 September 1939; Morag Chisholm Papers, Correspondence.

31 Imperial War Museum at http://collections.iwm.org.uk/server/show/ConWebDoc.1318.

32 Personal communication from Anne Crosbie.

33 Personal communication from his former student, Alex Beveridge, who has forgotten the name of the relevant organisation. Beveridge is also the source of the information regarding Chisholm's support for Crosbie, which has yet to be verified elsewhere.

34 E. Chisholm, 'What Life Has Taught Me', interview with Cyril Watling, *Cape Times Weekend Magazine*, 16 May 1964.

35 E. Chisholm, 'My Job in War-time', undated typescript of BBC broadcast, but (given the reference to rehearsals of his Piano Concerto) probably the second or third week in January 1940. He refers to this broadcast as having taken place 'early in 1940' in a later broadcast script, 'A Musician in Wartime', which was recorded on 3 February 1950. Both scripts in Morag Chisholm Papers.

36 Chisholm, 'My Job in War-time'.

37 Letter to Dr Henry George Farmer, 30 September 1955, Glasgow University Library, Farmer Collection 888.

38 Ibid.

39 Probably in 1941. A typescript of Chisholm's works, possibly made for him in Cape Town, has reversed the probable dates, giving 1941 as the date of composition and 1940 as the date of performance; Morag Chisholm Papers.

40 See typescript and sketches for *Babar* narrator's part; Chisholm Papers, Box 29, 230.

41 Chisholm's own handwritten catalogue of his works; Chisholm Papers, Box 16, 127.

42 Loose opening page of full score, original MS, with dedication 'For Sheila' above title; Chisholm Papers, sketches for *Adventures of Babar*, TPA 782.70 79/444.

43 Personal communication from Sheila Chisholm.

44 Chisholm, *Men and Music – Donald Tovey*; Morag Chisholm Papers.

45 Leader in *Glasgow Herald*, 4 December 1940, p. 6. Correspondence on 3rd, p. 6; 5th, p. 3; 6th, p. 3; 7th, p. 2; 9th, p. 3; 10th, p. 3; 11th, p. 5; 12th, p. 3.

46 H. S. Roberton, *Orpheus with His Lute*, Oxford, 1963, Appendix 1, pp. 297–302, which includes quotations from press reports.

47 H. Phillips, *The University of Cape Town 1918–1948: The Formative Years*, Cape Town, 1993, p. 288.

48 UCT University Archives, Chair of Music 1939–45, Box 12.1.5.

49 Undated copy of testimonial from Tovey, Hedenham Lodge, Bungay, Suffolk, UCT University Archives, Chisholm personal file.

50 Partly dated copy of letter from William Walton, Ashby St. Ledgers, Rugby, 1938, UCT University Archives, Chair of Music 1939–45, Box 12.1.5.

51 Copy of testimonial partly dated and addressed from Bax, London, 1938, UCT University Archives, Chair of Music 1939–45, Box 12.1.5.

52 Letter to Chisholm from Frederic Lamond, 7 October 1939; Chisholm Papers, Correspondence G–Z.

53 UCT Senate Minutes, 21 March 1939, p. 5.

54 University of Cape Town Calendars, 1939–47.

55 Letter from W. B. M. to Chisholm, 30 September 1939; Morag Chisholm Papers.

56 Concert programme of the Choral and Orchestral Union of Glasgow, 20 January 1940, pp. 249–55; Chisholm Papers, Programmes Box 5, 26.

57 Mitchell Library, Gc 792.809 41435, CEL Celtic Ballet Programmes.

58 Our Music Critic, 'The Scottish Orchestra', *Glasgow Herald*, 13 December 1937.

59 Morris, *My Life in Movement*, p. 100.

60 Information from Jonathan Burnett, 7 January 2004.

61 MacLellan, 'Reminiscences of the Celtic Ballet', p. 19.

62 Chisholm/Stephens, *Isle of Youth*, Glasgow, no date, but accessioned by the Mitchell Library, Glasgow, in 1943.

63 Anon., 'The Forsaken Mermaid', *Glasgow Herald*, 7 December 1940.

64 Letter from Chisholm to an unidentified lady. Judging from the contents of the letter, presumably she was a Secretary of some committee giving out funds for cultural projects. The letter is dated 27 May 1960 – an error for 1940. Photocopy in Morag Chisholm Papers, from Chisholm Papers, Archival Box 12.

65 D. Talbot, *For the Love of Singing*, Cape Town, 1978, p. 21.

66 Letter from Chisholm at UCT to Dr Henry George Farmer, 30 September 1955, Glasgow University Library, Farmer Collection 303; and 'B.M.' (Beatrice Marx, music critic for the *Cape Times*), Erik Chisholm Arrives, unidentified Cape Town newspaper clipping, 1946; Chisholm Papers, Box 21, 157. However, in Chisholm's typescript of a Curriculum Vitae; Chisholm Papers, Box 16, 127, p. 1, it is stated that 'In 1939, helped to reorganise the Carl Rosa Opera Company and went on tour with the company as conductor (including a London Winter garden season) and later as advance publicity manager: worked in this latter capacity for the International Ballet Co., and as touring extra-mural lecturer on different musical subjects'.

67 'B.M.' (Beatrice Marx), Erik Chisholm Arrives, unidentified Cape Town newspaper clipping, 1946; Chisholm Papers, Box 21, 157.

68 *Clàr-Cuimhneachais* (souvenir programme), *The Earth Shapers*, p. 8, which contains black and white photographs of Midyir and the Earth Spirit in costume, and of Angus and the Mopopoise with the Water Spirits, also in costume; Morag Chisholm Papers. Crosbie's original watercolours for the sets are in the Morag Chisholm collection.

69 Lewis Foreman's liner notes for the CD (Erik Chisholm, Symphony No. 2, *Ossian*, Epoch Dutton CDLX 7196, tracks 1–6) treat the first movement as an Introduction on the grounds that the *Scherzo-Toccata* (track 3 on the CD) is marked 'ii'. However the *Andante maestoso* (track 4 on the CD) is clearly marked 'iv' in the full score.

70 Scenario for Scene IV, *Clàr-Cuimhneachais* (souvenir programme), *The Earth Shapers*, p. 8; Morag Chisholm Papers.

71 'M. L.' [Maurice Lindsay], 'Weekend Concerts', *Glasgow Bulletin*, 12 December 1949; Chisholm Papers, Box 1, 22. Also,

'Erik Chisholm's New Work', 'By Our Music Critic' [Maurice Lindsay], *Glasgow Herald*, 12 December 1949; Chisholm Papers, Box 1, 22.

72 Anon., 'Celtic Ballet in Glasgow', unidentified newspaper cutting (possibly *Glasgow Herald*), 29 November 1941.

73 Lewis Foreman, liner notes for Erik Chisholm, Symphony No. 2, *Ossian*, Epoch Dutton CDLX 7196, p. 6.

74 Chisholm, 'The Composer in Scotland', pp. 3 and 4 of the typescript.

75 Letters from Arthur Geddes at 70, Cluny Gardens, Edinburgh, 30 April 1942 and 25 May 1942; Chisholm Papers, Uncatalogued, Box, Opera 42, Folder, 'The Making of the Tartan.'

76 Letter from Chisholm to Mr Sanderson, 3 November 1942, Fiona Chisholm Papers.

77 Ibid.

78 Chisholm, typescript for 'A Musician in Wartime'.

79 Unidentified newspaper clippings, one referring to Southsea with blue pencil mark 'Nov '43'; Chisholm Papers, Box 16, 136. Also roughly dated newspaper clippings in Morag Chisholm Papers, Ballet Box.

80 Chisholm, Typescript of a Curriculum Vitae, p. 1; and K. Wright, 'Erik Chisholm: A Tribute', *Composer*, 17, October 1965, pp. 34–5. However, Virginia Fortescue throws doubt on the 'several' – letter to the author, 30 July 2006.

81 A. Walker, 'Erik Chisholm', *Stretto*, Summer 1986, p. 9.

82 Typescript of a list of Chisholm's compositions; Morag Chisholm papers. The title of the orchestral versions is *Nine Orchestral Preludes*. They are scored for double wind, timpani, percussion, piano, harp and strings.

83 The piano version of 'Stravaiging' is numbered 19 and 'The Hour of the Sluagh' is numbered 24, in Box Piano 9tpa 781.4 Chis 2002/12662.

84 Agnes Walker, 'Dr. Erik Chisholm', *Glasgow Illustrated*, August 1965, and typescript of list of Chisholm's compositions; Morag Chisholm Papers.

85 Undated letter from Morag Chisholm to her father, thought to be 1943; Morag Chisholm Papers.

86 My thanks to George MacIlwham for bringing this piece to my attention.

87 Virginia Fortescue, letter to the author, 30 July 2006.

88 Chisholm's opinion of the Anglo-Polish Ballet is to be found in an article he wrote for the *Evening News of India*, 1 November 1945; Chisholm Papers, Box 29, 223. The article is full of interesting observations on ballet in general.

CENTRE-PIECE *Pictures from Dante & Night Song of the Bards*

1 Golden Jubilee Music Festival Programme for 25 and 30 August 1960, final symphony concert; Chisholm Papers, Box 28, 206.

2 Ibid.

3 Concert programme for the Golden Jubilee of the South African College of Music, 30 August 1960; Chisholm Papers, Box 2, 13.

4 Pictures from Dante; Chisholm Papers, Orchestra 3.

5 Typescript classified list of compositions, undated but presumably late 1951, as the Violin Concerto is described as having a 'forthcoming first performance' in March 1952; Chisholm Papers.

6 Curriculum vitae and list of works in Chisholm's hand, undated but post-1962; Chisholm Papers, Box 16, 127.

7 Ibid.

8 James Macpherson, 'Croma: A Poem', in *Fingal, an Ancient Epic Poem in Six Books Together with Several Other Poems, Composed by Ossian the Son of Fingal*, Translated from the Gaelic Language by James Macpherson, Dublin, 1763, p. 246.

9 S. Johnson, *A Journey to the Western Highlands*, London, 1974, pp. 104–7.

10 For those readers unaware of the antiquity of this literature, I recommend browsing the publications of the Dublin Institute of Advanced Studies, and James F. Kenney's *The Sources for the Early History of Ireland: Ecclesiastical*, Dublin, 1997.

11 Derick S. Thomson, *The Companion to Gaelic Scotland*, Oxford, 1983, p. 60.

12 A most useful study of the degree of indebtedness or otherwise of Macpherson to his sources is Derick S. Thomson's *The Gaelic Sources of Macpherson's 'Ossian'*, Aberdeen University Studies, no. 130, Edinburgh and London, 1951, but it does not deal with the passage referred to here and, in a personal communication with the author, Derick Thomson was unable to add further information.

13 E. A. Sharp and J. Matthay (eds.), *Lyra Celtica*, Edinburgh, 1932, pp. 31–4.

14 J. G. Campbell, ' "Oidhche Dhoirbh", from the Telling of Allan MacDonald, Mannal, Tiree', in *The Fians ... Waifs and Strays of Celtic Tradition*, Argyllshire Series no. IV, London, 1891, pp. 101–3. See also J. Purser, 'Sources for Macpherson's "Night Song of the Bards" ', paper given at *Rannsachadh na Gàidhlig 2006*, Sabhal Mòr Ostaig, 20 July 2006.

15 A. H. Fox Strangways, *The Music of Hindostan*, Oxford, 1914, pp. 162, 324. Chisholm refers to this book in E. Chisholm, 'Some Aspects of European and Hindustani Music', *Evening News of India*, Saturday 13 August 1945, p. 4, in which the name 'Strangways' is misprinted as 'Strangeways'; Chisholm Papers, Box 29, 223.

16 Fox Strangways, *The Music of Hindostan*, p. 162.

17 E. Chisholm, *Men and Music – Béla Bartók*; Morag Chisholm Papers, p. 11.

18 Fox Strangways, *The Music of Hindostan*, pp. 184–5.

19 E. Chisholm, *The Inland Woman*, figure 21.

20 E. Chisholm, autograph list of his own operas; Morag Chisholm Papers. In a typewritten list the year is given as 1950.

21 BBC radio talk about Liszt as a teacher given by Frederic Lamond, 1947. Reproduced in *A Liszt Legend*, Embryo Cassettes, ISCN 085335 7005.

22 W. Wordsworth, 'Preface' to *Lyrical Ballads*, 1805.

CHAPTER 6 From Italy to India and Singapore

1 E. Chisholm, Typescript of a Curriculum Vitae; Chisholm Papers, Box 16, 127, p. 1.

2 K. Wright, 'Erik Chisholm: A Tribute', *Composer*, 17, October 1965, pp. 34–5.

3 Sheila Chisholm, radio interview on Fine Music Radio, Cape Town, 1 February 2004.

4 E. Chisholm, typescript for 'A Musician in Wartime'; Chisholm Papers, uncatalogued.

5 E. Chisholm, *Men and Music – Alfredo Casella*; Chisholm Papers, Box 15, 116. The whereabouts of this film is not known.

6 Chisholm, typescript for 'A Musician in Wartime'.

7 Letter from Chisholm to H. G. Farmer, 24 May 1945, Glasgow University Library, Farmer Collection 288/7.

8 Letter from Chisholm to H. G. Farmer, 11 June 1945, Glasgow University Library, Farmer Collection 288/8.

9 An alternative but unlikely date of 1943 is given in K. Wright, 'Erik Chisholm: A Tribute', *Composer*, 17, October 1965, pp. 34–5.

10 Letter to Chisholm from Sir Hector Hetherington, 11 July 1945; Morag Chisholm Papers.

11 Chisholm, typescript for 'A Musician in Wartime'.

12 Letter from Sheila Chisholm to her father, 20 July 1945; Morag Chisholm Papers.

13 *Evening News of India*, 15 September 1945; Chisholm Papers, Box 22, 164.

14 Letter from Lt. Colonel J. E. Hawkins for OC. ENSA, India and SEAC; Chisholm Papers, Box 22, 164.

15 Correspondence in ENSA file; Morag Chisholm Papers.

16 [To] Major Parkin, Accounts Department, ENSA, Green's Hotel, Bombay, 26.1. [1946].

Dear Major Parkin,

With reference to the account you sent me, re (1) the main burden of this, i.e. excess on my hotel accommodation at the Taj Mahal: will you please refer this to Colonel Hawkins who possesses a medical certificate given me by Dr. Shenken stating that owing to the conditions [*sic*] of my eyes it is essential that I should

always be provided with a single room.

You may recall a request of mine for an entertainment allowance of Rs. 100/- which I claimed in connection with the formation of our Symphony Orchestra. As I had no bills for this you were unable to do anything about it but suggested, in future, I should have additional sums for entertainment put on my bill. The sum in question was incurred for meals at the Taj Mahal for Lieut. Eric Rankin, a possible assistant conductor, Mr. Dawson – violin, and Captain Verga – cello.

The additions to my Delhi bills were for mineral waters served at meals: I was informed that drinking the water in the Swiss Hotel was ill-advised at the period of my visit there.

I trust this provides you with the necessary information.

Yours sincerely

[unsigned carbon copy of a typescript in the Chisholm Papers, Box 22, 164].

17 E. Chisholm, typescript for 'A Musician in Wartime'.

18 Ibid. See also E. Chisholm, 'University, Symphony Orchestra, Ballet, Drama and Revue', *Evening News of India*, 26 October 1945; Chisholm Papers, Box 29, 223.

19 Typescript, 15 April 1959, for a radio talk, 'The Music I Like' by Erik Chisholm; Chisholm Papers, Box 8, 32.

20 Typescript from Lily Savitz, headed 'TD 68/4 – From the estate of Dr. Erik Chisholm', January 1968; Morag Chisholm Papers.

21 Unidentified Cape Town newspaper cutting, 1949? Chisholm Papers, Box 1, 22.

22 Sheila Chisholm, radio interview on Fine Music Radio, Cape Town, 1.2.2004.

23 Chisholm's appointment, title and accommodation are confirmed in a letter from Lt. Col. L. Stokes-Roberts, Officer i/c ENSA Entertainments, Allied Land Forces, South East Asia; to Officer i/c ENSA Entertainments, No. 2 Area, SEAC, 27 October 1945; Morag Chisholm Papers.

24 Letter from Chisholm, Calcutta, to Colonel White, O.C. ENSA India & SEAC. Bombay, 6 November 1945; Chisholm Papers, Box 22, 164.

25 Letter to Chisholm from J. Studer, Joint

Honorary Secretary of the Bombay Choral & Philharmonic Society, 29 October 1945; Morag Chisholm Papers.

26 Jack Hawkins, famous for his roles in films such as *The Cruel Sea*.

27 Carbon copy of letter from Chisholm to Director of N.S.E. at the Theatre Royal in London, 29 October 1945; Morag Chisholm papers. Also carbon copy of a lengthy letter of protest and self-justification to Colonel White, 6 November 1945; Morag Chisholm Papers, Correspondence.

28 NAAFI posters for December 1945 and January 1946; Chisholm Papers, Programmes Box 5, 26.

29 See anonymous article, 'Singapore Symphony Orchestra' and Chisholm Papers, BC 129, Box 22, File 164, for correspondence.

30 Chisholm, typescript for 'A Musician in Wartime'.

31 Chisholm, letter of thanks to Lt. Col. R. E. Foulger, Commissioner of Police, Singapore, 10 April [1946]; Chisholm Papers, Box 22, 164.

32 Chisholm, letter of thanks to Sir Keith Park, 10 April 1946; Chisholm Papers, Box 22, 164.

33 Chisholm, letter to Ernest Dennis, 10 February 1946; Chisholm Papers, Box 22, 164.

34 Chisholm Papers, Box 22, 164.

35 Letter from Chisholm (in Singapore) to Professor Irving in Cape Town, 18 January 1946; Chisholm Papers, Box 22, 164.

36 Carbon copy of unsigned letter to Sgt. Maj. Simpson, 20 February 1946; Chisholm Papers, Box 22, 164.

37 Letter from Chisholm to Keith Park, 22 February; reply from Keith Park, 22 February 1946; Chisholm Papers, Box 22, 164.

38 Carbon copy of letter from Chisholm to Dr Sandre, unsigned, 25 February 1946; Chisholm Papers, Box 22, 164.

39 E. Chisholm, letter of thanks to the Manager of Raffles Hotel, 10 April 1946; Chisholm Papers, Box 22, 164.

40 Undated typescript headed, 'Lieut. Col. E. Dennis'; Chisholm Papers, Box 22, 164.

41 Chisholm, typescript for 'A Musician in Wartime'.

42 Letter from Chisholm (in Singapore) to Professor Irving in Cape Town, 18 January 1946; Chisholm Papers, Box 22, 164.

43 P. Abisheganaden, *Notes Across the Years – Anecdotes from a Musical Life*, Singapore, 2005, p. 113. I am grateful to Tou Liang Chang for drawing my attention to this work.

44 Alan Gordon, 'The Hardest Working Man in Singapore', undated, unidentified newspaper cutting; Morag Chisholm Papers, being a published version of the typescript.

45 Letter from the Secretary, South Africa House, Trafalgar Square, London WC2, 21 July 1945 to the Registrar at UCT. UCT University Archives, Chair of Music 1939–45, Box 12.1.5; and telegram from the High Commissioner of South Africa to the Registrar at UCT, 18 May 1945, on the back of which has been written by hand, 'Dr Kenneth Barritt considered best of local applicants ...', UCT University Archives, Chair of Music 1939–45, Box 12.1.5. In the event, Kenneth Barritt ended up in Glasgow at the Royal Scottish Academy of Music and Drama.

46 Letter from A. Goldsborough, to Bell, 8 July 1945, UCT University Archives, Chair of Music 1939–45, Box 12.1.5.

47 Carbon copy of telegram sent to the High Commissioner for South Africa, Trafalgar Square, London, 29 August 1945, UCT University Archives, Chair of Music 1939–45, Box 12.1.5.

48 Letter from Chisholm at ENSA Headquarters, Green's Hotel, Bombay, 26 September 1945 addressed 'Sir' – presumably the registrar at UCT, UCT University Archives, Chair of Music 1939–45, Box 12.1.5.

49 Unsigned letter to Chisholm, on Jashf Dolotine's notepaper, 7 September 1945; Morag Chisholm Papers, Correspondence. Also letter with damaged date – probably 1945 – signed 'Jashf' to Diana Chisholm; Morag Chisholm Papers, Letters from Musical Celebrities. Virginia Fortescue identifies the correspondent as Jashf Crandall. The name 'Dolotine' is not explained.

50 Carbon copy of a TS letter from Chisholm, 18 January 1946, to Irving at the Medical School, Mowbray, Cape Town; Chisholm Papers, Box 22, 164.

51 UCT Minutes of the Board of the Faculty of Music, 17 June 1946 at the University Office, UCT University Archives, Music1923–47.

52 Letter from J. Cameron Taylor to Chisholm, 8 February 1946; Chisholm Papers, Correspondence G–Z.

53 Travel permit for 30 April 1946; Morag Chisholm Papers, ENSA Box.

CHAPTER 7 Under Table Mountain

1 An interview in the Cape Argus of 15 May 1946 provides a *terminus post quem*; Chisholm Papers, Newspaper clippings, Box 21, 157.

2 'B.M', 'Dr. Erik Chisholm Arrives', unidentified Cape Town newspaper clipping, 1946; Chisholm Papers, Newspaper Clippings, Box 21, 157.

3 Travel permit for 30 April 1946; Morag Chisholm Papers, ENSA Box.

4 University of Cape Town, *Calendar 1948–1949*, 'Faculty of Music', Cape Town, 1948, p. 2.

5 Chisholm, 'What Life Has Taught Me', interview with Cyril Watling, *Cape Times Weekend Magazine*, 16 May 1964.

6 University of Cape Town, *Calendars*, 1939–47.

7 Letter from J. Cameron Taylor to Chisholm, 8 February 1946; Chisholm Papers, Correspondence G–Z.

8 Letter from Chisholm to Cameron Taylor, 29 March 1946; Chisholm Papers, Box 22, 164.

9 Ibid.

10 Letter from Chisholm to Admiral Lord Louis Mountbatten, 10 April 1946; Chisholm Papers, Box 22, 164.

11 Personal communication from Morag Chisholm.

12 Personal communication from Morag Chisholm.

13 Letter from John Andrews, 27 November 61 addressed to 'My Dear Volcanic, Earthquaking Tornado, named for short, Erik'; Chisholm Papers, Correspondence A–I.

14 Personal communication from Morag Chisholm.

15 Ernest Newman, 'The Edinburgh Festival', *Sunday Times*, 31 August 1947; Chisholm Papers, Writings about EC, Box 1, 22.

16 Information from Virginia Fortescue, letter to the author 30 July 2006.

17 Minutes of UCT Council's Finance Committee, 13/8/1947, appendix.

18 A. Gobbato, Lecture given at 54th UCT Summer School, Baxter Theatre, 27 January 2004, and University of Cape Town, *Calendar 1948–1949*, 'Faculty of Music', Cape Town, 1948, p. 2.

19 H. Phillips, *The University of Cape Town 1918–1948: The Formative Years*, Cape Town, 1993, pp. 288–90.

20 D. Talbot, *For the Love of Singing*, Cape Town, 1978, p. 21.

21 Ibid., p. 9.

22 UCT Administration Archives, file on Chair of Music, 1945, Chisholm to Carter, 14 January 1946.

23 Memorandum attached to the Minutes of the UCT Board of the Faculty of Music meeting, 3 June 1946, pp. 2–3, UCT Archives.

24 M. Brimer, 'Music, Opera and Ballet', in *UCT at 150: Reflections*, Cape Town, 1979, pp. 73–6.

25 Unsigned copy of submission to the Registrar, 29 September 1947, UCT Archives.

26 Diana Chisholm, interview with S. S. Buis, 1979; Morag Chisholm Papers.

27 *Cape Argus*, 17 September 1947.

28 *Varsity*, 3 April 1947.

29 Giuseppe Paganelli was voice teacher at the Cape Town College of Music from 1926–44: see Talbot, *For the Love of Singing*, chapters 1 and 2.

30 Brimer, 'Music, Opera and Ballet', pp. 73–6.

31 Gobbato, lecture given at the 54th UCT Summer School.

32 Talbot, *For the Love of Singing*, p. 24.

33 Personal communication from Robin Harvey.

34 Concert programme, Hiddingh Hall, Cape Town, 13 December 1946; Chisholm Papers, Programmes Box 29, 228.

35 Anon., 'Fiasconaro and Talbot', *Probe*, 7 (1), 30 July 1959, p. 1; Chisholm Papers, Box 16, 136.

36 Concert programme, Hiddingh Hall, Cape Town, 13 December 1946; Chisholm Papers, Box 3, 18.

37 Gc 792.809 41435 CEL Celtic Ballet Programmes, Mitchell Library, Glasgow. The performance was in 1948.

38 M. Morris, *My Life in Movement*, London, 1969, and The International Association of MMM Ltd. Garelochhead, 2003, pp. 107–8.

39 Personal communication from Morag and Fiona Chisholm.

40 Letter from John Chisholm to Erik Chisholm, 1 May 1949; Chisholm Papers, Box 16, 126.

41 Personal communication from Morag and Fiona Chisholm.

42 M. Lindsay, 'Week-End Concerts', *The Glasgow Bulletin*, 12 December 1949; Chisholm Papers, Box 1, 22.

43 Letter from Chisholm to Clinton Gray-Fisk (Chisholm spells his name Clifton Gray-Fiske), 21 January 1953, carbon copy in Chisholm Papers, Correspondence G–Z.

44 E. Chisholm, 'The Music I Like', 15 April 1959. This is the third of three draft typescripts of a radio talk – evidenced by the suggested experiment in paragraph three of the typescripts – all three substantially corrected and the latest one with many cuts indicated, possibly to meet time or space exigencies. This transcription includes all the material intended to be cut and also silently includes pencil alterations, all made in Chisholm's hand; Chisholm Papers, Box 8, 32.

45 Typescript from Lily Savitz, headed 'TD 68/4 – From the estate of Dr. Erik Chisholm', January 1968; Morag Chisholm Papers.

46 Chisholm Papers, TPA 781.7 CHI 80/446.

47 Concert programmes, ISCM concert, Hiddingh Hall, 22 November 1949; Chisholm Papers, Box 3, 18.

48 Anon., but almost certainly Christopher Grier (see following), 'New Piano Concerto', *The Scotsman*, 7 February 1950; Chisholm

Papers, Box 1, 22. A more extended version of this review, but one that adds little except general admiration, was broadcast on the Scottish Home Service from Edinburgh on Wednesday 1 March 1950, 10.00–10.45, as part of the 'Arts Review' programme; Chisholm Papers, Box 1, 22.

49 Erik Chisholm, Concerto for Piano and Orchestra, No. 2, arranged for two pianos, London, 1951.

50 *Radio Times* for the week beginning 11 September 1953.

51 Letter from Chisholm to Gray-Fiske, 8 April 1953; Chisholm Papers, Correspondence G–Z.

52 Carbon copy of unheaded letter from Chisholm to Dr Antony Baldwin, 12 September 1952; Chisholm Papers, Correspondence A–I.

53 Letter from Chisholm to Clinton Gray-Fisk, 21 January 1953.

54 Asad Ali Khan, liner notes for cassette tape, *Maestro's Choice, Series One, Asad Ali Khan*, Music Today, A91012.

55 Prakriti Dutta in conversation with John Purser, BBC Radio Scotland *Scotland's Music*, programme 42, 'A Trip to Hindustan', broadcast 28 October 2007.

56 Ibid.

57 Maharana Vijayadevji of Dharampur, *Sangit Bhâva*, Bombay, 1939, p. 27 (copy in University of Cape Town Library).

58 Ibid., p. 29.

59 The characteristics associated with the various râgas are derived from the relevant comments in *Sangit Bhava* and from Alain Daniélou's *The Râgas of Northern Indian Music*, London, 1968, Part II.

60 Ernest Fleischman, in an otherwise thoroughly laudatory review, wrote that 'The insistent ground of the sixth [variation] (for piano solo) tended to pall somewhat, though.' 'E. F', 'First Performance of Chisholm Concerto', *Cape Times*, 23 November 1949.

61 The spelling 'Buresca' in the full score is a simple error on Chisholm's part.

62 'The Music Critic', 'Szymon Goldberg in First Performance of Chisholm Concerto', *Cape Argus*, 19 March 1952; Chisholm Papers.

63 Maharana Vijayadevji of Dharampur, *Sangit Bhâva*, p. 67.

64 A. H. Fox Strangways, *The Music of Hindostan*, Oxford, 1914, p. 162.

65 Typescript draft entitled 'Why I Am Not a Christian', with corrections in ink and pencil, dated 12 May 1959, and partial typescript incorporating the corrections up to clause (g); Chisholm Papers, Box 8, 32.

66 Concert programme, ISCM, Hiddingh Hall, 8 August 1950.

67 Typescript classified list of compositions, undated but presumably late 1951, as the Violin Concerto is described as having a 'forthcoming first performance' in March, 1952; Chisholm Papers.

68 Faculty of Music 1923–50, brochure; Chisholm Papers, Box 27, 200.

69 Gobbato, lecture given at 54th UCT Summer School, Baxter Theatre, 27 January 2004, and University of Cape Town, *Calendar 1948–1949*, 'Faculty of Music', Cape Town, 1948, p. 2.

70 Concert programme, UCT University Music Society, Hiddingh Hall, 13 September 1950; Chisholm Papers, Box 3, 18.

71 Souvenir programme, UCT Arts Festival, 1951, in possession of Lily Savitz.

72 Letter from Ernest Fleischman to Lily Savitz, 16 September 1992, courtesy of Lily Savitz.

73 Typescript list of Chisholm's works; Morag Chisholm Papers.

74 Letter from Chisholm to William Adam, 30 March 1950; Morag Chisholm Papers, Correspondence.

75 TS of notes compiled by Chisholm; Chisholm Papers, T780.941 55/131.

76 Flyer for recital series of Hindemith quartets, which refers back to the Bartók series; Chisholm Papers, Box 1, 7.

77 Carbon copy of letter from Chisholm to Christopher Grier at *The Scotsman*, 20 January 1951; Chisholm Papers, Correspondence G–Z.

78 Letter from Christopher Grier to Chisholm, 10 February 1951; Chisholm Papers, Correspondence, G–Z.

79 Carbon copy of unheaded letter from Chisholm to Dame Ninette de Valois at Sadlers Wells, London, 7 August 1952; Chisholm Papers, Correspondence, A–I.

80 Letter from Dame Ninette de Valois, Royal Opera House, Covent Garden, London, to Chisholm at UCT, 20 August 1952; Chisholm Papers, Correspondence, A–I.

81 Letter from Chisholm to J. Gibson at J. & W. Chester Ltd., 3 November 1952, and replies from Gibson to Chisholm, 24 September and 15 October 1952; Chisholm Papers, Correspondence, A–I.

82 Carbon copy of letter from Chisholm to Paul Hindemith, Music Department, Yale University, Newhaven, Conn., 21 August 1952; Chisholm Papers, Correspondence, G–Z.

83 Christmas card from Paul Hindemith to Chisholm, Christmas/New Year 1952/3; Chisholm Papers, Correspondence G–Z.

84 Carbon copy of letter from Chisholm to Paul Hindemith, Music Department, Yale University, Newhaven, Conn., 24 June 1953; Chisholm Papers, Correspondence, G–Z.

85 Flyer for recital series of Hindemith quartets, which took place on 14 and 21 November and 5 December 1952; Chisholm Papers, Box 1, 7.

86 Carbon copy of unheaded letter from Chisholm to Francis Judd Cooke at the New England Conservatory, Boston, 27 November 1952, p. 2; Chisholm Papers, Correspondence, A–I.

87 Undated recorded interview between Morag and Fiona Chisholm and Michael Whiteman.

88 Typescript of productions in Chisholm Papers, 1.3.5, formerly Box 27, 200.

89 Talbot, *For the Love of Singing*, p. 39.

90 'News, South Africa', *Opera*, 5 (10), October 1954, pp. 629–30; Chisholm Papers, Box 2, 15.

91 Carbon copy of letters from Chisholm to Clinton Gray-Fisk, 21 January 1953, 8 April 1953 and letter to Chisholm from Gray-Fisk, 9 February 1953; Chisholm Papers, Correspondence, G–Z (see letters to and from for fuller texts).

92 Carbon copy of letter from Chisholm to Rafael Kubelik, at the Chicago Symphony Orchestra, 28 February 1953, and reply from Kubelik, 7 May 1953; Chisholm Papers, Correspondence, G–Z.

93 Letter from L. M. Gilbert, 23 March

1953, to Chisholm at UCT; Chisholm Papers, Correspondence, G–Z.

94 Carbon copy of letter to L. M. Gilbert, 27 March 1953; Chisholm Papers, Correspondence, G–Z.

95 Personal communication from Sheila Chisholm.

96 Typescript draft entitled 'Why I Am Not a Christian', with corrections in ink and pencil, dated 12 May 1959, and partial

typescript incorporating the corrections up to clause (g); Chisholm Papers, Box 8, 32.

97 Personal communication from Morag Chisholm.

98 Unidentified article with 'article by Watson Lyle – 1932' in ink, in Chisholm's hand, written beside it; Chisholm Papers, Box 16, 126. The relevant passage is quoted in Chapter 1.

99 Talbot, *For the Love of Singing*, p. 50.

CHAPTER 8   On Tour in the USA and Europe

1 Letter from the Vice-Chancellor of Queen's University, Belfast, Eric Ashby, 17 September 1953 to Chisholm suggesting a meeting there in January; Chisholm Papers, Correspondence A–K, 219.

2 Letter from Chisholm to Christopher Grier, music critic, *The Scotsman*, Edinburgh, 16 June 1953; Chisholm Papers, Correspondence G–Z, 220.

3 K. A. Wright, 'Dark Sonnet', television programmes for Tuesday 29 January 1954, *Radio Times*, p. 26.

4 Carbon copy of an unheaded letter from Chisholm to Miss Joan Cross, 4 March 1953; Chisholm Papers, Correspondence A–I, – 'now renamed "Dark Sonnet" with the author's approval'.

5 Carbon copy of unheaded letter from Chisholm to Francis Judd Cooke at the New England Conservatory, Boston, 27 November 1952, p. 2; Chisholm Papers, Correspondence A–I, p. 3.

6 Carbon copy of letter to Christopher Grier, music critic, *The Scotsman*, 12 August 1952; Chisholm Papers, Correspondence A–I.

7 Opera programme, Stellenbosch Town Hall, 29 October 1952; Chisholm Papers, Box 3, 16.

8 'B.M.', 'Well-deserved Success at Little Theatre', *Cape Times*, 20 October 1952; Chisholm Papers, Box 21, 159.

9 Pencil markings on the vocal score indicate such a performance, though it may simply have been as part of a lecture on the work, for they are in the same hand as that which outlined the appearances of the motifs on the flyleaf; Chisholm Papers,

Simoon vocal score, uncatalogued but with TD 68/4 pencilled in facing frontispiece.

10 Carbon copy of unheaded letter from Chisholm to Francis Judd Cooke at the New England Conservatory, 27 November 1952, p. 2; Chisholm Papers, Correspondence A–I. *Simoon* was planned as part of a group of operas whose subject matter was murder. In this, Chisholm no doubt recalled his youthful fascination with the macabre character of Grand Guignol. However, the order of the operas seems to have been fluid to say the least, as the month before he wrote this letter he had placed *The Pardoner's Tale* as 'the first part' of a '3-Act opera "Murder in 4 Keys"'. It also is not clear why this fluid group is sometimes described as 'Murder in 4 Keys' and other times 'Murder in 3 Keys'.

11 A guide to the appearances of these motifs has been pencilled inside the cover of the vocal score (TD 68/4) as follows: Biskra, 13, 17, 22, 23, 25, 27, 33, 37, 38, 101. Yusuf, 15. Hate, 21, 22, 24, 30, 37, 38, 39. Love, 24–36. Pride, 26, 100. Magic, 29. Spring, 28–32. Guimard, 29, 36, 43–6, 50–2, 87, 89, 90, 94, 98, 100. It is not clear in whose hand this guide has been written.

12 Frontispiece of full score of *Simoon*; Chisholm Papers, uncatalogued, but with TD 68/4 pencilled in facing frontispiece.

13 Vocal score of *Simoon*; Chisholm Papers, uncatalogued, but with TD 68/4 pencilled in facing frontispiece.

14 In the vocal score, Yusuf's line in bar 497 is marked back one beat, starting therefore on the last quaver of bar 496. This is not marked in on the full score.

15 Letter to Christopher Grier, music

critic, *The Scotsman*, 23 July 1954; Chisholm Papers, Correspondence G–Z.

16 Letter from Chisholm to H. G. Farmer, 30 September 1955, Glasgow University Library, Farmer Collection 303.

17 Letter to Leonard Sargent at UCT, 27 December 1953, airmailed from Southampton 28 December 1953.

18 'Dear Mr. Copland, If you have got a marvellous memory, you will recall having met me in a tea-shop in New York sometime in January '54.' But this seems impossible unless Chisholm returned to the USA. Letter from Chisholm to Aaron Copland, 3 September 1959; Chisholm Papers, B.1.1.1, Box 23, 165.

19 Letter from *Queen Mary* to Leonard Sargent at the Department of Extra-Mural Studies, UCT, 27 December 1953; Chisholm Papers Box 1, 22.

20 'Passer-By', 'Pertinent and Otherwise', *The Bulletin*, 11 September 1953; and 'M. B.', 'Erik Chisholm Operas', *The Glasgow Herald*, 16 September 1953.

21 Carbon copy of unheaded letter to Valerie Fletcher, secretary to Eliot, at Faber & Faber, 9 March 1954; and typescript copy of headed letter to T. S. Eliot, Esq., S.S. 'Pretoria Castle', Docks, CAPE TOWN, 25 February 1954; Chisholm Papers, Correspondence A–K.

22 E. Chisholm, typescript of article written by the composer for publicity in connection with the New York production; Chisholm Papers, Box 16, 131, p. 1.

23 Ibid., p. 2.

24 Carbon copy of letter from Chisholm to William MacLellan, 14 December 1960; Chisholm Papers, Correspondence G–Z.

25 D. Talbot, *For the Love of Singing*, Cape Town, 1978, p. 43.

26 Letter from Chisholm to Professor Douglas Clarke, Dean of the Faculty of Music, McGill University, 22 December 1954; Chisholm Papers, Correspondence A–K.

27 M. Ballinger, *From Union to Apartheid*, Cape Town, 1969, p. 309; and R. De Villiers, 'Afrikaner Nationalism', in M. Wilson and L. Thompson (eds.), *The Oxford History of South Africa*, Oxford, 1971, vol. II, p. 406.

28 Carbon copy of letter of 23 July 1954

to Miss Agnes Duncan (no address given); Chisholm Papers, Correspondence A–K.

29 Letter from Chisholm to Dr Henry George Farmer, c/o The Library, University of Glasgow, 30 September 1955, Glasgow University Library, Farmer Collection 303.

30 'Forgotten Scot Back As Leader, by Daily Mail Reporter', *Daily Mail*, 7 March 1950; Chisholm Papers, Box 1, 22.

31 Letter to Chisholm from Percy Grainger at 7 Cromwell Place, White Plains, NY, 25 August 1955; Chisholm Papers, Correspondence G–Z.

32 Carbon copy of letter to the Editor, *Cape Times*, 24 April 1956; Chisholm Papers.

33 Carbon copy of letter to the Editor, *Cape Times*, 17 May 1956; Chisholm Papers.

34 Information kindly supplied by Virginia Fortescue in a letter to the author of 30 July 2006.

35 Carbon copy of undated typescript in Chisholm Papers, Box 8, 32.

36 Carbon copy of Memo PMcD/RW, 8 November 1956, unsigned, but for Registrar, UCT University Archives, Chisholm personal file.

37 Unattributed article, 'Wigmore Hall', *The Times*, 1 January 1957, p. 3e.

38 Unattributed article, 'Wigmore Hall', *The Times*, 31 December 1956, p. 3g.

39 Unattributed article, 'Wigmore Hall', *The Times*, 3 January 1957, p. 4g.

40 Unattributed article, 'Wigmore Hall', *The Times*, 7 January 1957, p. 12d.

41 Undated typescript; Chisholm Papers, Box 17, 139.

42 Ibid.

43 Information kindly supplied by Virginia Fortescue in a letter to the author of 30 July 2006.

44 Letter from Peter Bartók to Chisholm, 23 October 1956; Chisholm Papers, BC129, Correspondence A–I.

45 Dunedin Society, Glasgow Festival of Opera and Chamber Music programme, 22–30 January 1957; Chisholm Papers, Box 29, 228.

46 M. Lindsay, Francis George Scott and the Scottish Renaissance, Edinburgh, 1980, p. 139.

47 Typescript programme of recital of

songs and piano music from Erik Chisholm's *Celtic Song Book*, 3 May 1957; Chisholm Papers, Box 2, 242.

48 M. Lindsay, 'Erik Chisholm's Collection', *The Glasgow Bulletin*, 26 January 1957.

49 E. Chisholm, '1st Lecture on A Celtic Song Book'; Chisholm Papers Box 9, 241.

50 For instance, No. 10, *Sud air m' aigne fo ghruaim* is a 9/8 version of the tune used for Iain Luim's *Oran do Dhòmhnall Gorm*; No. 20 is the air for Roderick Morison's *Creach na Ciadaoin*; No. 21, *A' bhliadhna gus an aimsir so*, goes with Duncan Ban MacIntyre's *Oran an t-Samhraidh*; No. 49, *'S e Coinneach òg a fhuair an togail* belongs to Iain Luim's *Oran do Choinneach Og Iarla Shìoford*; No. 61, *Keapach 'na fasach* goes

with Iain Luim's *Murt na Ceapaich*; No. 65, *Imir sein, a Choinnich chridhe* is used for the 'Ness Rowing Song'; No. 101, *Tha mo chion air an ùr ghibht* is probably the correct air for Sìleas na Ceapaich's *Comhairle air na Nigheanan Òga*; No. 132, *Coir a' cheathaich* belongs to Duncan Ban MacIntyre's *Oran Coire a' Cheathaich*; No. 139, *Màraidh bhàn òg*, is the air for Duncan Ban MacIntyre's *Oran d' a Cheile Nuadh-Phosda*; No. 140, *Scian 'sgur fad tha mi m' thàmh* is the air for Iain Luim's *Cumha do Shir Dòmhnall Shléite*; No. 166, *A 'cheud luan do'n ràidh* has famous words by Roderick Morrison.

51 Chisholm, '1st Lecture on A Celtic Song Book'.

CHAPTER 9   Soviet Ambassador

1 Carbon copy of letter from Diana Chisholm to the Editor, 'OPUS', Johannesburg, 12 August 1966; Morag Chisholm Papers, and article by E. Chisholm, 'We Lived in Luxury in Moscow', *Cape Argus*, 10 September 1957.

2 Hanns Eisler was the Deputy Chairman, and Kilpinen was also on the jury. Typescript of results; Chisholm Papers, Box 6, 221.

3 Anon., 'Russians Bubbling Over with Friendship and Hospitality', *New Age*, 5 September 1957; Chisholm Papers, Box 16, 136.

4 E. Chisholm, two articles in the *Cape Argus*, the first ('We Lived in Luxury in Moscow') dated 10 September 1957; the second ('Russians Queuing for Music Records Are like Bargain-hunters'), undated, but presumably later in September 1957.

5 Typescript draft entitled 'Why I Am Not a Christian', with corrections in ink and pencil, dated 12 May 1959, and partial typescript incorporating the corrections up to clause (g); Chisholm Papers, Box 8, 32.

6 Postcard from Chisholm to Phyllis Brodie, 6 August 1957; Morag Chisholm Papers.

7 Letter from Oda Slobodskaya to Chisholm, postmarked 2 December 1954; Morag Chisholm Papers, Letters from Musical Celebrities.

8 Letter from Chisholm to Oda

Slobodskaya, 17 January 1955; Morag Chisholm Papers, Letters from Musical Celebrities.

9 Letter from Nicolas Slonimsky to Chisholm, 25 January 1958; Morag Chisholm Papers, Correspondence.

10 Letter from Henry Cowell to Chisholm, 16 January 1958; Chisholm Papers, Correspondence A–K.

11 Carbon copy of unheaded letter from Chisholm to Dr Lubomir Doruzka, c/o Shv State Publishing House of Music, Palackého 1, Prague 1, Czechoslovakia, 19 January 1965; Chisholm Papers, Correspondence A–I.

12 Letter to Chisholm from the registrar UCT, 16 June 1958, ref. PWL/RW, UCT Archives, Chisholm personal file.

13 Letters to Chisholm from the registrar UCT, 26 January 1961, ref. PWL/EJH and 9 June 1961 from J. G. Benfield, ref. PWL/EJH, UCT Archives, Chisholm personal file.

14 Personal communication from Morag Chisholm.

15 Letter from Morag Chisholm to her father, 9 August 1958; Morag Chisholm Papers.

16 Typescript of letter from Chisholm to the editor, *Cape Times*, 12 June 1958. 'B.G.' was Blanche Gerstman, a former student at the College of Music, a composer and bass player (information from Virginia Fortescue).

17 UCT Opera Company, opera season

1958, *Souvenir Programme*; Chisholm Papers, 1.3.5, formerly Box 27, 200.

18 Personal information from Sheila and Fiona Chisholm, and *Varsity*, 5 March 1959, p. 5.

19 (Cape) *Sunday Times* correspondents, 'Festival Troubles', *Sunday Times*, 5 July 1959; Chisholm Papers, Box 16, 136.

20 F. Chisholm, 'Conductor Loved Controversy', *Cape Argus Tonight*, 23 January 2004, 'People' section, p. 8.

21 Personal communication from John Joubert.

22 E. Chisholm, 'Foreword' in the *Souvenir Programme* of the Golden Jubilee Year of the UCT South African College of Music; Chisholm Papers Box 4, 19, pp. 7, 9. Chisholm also wrote to the USSR State Publishing House enclosing a catalogue of '100 L.P. records in forty-three African languages: also a list of some relevant books' in a letter dated 9 March 1961; Chisholm Papers, Box 9, 245.

23 See Hindemith correspondence; Chisholm Papers, Correspondence G–Z.

24 Handwritten translation of a (missing) original, Minister, Office of Culture, USSR, Moscow, 28 June 1959; Chisholm Papers, Box 23, 165.

25 Letter from Kabalevsky (plus handwritten translation) to Chisholm, 30 July 1959; Chisholm Papers, Box 23, 165.

26 Letter and translation from L. Soupagin at the USSR Ministry of Culture, to Chisholm, 21 September 1959; Chisholm Papers, Box 23, 165.

27 Correspondence from Chisholm to Mr Ivanian, 28 August 1959; Minister Boni, 14 December 1959 and 26 February 1960; to Ivanov, 31 March 1960; to Mr Boni, 12 May 1960, 18 May 1960 and 3 June 1960; and to Mr Sergei Molochkov, 30 May 1960. Reply from L. Soupagin, 15 July 1960; Chisholm Papers, Box 23, 165.

28 Seiber came as a lecturer for the Students' Visiting Lecturers Trust Fund, and as a composer and conductor for the College. Letter from Chisholm to Professor W. H. Hutt, 10 June 1960; Chisholm Papers, Box 28, 215.

29 Golden Jubilee Music Festival, programme for 25 and 30 August 1960, final symphony concert; Chisholm Papers,

Golden Jubilee Festival Programme, Box 28, 206.

30 Sundry correspondence from Stanley Glasser in the spring of 1960; Chisholm Papers, B1.1.2, formerly Box 23, 170.

31 Sundry correspondence from and to Chisholm, spring 1960; Chisholm Papers, Box 27, 129.

32 Memorial notice in the UCT *Staff Newsletter*, December 1963.

33 *Varsity*, 11 May 1960, p. 4; 18 May 1960, p. 4; 25 May 1960, p. 4.

34 Letter from K. P. Ranindranathan, Government of India, Under-Secretary to the Ministry of Scientific and Cultural Affairs, New Delhi, 25 June 1960.

35 Carbon copy of letter from Chisholm to Mr William MacLellan, 240 Hope Street, Glasgow, 10 February 1960; Chisholm Papers, Correspondence G–Z.

36 Letter to William MacLellan, 30 November 1960; Chisholm Papers, Correspondence G–Z.

37 E. Chisholm, *Men and Music – Medtner*; Morag Chisholm Papers.

38 Autograph notes for a speech delivered in Riga, no date, but presumably September, 1962; Morag Chisholm Papers.

39 Postcard from Chisholm to Morag Chisholm, 29 September 1962; Morag Chisholm Papers.

40 Autograph notes for a speech delivered in Riga, no date, but presumably September, 1962; Morag Chisholm Papers.

41 E. Chisholm, 'The Wonder of English'; Chisholm Papers, Box 8, 32.

42 Ibid.

43 Letter from Nevill Coghill at Merton College, Oxford, to Chisholm, 18 January 1962; Chisholm Papers, Correspondence, A–I.

44 A. Gobbato, Lecture given at 54th UCT Summer School, Baxter Theatre, 28 January 2004.

45 A computer typeset version of the vocal score published by Studio Holland (PTY) Ltd., Music Printers at Parow, held at SMC and UCT, appears to be based upon an early MS vocal score TD 383 TPA 780.7 CHI 61/538 in UCT dated 'end Feb. 8 1961 at Wellington Rd. Durbanville at Sheila Smit's place'. This score is marked in Chisholm's hand with

many alterations and additions, which have not been incorporated into the computer typeset version. Moreover, this version is full of errors and anomalies, particularly with regard to bar lengths and time signatures. It is possible that this version was based upon another early vocal score.

46 Letter from Chisholm to Morag Chisholm, 12 January 1961; Morag Chisholm Papers.

47 Gobbato, Lecture given at 54th UCT Summer School.

48 See H. E. Wooldridge, *Early English Harmony*, 1897, vol. I, plate 23.

49 Typescript in Chisholm Papers, Box 8, 37.

50 Letter from Nevill Coghill at Merton College, Oxford, to Chisholm, 14 January

1962; Chisholm Papers, Correspondence A–I.

51 Letter from Chisholm to Morag Chisholm, 2 March 1961; Morag Chisholm Papers.

52 Chisholm Papers, Opera 30, TPA 782.7.

53 Chisholm Papers, Opera 30, TPA 780.7 CHI 80/325.

54 Chisholm Papers, Box 8, 37.

55 Note in the full score, pp. 104–5; Chisholm Papers, Opera 30, TPA 782.7.

56 Chisholm Papers, Opera 28, TPA 782.7.

57 Letter from Chisholm to Diana, 2 March 1962; Morag Chisholm Papers.

58 Letter from Nevill Coghill at Merton College, Oxford, to Chisholm, 14 January 1962.

INTERLUDE   The Love of Janáček

1 I am indebted to Mrs Irene Ferguson, Assistant to the Edinburgh University Archivist at Special Collections, for this information.

2 E. Chisholm, 'Creative Education in Music', *Colston Papers*, XIV, being the Proceedings of the Fourteenth Symposium of the Colston Research Society held in the University of Bristol, April 2–5, London, 1962, p. 198.

3 K. Wright, 'Erik Chisholm: A Tribute', in E. Chisholm, *The Operas of Leoš Janáček*, Oxford, 1971, p. xx.

4 E. Chisholm, 'The Music I Like'; Chisholm Papers, Box 8, 32.

5 D. Talbot, *For the Love of Singing*, Cape Town, 1978, pp. 168–9.

6 J. Tyrrell, 'Reviews of Books – The Operas of Leoš Janáček', *Music and Letters*, 1972, pp. 74–7.

7 Personal interview with Marjorie and Ronald Stevenson, 11 May 2004.

8 M. Rayment, 'Penetrating Study of Janáček's Operas', *Glasgow Herald*, no date, cutting in Morag Chisholm Papers.

9 K. Wright, 'Editorial Note', in Chisholm, *The Operas of Leoš Janáček*, p. xv.

10 Chisholm, *The Operas of Leoš Janáček*, p. 8.

11 Ibid., pp. 314–15.

12 Wright, 'Editorial Note', p. xvi.

CHAPTER 10   Chasing a Restless Muse

1 It is not clear whether this was at Erik's insistence or the result of her own volition. Erik wrote, 'I refuse to go on with bickering life with her any more', and in a later letter wrote, 'By the way Mum furnished her flat by denuding our 14 York Rd place': letters from Chisholm to Morag Chisholm, 21 June 1961 and 28 October 1961; Morag Chisholm Papers.

2 Letter from Chisholm to Morag Chisholm, 30 June 61; Morag Chisholm Papers.

3 Letter from Chisholm to Morag Chisholm, 12 January 1961; Morag Chisholm Papers.

4 Letters from Chisholm to Morag Chisholm, 6 May 1961 and 30 June 1961; Morag Chisholm Papers.

5 Carbon copy of unheaded letter from Chisholm to Mr. G. Feldman, Chairman, Robert Burns Friendship Club, Pushkin School, No. 353, Moscow, 20 June 1963 [date added in ink by unknown hand]; Chisholm Papers, Correspondence A–I.

6 Morag and Sheila Chisholm, personal communication.

7 This whole sensitive matter has been discussed frankly with the three Chisholm daughters, Morag, Sheila and Fiona. Their different perspectives – and they are different – have never once inhibited my research, and I wish here especially to record my gratitude and admiration for their collective and individual honesty, even where their testimony has been slightly at odds.

8 Chisholm responding to Cyril Watling, *Cape Times Weekend Magazine*, 16 May 1964.

9 Among these were Noreen Cargill and Pat Montgomery – letter from Sheila Chisholm to her sister Morag, 25 September 2002; Morag Chisholm Papers.

10 Letters from Margaret May to the author, 20 September 2004 and 8 October 2004.

11 Letter from Gunter Pulvermacher, 15 December 1962, to Chisholm at UCT; Chisholm Papers, Correspondence G–Z.

12 Personal information from Lillias Scott.

13 Ibid.

14 Morag Chisholm, personal communication and letter from Lillias Scott Forbes to the author, 1 July 2005.

15 Chisholm, 'What Life Has Taught Me', interview with Cyril Watling, *Cape Times Weekend Magazine*, 16 May 1964.

16 Neil Solomon to the author, 2 November 2004.

17 Letter from Chisholm in Oxford to Mrs Diana Chisholm at 5 Astra Court, Mowbray, in Cape Town, wrongly dated by Chisholm as '9.II.63', but postmarked 9 February 1962; Morag Chisholm Papers.

18 Photocopy of letter from Chisholm to Phyllis Brodie, 14 December 1962; Morag Chisholm Papers.

19 Ibid.

20 Concert programme, University of Manchester, Faculty of Music, in the hall of the faculty, 16 November 1962; Chisholm Papers, Box 29, 228.

21 Letter to Chisholm from William MacLellan, 31 December 1962; Chisholm Papers, Correspondence G–Z.

22 Letter from Tom Price at UCT, 6 December 1962, to Chisholm at Oxford.

23 Letter to Chisholm at Oxford from M. Glasser at Wynberg, 16 January 1963.

24 *Standard Encyclopaedia of Southern Africa*, Cape Town, 1972, vol. 6, p. 36; and R. Davenport and C. Saunders, *South Africa – A Modern History*, 5th edition, Basingstoke, 2000, p. 378.

25 Letters from Chisholm dated 10 and 11 January were received by Fiasconaro, but their whereabouts are not known. Fiasconaro refers to them in his letter to Chisholm of 16 January 1963, Fiona Chisholm Papers.

26 Letter from Fiasconaro to Chisholm, 16 January 1963, Fiona Chisholm Papers.

27 Ibid.

28 Lillias Scott Forbes stated that they 'got on very well … and accepted each other's line of action' (letter to the author, 1 July 2005).

29 Letter from Fiasconaro to Chisholm, 26 January 1963, Fiona Chisholm Papers.

30 Letter from Virginia Fortescue to Chisholm, 31 January 1963; Chisholm Papers Correspondence A–K.

31 Suggestions that they were lovers are denied by Virginia Fortescue herself, who found him 'unattractive physically' (letter to the author, 30 July 2006). The suggestion was made by Lionel Bowman and is recorded in notes taken by H. Phillips from an interview with Lionel Bowman, 6 November 1992 (information and copy of his notes are courtesy of H. Phillips). Others have made similar suggestions, but rumour is no substitute for evidence.

32 Letter to Chisholm from Annette Rousseau, at the South African College of Music, 5 June 1962; Chisholm Papers, Correspondence G–Z.

33 Final order of Divorce Case No. I. 539/1963, witnessed 27 March 1963; Morag Chisholm Papers.

34 Letter from Chisholm to Morag Chisholm, 3 June 1963; Morag Chisholm Papers.

35 Ibid.

36 Undated, incomplete letter from Chisholm to Morag Chisholm; Morag Chisholm Papers. Fiona Chisholm questions

the reality of this caving in (personal communication), and Lillias Scott Forbes was unaware either of being cut or of any change of attitude (letter to the author, 1 July 2005).

37 Anon., 'Proposed Opera on Robert Burns', *The Times*, 22 January 1957, p. 2.

38 Dated in autograph list of works; Chisholm Papers, Box 16, 127.

39 Vocal score; Chisholm Papers, Opera 33, TPA 782.7 CHI 79/480.

40 Carbon copy of letter from Chisholm to Frank O'Connor, c/o Caedmon Publishers, 12 December 1960; Chisholm Papers, Celtic Song Book Correspondence, Box 9, 245.

41 Score, libretto and parts are in the Chisholm Papers, Opera 33, TPA 782.7 CHI 79/480.

42 B. Kennelly (ed.), 'Introduction', in *The Penguin Book of Irish Verse*, Harmondsworth, 1970, p. 34.

43 Carbon copy of unheaded letter from Chisholm to Mr G. Feldman, Chairman, Robert Burns Friendship Club, Pushkin School, No. 353, Moscow, 20 June 1963 [date added in ink by unknown hand]; Chisholm Papers, Correspondence A–I. A draft libretto in the Chisholm Papers (Own Music, Box 19, 153) was entered into a diary in Irish for 1957 which has a very few engagements entered in another hand than Chisholm's – a hand used to Irish orthography – but there is no indication to whom it belonged. Chisholm has cut and pasted in copies made from a life of Burns and has added his own notes in various inks and pencil. There is no indication that MacDiarmid has had a hand in this draft.

44 Autograph list of works; Chisholm Papers, Box 16, 127.

45 Chisholm Papers, Opera 51.

46 Personal interview with Marjorie and Ronald Stevenson, 11 May 2004.

47 Letter from Chisholm to Morag Chisholm, 23 April 1963; Morag Chisholm Papers.

48 Personal interview with Marjorie and Ronald Stevenson, 11 May 2004.

49 Concerts programme for UCT Faculty of Music, Hiddingh Hall Concerts and Lectures, August–December, 1963, programme for 19 November; Chisholm Papers, Box 29.

50 Chisholm Papers, Box 16, 136.

51 Letter from Chisholm to Morag Chisholm, 23 April 1963; Morag Chisholm Papers; and personal interview with Marjorie and Ronald Stevenson, 11 May 2004.

52 Personal interview with Marjorie and Ronald Stevenson, 11 May 2004.

53 Letter from Chisholm to Morag Chisholm, 8 March 1963; Morag Chisholm Papers.

54 Chisholm Papers, Opera 10–20, TPA 782.7 CHI 79.434,435,456,461; CHI 80.432,433.

55 Autograph list of works; Chisholm Papers, Box 16, 127.

56 Dedication on score; Chisholm Papers, TPA 782.7.

57 Note on score of *The Importance of Being Earnest*; Chisholm Papers, TPA 782.7.

58 Apparently Curwen had agreed to publish it, but there are no orchestral parts. A performance was proposed for September 1964, possibly by the English Opera Group under their then director, Meredith Davies, but it seems not to have taken place, although a number of vocal scores were prepared. Chisholm refers to a letter from Meredith Davies in this connection in his autograph list of works; Chisholm Papers, Box 16, 127. Fourteen vocal scores, not all complete, are in the Chisholm Papers, along with the opera.

59 Personal interview with Ronald and Marjorie Stevenson, 21 May 2004.

60 Personal interview with Marjorie and Ronald Stevenson, 11 May 2004.

61 Personal communication from Morag Chisholm.

62 Personal interview with Marjorie and Ronald Stevenson, 11 May 2004.

63 Ibid.

64 Copy of a letter from Chisholm to Sorabji, 31 July 1964; Morag Chisholm Papers, Sorabji Box.

65 Personal interview with Marjorie and Ronald Stevenson, 11 May 2004.

66 Copy of a letter on UCT notepaper from Chisholm to Stevenson, 6 August 1964; Morag Chisholm Papers.

67 H. MacDiarmid, letter to Ronald and Marjorie Stevenson, 27 June 1964, in

New Selected Letters, ed. Dorian Grieve, Owen Dudley Edwards and Alan Riach, Manchester, 2001, p. 397. He did, however, write to Lillias in November of that year, 'restating the variance of approach to musical matters' of Scott and Chisholm (letter from Lillias Scott Forbes to the author, 1 July 2005).

68 MacDiarmid, letter to Ronald and Marjorie Stevenson, 27 June 1964.

69 Chisholm, 'What Life Has Taught Me'.

70 See J. Purser, *Scotland's Music*, Edinburgh, 2007, chapter 15, esp. pp. 231–3.

71 Neil Solomon to the author, 2 November 2004.

72 L. Scott Chisholm, *Poems of Love*, Edinburgh, 1966, dedication.

73 Personal information from Lillias Scott Forbes.

74 Ibid.

75 See E. Bunting, *Ancient Irish Melodies*, Dublin, 1840, p. 83, footnote a.

76 Personal information from Lillias Scott Forbes.

77 Letter from Chisholm to Morag Chisholm, 17 January 1965; Morag Chisholm Papers.

78 Letter from Erik Chisholm to Mrs Diana Chisholm, 18 January 1965; Morag Chisholm Papers.

79 Ibid.

80 Letter from Lillias Scott (Chisholm) to Morag Chisholm, 26 July 1965; Morag Chisholm Papers.

81 *Varsity*, 12 May 1965, p. 3.

82 UCT, *News Diary*, 2 (5), 1965, p. 7.

83 Letter from Fiona Chisholm to Morag Chisholm, 9 June 1965; Morag Chisholm Papers.

84 Photostat copy of short death certificate, Chisholm, personal file, UCT Archives.

85 'Students Honour Dr. Chisholm', *Cape Times*, 11 June 1965; Chisholm Papers, BC 129, A9, formerly Box 17, 141.

86 Agnes Walker, 'Dr. Erik Chisholm', *Glasgow Illustrated*, August 1965, and memorial notice in the UCT *Staff Newsletter*, December 1963.

87 Obituaries, telegrams and letters are in a scrapbook in the Chisholm Papers, A9, formerly Box 17, 141.

88 Personal communication from Sheila Chisholm.

89 Anon., 'Prof. Chisholm, Composer and Conductor, Dies', *Cape Times*, 9 June 1965.

90 Letters to the editor, *Cape Times*?, 9 June 1965; Chisholm Papers, A9, formerly Box 17, 141.

91 Copy of tribute from Virginia Fortescue in letter to the author 30 July 2006.

92 'Obituary, Dr. Erik Chisholm', *The Times*, no date, but presumably on or shortly after 9 June 1965; Chisholm Papers, A9, formerly Box 17, 141.

93 D. Galloway, 'Dr. Erik Chisholm, *Opus*, 1 (4); Chisholm Papers, Box 2, 15.

94 Diana Chisholm, interview with S. S. Buis, 1979; Morag Chisholm Papers.

Select Bibliography

A COMPLETE BIBLIOGRAPHY OF ERIK CHISHOLM'S WRITINGS AND the writings about him and his works would constitute a small book on its own. This selection has substantially been made using clippings from a variety of sources – chiefly the Morag Chisholm Papers and the Chisholm Papers in the University of Cape Town at www.lib.uct.ac.za/mss/. Many of the clippings in these archives are unidentified or undated. Further references will be found in the endnotes, with details of current locations.

■ Books by Erik Chisholm (published)

The Operas of Leoš Janáček, Oxford, 1971.

■ Books by Erik Chisholm (unpublished)

Men and Music – a series of essays about the following, some of whom share an essay: Arnaud, Bartók, Bax, Busch (Adolf and Fritz), Casella, Grainger, Goossens (Eugene), Hindemith, Ireland, Lamond, Makushina, Medtner, Petri, Schmitt, Scott (Cyril), Shostakovich, Sorabji, Szymanowski, Tovey, Van Dieren, Walton.

■ Selected articles by Erik Chisholm (published)

'An Outstanding Work by a Native Composer – Mr Ian Whyte's Quintet', *The Scottish Musical Magazine*, XI (10), August 1930, pp. 184–5.

'The Active Society for the Propagation of Contemporary Music, Glasgow – First Concert', *The Scottish Musical Magazine*, XI (12), October 1930, pp. 222–3.

'The Active Society for the Propagation of Contemporary Music, Glasgow – Second Concert', *The Scottish Musical Magazine*, XI (12), October 1930, pp. 229–30.

'Third Concert of the Active Society', *The Scottish Musical Magazine*, XII (1), November 1930, pp. 5 *et seq.*

'Active Society's Concert, January 21st', *The Scottish Musical Magazine*, XII (3), January 1931, pp. 44–7.

'About Music – New Pieces for City', *Weekly Herald*, October 1935?

'About Music – Music in Soviet Russia No. I', *Weekly Herald*, 9 November 1935.

'About Music – Music in Soviet Russia No. II', *Weekly Herald*, 16 November 1935.

'About Music – Music in Soviet Russia No. III', *Weekly Herald*, 23 November 1935.

'About Music – The Operas of Feruccio Busoni', *Weekly Herald*, 30 November 1935.

'About Music – Busoni on the Possibilities of Music', *Weekly Herald*, 7 December 12 1935.

'About Music – Programme Builders', *Weekly Herald*, no date.

'About Music – On Jazz', *Weekly Herald*, no date.

'About Music – Where the Organ Fails', *Weekly Herald*, no date.

'About Music – Reviving Opera', *Weekly Herald*, no date.

'About Music – The Problem of Opera', *Weekly Herald*, no date

'About Music – Romance of Neglected Masterpieces', *Weekly Herald*, no date

'About Music – The Scandal of the Church Organist', *Weekly Herald*, no date

'Kaikhosru Sorabji – An essay by Erik Chisholm, with a descriptive catalogue of his works', London *c.* 1938, reprinted privately *c.* 1964.

'The Composer Sorabji' (with Frank Holliday) – transcript of a recorded talk, printed privately, 1970.

'Is Music a "Teachable" Subject?', *Evening News of India*, no date, Autumn 1945?

'Is Music a "Teachable" Subject?, II', *Evening News of India*, no date, Autumn 1945?

'How Music is Taught In British Schools, I and II', *Evening News of India*, no date, Autumn 1945?

'The Music of Kaikhosru Sorabji, a Parsi Composer', *Evening News of India*, no date, Autumn 1945?

'Raymond O'Connell's Piano recital', *Evening News of India*, no date, Autumn 1945?

'Some Aspects of European and Hindustani Music', *Evening News of India*, Saturday 11 August 1945.

'An Adjudicator's Report on a Performance by the Bombay Symphony Orchestral Society', *Evening News of India*, 15 September 1945, plus correspondence and reply by Chisholm in two subsequent undated issues.

'Letter – Harmony in Hindustani Music', *Evening News of India*, no date [August/September 1945].

'Hints to Chamber Music Players', *Evening News of India*, no date [not before 26 September 1945].

'University, Symphony Orchestra, Ballet, Drama and Revue', *Evening News of India*, Friday 26 October 1945.

'Some Afterthoughts on a Concert by the Philharmonic Society', *Evening News of India*, no date, Autumn 1945?

'Activities in a P.O.W. Camp', *Evening News of India*, no date, Autumn 1945?

'Ballet in England', *Evening News of India*, Thursday 1 November 1945.

'String Quartet and Organ Recitals', *Evening News of India*, Monday 5 November 1945.

Unpublished and undated typescript: 'Article written by the composer for publicity in connection with the New York production', Chisholm Papers, Box 16, 131, Writings by EC.

First Cramb Lecture: TSS Chisholm Papers, Lectures and Talks, Box 8, 30. 29
April 1957.

'We Lived in Luxury in Moscow for Three Weeks', *Cape Argus*, 10 September
1957?

'Russians Queuing for Music Records Are like Bargain-hunters', *Cape Argus*,
September 1957?

'Creative Education in Music', offprint from *Colston Papers*, XIV, being the
Proceedings of the Fourteenth Symposium of the Colston Research Society,
University of Bristol, 2–5 April 1962.

'What Life Has Taught Me', interview with Cyril Watling, *Cape Times Weekend
Magazine*, 16 May 1964.

Selected articles by Erik Chisholm (unpublished)

'The Composer in Scotland' (MS notes in Chisholm Papers, Writings by EC,
Box 16, 129. Paper given at a club in central Glasgow shortly before the
performances of *The Earth Shapers* in November 1941 – see pp. 3 and 4 of
the typescript.)

'The Music I Like' (third of three draft typescripts for a radio talk, Chisholm
Papers, Writings by EC, Box 8, 32).

'A Musician in Wartime' (script for a BBC broadcast, recorded 3 February
1950 for the Scottish Home Service. See BBC contract letter to Chisholm, 3
February 1950, Morag Chisholm Papers, Letters from Musical Celebrities).

'My Job in Wartime' (undated typescript of BBC broadcast, but, given the
reference to rehearsals of his Piano Concerto, probably the second or third
week in January 1940. He refers to this broadcast as having taken place 'early
in 1940' in a later broadcast script, 'A Musician in Wartime'. Morag Chisholm
Papers.).

'Piobaireachd – A Neglected Art' (undated typescript taken from dictation or
tape by someone unfamiliar with the subject, Morag Chisholm Papers).

'Politics in Music' (typescript in Chisholm Papers, Writings by EC, Box 16, 131
no date).

'The Wonder of English' (Chisholm Papers, Writings by EC, Box 8, 32).

'Why I Am Not a Christian' (Chisholm Papers, Writings by EC, Box 8, 32).

Selected books, articles and reviews dealing with Erik Chisholm or providing background information

'A.P', 'Amateur and School Performances', *Opera*, January? 1957, pp. 193–4.

Annand, Louise, *J. D. Fergusson in Glasgow 1939–1961*, Abingdon, 2003.

Anon., 'Musicians from South Africa', *The Times*, 21 December 1956, p. 9.

Anon., 'Musicians from South Africa', *The Times*, 31 December1956, p. 3.

Anon., 'Wigmore Hall, South African Festival', *The Times*, 1 January 1957, p. 3.

Anon., 'Wigmore Hall, Festival of South African Music', *The Times*, 3 January
1957, p. 4.

Anon., 'Music from the Cape', *The Times*, 7 January 1957, p. 12.

Anon., 'Rudolf Steiner Theatre, "The Consul"', *The Times*, 10 January 10, p. 4.

Anon., 'South African Singers', *The Times*, 17 January 1957, p. 3.

Anon., 'Proposed Opera on Robert Burns', *The Times*, 22 January 1957, p. 2.

Anon., 'The Bombay Man's Diary', *Evening News of India*, Monday 5 November 1945, and undated.

'The Baillie', 'The Man You Know – Dr. Erik Chisholm – A Scottish Musician', *Weekly Herald*, 7 December 1935.

Brimer, M., 'Music, Opera and Ballet', in *UCT at 150: Reflections*, Cape Town, 1979.

Hogarth, B., 'A Thoroughly National Composer, Erik Chisholm: Tone Poet of the Highlands', *The Scottish Musical Magazine*, XI (11), September 1930, p. 197.

'J.W.', 'Music in Glasgow', *The Scottish Musical Magazine*, VII (7), 1 March 1926, pp. 135–6.

'J.W.', 'Music in Glasgow', *The Scottish Musical Magazine*, X (5), February–March 1929, p. 90.

'J.W.', 'Music in Glasgow', *The Scottish Musical Magazine*, XI (5), March 1930, p. 90.

Lindsay, M., *Francis George Scott and the Scottish Renaissance*, Edinburgh, 1980.

MacDiarmid, H., *The Company I've Kept*, London, 1966.

MacDiarmid, H., *Hugh MacDiarmid – Contemporary Scottish Studies*, ed. A. Riach, Manchester, 1995.

MacDiarmid, H., *Hugh MacDiarmid – Albyn*, ed. A. Riach, Manchester, 1996.

MacDiarmid, H., *Hugh MacDiarmid – The Raucle Tongue*, ed. A. Calder, G. Murray and A. Riach, Manchester, 1998.

MacDiarmid, H., *New Selected Letters*, ed. Dorian Grieve, Owen Dudley Edwards and Alan Riach, Manchester, 2001.

MacLellan, W., 'Scottish Composers – II Erik Chisholm', *Con Brio*, I (3), 1947, pp. 12–13.

MacLellan, W., 'Reminiscences of the Celtic Ballet', in *Margaret Morris Drawings and Designs and the Glasgow Years*, Glasgow, 1985.

McQuaid, J., 'Scottish Composers – II Erik Chisholm', *Con Brio*, I (3), 1947, pp. 13–16.

Morris, M., *My Life in Movement*, London, 1969, and The International Association of MMM Ltd., Garelochhead, 2003.

Phillips, H., *The University of Cape Town 1918–1948: The Formative Years*, Cape Town, 1993.

Purser, J., 'Erik Chisholm and Piobaireachd', *Piping Today*, 10, pp. 46–9.

Purser, J., 'Night Song of the Bards', McCulloch, M. (ed.), *Scottish Studies Review*, 6 (1), Spring 2005, pp. 43–58.

Purser, J., Is The Red Light On? – The Story of the BBC Scottish Symphony Orchestra, Glasgow, 1987.

Purser, J., 'Sources for Macpherson's "Night Song of the Bards" ', paper given at
    Rannsachadh na Gàidhlig 2006, Sabhal Mòr Ostaig, 20 July 2006.
Purser, J., 'Erik Chisholm's "Hindustani" Piano Concerto', Proceedings of Musica
    Scotica Conference, 28 April 2007 at Glasgow University, forthcoming.
Purser, J., *Scotland's Music*, Edinburgh, 2007.
Purser, J., 'Chasing a Restless Muse – Part I', *British Music Society News*, 116,
    December 2007, pp. 233–40.
Purser, J., 'Chasing a Restless Muse – Part II', *British Music Society News*, 116,
    March 2008, pp. 278–86.
Roberton, H. S., *Orpheus with His Lute*, Oxford, 1963.
Saunders, W., 'Scottish Chiefs, no. XV. A Chief Composer', *The Scots Magazine*,
    1933, pp. 17–20.
Shannon, P. 'The Active Society for the Propagation of Contemporary Music',
    letter in *The Scottish Musical Magazine*, XI (10), August 1930, p. 186.
Wright, Kenneth, 'Erik Chisholm, A Tribute', *Composer*, 17, October 1965,
    pp. 34–5.
Talbot, D., *For the Love of Singing*, Cape Town, 1978.
Tyrrell, J., 'Reviews of Books – The Operas of Leoš Janáček', *Music and Letters*,
    1972.

◼ Reviews of Erik Chisholm's music on CD

Anderson, M., Review of DRD0219 and DRD0222, *Piano International*, 8 (37), 20
    January 2005, pp. 80–1.
Anon., 'Erik Chisholm', review of DRD0223, *British Music Society News*, 106,
    June 2005, pp. 342–3.
Clarke, C., 'Erik Chisholm, Music for Piano Volume 2', available online at: www.
    musicweb_international.com/classrev/2005/June05/Chisholm_ DRD0223.
    htm.
Johnson, D. H., 'Erik Chisholm', review of DRD0222, *British Music Society News*,
    103, September 2004, pp. 219–20.
Jones, M., 'Piano Music of Erik Chisholm and His Friends', *Tempo*, 59 (231),
    January 2005, p. 72.
Lidiard, P., 'CD Reviews', review of DRD0222 and DRD0219, *Piano Professional*,
    January 2005, p. 34.
March, I., 'Chisholm, "Music for Piano, Volume 1" ', *The Gramophone*, 82,
    February 2005, p. 64.
MacDonald, C., 'Dunelm records', review of DRD0219, *International Record
    Review*, 5 (2), July/August 2004, p. 63.
MacDonald, C., 'Chisholm: Piano Works, Volume 2', *International Record
    Review*, 5 (11), May 2005, p. 58.
Woolf. G., 'Chisholm and His Friends', available online at: www.musicalpointers.
    co.uk/reviews/cddvd/ChisholmBusoniCD.htm.

Discography

■ Published recordings

Olympia

OCD 639 *Erik Chisholm (1904–1965): Piano Music*
　Third Sonatina on Four Ricercars
　Cameos (1926)
　Scottish Airs
　Sonatine Écossaise
　Night Song of the Bards
　　Murray McLachlan (Piano)

Claremont GSE

CD GSE 1572 *Songs for a Year and a Day*
　Lillias Scott settings:
　'Love's Reward'
　'Johnnie Logie'
　'Skreigh O' Day'
　'Fragment'
　'Prayer'
　'The White Blood of Innocence'
　'Hert's Sang'
　　Brad Liebl (Baritone) Thomas Rajna (Piano)

Koch Schwann

3-1590-2 *Essentially Scottish*
　Harris Dance

Epoch Dutton

CDLX 7196
　Symphony No. 2, *Ossian*
　　BBC Concert Orchestra/Martin Yates

Dunelm Records (to be transferred to the Divine Art label)

DRD0174 *Erik Chisholm*
Piano Concerto No. 1, *Piobaireachd*
Star point
Sonatina in G minor
Elegies 1–4
Sonatina No. 4
'With Cloggs On'
  Murray McLachlan (Piano)

DRD0219 *Piano Music of Erik Chisholm and His Friends*
Sonata in A, 1939 – *An Rioban Dearg* (Unabridged)

DRD0222 *Erik Chisholm, Music for Piano, Volume 1*
Straloch Suite
Scottish Airs for Children
Sonata in A, 1939 – *An Rioban Dearg* (Abridged)
  Murray McLachlan (Piano)

DRD0223 *Erik Chisholm, Music for Piano, Volume 2*
From 'Twenty-four Preludes from the True Edge of the Great World', 1–6, 8,
    19, 23, 24.
Airs from the Patrick MacDonald Collection, i–xxvi.
Five Movements from the *Petite Suite* – consisting of nos. xxvii–xxxi of *Airs*
    (above).
  Murray McLachlan (Piano)

DRD0224 *Erik Chisholm, Music for Piano, Volume 3*
Piobaireachd 1–4
Sonatinas 1 and 2
Two *Piobaireachd* Laments
Cornish Dance Sonata
  Murray McLachlan (Piano)

DRD0225 *Erik Chisholm, Music for Piano, Volume 4*
Piobaireachd 5–8, 10–13
Sonatina 3
Cameos
Highland Sketches
Portraits
  Murray McLachlan (Piano)

The following Dunelm Recordings are forthcoming, transferred to the Divine Art label

DRD0226 *Erik Chisholm, Music for Piano, Volume 5*
  Piobaireachd 14, 16, 17, 19–23
  Sonatinas 5 and 6
  Cameos
  Sonatine Écossaise
  Harris Dance
  Tango
  Sonata 'Elektra'
  Dance Bacchanal
    Murray McLachlan (Piano)

Erik Chisholm, Music for Piano, Volume 6
  Ceol Mór Dances
  Dunedin Suite
  Scottish Airs
  Dance of the Princess Jaschya-Sheena
  Wisdom Book
  Nocturnes: *Night Song of the Bards* 1–6
    Murray McLachlan (Piano)

Erik Chisholm, Music for Piano, Volume 7
  Elegies
  Peter Pan Suite
  Sonatina 4
  Suites 1–3
    Murray McLachlan (Piano)

■   Unpublished recordings

The following unpublished recordings can be accessed at the institutions named:

Opera: *Dark Sonnet*, soprano and orchestra conducted by Erik Chisholm (University of Cape Town MSS and Archives Dept).

Operas: *Dark Sonnet* and *The Pardoner's Tale* (University of Cape Town Opera School, 2004).

Opera: *The Inland Woman* (piano reduction version) (University of Cape Town MSS and Archives Dept).

Hindustani Piano Concerto, Adolph Hallis, piano, and Erik Chisholm conducting the BBC Scottish Orchestra, 9 February 1950 (University of Cape Town MSS and Archives Dept).

Hindustani Piano Concerto, Ronald Brautigam, piano, and Clark Rundell conducting the BBC Scottish Symphony Orchestra (BBC Radio Scotland, 2007).

Pictures from Dante, Clark Rundell conducting the BBC Scottish Symphony Orchestra (BBC Radio Scotland, 2007).

Babar, Erik Chisholm conducting the Cape Town Symphony Orchestra (University of Cape Town MSS and Archives Dept).

The Forsaken Mermaid, 1, Richard Black and Michael Jones, 2–11 Erik Chisholm and Wight Henderson, recording made in the 1930s (Erik Chisholm Trust).

'The Fisherman's Dance' from *The Forsaken Mermaid*, Jean Hucheson and Jack Keaney (BBC Radio Scotland, 1992).

Piobaireachd Variations from Two *Piobaireachd* Laments – No. 2, Agnes Walker (Erik Chisholm Trust).

Night Song of the Bards, Nos. 3, 4, 5, Nina Schumann, (South African Broadcasting Corporation, 1991).

■   The following recordings are held by the Erik Chisholm Trust

A Scotch Titbit, David Hackbridge Johnson (violin) and Michael Jones (piano), The Warehouse, London, 10 July 2001.

'Stravaiging', *Rudha Ban*, 'Song of the Mavis', Michael Jones (piano), The Warehouse, London, 10 July 2001.

Fair Headland (British Library, National Sound Archive).

The Welter of the Waters (British Library, National Sound Archive).

Erik Chisholm, talk on contemporary music, B-SABC 20/5/49.

Tribute to Erik Chisholm by Gunter Pulvermacher, 1965 (source unidentified).

Tribute to Erik Chisholm by Gideon Fagan, South African Broadcasting Corporation, ABC, 8 July 1965, in English and Afrikaans.

Selected Compositions

A COMPREHENSIVE CATALOGUE OF CHISHOLM'S COMPOSITIONS AND drafts is currently in preparation. The cataloguer is Michael Tuffin, working for the Erik Chisholm Trust and the University of Cape Town Libraries, Manuscripts and Archives Department under Lesley Hart. It should become available, including online, in 2009. In the meantime, the Erik Chisholm website reproduces the relevant catalogue entries of the Scottish Music Centre, where they can also be consulted on-line. See www.erikchisholm.com and www.scottishmusiccentre. com/erikchisholm.

At this stage, then, a catalogue in this book would be unnecessary and soon out of date. What follows is a list of selected compositions according to genre, with their dates of composition or completion.

▪ Operas

The Wolfings, 1920s? (after Morris)
The Feast of Samhain, 1941 (after Stephens)
The Inland Woman, 1950 (after Lavin)
Dark Sonnet, 1952 (after O'Neill)
Simoon, 1953 (after Strindberg)
Black Roses (*Sweeney Agonistes*), 1954 (Chisholm; *Sweeney Agonistes* version after Eliot)
The Pardoner's Tale, 1961 (after Chaucer)
The Nun's Priest's Tale, 1961 (after Chaucer)
The Wyf of Bath's Tale, 1962 (after Chaucer)
The Importance of Being Earnest, 1963 (after Wilde)
The Caucasian Chalk Circle, 1963 (after Brecht)

▪ Ballad opera

The Life and Loves of Robert Burns, 1963 (after Burns)

▪ Narrator and orchestra

The Adventures of Babar, 1941

▪ Ballets

The Pied Piper of Hamelin, 1937 (after Browning)
Piobaireachd, 1940–1 (Chisholm)
The Earth Shapers, 1941 (Chisholm)
The Forsaken Mermaid, 1942 (Chisholm and Morris)
The Hoodie Craw, 1947 (Chisholm)

▓ Symphonies

Symphony No. 1, *Tragic*, 1937–8
Symphony No. 2, *Ossian*, 1939

▓ Other orchestral works

Straloch Suite, 1933
The Freiris of Berwick, Overture, 1933
A Celtic Wonder Tale, 1939
Ceol Mór Dances, 1943
Preludes, *From the True Edge of the Great World*, 1943
Pictures from Dante, 1948

▓ Concertos

Dance Suite for Piano and Orchestra, 1932
Piano Concerto No. 1, *Piobaireachd*, 1936
Piano Concerto No. 2, *The Hindustani* (also known as *The Indian*), 1948–9
Concerto for Violin and Orchestra, 1950
Van Riebeeck Concerto, 1951 (for orchestra)

▓ String orchestra

Dunedin Suite, 1944

▓ Chamber works

Double Trio, 1930

▓ Piano solos

Cornish Dance Sonata, 1926
Cameos, 1926
Portraits, 1924–9
Straloch Suite, 1933
Piobaireachd 1930s?
Sonata, *An Rioban Dearg*, 1939
Scottish Airs for Children, 1940s?
Preludes, *From the True Edge of the Great World*, 1943
Night Song of the Bards, 1944–51
E Praeterita – Six Sonatinas for Piano, 1947
Two *Piobaireachd* Laments, 1951
Airs from the Patrick MacDonald Collection, 1951
Scottish Airs, 1951
Petite Suite, 1951
Sonatine Écossaise, 1951
Highland Sketches, 1951
Four Elegies, 1951

Index

Music examples are indicated by **bold** page numbers. Endnotes are indexed when the name or subject is not clear from the text relating to the referent.